Engaging
Theories
in
Family
Communication

Engaging Theories in
Family
Communication
Multiple Perspectives

Editors

Dawn O. Braithwaite
University of Nebraska–Lincoln

Leslie A. Baxter
University of Iowa

SAGE Publications
Thousand Oaks ▪ London ▪ New Delhi

For information:

Sage Publications, Inc.
2455 Teller Road
Thousand Oaks, California 91320
E-mail: order@sagepub.com

Sage Publications Ltd.
1 Oliver's Yard
55 City Road
London EC1Y 1SP
United Kingdom

Sage Publications India Pvt. Ltd.
B-42, Panchsheel Enclave
Post Box 4109
New Delhi 110 017 India

Printed in the United States of America on acid-free paper

Library of Congress Cataloging-in-Publication Data

Engaging theories in family communication : multiple perspectives / Dawn O. Braithwaite, Leslie A. Baxter, editors.
    p. cm.
Includes bibliographical references and index.
ISBN 0-7619-3060-4 (cloth : alk. paper) — ISBN 0-7619-3061-2 (pbk. : alk. paper)
    1. Communication in the family. I. Braithwaite, Dawn O. II. Baxter, Leslie A.
HQ734.E646 2006
306.87—dc22

                                2005008164

05   06   07   08   09   10 9 8 7 6 5 4 3 2 1

Acquiring Editor:	Todd R. Armstrong
Editorial Assistant:	Deya Saoud
Production Editor:	Sanford Robinson
Typesetter:	C&M Digitals (P) Ltd.
Copy Editor:	Nancy Sixsmith, Freelance Editorial Services
Indexer:	John Hulse
Cover Designer:	Ravi Balasuriya

Contents

Preface

We began this book project several years ago in reaction to questions concerning whether family communication had its own unique stamp; it had grown largely out of interpersonal communication in our home discipline of communication studies and from the work in sister disciplines of psychology, sociology, and family studies. A turning point in our desire to pursue this project came when one of us read a prospectus for a family communication book in which a scant 13% of the citations came from communication scholars. While we knew that family communication was certainly a sibling, we were more convinced than ever that we wanted to contribute to its identity and development.

This book also grew out of our frustration at the lack of theory guiding some of the research we were reading. While this is not an issue affecting the discipline of communication alone, nor family communication within our discipline, we desired to learn more about the use of theory in family communication scholarship. Our sense was that the strength of family communication would be reflected in the theories that guide its research. We knew that a variety of theories were being used, coming out of both communication studies and from other disciplines, but we did not have a clear picture of the landscape. We also believed that there were theories out there, both from communication and other disciplines, that were underused or yet to be discovered by family communication scholars. Thus the current project was born.

Readers will learn about our interpretation of the landscape of family communication theory in Chapter 1. We are grateful to Dr. Chad McBride of Creighton University, who, while a doctoral student at the University of Nebraska–Lincoln, undertook a study of all family communication scholarships from 1990 to 2003. This was a challenging task, and Chad helped us tremendously to lay the groundwork for this book. We thank Emily Lamb and Aimee Miller, doctoral candidates at the University of Nebraska–Lincoln, who helped complete the literature search. Taking all these data, our goal in the first chapter is to couch the theories within the larger discussion of metatheory or paradigms. Readers will see an Editors' Note at the start of each chapter, giving our sense of the origins and paradigmatic home of each theory in the book.

We express our heartfelt thanks to the 35 scholars who joined us on this project as authors of the 20 theory chapters. This is a superior set of scholars and we would not have a book without their expertise and cooperation. We also appreciate the foreword to this volume authored by Anita Vangelisti, and we point readers to the substantive contribution she makes to the book. We join with Sage in thanking the reviewers Douglas Kelley, Arizona State University; Marceline Thompson-Hayes, Arkansas State University; and Lynn H. Turner, Marquette University, for their insightful comments and suggestions. We also recognize the important contributions of Todd Armstrong, Senior Editor of Communication Studies at Sage Publications, along with Deya Saoud, Senior Editorial Assistant at Sage.

Finally, this book project also reflects and contributes to our own personal sense of family and family communication. Between us, we represent many types of family experiences at different points in our lives: adoptive, stepfamily, multiethnic, traditional nuclear, single parent, and voluntarily child-free. We are coeditors and coauthors, close friends, and family—fictive kin, if you will. Our work together helps us explore just what family means to us. Dawn thanks Leslie for many years of friendship and almost daily phone calls, and she loves being "Auntie Dawn" to Emma. She dedicates this book to Charles Braithwaite for 21 years of family, love and support and to her father, Tom Ohlendorf, who loved his family with all his heart. Leslie thanks Dawn for her many years as friend and colleague, and dedicates this book to her daughter, Emma, "just because."

—*Dawn O. Braithwaite & Leslie A. Baxter*

Foreword: Variations and Challenges

Anita L. Vangelisti

There are countless theories that explain interpersonal processes relevant to families, many that describe the development of family relationships, and a number that highlight communication processes as they occur in family contexts. *Engaging Theories in Family Communication* is the first edited volume to bring together a selection of these theories and to demonstrate the various ways they might be used to illuminate family interaction for researchers and students.

Twenty different theories are covered in the volume. The volume's editors, Dawn O. Braithwaite and Leslie A. Baxter, divide these theories into two sections: one that includes theories originally put forth by scholars within the field of communication, and the other composed of theories developed by scholars from fields such as social psychology, family studies, and sociology. Eminent researchers in their own right, Braithwaite and Baxter selected these theories based on their "demonstrated or potential value to the study of family communication." The selections made by Braithwaite and Baxter are instructive and offer readers a broad, comprehensive survey of some of the theories that have been used—as well as those that might be used in the future—to study the ways family members communicate.

The theories included in the volume vary in terms of the degree to which they (a) are employed by those who study family communication, as opposed to communication in other contexts; (b) were developed to explain dyadic interactions, as opposed to family interactions; and (c) target specific social issues, as opposed to general social processes. For instance, some of the theories covered are those that informed readers will expect to see; these are theories that have been employed frequently in research on family communication and that are foundational to most textbooks on the topic. Family systems theory, a staple in most graduate and undergraduate courses on family communication, is treated by Kathleen Galvin, Fran Dickson, and Sherilyn Marrow. These authors provide an overview of the theory and note its underlying assumptions, strengths, and weaknesses. Tamara Afifi and Jon Nussbaum cover family career theories and describe the way those theories might be used to explain family communication in the face of stressors that occur at various points in the family lifecycle. April Trees offers a review of attachment theory, foregrounding the central role of communication in the formation of individuals' beliefs about relationships. Relational dialectics are dealt with by Leslie Baxter, who addresses the historical roots of the theory, describes its major claims, and clarifies a number of issues that have been raised in prior work.

In addition to theories that are commonly used by those who study and teach family communication, Dawn Braithwaite and Leslie Baxter include several theories that typically are employed to study communication in contexts other than the family. For example, Kathleen Krone, Paul Schrodt, and Erika Kirby describe structuration theory—a theory put forth by sociologist Anthony Giddens and adopted by scholars studying organizational and group communication. Dawn Braithwaite, Paul Schrodt, and Jody Koenig Kellas provide an overview of Symbolic Convergence Theory. This theory, as the authors note, originated with Ernest Bormann's research on small group communication and has yet to be systematically applied to the study of families. Kory Floyd and Mark Haynes review evolutionary theories. Although theories focusing on evolutionary processes have been employed to study mate selection, pair bonding, and parent-child relationships, they have not been widely used by communication researchers who study families. In each of these chapters the authors describe how the theories might be applied to the study of family communication and offer innovative ideas for future research.

A number of the theories, although commonly used by those who study family communication, were developed to explain dyadic interactions rather than interactions that occur specifically in the context of families. For example, social exchange and equity theories are reviewed by Marianne Dainton and Elaine Zelley. These theories employ economic concepts and metaphors to explain the decisions people make in the development and maintenance of dyadic relationships. Jake

Harwood, Jordan Soliz, and Mei-Chen Lin describe communication accommodation theory, a theory that "was originally developed to understand how and why individuals adjust their communication to their interlocutors' communication style." Sandra Petronio and John Caughlin offer an overview of communication privacy management theory. This theory, as evidenced by the authors' review, has been used by researchers to understand communication patterns in families, but was developed to provide a more general understanding of how people manage private information in dyadic relationships. Goals-plans-action theories are covered by Steven Wilson and Wendy Morgan. These authors note that because people have goals and plans whenever they communicate, the theories "address general questions about communication rather than issues unique to families." Although the authors of each of these chapters acknowledge that the theories they describe were intended to explain dyadic phenomena, each of the authors also provides clear, vivid examples of how the theories have been, and might be, used to explain family communication.

In contrast to theories that were developed to address dyadic interactions, several of the theories in the book were conceived specifically to explain what happens when family members interact. For example, family communication patterns theory, presented by Ascan Koerner and Mary Anne Fitzpatrick, was developed as a way to explain how family members create a shared social reality via cognitive and behavioral processes. Inconsistent nurturing as control theory, described by Beth LePoire and René Dailey, offers a framework for examining communication in families that include a member who engages in undesirable compulsive behavior (e.g., substance abuse). Edna Rogers's review of relational communication theory clearly demonstrates that the theory emerged out of an effort to understand the constitutive association between family interaction and family relationships. Similarly, as April Trees notes, attachment theory was put forth to explain the emotional bonds that develop between infants and their primary caregivers.

Some of the theories included in the volume were proposed not only to explain patterns of family communication but also to provide an understanding of specific social concerns that affect families. Inconsistent nurturing as control theory is a good example. As Beth Le Poire and René Dailey note, the theory describes the ways in which some family members may unwittingly reinforce undesirable compulsive behavior in others. Le Poire and her colleagues have used the theory to predict communication sequences associated with substance abuse and eating disorders. Another example is emotion regulation theory. This theory, as described by William Cupach and Loreen Olson, was developed to explain the influences of both marital interaction and parent-child interaction on the emotional development of children. Cupach and Olson offer a compelling application of the theory to issues associated with family conflict and violence.

Rather than focus on specific social concerns, several of the theories center around more general social processes. For instance, social learning theory, reviewed by Adrianne Kunkel, Mary Lee Hummert, and Michael Dennis, describes the processes by which individuals acquire behaviors by observing and modeling the behaviors of others. Attribution theory, discussed by Valerie Manusov, focuses on the explanations and interpretations that individuals formulate concerning their own, and others', behavior. Critical feminist theories, as described by Julia Wood, question the processes and practices that create and maintain patriarchal ideologies. Kristin Langellier and Eric Peterson's discussion of narrative performance theory suggests that the theory treats family as a "production of communication practices." Similarly, Wendy Leeds-Hurwitz notes that social constructionism and symbolic interactionism emphasize the interactive processes by which people understand and construct their social worlds.

Whether the theories covered by the authors target specific social issues or general social processes, were developed to explain dyadic or family interactions, or are typically used by those who study family communication, they all offer interesting lenses through which to examine family interaction. The usefulness of each of the theories is highlighted as authors not only offer a description of the relevant theory but also an explanation of how it has been or might be applied to the study of family communication and an outline of its various strengths and weaknesses. This will be especially helpful to students of family communication.

Reviewing the applications, strengths, and weaknesses of each of the theories reveals several challenges that face researchers and theorists who seek to understand family communication. Many of these challenges involve the unique characteristics of family relationships and the social contexts in which those relationships are embedded. For instance, researchers frequently note that family relationships are involuntary and difficult, if not impossible, to dissolve. The involuntary nature of family relationships as well as their "staying power" place tight constraints on individuals' relational alternatives. In the best of worlds, when family members are happy and well-adjusted, these constraints may increase members' commitment to each other and to the family as a whole. However, in the worst of worlds, when family members are distressed, psychologically troubled, or abused, the same restrictions may place them at a great deal of risk. In either case, the constraints inherent in family relationships are likely to influence the ways individuals interpret their family members' behaviors.

Some of the theories reviewed in this volume are particularly well-suited to explain the nature of the relational constraints experienced by family members and the influence of those constraints on family relationships. Indeed, critical feminist theories deal directly with such restrictions. Social constructionist, symbolic interaction, and narrative performance theories all address the ways that communication, and the constraints associated with it, embody and create interpersonal relationships. Family systems theory and relational communication theory similarly acknowledge the influence that variations in relational alternatives may have on family interaction. However, other theories—particularly those that were not originally put forth to explain family communication—have less to say about this issue. How might the constraints associated with family relationships affect the ways members interpret and explain each other's behavior? Attribution theory certainly allows for variations in the explanations that family members generate, but it does little to illuminate the ways that, for example, individuals who are abused by a family member are constrained in explaining their abuser's behavior (but see Herbert, Silver, & Ellard, 1991). Similarly, social exchange theory accounts for variations in members' decisions based on the alternatives they have to their family relationships, but it does less to explain how children, who are accorded little to no decision-making power, respond to situations when they have few, if any, relational alternatives.

Another challenge that emerges from a reading of the chapters in the present volume involves the influence of time on the ways family members interact. Family relationships take place over a more extended period of time than almost any other type of relationship. The relatively lengthy nature of many family relationships raises two issues with regard to time that should influence theorizing about family communication. First, whenever family members interact, they bring with them a long history and anticipate a relatively lengthy future. Thus, each utterance is shaped by the myriad of utterances that came before it as well as those that are expected to come after it. A conversation between two adult siblings may be influenced by an interaction that occurred on a playground 20 years earlier as well as by the aggregation of interactions that have occurred between the two during the course of their lifetime. Even communication between family members with relatively brief histories (e.g., a new stepparent and her stepchild) will be affected by the expectation that it will be followed by many interactions in the future. Second, because family relationships take place over an extended time period, they are exposed to change. Changes in individuals, their family relationships, and their social environment influence the ways family members communicate. Thus, for example, an interaction between an adult son and his aging father is influenced not only by the interactions that preceded and are likely to follow it but also by changes in the way the son and his father have related to each other over time.

Many, if not most, of the theories selected by Braithwaite and Baxter allow space for researchers and theorists to discuss the influence of time on family communication. Some, such as family career theories, are based on the notion that family members and their relationships change over time. Others, including attribution theory and goals-plans-action theories, look to individuals' perceptions of the past or the future to explain family members' behavior. Yet others, like relational communication, inconsistent nurturing as control, and symbolic convergence theories, focus on sequences of interaction that unfold over time. While most of these theories allow space for the inclusion of time in one form or another, very few identify time as a central element in shaping family interaction. Family communication is situated within, and influenced by, interactions that have occurred in the past, are taking place in the present, and may come about in the future. Understanding changes in family members' communication, the influence of those changes on family relationships, and the effects of past and future interactions on current conversations obviously is no easy task, but it is one that theorists need to tackle.

A further challenge facing researchers, theorists, and students who study family communication involves the influence of relational and cultural contexts on family members' interactions. Most scholars agree with the proposition that these contexts shape the ways family members communicate. Research clearly demonstrates that members adjust their communication behaviors to different constellations of family relationships: Even infants behave differently when they are in the presence of a parent than they do when in the presence of both a parent and a sibling (Barton & Tomasello, 1991). Similarly, the cultural backgrounds that family members bring to interactions affect the way they enact and interpret communication: Studies suggest that African American spouses may be more accepting of negativity and more likely to interpret it as a normal part of family life than are European Americans (Orbuch & Veroff, 2002).

In spite of clear evidence that relational and cultural contexts affect family interaction, few theories directly address the pivotal role of these variables in shaping the ways in which family members communicate and interpret communication. A number of the theories covered in the present volume acknowledge that relational and cultural variables influence communication processes. For instance, communication privacy management theory suggests that rules for managing private information may vary from one relationship to another. Relational dialectics theory similarly recognizes variation in the ways family members manage dialectical tensions. Emotion regulation theory might be used by researchers to examine cultural differences in the influence of marital communication on children's ability to regulate their emotions, whereas communication accommodation theory might be employed to look at variations in the degree to which family members from different cultures adjust to each other's styles of communication. Although these and other theories recognize the possible influence of relational and cultural contexts on family interaction, most do not explain how those influences occur. Relational and cultural contexts give meaning to communication behavior. They provide cues for interpreting communication and guidelines for how and what to communicate. Given this, explaining how these contexts impart meaning is an important task for those who study family communication. Accomplishing this task will help researchers not only to understand the meanings that relational and cultural contexts impart but also the ways in which family interaction is influenced by these meanings.

It is important to note that the three challenges outlined in this foreword are not offered as an indictment of the field. Rather, they are put forth as a set of issues that researchers and theorists who study family communication ought to consider as they move forward with their work. The fact that Braithwaite and Baxter were able to bring together a distinguished group of authors to write about 20 different theories that might be used to inform the study of family communication is evidence that the field is maturing. We are ready now, not only to use existing theories to guide our research and our knowledge as students of family communication, but to expand upon those theories so that they capture more of the unique qualities of family interaction.

REFERENCES

Barton, M. E., & Tomasello, M. (1991). Joint attention and conversation in mother-infant-sibling triads. *Child Development, 62,* 517–529.

Herbert, T. B., Silver, R. C., & Ellard, J. H. (1991). Coping with an abusive relationship: I. How and why do women stay? *Journal of Marriage and the Family, 53,* 311–325.

Orbuch, T. L., & Veroff, J. (2002). A programmatic review: Building a two-way bridge between social psychology and the study of the early years of marriage. *Journal of Social and Personal Relationships, 19,* 549–568.

1

Introduction: Metatheory and Theory in Family Communication Research

Leslie A. Baxter

Dawn O. Braithwaite

We envision this volume as a resource to students and researchers who are interested in family communication. Rather than providing the reader with a summary of research findings as one would find in a handbook (e.g., Vangelisti, 2004), our goal is to provide an overview of important theories that are, or have the potential to be, useful in the study of family communication.

But what is a "family"? As any scholar of family can tell us, defining family is far from simple! White and Klein (2002) argued that a family is a social group whose distinctiveness from other social groups tends to be a matter of degree. They explained, "Nonfamily groups, such as networks of friends or coworkers, usually have some family properties but fewer of these properties or in less obvious amounts" (p. 21). What then are the "family properties" of relevance? White and Klein identified several properties, although family scholars differ with respect to which properties are requisite in conceptualizing a family.

We present a list of these properties before articulating our own definition of "family:"

- *Long-term commitment.* Although a marriage can be ended and family members can be estranged, the concept of "family" generally involves an expectation of long-term endurance. Other social groupings may demonstrate long-term commitment, but without any necessary expectation for that outcome. For example, we don't have to make a lifelong commitment to a friend, although we might end up having a friend for life. The degree to which this commitment is voluntary, and thus able to be severed, depends on the nature of the bond, which is the property to which we turn next.
- *Relations created through biology, law, or affection.* Family scholars vary in the kind of bond that produces the long-term commitment associated with family. For some, a biological, or blood, link is requisite for family membership. For others, affinal bonds such as adoption or legally recognized unions are requisite. For others, affection is the criterial bond; that is, the parties must have an affection-based, long-term commitment to one another (e.g., a long-term, committed cohabiting pair). Clearly, biological bonds are involuntary, whereas affectional bonds are entirely voluntary. Legal bonds can be changed, but their presumption is in favor of long-term stability once formed.
- *Enmeshment in a kinship organization.* Some scholars argue that a family is unique among social groups in having an "outward extension" into a broader kinship organization. For example, we acquire a "cousin" because a parent's sibling has a child. A spouse gains in-laws upon marriage. A child has an honorary "auntie" that comes from her mother's friendship with a best friend.
- *Ongoing interdependence.* This property emphasizes that family members live together, interact on a frequent basis, or otherwise create lives of interdependence in which they affect one another in some meaningful way.
- *Institutionalization.* This property underscores that a family is recognized as a legal institution and as such has normalized connections with other institutions such as schools, the workplace, and government agencies.

Our own definition of family is guided by a preference for the most inclusive definition possible. Our definition thus privileges the properties of long-term commitment and interdependence above all others. For our purposes, a "family" is *a social group of two or more persons, characterized by ongoing interdependence with long-term commitments that stem from blood, law, or affection.*

For our purposes, the definition of "communication" is more straightforward and refers to symbol use between persons through verbal or nonverbal means. But what are communication theories and what is the work they should do in the scholarly enterprise? At its most basic level, a communication theory can be understood as a set of statements that renders intelligible some communication phenomenon or process (Baxter & Babbie, 2004). But we frankly don't find such a general statement to be very helpful. Instead, we have found that the theory concept is not a neutral one; conceptions of what counts as a theory and what a theory is supposed to do are embedded in broader philosophical systems of inquiry, or metatheoretical discourses, about reality and how one produces knowledge claims. To understand the concept of theory, then, we think it is important to provide, however briefly, a backdrop of the primary philosophical perspectives that circulate in the family communication literature. These metatheoretical backdrops are not unique to the family communication domain; they can be found in many of the subfields of communication studies as well as in complementary disciplines such as sociology, psychology, and family studies.

METATHEORETICAL DISCOURSES
OF FAMILY COMMUNICATION

For our purposes, a discourse is a linguistic system of distinctions and the values enacted in those distinctions (Deetz, 2001). Metatheoretical discourses of family communication are best thought of as alternative ways to talk (and think) about family communication. It is not fruitful to engage the question of which discourse is correct (for this is an impossible undertaking). Rather, the issue is to appreciate the intellectual resources embedded in a given metatheoretical discourse—the stock arguments if you will, often implicit, that provide warrants for why certain research questions are more interesting than others, why certain methods are valued over others, and which conceptions of theory are valued over alternative conceptions. Following Bochner (1985), we have identified three basic discourses in family communication: logical-empirical, interpretive, and critical.

Logical-Empirical Perspective

Logical-empiricism presumes an objective reality that can be discovered through appropriate methods. The goal of logical-empirical theory and research is to advance predictions and to offer generalized, law-like cause-effect explanations or functional explanations about how variables or structures are interdependent with one another. Researchers committed to the discourse of logical empiricism favor an a priori process in which they initially identify a theory relevant to the phenomenon they want to explain and predict. Theories should consist of law-like statements, which apply across situations, about how variables or structures relate, causally or functionally. Logical-empiricism is committed to value-neutral theorizing in which researcher subjectivity should be controlled or neutralized.

In its idealized form, the researcher's task is to deduce testable hypotheses from a theory. For example, a researcher adopting this perspective might be interested in studying how the communication norms of one's family of origin affect the development of communication norms in one's own family. The researcher would begin with a theory relevant to this phenomenon (e.g., social learning theory), in which variables have been logically linked causally or functionally. From this theory, the researcher would derive testable hypotheses relevant to the transmission of communication norms. For instance, the researcher might reason that there will be a positive correlation between preferred conflict strategies in participants' families of origin and immediate families. The researcher would deduce this hypothesis by using social learning theory and reasoning that children model their parents' communication behaviors. Thus, a grown-up child would reproduce the conflict strategies that were modeled during childhood. The researcher would determine whether the hypothesis was supported by the observations, and thus whether the theory of social learning gained support in the context of intergenerational transmission of conflict strategies.

Interpretive Perspective

By contrast, the metatheoretical discourse of interpretivism rejects a single objective view of reality that can be discovered. From the interpretive perspective, the social world consists of multiple realities according to the subjective position of the person or group. Humans are agents who act on their world in light of their subjective positions, and although humans often act to reproduce existing patterns they can also choose to change those patterns. Interpretive researchers are committed to a detailed understanding of how particular social realities are produced and maintained through the everyday practices of individuals. Researchers committed to the discourse of interpretivism value the "native's point of view"—the perspectives and language choices of the individuals being studied. In addition, they tend to value context- or situation-specific research. Because the interpretive project is committed to local meanings and rule-governed meaning-making processes, the theories valued by interpretive researchers are those focused on meanings and meaning-making.

Interpretive theories might be used by researchers as sensitizing devices or guides to getting started in a research study and subsequently put into conversation with locally emergent meanings. The goal is not to test a theory in a specific situation but rather to engage the theory in conversation with the emergent observations and interpretations that flow from the natives' experiences. Thus, from an interpretive perspective, a theory is a heuristic device, useful in sensitizing a researcher; it is a conversational partner, if you will. It is open to transformation when put into play with the natives' point of view and the interpretations of the researcher.

For example, an interpretive researcher interested in the intergenerational transmission of communication norms might start with a general theory of how social realities are reproduced (e.g., structuration theory) and use this theory as a sensitizing device, helpful in guiding preliminary interview questions or in making findings intelligible at the analysis stage of the study. However, the researcher would not test hypotheses derived from the theory. In the end, the researcher would conclude that the theory was more or less useful in illuminating the natives' experiences.

Alternatively, an interpretive researcher might prefer to operate entirely inductively, developing a theory from the "bottom up" from observations. This process is often referred to as grounded-theory construction. Returning to our example of the intergenerational transmission of communication norms, our interpretive researcher might adopt an exclusively inductive approach with the goal of developing a grounded theory of intergenerational meaning-making in families by asking family members to describe, in their own terms, what similarities and differences they saw in communication across the generations of their family and in what ways these were meaningful to them.

Critical Perspective

In contrast to both logical-empirical and interpretive researchers, a critical scholar would view the family as a social/historical creation in which various power struggles take place. A critical researcher would rely on a theory of discursive, institutional, or ideological power to provide the analytic guide to uncover silenced voices and to inform his or her understanding of the process by which other voices become dominant from one generation to the next. Key to this analysis would probably be the role of various discourse systems, societal structures, and ideologies (for example, an ideology of patriarchy) in affecting the communicative dynamics of particular families. Critical researchers often focus on the interests of predetermined, identifiable groups, such as women and people of color, or nonelite social classes, such as people with disabilities. The work of critical researchers is often characterized by an emancipation or enlightenment goal and an activist, social-change agenda.

Returning to the intergenerational transmission example one final time, a critical researcher would be interested in determining whose norms were legitimated and whose norms for communicating were silenced or delegitimated. The researcher might find critical feminist theories useful in this enterprise; for example, to help us understand why fathers appear more influential than mothers in influencing inter-generational transmission of communication norms. The researcher's goal would be the recovery of perspectives and norms that were silenced in the power-filled dynamics of family life. In the context of our hypo-thetical example, this would involve an effort to empower the voices of mothers and grandmothers, perhaps.

To this point in our essay, we have been operating at quite an abstract level—such is the nature of metatheoretical discourses. How-ever, researchers rarely articulate their metatheoretical commitments explicitly (and perhaps they should more than they do). Rather, schol-ars' philosophical alignments often float at a latent level, between the lines of their prose. The sophisticated reader needs to know how to interpret a given researcher's choices in order to infer what his or her metatheoretical commitments are in a given study. Once one knows what key signs to look for, it is possible to locate a given researcher's commitments. Why is this helpful and important? Because it tells the reader what the researcher values about theory and how theory should be used and evaluated in the given study. Thus, in this book, we begin each chapter with an editors' note in which we locate a given theory, or cluster of theories, within its appropriate metatheoretical discourse. As you read each chapter in this book, we encourage you to work through the intellectual exercise of identifying the specific ways in which a metatheoretical discourse "seeps through" in the articulation of that chapter's theory(ies).

But let's bring down the level of abstraction a bit and turn our attention to family communication research. In doing so, we will note some interesting patterns and trends with respect to both theories and the metatheoretical discourses in which they are embedded.

FAMILY COMMUNICATION RESEARCH, 1990–2003

For the purposes of this book, we undertook an empirical study of published family communication research conducted by researchers who professionally identify with the communication studies discipline.[1] Unlike others (e.g., Stephen, 2001), we did not include research in interpersonal communication unless the focus of the study met our criterial properties for "family." Thus, for example, if in a given study researchers compared marital couples to nonfamilial relationship types (e.g., dating couples), we included it in our sample because it was a comparison of familial and nonfamilial relationship types. However, if researchers focused their study on romantic relationships and combined marital couples with other couple types (e.g., dating pairs) into a single sample, we did not include it in our examination because the relationship type that was studied did not meet our criteria for "family." In addition, we chose to focus on the field of family communication, unlike others (e.g., Stamp, 2004) who have focused more broadly on the interdisciplinary literature on marriage and the family. Our focus is thus narrower than the analyses by others (Stamp, 2004; Stephen, 2001). Because family communication was formally recognized as a distinct scholarly domain in 1989 with the formation of the Family Communication Division in the National Communication Association (NCA), we used 1990 as our starting point, surveying research published through 2003. In particular, we examined 21 journals most likely to contain the published research of family communication scholars. We included in our search 13 communication journals sponsored by the International Communication Association (ICA), the National Communication Association, or the regional NCA affiliates' professional communication associations: *Communication Monographs, Communication Quarterly,*

Communication Reports, Communication Research Reports, Communication Studies, Human Communication Research, Journal of Applied Communication Research, Journal of Communication, Qualitative Research Reports in Communication, Quarterly Journal of Speech, Southern Communication Journal, Text and Performance Quarterly, and *Western Journal of Communication.* In addition, we included five journals edited by communication scholars: *Communication Research, Journal of Family Communication, Journal of Language and Social Psychology, Research on Language and Social Interaction,* and *Women's Studies in Communication.* We also included family communication research articles authored by communication scholars that appeared in the two interdisciplinary journals on social and personal relationships: *Journal of Social and Personal Relationships* and *Personal Relationships.* Last, we included family communication research articles authored by communication scholars that were published in the leading interdisciplinary journal on marriage and the family: *Journal of Marriage and the Family.* Because researchers in other disciplines publish work on family communication, critics might regard our rules of exclusion as xenophobic. Although we certainly value the communication work by others from outside the communication discipline, we wanted to access the work done by the community of scholars whose primary intellectual affiliation is communication studies. A total of 289 research-based articles were identified for inclusion. We excluded conceptual essays from our sample, because our goal was to assess the role of metatheory and theory in qualitatively oriented or quantitatively oriented research.

Metatheoretical Commitments

We read the corpus of research articles included in the analysis to first determine the metatheoretical commitments of family communication researchers. A total of 220, or 76.1%, of published family communication research articles were embedded in a logical-empirical discourse. A total of 59, or 20.4%, of family communication studies were interpretive in nature. A modest 3.5%, or 10 articles, displayed a critical perspective. To date, family communication research thus has been deeply embedded within a discourse of logical empiricism. The goal of logical empirical research is to identify generalized claims about the causal or functional relationship among observed variables. To date, fewer family communication scholars have adopted an interpretive perspective, displaying a commitment to localized and situated understanding of family communication in which the "native's point of view" is privileged. Even more rare were critical studies in which the goal of the researcher was to emancipate silenced or muted voices or perspectives.

Our findings, in general, are similar to those reported by Stamp (2004) in his survey of the broader research literature on marriage and family (including but not limited to family communication), most of which was derived from research published in the *Journal of Marriage and the Family*. Although we, like Stamp, found logical-empirical work to be dominant, this work occupied a smaller percentage of the family communication research (76.1%), as opposed to the broader literature on marriage and the family (91.9%). We found that interpretive work was more common in family communication research (20.4%), as opposed to the broader literature on marriage and the family (6.5%). Critical work was slightly more evident in family communication research (3.5%), as opposed to the broader literature on marriage and the family (1.6%).

Which general topic areas were investigated within these metatheoretical domains? The overwhelming proportion of work focuses on the family subsystems of parent-child communication (105 articles) or marital communication (102 articles). Other subsystems received much less scholarly attention: sibling communication (15 articles); grandparent-grandchild communication (12 articles); in-law communication (1 article). Relatively few articles were focused on the family as a whole system or unit of analysis (42 articles). Traditional, first-married families dominated the research; stepfamilies (11 articles) and divorced families (7 articles) received less attention.

Theoretical Commitments

Although all research is embedded in a metatheoretical discourse, we wanted to know how much of the research displays theoretical presence in which a specific theory(ies) has been invoked by the researcher to render intelligible a given phenomenon or process. Our threshold for evaluating theoretical presence was generous: We included articles in which the author mentioned at least one theory in the introductory warrant/argument for the study, employed at least one theory as a framework to analyze data, developed a grounded theory, and/or discussed at least one theory in the article's conclusion as a way to make post hoc sense of findings or to address the implications of the findings. Although the threshold we used departs little from the idealized use of theory among interpretive or critical theorists, it is generous with respect to logical-empirical work; we found theoretical presence in many logical-empirical studies that did not deduce testable hypotheses from an identified theory.

Overall, 42.9% ($n = 124$) of published research in family communication displayed theoretical presence; by contrast, 57.1% ($n = 165$) evidenced no theoretical presence. The most frequently identified theories were, (in descending order of frequency) relational dialectics theory (21), the typological theory of family communication patterns (20), the theory of marital types (15), narrative theory (9), relational control theory (8), communication privacy management theory (8), uncertainty reduction theory (8), socioevolutionary theory (6), critical feminist theory (6), social learning theory (5), social exchange-based theory (5), attachment theory (5), performative theory (5), social constructionist theory (5), confirmation theory (5), systems theory (4), communication accommodation theory (4), metaphor theory (4), attributional accounts theory (3), and ritual theory (3). The remaining list of cited theories, large in number, consisted of theories that were invoked no more than twice.

Not surprisingly, there are both similarities and differences in the theoretical presences identified in family communication research as opposed to the broader literature in marriage and the family (Stamp, 2004). Ten theories are common to both lists of frequently cited theories, albeit with different relative frequencies: relational dialectics theory, the theory of marital types, narrative theory, critical feminist theory, social learning theory, social exchange–based theory, attachment theory, social constructionist theory, systems theory, and attributional accounts theory. With the exception of the first two of these theories, most of the theories originated from scholars outside the communication discipline and have been imported productively into family communication research. Some theories appear uniquely in the family communication research and do not appear with frequency in the broader marriage and family domain: the typological theory of family communication patterns, relational control theory, communication privacy management theory, uncertainty reduction theory, socioevolutionary theory, confirmation theory, performative theory, and communication accommodation theory. Many of these theories have been developed by scholars from within the communication studies discipline. Last, some theories that have a presence in the broader marriage and family domain have not been used with much frequency by communication researchers: family life course theory, role theory, network theory, and symbolic interactionism.

Implications

As editors of a book devoted to theories of family communication, we are biased in favor of theoretically centered research as opposed to atheoretical research. We appreciate that not all scholars share our opinion; some think it sufficient to embed a given study in the conversation of accumulated findings from others' studies. We favor theoretically centered research for two simple reasons. First, theory provides us with a way to bring coherence and intelligibility to a set of findings. Several atheoretical studies can produce a common finding, but it is theory that makes that finding intelligible, although quite differently from one theory to the next. Theory provides us with a lens: to provide a causal or functional explanation of why that finding emerged (logical-empirical), to provide us with an understanding of what it means or how it came to mean within a given situated group (interpretive), or to direct us toward emancipatory social change (critical). Second, theory helps us launch new research, either by providing the basis of testable hypotheses (logical-empirical) or by providing us with a heuristic sensitizing device (interpretive and critical).

In light of our pro-theory bias, we are concerned that only a minority of family communication research displays theoretical presence of any kind. We will discuss here three implications from our survey of family communication research from 1990 to 2003. The first implication of our review of family communication research from 1990 to 2003 is thus a call for a more significant place for theory. Our primary goal for this book is to present theories that currently have a presence in family communication research and to offer theories that we think hold much potential for family communication research. We hope that in some modest way, readers of this volume will increasingly bring theory-based sensibilities to their research activity.

The second implication of our survey of family communication research is a call for a better balance among metatheoretical commitments. Family communication researchers have a slightly better balance among logical-empirical, interpretive, and critical discourses than what is found in the broader marriage and family domain, but it is still dominated by one perspective—that of logical empiricism. We certainly believe that this metatheoretical discourse is a valuable one, but our bias favors a more balanced representation of all perspectives. Our view is that the collective ability of our field to render family communication intelligible rests on a conversation among perspectives, and we believe that all perspectives should have a comparable presence at the scholarly table. Thus, we hope that interpretive and critical research on family communication is increasingly in evidence. Toward that end, we have intentionally included theories in this book that hold relevance for interpretive and critical scholars, in addition to those theories important to scholars with logical-empirical, metatheoretical commitments.

The third implication of our survey of family communication research is that family communication is coming into its own as a distinct subfield of study. Although communication researchers continue to find value in theories of marriage and the family originating in other disciplines, they increasingly rely on a variety of "home-grown" theories that originate within the communication discipline. It is our view that all of these theories—those imported from outside the discipline as well as those home-grown within the discipline—needed to be gathered together in a single volume to inform students and researchers with an interest in family communication.

THE ORGANIZATION OF THE BOOK

The theories included in this volume were selected based on two criteria: (1) the theory demonstrated theoretical presence in the family communication literature, and (2) our belief that the theory holds substantial heuristic value in informing the study of family communication. Most of the most frequently identified theories in our examination of the research from 1990 to 2003 have been included. In addition, we have included theories, especially those embedded in underrepresented metatheoretical discourses, that we believe hold potential to enrich the theoretical landscape in the family communication literature. Nonetheless, we were forced to make difficult choices in light of page limitations for the volume. We recognize that we were not able to cover all possible theories in this one book.

One apparent omission on our part deserves explicit comment. Work in family communication or family studies more generally is often organized, if not informed, by a developmental or life-span perspective. This perspective is often captured in a variety of theoretical labels, including life-span family theory, family development theory, or family life course theory (White & Klein, 2002). Our sense of this body of work is that it could be productively folded into a more general chapter on theories of family stress and adaptation. Some stressors faced by families are predictably related to the developmental life course of families (e.g., the transition to parenthood, caregiving for an elderly parent, and so on). Other stressors are less predictable (e.g., divorce, stepfamily formation, drug addiction in a family member). We have combined both predictable and unpredictable stressors into a single chapter in part to save space, but also because we believe that these two bodies of work share the common theoretical question of how families change. This combination chapter is not the only one in which we asked authors to engage in creative combinations.

Thus, the 20 theory-based chapters that comprise this volume represent more than 20 theories. Both for the practical reason of economizing on space and for the purpose of positioning similar theories alongside one another, we asked several authors to address multiple theories. In all instances, it is our view that the theories clustered together into a given chapter share a common theoretical focus.

As anyone who has ever edited a book can attest, there is no single "best" way to organize chapters. We decided against an organizational structure that could reify compartmentalization of family communication into a set of subsystem studies (e.g., theories of marriage, theories of parent-child communication, and so forth). Middle-range theories of subsystems are valuable and necessary, but one risk they carry is that scholars might find it difficult to see common phenomena or processes across several subsystems, including the family system as a whole. Furthermore, several theories are not easily compartmentalized into a single subsystem.

We also decided against an organizational structure driven by metatheoretical commitments—a section devoted to logical-empirical theories, a section on interpretive theories, and a section on critical theories. Some theories cross over and are invoked by researchers of different metatheoretical sensibilities (e.g., structuration theory). Furthermore, as Deetz (2001) observed in the context of organizational communication research, and which applies as well to family communication research, metatheoretical discourses "are not themselves sealed off from each other. They pose problems for each other and steal insights across the lines" (p. 16).

Our goal is not to instantiate a view that metatheoretical discourses are in separate, isolated camps but to place them in proximity to one another so as to encourage "insights across the lines."

We also decided against an organizational structure in which theories were grouped by scope. Some theories are very broad in orientation—so-called grand theories. Other theories are more narrowly focused—for example, theories centered on particular social problems such as violence or drug abuse. We think the scope of any theory is a function of the imaginations of those researchers who apply and extend it, thus limiting the value of "scope" as an organizing mechanism.

In the end, we decided on a simpler way to organize the chapters. Section I, organized alphabetically, provides coverage of theories relevant to family communication that originated from within the communication discipline. Section II, organized alphabetically, provides coverage of theories relevant to family communication that originated in other disciplines of study, particularly family studies, psychology, and sociology. In both sections, readers will encounter theories that have been used with some frequency in family communication research from 1990–2003, in addition to new or overlooked theories that we, as editors, find valuable to the study of family communication.

All the theories included in the volume hold potential or demonstrated relevance for understanding family communication, yet few of the theories originated with the explicit goal of understanding family communication per se. The majority of theories in Section I, for example, were developed by interpersonal communication scholars interested in understanding interpersonal communication more generally. A similar state of affairs exists with respect to the theories of the second section; these theories for the most part did not originate as theories of family communication. Thus, this volume is one of theories in family communication more so than theories of family communication. As the field of family communication matures, we anticipate that subsequent theory books will evidence a higher proportion of theories developed explicitly with family communication in mind.

NOTE

1. The editors would like to thank Dr. Chad McBride, Assistant Professor of Communication Studies, Creighton University, for his assistance in compiling the data for this analysis. Any interpretations or errors are those of the editors.

REFERENCES

Baxter, L. A., & Babbie, E. (2004). *The basics of communication research*. Belmont, CA: Wadsworth.

Bochner, A. P. (1985). Perspectives on inquiry: Representation, conversation, and reflection. In M. L. Knapp & G. R. Miller (Eds.), *Handbook of interpersonal communication* (pp. 27–58). Beverly Hills, CA: Sage.

Deetz, S. (2001). Conceptual foundations. In F. M. Jablin & L. L. Putnam (Eds.), *The new handbook of organizational communication: Advances in theory, research, and methods* (pp. 3–46). Thousand Oaks, CA: Sage.

Stamp, G. H. (2004). Theories of family relationships and a family relationships theoretical model. In A. L. Vangelisti (Ed.), *Handbook of family communication* (pp. 1–30). Mahwah, NJ: Lawrence Erlbaum.

Stephen, T. (2001). Concept analysis of the communication literature on marriage and family. *Journal of Family Communication, 2*, 91–110.

Vangelisti, A. L. (Ed.). (2004). *Handbook of family communication*. Mahwah, NJ: Lawrence Erlbaum.

White, J. M., & Klein, D. M. (2002). *Family theories* (2nd ed.). Thousand Oaks, CA: Sage.

PART I

Theories Originating in Communication

as the establishment of an Intergroup Communication Interest Group in the International Communication Association demonstrate that such attention is growing (Harwood & Giles, in press). Our first goal in this chapter is to outline the benefits that accrue from taking an intergroup approach to family communication. Second, we summarize Communication Accommodation Theory (CAT) and illustrate ways in which this theory provides a framework for viewing family communication through an intergroup lens. Finally, we consider how broad cultural group memberships influence certain structural dynamics of families, which in turn influence accommodation within those families. Our goal is to place communication in family relations in the context of broader social and cultural group memberships, and to illustrate how communication between individuals in families is in part determined by those broader sociostructural phenomena.

A consequence of looking beyond interpersonal characteristics and focusing on group memberships is an enhanced understanding of how phenomena such as prejudice and stereotyping may be usefully considered as part of the family communication dynamic. In most cultural contexts, the prototypical family involves multiple generations with some biological or legal relationship living in some degree of proximity. Thus, families are by definition *intergroup* structures; they are defined by intergenerational relations. Hence, communication within many family relationships involves intergenerational linkages that may be imbued with age-related categorizations and stereotypes (e.g., grandparent-grandchild, parent-child, and even older-younger sibling relationships). Other group differences may also pervade the family context. Influences of gender in family dynamics have been well-established (e.g., Tannen, 2003). Multicultural families are also growing more common. Communication within such families varies in degree of group salience. Some interactions may be "purely" interpersonal, driven almost exclusively by considerations of individual characteristics and proclivities. At other times, cultural differences may predominate; for example, when partners in intercultural marriages must manage and negotiate issues related to their diverse backgrounds (Killian, 2001). Interracial/interethnic marriages also result in children who possess multiethnic/multiracial backgrounds. According to Rockquemore and Brunsma (2002), these children may "choose" between identifying with one of their parents' racial/ethnic groups, adopting a biracial/multiethnic identity wherein they identify with other multiethnic individuals, a protean identity (i.e., switching identity between the available "options" dependent on context), or a transcendent identity (rejecting any racial/ethnic identity) (see also Phinney & Alipura, 1996). Communication in the family is important in the development of one's racial/ethnic identity (Socha & Diggs, 1999), yet little research has focused on the role of family communication in identity development in multiracial/multiethnic individuals.

An intergroup approach to communication derives from Tajfel's work on SIT (Tajfel, 1978; Tajfel & Turner, 1986). More recent developments of SIT continue its socio-psychological approaches to examine issues such as prejudice and stereotyping (Brown & Gaertner, 2003; Turner & Reynolds, 2003), and advance theories developed from work at the interface of language and social psychology (Robinson & Giles, 2001). Space is not available for a lengthy exposition of the intergroup approach here (Harwood & Giles, in press); however, the essence of the theory is quite simple. In short, Tajfel's work demonstrated that individuals gain a sense of identity from their memberships in social groups (e.g., ethnic, linguistic, gender, age, etc.), and that those identifications (*social* identities) become an important aspect of their sense of self. In certain circumstances, for example, when groups are threatened or when some aspect of context makes groups salient, individuals may behave in terms of their group memberships to protect and support their social identities. This behavior will include consciously or unconsciously communicating in group-relevant terms; for example, when a teenage child adopts age-specific slang during conflict with a parent. As has become clear from recent theorizing, acting in terms of social group memberships is neither rare, nor is it aberrant behavior (Harwood, in press; Turner & Reynolds, 2003). Indeed, behaving with *no* regard to social group memberships is probably the exception, rather than the rule; the occasions on which social groups can be truly said to have no influence on our communication are very rare, different only in degrees.

An intergroup approach to the family sensitizes us to the ways in which age and cultural differences influence interpersonal communication within the family. In addition, it raises theoretically interesting questions concerning the ways in which shared identification with the family unit intersect with nonshared (age or cultural) identities within the family. Empirically, we know little about how the various identity "options" available are managed communicatively inside the family unit. The idea of family communication styles, standards, or patterns has become widespread in the literature (e.g., Caughlin, 2003;

Fitzpatrick & Ritchie, 1994), but little attention has been paid to the theoretical means by which such patterns and family identities are mutually influential. A focus on group identity provides greater understanding of the means by which family communication patterns emerge and are sometimes rejected.

COMMUNICATION ACCOMMODATION THEORY

CAT was originally developed to understand how and why people shift their communication to or from those with whom they interact (Giles, 1973; Giles & Powesland, 1975; Shepard, Giles, & LePoire, 2001). A broadly convergent orientation (seeking affiliation, social approval, compliance, communication effectiveness) is associated with the tendency to converge one's speech style along various dimensions (e.g., speech rate, accent, etc.). A divergent orientation (seeking distinctiveness, expressing social disapproval) is associated with divergence along those same dimensions. The general notion of adaptation to an interlocutor's communication has been studied from other perspectives (e.g., see Burgoon, Stern, & Dillman, 1995; Hatfield, Cacioppo, & Rapson, 1994); however, none has achieved the longevity or heuristic power of CAT.

CAT was the first communication theory to draw largely on SIT and to take a truly intergroup approach to interpersonal communication. The theory was examined extensively in numerous interethnic contexts, demonstrating that individuals' social identities were reflected in their accommodative style (Gallois, Giles, Jones, Cargile, & Ota, 1995; Street & Giles, 1982). Recipients of accommodation were shown to interpret their interlocutor's speech in ways that were consistent with the premises of the CAT; for example, the failure to converge was seen as a sign of social disapproval and intergroup hostility. In a classic study, Bourhis and Giles (1976) examined responses to a public address announcement in a Cardiff theater that was made in Welsh, Welsh-accented English, or RP English (the high-status national variety). Local Welsh-speaking patrons responded more positively to the announcement in Welsh, whereas local English-speaking patrons responded more positively to an RP or a mild Welsh-accented English. Thus, CAT provides a powerful explanatory and predictive model for understanding the ways in which micro-level interpersonal adjustments are influenced by broader social group memberships, and for examining the ways in which such micro-level adjustments send messages about group identifications and intergroup dynamics.

Recent theoretical developments have elaborated CAT and outlined four specific *sociolinguistic encoding strategies* within the theory: approximation strategies (i.e., convergence and divergence), interpretability strategies, discourse management, and interpersonal control (Coupland, Coupland, Giles, & Henwood, 1988). In the following sections we briefly describe each of these strategies. In doing so, we provide examples of how this theoretical framework might be usefully applied in the family context to understand communication behaviors on both an interpersonal and intergroup level.

Approximation Strategies

Approximation is accommodation to the interlocutor's *productive performance* (i.e., the partner's speech style). In the past, this has been most commonly discussed in terms of convergence (a "moving toward" the other's speech style) and divergence ("moving away from" the other's speech style). Previous studies have shown, for instance, that individuals who adjust their speech rate to speak at a rate more similar to their partner's are evaluated positively (Giles & Smith, 1979). In the family, evidence of accommodative tendencies would be apparent in children's adoption of parental communicative styles and behaviors. In many cases, children's "imitation" of parents' behaviors has been considered from a more general socialization approach (e.g., modeling or social learning; see Bandura, 1977). These approaches have been productive. However, CAT offers some additional predictive power, both in terms of the conditions under which adoption of parental styles might be more likely to occur (e.g., affiliation, compliance-seeking, shared family identification) and the conditions under which it might be consciously avoided or rejected (e.g., seeking differentiation, independence, rebellion, etc.). Thus, a child who is strongly identified with her family and loves her parents is considerably more likely to adopt the family communication style than one who is disengaged or alienated from the family unit. Similarly, convergences and divergences in spousal communication might be revealing as to the state of psychological engagement or disengagement with the relationship. Such motivational dynamics for shifting toward and away from a family communication style have not been examined carefully in the family communication literature. In particular, the role of a *shared family identity* in influencing shared communication styles seems like rich ground for future research. CAT predicts increasing levels of convergence with a perception of shared group identification and high levels of personal identification with the group (see Banker & Gaertner, 1998, for work on family identity as group identity). Thus, in a sense CAT becomes a useful linguistic tool to mark the family territory at the psychological level.

Approximation can also be used in understanding certain communication patterns related to interracial/interethnic marriages. For example, in cases where a partner's family speaks a different language, converging toward a partner's language may be a method for displaying recognition and/or appreciation for the spouse's cultural background. Although it is unlikely that a spouse would become fluent in a language for this purpose, using certain words or phrases (e.g., greetings, terms of endearment) may be a strategy used by partners in an attempt to illustrate recognition and appreciation. This is important because one issue relevant to interracial/interethnic couples is family approval or acceptance (Killian, 2001). In this sense, family members of an interracial/interethnic couple may use language in a divergent orientation by alienating a nonspeaker if they disapprove of the relationship. On the other hand, the family may attune their speaking style (or more specifically, their language) as a way to show approval and acceptance. For many groups, native language use can be an important tool for maintaining racial/ethnic group membership, identification, and solidarity (Giles & Johnson, 1987). For instance, a bilingual Mexican-American mother-in-law might speak English to her new native English-speaking son-in-law to signal his acceptance in the family and a desire to establish interpersonal ties. In contrast, repeated use of Spanish might signal (or at least be heard to signal) dissociation and an unwillingness to establish ties independent of cultural differences.

Interpretability Strategies

Interpretability strategies involve accommodating to the partner's perceived *interpretive abilities*—the ability to understand. Within the family context, interpretability strategies are apparent in parents' accommodations to their young children. Parents are acutely aware of what their children can understand, and carefully attune their speech to their children's level (Robinson & Rackstraw, 1972). This "baby talk" has been shown to be functional, at least along some dimensions, in facilitating children's language learning and comprehension (Snow, 1986).

Despite such appropriate accommodations to interpretive ability, interpretability strategies have most commonly been discussed in terms of *over*accommodation. Overaccommodation occurs when one party perceives an interpretive deficit in the partner and attempts to overcome it by simplifying speech (e.g., reducing grammatical complexity or simplifying grammar) or using other techniques (e.g., talking excessively loud). To the extent that such speech goes *beyond* what is required by the interlocutor, it is termed "overaccommodation." Overaccommodation has been discussed in communication with persons who are mentally impaired (Hamilton, 1991) and with non-native language speakers (DePaulo & Coleman, 1986). Overaccommodation has received most attention in intergenerational communication, in which it has been shown to be associated with negative stereotypes of aging (Caporael, 1981) and can lead to negative outcomes for older recipients (Ryan, Giles, Bartolucci, & Henwood, 1986).

In their study of overaccommodation, Montepare, Steinberg, and Rosenberg (1992) found evidence of age-related overaccommodations in grandchildren's speech to their grandparents, as compared with their talk to parents. Although data suggest that overaccommodations are less common in the family context than with strangers (Ng, Liu, Weatherall, & Loong, 1997), we can also imagine that they might be particularly *harmful* when they do occur in the family (Harwood, 2000). Older persons might view the family as a site in which they can escape the negative stereotyping of age that they encounter outside, and they might expect their family members to treat them as an individual rather than in terms of group membership as an older person. In this case, the older person and other family members are simultaneously negotiating relational as well as identities issues in their interactions. More generally, this points to the possibility that others may be stereotyped and overaccommodated within the family; for example, adolescents resenting being treated "like children" or family members from different cultural groups being addressed in simplified English.

Discourse Management Strategies

These strategies focus on the other person's conversational *needs* and are often discussed in terms of topic selection, face management, and the like. For instance, in the intergenerational context, a younger person asking an older person about an event in the past might be classified as a discourse management strategy. The young person is tailoring the conversation to the perception of the other person's expertise and interests. In the family context, a grandparent opening a conversation with a grandchild by asking about school could also be seen as engaged in discourse management, assuming that school is an unproblematic topic and that the grandchild is not failing classes (Lin, Harwood, & Bonnesen, 2002).

Discourse management is also relevant to communication in interracial/interethnic couples. Discussing topics of historical interest as well as traditions and holidays may be a way of showing appreciation and recognition of a partner's heritage. However, in certain situations (e.g., when there is a negative historical relationship between the racial/ethnic groups), some topics may be avoided as a way to steer clear of potential conflicts in the relationship (Killian, 2001). Hence, the manner in which partners and their families' topics of conversation can provide insight into the way in which the couple and the extended family seek balance interacting with one another as members of the same family and, at the same time, as separate racial/ethnic group members.

Discourse management can also be seen as a useful frame for understanding identity development in children from multiracial/cultural families. Building on Orbe (1999) and Rockquemore and Brunsma (2002), we hypothesize that the ways in which ethnicity and culture are talked about in families will be associated with the development of cultural identities. In families that embrace the experience of one racial/ethnic group, the children will tend to carry a singular identity, whereas families that highlight the insignificance of racial/ethnic identity are more likely to raise children with transcendent identities. Families that emphasize the multiracial/multiethnic diversity within the family will be more likely to raise children who are proud to have multicultural identities and are sensitive to their diverse heritage. Of course, children's identification will be influenced by numerous other factors (including their levels of family identification, physical appearance, friends, relations with extended family, etc.). We would argue that assessing discourse management strategies provides a lens for understanding how individuals balance the interpersonal and intergroup nature of their multiethnic family relationships; and through which individuals obtain desired family, ethnic, and cultural identities.

Interpersonal Control

These strategies attempt to direct the course of a particular conversation, or more generally a relationship, by strategies such as interruption or even direct power claims. The paradigm case is what Ryan et al. (1986) refer to as dependency-related overaccommodation. This phenomenon encompasses situations in which older adults are patronized or "baby-talked" as a function of their relative powerlessness in an institutional setting. Hence, the overaccommodation is not merely an inappropriate adjustment based on perceptions of interpretive ability; rather, it is an explicit attempt to control and manipulate the recipient, in the case of baby talk to an older adult to encourage passivity (Ryan et al., 1986).

Control strategies are common in some family contexts, such as parents' attempts to control children, or in adult children's caregiving interactions with their aging parents (Morgan & Hummert, 2000). Similar patterns can be found in other types of family relationships. For instance, although a heterosexual marriage is in many regards a highly interpersonal relationship featuring intimate knowledge and a highly individuated conception of the spouse, gender differentiation is common and usually taken for granted. Men have a greater tendency to engage in "one-up" power moves in marital communication (Millar & Rogers, 1988; see Tannen, 2003 for a complex discussion of gender roles in family relations). Thus, even within this personalized intimate relationship, there are tendencies that are identifiably tied to power and control needs, and those needs are linked to broader social group memberships. This communicative exercise of power reveals an accommodative orientation that is rooted in social group status hierarchies and accommodates those differences in creative ways.

Covering these four accommodative strategies has provided insight into the ways in which individuals adjust their communication to one another within the family context, and through the examples we have illustrated the ways in which broad group memberships influence such adjustments. However, it is also important to understand more about the cultural context in which such family interactions are embedded. Specifically, different accommodation strategies will have different meanings in different cultural contexts, and to the extent that individuals identify with the broad cultural context within which they are embedded, they will shape their interactions based on local cultural norms to a greater or lesser extent. Hence, the final section of this chapter examines such cultural influences.

Cultural Influences on Family
Relations and Accommodation Strategies

A need to recognize cultural variability in family structures and relations is evident given that family cultures are subsumed within their broader cultural value and belief systems (Parke, 1994). One of the most well-cited dimensions that characterize cultural differences is Hofstede's (1980) individualism versus collectivism. In general, individualistic cultures emphasize personal independence, autonomy, and achievement and place a person as the unit of the society and center of interpersonal relationships. Collectivism stresses interdependence and obligation to/sacrifice for the ingroup. Thus, the ingroup is the fundamental unit of society. This dimension has been used in studies as a conceptual framework of cultural variability to account for significant behavioral and perceptual differences (Cai, Wilson, & Drake, 2000; Markus & Kitayama, 1991; Triandis, Bontempo, Villareal, Asai, & Lucca, 1988).

The individualist-collectivist dimension contributes to fundamental differences in self-concept as independent versus interdependent, and to the ways in which people relate to others (Bochner, 1994; Triandis, 1989; Yamagishi, Jin, & Miller, 1998; Yum, 1988). In terms of family dynamics, Gudykunst and Lee (2001) highlighted the manner in which ethnic/cultural identities may work together with this independent versus interdependent orientation to influence cohesiveness and adaptability in marital relationships, intergenerational relationships, and family communication styles. Thus, considerable work leads to the conclusion that the family may be a more influential ingroup in collectivist cultures than in individualist cultures, and thus perhaps that accommodation within the family carries more weight in such cultural contexts (Chuang, 1998; Gao, 1996).

One demonstration of possible cultural variations in accommodation practices and evaluations emerged from the studies by Harwood (2000), and Lin and Harwood (2003). Using items derived from Williams, Ota, Giles, Pierson, Gallois, Ng, Lim, Ryan, Somera, Maher, Cai, and Harwood (1997), both studies examined grandchildren's and grandparents' perceptions of accommodation behaviors in the grandparent-grandchild relationship. Harwood (2000) found that in North America the best predictor of relational solidarity was perception of the partner's perceived accommodation solidarity, whereas Lin and Harwood (2003) found that one's *own* accommodation behavior was the best predictor in Taiwan. Such findings reflect the individualist-collectivist divide. The collectivist culture in these studies revealed a greater willingness to view the communication as a "shared" responsibility and the relationship as "belonging" to both people; hence, self is seen as responsible for relational maintenance.

Beyond this illustration, other cultural variables may influence accommodation strategies within the family. For instance, in a culture in which role relations in the family are highly structured, interpersonal control strategies may be used, especially when hierarchical structures are challenged. For example, in intergenerational conflicts in Chinese culture, older family members may adopt language devices such as long pauses, silence, interruption, or condescending terms to signal their disapproval or create a tension in conversation (Zhang & Hummert, 2001). By the same token, discourse management strategies, such as turn-taking, may presumably be more structured and predetermined in a hierarchical-oriented culture (Lin, Zhang, & Harwood, in press). Making matters more complicated, apparently divergent strategies (e.g., tones, word choices, or eye contact) may be used to signal proper role relations. For example, a grandson may respond to his grandfather's lengthy question with a very short answer. In this case, diverging from the high-status family member signals appropriate deference and respect for the power structure. This pattern is somewhat analogous to the "complementarity" pattern described by CAT scholars (Giles, 1980; Hogg, 1985; Street, 1991) whereby men and women "diverge" toward typical gender roles, thus signaling mutual attraction. The CAT framework thus may be a useful way to understand accommodation toward family communication *norms* in certain cultures.

CONCLUSION

Accommodation strategies provide us with a useful set of tools for understanding a broad range of family communication and for linking that communication to underlying socio-psychological processes. Due to our interest in encouraging attention to intergroup influences on interpersonal behavior, we have focused on intergroup communication processes. However, CAT also has great power in understanding the more traditional realm of interpersonal processes in the family, such as divergence during marital conflict. In addition, it is important to understand that the various strategies described may be used simultaneously. For instance, an older sibling converging toward a younger person's speech style and accommodating his/her conversational needs might be carefully paving the way to obtain compliance with some forthcoming request (i.e., in this case the use of approximation and discourse management strategies might be operating as "setups" for an interpersonal control move).

Detailed examinations of family communication episodes from the CAT perspective would be useful. The theory encourages simultaneous examination of communication at a micro level (e.g., speech rate, subtle changes in accent) as well as at the broader discourse level (e.g., facework, compliance seeking). Few other theoretical perspectives prescribe such breadth in the study of interaction, so few provide the range of insight that CAT brings to family communication. Unlike other communication theories, CAT is also well-equipped to handle processes influenced by personal and social identities (i.e., interindividual and intergroup behavior). For the future, we advocate three specific directions. First, scholars should examine accommodation processes within multiethnic families. We see great scope for understanding the ways in which cultural, age, and family identities are emphasized and negotiated using accommodation strategies. Second, CAT could help us understand more about the negotiation of identities in stepfamily relationships by examining the ways in which members of the "subfamilies" involved converge or diverge with regard to others. Finally, we suggest more attention to "real" interaction rather than the self-report data common in the CAT research to identify patterns of communication within a family or to examine specific episodes when certain accommodation strategies are adopted to achieve relational or identity goals.

We have illustrated the ways in which an intergroup approach is a good way to approach even the most apparently "interpersonal" relationships. CAT considers the interpersonal-relational issues involved in family communication and enhances our understanding of how people are relating to one another along numerous dimensions, some of which are the respective social group memberships of each party.

REFERENCES

Bandura, A. (1977). *Social learning theory.* Englewood Cliffs, NJ: Prentice Hall.
Banker, B. S., & Gaertner, S. L. (1998). Achieving stepfamily harmony: An intergroup-relations approach. *Journal of Family Psychology, 12,* 310–325.

Bochner, S. (1994). Cross-cultural differences in the self-concept: A test of Hofstede's individualism/collectivism distinction. *Journal of Cross-Cultural Psychology, 25*, 273–283.

Bourhis, R. Y., & Giles, H. (1976). The language of co-operation in Wales: A field study. *Language Sciences, 42*, 13–16.

Brown, R., & Gaertner, S. (Eds.). (2003). *Blackwell handbook of social psychology: Intergroup processes.* Malden, MA: Blackwell.

Burgoon, J. K., Stern, L. A., & Dillman, L. (1995). *Interpersonal adaptation: Dyadic interaction patterns.* New York: Cambridge University Press.

Cai, D. A., Wilson, S. R., & Drake, L. E. (2000). Culture in the context of intercultural negotiation: Individualism-collectivism and paths to integrative agreements. *Human Communication Research, 26*, 591–617.

Caporael, L. R. (1981). The paralanguage of caregiving: Baby talk to the institutionalized aged. *Journal of Personality and Social Psychology, 40*, 876–884.

Caughlin, J. P. (2003). Family communication standards: What counts as excellent family communication and how are such standards associated with family satisfaction? *Human Communication Research, 29*, 5–40.

Chuang, Y.-C. (1998). The cognitive structure of role norms in Taiwan. *Asian Journal of Social Psychology, 1*, 239–251.

Coupland, N., Coupland, J., Giles, H., & Henwood, K. (1988). Accommodating the elderly: Invoking and extending a theory. *Language in Society, 17*, 1–41.

DePaulo, B. M., & Coleman, L. M. (1986). Talking to children, foreigners, and retarded adults. *Journal of Personality and Social Psychology, 51*, 945–959.

Fitzpatrick, M. A., & Ritchie, L. D. (1994). Communication schemata within the family: Multiple perspectives on family interaction. *Human Communication Research, 20*, 275–301.

Gallois, C., Giles, H., Jones, E., Cargile, A., & Ota, H. (1995). Accommodating intercultural encounters: Elaborations and extensions. In R. L. Wiseman (Ed.), *Intercultural communication theory* (pp. 115–147). Thousand Oaks, CA: Sage.

Gao, G. (1996). Self and other: A Chinese perspective on interpersonal relationships. In W. B. Gudykunst, S. Ting-Toomey, & T. Nishida (Eds.), *Communication in personal relationships across cultures* (pp. 81–101). Thousand Oaks, CA: Sage.

Giles, H. (1973). Accent mobility: A model and some data. *Anthropological Linguistics, 15*, 87–105.

Giles, H. (1980). Accommodation theory: Some new directions. *York Papers in Linguistics, 9*, 105–136.

Giles, H., & Johnson, P. (1987). Ethnolinguistic identity theory: A social psychological approach to language maintenance. *International Journal of the Sociology of Language, 68*, 66–99.

Giles, H., & Powesland, P. (1975). *Speech style and social evaluation.* London: Academic Press.

Giles, H., & Smith, P. M. (1979). Accommodation theory: Optimal levels of convergence. In H. Giles & R. St. Clair (Eds.), *Language and social psychology* (pp. 45–65). Oxford: Blackwell.

Gudykunst, W. B., & Lee, C. M. (2001). An agenda for studying ethnicity and family communication. *Journal of Family Communication, 1,* 75–85.

Hamilton, H. E. (1991). Accommodation and mental disability. In H. Giles, J. Coupland, & N. Coupland (Eds.), *Contexts of accommodation: Developments in applied sociolinguistics* (pp. 157–186). New York: Cambridge University Press.

Harwood, J. (2000). Communicative predictors of solidarity in the grandparent-grandchild relationship. *Journal of Social and Personal Relationships, 17,* 743–766.

Harwood, J. (in press). Communication as social identity. In G. Shepherd, J. St. John, & T. Striphas (Eds.), *Communication as . . . : Stances on theory.* Thousand Oaks, CA: Sage.

Harwood, J., & Giles, H. (in press). *Intergroup communication: Multiple perspectives.* New York: Peter Lang.

Hatfield, E., Cacioppo, J. T., & Rapson, R. L. (1994). *Emotional contagion.* New York: Cambridge University Press.

Hofstede, G. (1980). *Culture's consequences.* Beverly Hills, CA: Sage.

Hogg, M. (1985). Masculine and feminine speech in dyads and groups: A study of speech style and gender salience. *Journal of Language and Social Psychology, 4,* 99–112.

Killian, K. D. (2001). Reconstituting racial histories and identities: The narratives of interracial couples. *Journal of Marital and Family Therapy, 27,* 27–42.

Lin, M.-C., & Harwood, J. (2003). Predictors of grandparent-grandchild relational solidarity in Taiwan. *Journal of Social and Personal Relationships, 20,* 537–563.

Lin, M.-C., Harwood, J., & Bonnesen, J. L. (2002). Topics of conversation in the grandparent-grandchild relationship. *Journal of Language and Social Psychology, 21,* 302–323.

Lin, M.-C., Zhang, Y. B., & Harwood, J. (in press). Taiwanese younger adults' intergenerational communication schemas, *Journal of Cross-Cultural Gerontology.*

Markus, H., & Kitayama, S. (1991). Culture and the self. *Psychological Review, 98,* 224–253.

Millar, F. E., & Rogers, L. E. (1988). Power dynamics in marital relationships. In P. Noller & M. A. Fitzpatrick (Eds.), *Perspectives on marital interaction* (pp. 78–97). Philadelphia, PA: Multilingual Matters.

Montepare, J. M., Steinberg, J., & Rosenberg, B. (1992). Characteristics of vocal communication between young adults and their parents and grandparents. *Communication Research, 19,* 479–492.

Morgan, M., & Hummert, M. L. (2000). Perceptions of communicative control strategies in mother-daughter dyads across the life-span. *Journal of Communication, 50,* 48–64.

Ng, S. H, Liu, J. H., Weatherall, A., & Loong, C. F. (1997). Younger adults' communication experiences and contact with elders and peers. *Human Communication Research, 24,* 82–108.

Orbe, M. P. (1999). Communicating about race in interracial families. In T. J. Socha & R. C. Diggs (Eds.), *Communication, race, and family: Exploring communication in black, white, and biracial families* (pp. 167–180). Mahwah, NJ: Lawrence Erlbaum.

Parke, R. D. (1994). Epilogue: Unresolved issues and future trends in family relationships with other contexts. In R. D. Parke & S. G. Kellam (Eds.), *Exploring family relationships with other social contexts* (pp. 215–230). Hillsdale, NJ: Lawrence Erlbaum.

Phinney, J. S., & Alipura, L. L. (1996). At the interface of culture: Multiethnic/multiracial high school and college students. *The Journal of Social Psychology, 136,* 139–158.

Robinson, W. P., & Giles, H. (Eds.). (2001). *The new handbook of language and social psychology.* Chichester, UK: John Wiley.

Robinson, W. P., & Rackstraw, S. (1972). *A question of answers.* London: Routledge.

Rockquemore, K. A., & Brunsma, D. L. (2002). Socially embedded identities: Theories, typologies, and processes of racial identity among black/white biracials. *The Sociological Quarterly, 43,* 335–357.

Ryan, E. B., Giles, H., Bartolucci, G., & Henwood, K. (1986). Psycholinguistic and social psychological components of communication by and with the elderly. *Language and Communication, 6,* 1–24.

Shepard, C. A., Giles, H., & LePoire, B. A. (2001). Communication accommodation theory. In W. P. Robinson & H. Giles (Eds.), *The new handbook of language and social psychology* (pp. 33–56). Chichester, UK: John Wiley.

Snow, C. E. (1986). Conversations with children. In P. Fletcher & M. Garman (Eds.), *Language acquisition* (2nd ed., pp. 69–89). Cambridge, UK: Cambridge University Press.

Socha, T. J., & Diggs, R. C. (1999). At the crossroads of communication, race, and family: Toward understanding black, white, and biracial family communication. In T. J. Socha & R. C. Diggs (Eds.), *Communication, race, and family: Exploring communication in black, white, and biracial families* (pp. 1–24). Mahwah, NJ: Lawrence Erlbaum.

Street, R. L. (1991). Accommodation in medical consultations. In H. Giles, J. Coupland, & N. Coupland (Eds.), *Contexts of accommodation* (pp. 131–156). Cambridge, UK: Cambridge University Press.

Street, R. L., & Giles, H. (1982). Speech accommodation theory: A social cognitive approach to language and speech behavior. In M. Roloff & C. R. Berger (Eds.), *Social cognition and communication* (pp. 193–226). Beverly Hills, CA: Sage.

Tajfel, H. (1978). Social categorization, social identity, and social comparison. In H. Tajfel (Ed.), *Differentiation between social groups: Studies in the social psychology of intergroup relations* (pp. 61–76). London: Academic Press.

Tajfel, H., & Turner, J. C. (1986). The social identity theory of intergroup behavior. In S. Worschel & W. G. Austin (Eds.), *The social psychology of intergroup relations* (2nd ed., pp. 7–24). Chicago: Nelson-Hall.

Tannen, D. (2003). Gender and family interaction. In J. Holmes & M. Meyerhoff (Eds.), *The handbook of language and gender* (pp. 179–201). Malden, MA: Blackwell.

Triandis, H. C. (1989). The self and social behavior in differing cultural contexts. *Psychological Review, 96,* 506–520.

Triandis, H. C., Bontempo, R., Villareal, M. J., Asai, M., & Lucca, N. (1988). Individualism-collectivism: Cross-cultural perspectives on self-in-group relationships. *Journal of Personality and Social Psychology, 54,* 323–338.

Turner, J. C., & Reynolds, K. J. (2003). The social identity perspective in intergroup relations: Theories, themes, and controversies. In R. Brown & S. Gaertner (Eds.), *Blackwell handbook of social psychology: Intergroup processes* (pp. 133–152). Malden, MA: Blackwell.

Williams, A., Ota, H., Giles, H., Pierson, H. D., Gallois, C., Ng, S. H., Lim, T. S., Ryan, E. B., Somera, L., Maher, J., Cai, D., & Harwood, J. (1997). Young people's beliefs about intergenerational communication: An initial cross-cultural comparison. *Communication Research, 24,* 370–393.

Yamagishi, T., Jin, N., & Miller, A. (1998). In-group bias and culture of collectivism. *Asian Journal of Social Psychology, 1,* 315–328.

Yum, J. O. (1988). The impact of Confucianism on interpersonal relationships and communication patterns in East Asia. *Communication Monographs, 55,* 374–388.

Zhang, Y. B., & Hummert, M. L. (2001). Harmonies and tensions in Chinese intergenerational communication. *Journal of Asian Pacific Communication, 11,* 205–230.

3

Communication Privacy Management Theory: Understanding Families

Sandra Petronio

John P. Caughlin

Editors' Note: Communication Privacy Management (CPM) theory comes from the discipline of communication studies, growing out of earlier work on self-disclosure from social psychology. This is a logical-empirical theory focused on boundaries in dyadic, family, group, or organizational systems. Interpretive scholars have also made use of the theory.

In today's world, families deal persistently with questions about private information. Parents are not sure what to tell their children about the circumstances surrounding their adoption, adult children are afraid to tell their parents about their HIV status, and recently divorced couples quickly tell whoever is available about their ex-spouse. Families with a member struggling to manage a stigmatized illness must judge whether to guard that information or reveal it to outsiders. Both keeping and telling information in different situations may be either beneficial or detrimental to individual family members and the family as a whole. Although managing privacy with outsiders is critical for family members, even within families, individuals frequently make decisions about how much to share and how much to keep private from other family members. Dealing with privacy in families, although complex, is critically important.

Indeed, family privacy is essential to family functioning because it often furnishes self-protection from public view, grants a degree of latitude for interpreting social norms, and affords a buffer zone from social pressures (Berardo, 1974). To understand how privacy works in families, this chapter presents the Communication Privacy Management (CPM) theory giving us a comprehensive view that includes both a definition of privacy (what it is) and an understanding of the process (how it works Petronio, 2002). Underpinning CPM is attention to the changeability of privacy choices (people often have a difficult time making a decision about whether they should tell someone something private or keep it a secret) and awareness of the dialectical nature found in private disclosures (also see Altman, Vinsel, & Brown, 1981). By saying that privacy is dialectical in nature, we mean that in making these difficult choices, there is a simultaneous push and pull between both wanting to tell and wanting to keep something to ourselves. CPM theory helps us learn how people regulate that push and pull of private disclosures. Particularly for family interactions, CPM provides a structure that captures the dynamic sense of family communication patterns found in private disclosures, yet allows us to examine the process in an understandable way (Caughlin & Petronio, 2004). This chapter presents an overview of CPM theory that illustrates how families manage the communicative activities regulating the dialectical tension of privacy and disclosure.

For the past 25 years, Petronio has worked to develop the theory of Communication Privacy Management. She began working on it because she was unhappy with the existing self-disclosure research (Petronio, 1991; Petronio, 2002). She found that telling everything about oneself was not always positive in the way that some literature suggested, and she was convinced that there was another way to conceptualize the process. For the next 25 years, Petronio conducted research, testing ideas with colleagues and students and building the theory you read about today (Petronio, 2002).

CPM is a practical theory constructed to permit applications that give us an opportunity to understand everyday problems and events that people encounter in families. CPM also assumes that privacy is *not* a singular concept; rather we can understand it most effectively in terms of a dialectical tension with disclosure. This dialectical relationship makes sense because it is difficult to conceive of disclosure without the nature of privacy. If all information is available, the notion of privacy becomes invalid. Likewise, if all information were restricted, disclosure would not exist. Together, each concept helps define the domain of the other (Petronio, 2002).

In determining a basic definition of privacy, CPM proposes that people characterize private information as something they own. However, people often bestow various degrees of ownership to others when disclosure takes place, making them shareholders. Because of this communicative process, private information can move from being personal to collective as individuals disclose to others (Petronio, 1991). For example, if Pam tells Dana that she wants another child but her husband does not, Pam's desire to have another child moves from being Pam's own private feeling to information she shared with Dana. Through the telling or disclosure, Pam makes this information dyadic and forms a boundary around the information that includes only Pam and Dana. Dana now knows something about Pam that Pam does not want shared with others. When people become shareholders of disclosed information, knowing the information renders them accountable for further revelations to third parties. Given this dynamic process, CPM uses a metaphoric boundary to illustrate the two conditions (personal and collective private information). In other words, CPM theory envisages a personal boundary surrounding information belonging solely to an individual, and collective boundaries including those that are dyadic—such as the one created with Pam and Dana (Petronio, 2002).

We expect to have complete control over the private information that is personal. When we move information from the personal level to the collective level through disclosure, however, we create a shared system that accounts for layers of jointly owned private information. Developing a shared boundary system does not mean that we give up all our private information; instead, we most certainly retain a personally private boundary. However, within the collective boundaries that we co-own, we add to the shared information we have responsibility for or we give responsibility to others by enacting third-party disclosures.

When we own personally private information or share in collectively owned private information, the way we control boundary accessibility is through rules. Perhaps one of the most important dimensions of CPM is the development of our understanding about privacy rules (Petronio, 2002). The decisions to reveal or conceal are predicated on rules that stem from many different spheres of influence. The calculus used to judge the scope of disclosure to others might take into account cultural issues, motivations, situational factors, gender criteria, or the cost of revealing. For example, we may develop rules based on the motivations for disclosure. If an adolescent daughter does not want her mother to know about her dating experiences, she may implement rules that limit the amount of information she typically gives her mother about dating.

These criteria used to generate privacy rules combine in complex ways to affect individuals' decisions regarding privacy in families. Caughlin and Afifi's (2004) research, for example, suggests that various motivations, such as wanting to protect one's relationship or wishing to disclose only to a responsive and competent confidant, can influence the extent to which typical privacy rules for topic avoidance apply. In particular, they found that when college students and their parents considered avoiding communication as motivated by desires to protect their relationship, they tended to be less dissatisfied by avoidance. This implies that although avoiding interaction is typically seen as counter-productive to parent-child relationships, when the motivation is to pro-tect that relationship, the rule about avoidance is suspended or at least diminished in importance. Conversely, parents and children tended to be particularly dissatisfied by topic avoidance if they viewed the other as incompetent to discuss the topic. This finding suggests that if one feels forced to accept avoidance due to the incompetence of the other, it makes the general rule against too much avoidance even more salient.

When boundaries become collective in nature, people negotiate pri-vacy rules or they are socialized to learn existing rules. This is important to families because parents, for example, want their children to learn the privacy rules that they value. However, to manage these boundaries successfully, people must execute synchronized boundary coordination. Boundary coordination operates through three processes (Petronio, 2002). First, people use privacy rules to determine who is going to receive personally private information through disclosure; in other words, which people are *linked* into a privacy boundary. Once this occurs, however, the boundary around that information does not remain personal. Instead, the borders expand into a dyadic or group boundary rendering the information collectively held. The result is a reconfigured boundary around the shared information mutually held by the originator and target of disclosure. Therefore, those receiving disclosed private information become shareholders as they reside within the newly formed collective boundary. Second, privacy rules also govern the parameters of *co-ownership* parameters of the information within the collectively held boundary. Because these rules determine whether the confidant has full rights of ownership or a limited partnership, the recipient is giving more or less responsibility as caretaker of the disclosed information. Third, privacy rules drive the level of information that is divulged to establish a collective boundary and determine what information can be revealed to third parties. As a result, *permeability* rules regulate the flow of private information that goes out of the privacy boundary. Thus, Sergio tells John that he is going to ask his partner to marry him. Sergio links John into a dyadic boundary around this information in which he assumes that both he and John co-own the information together, although it is likely that Sergio does not define the ownership equally. In other words, he no doubt thinks that the information is still primarily his. If John has a different view of ownership, it may be that John feels he has the right to determine whom else he tells. Consequently, he may have a different rule for permeability than does Sergio. John may tell his buddies about the marriage proposal before Sergio asks his partner to marry him. In this way, all three processes are interdependent but distinguishable.

The development or use of rules may function smoothly and be synchronized among the shareholders. In this case, the boundaries are coordinated successfully. Unfortunately, we do not live a perfect world, and the potential for coordination diminishes at times. Consequently, CPM proposes boundary turbulence, a mechanism that allows for incidences when privacy rules are broken in families and boundaries are no longer maintained according to an original agreement (Petronio, 2002).

BOUNDARY COORDINATION
AND TURBULENCE IN FAMILIES

Families are particularly interesting for privacy scholars to study because the members not only preserve personal privacy boundaries, individuals must engage in managing multiple boundary spheres (Petronio, 1991). Theorizing and research has shown that family members control an exterior boundary regulating private information flow to those outside the family (Morr, 2002; Petronio, 2002). Members also control interior boundaries. In other words, families construct dyadic and group privacy compartments or cells within the interior family boundary as they share personal information with select family members. Accordingly, the borders of interior privacy cells shift and change at times to include some members who receive disclosures about an incident and at other times exclude those same members from other information. Interestingly, observers can frequently locate the networks within families by who is privy to what information (Petronio & Bantz, 1991). For example, rules that thwart access, such as when a sister says, "don't tell Grandma this," indicate that Grandma is not granted entrance to this inner cell between certain family members, whereas the sister being told the private information is clearly considered part of the inner boundary circle. Boundary coordination for both the interior and exterior family boundaries adjusts to the demands that families encounter. However, because too much change can result in instability for the family, the consistent use of certain rules forms the basis for family privacy orientations.

CPM argues that families represent a clear example of collectivities that use privacy rules repeatedly to form basic orientations to privacy choices. Research supports the identification of three orientations for internal and external boundaries (Morr, 2002; Petronio, 2002). First, families can have high permeability orientations, in that they are very open and disclose internally to other family members and externally to individuals outside their family. For example, some families expect that all information considered private by one person in the family is meant to be shared with every member. No information is considered to be solely within the domain of any one person; rather, all members believe that any information belonging to one person is everyone's personal information. In this way, the family is completely open with each other. Not all families with high permeability orientations are as open with those inside and outside their family. Some families are completely open only to those within their families and reserve the information for members of the family rather than telling outsiders. On occasion, families might also reverse the focus and be completely open with outsiders while restricting information internally with family members.

Second, families may have moderate permeability concerning the privacy boundaries. These families are more judicious with choices about who knows information about family members, both among the individuals within the family and those outside. Whereas the high permeability families are less guarded, moderate families have more rules and take more precautions in judging disclosure to others within or outside the family.

Third, families may have a low permeability orientation to privacy. For these family members, private information is highly restricted. They draw thick boundary lines around their information with each other and/or those outside the family. This orientation best reflects families who are more likely to keep secrets because they have many rules that disallow the transmission of information to others (Vangelisti, 1994).

As couples develop their relationship, they negotiate privacy rules that are acceptable to each partner and collectively as a couple (Petronio, 2002). This negotiation often takes place through a process of trial and error. A husband may assume it is acceptable to tell friends that his wife's parent is an alcoholic. However, if the husband mentions to his wife that her parent was discussed, the wife might find this action unacceptable and become angry with her husband. Because CPM argues that boundary coordination and boundary turbulence go hand in hand; the inevitable bumps in the road force people to adjust their assumptions about rules guiding personal ownership and expectations for collective shareholder responsibility. Returning to the example, this couple necessarily has to work through the issues to arrive at a common set of rules for when, how, and with whom information about the alcoholic parent may be shared.

Couples not only negotiate privacy rules with each other, but families often have to teach existing rules to new family members so they can be integrated into the family. Obviously, this type of socialization takes place both explicitly, through actively instructing new members, and implicitly, through enacting acceptable behaviors as a model for others to follow. One of the more interesting phenomena in this regard is found in Morr's (2002) research. Morr discovered that when couples are engaged or newly married, one way families acknowledge the status of the new member of the family is through disclosing family secrets (see also Vangelisti & Caughlin, 1997; Vangelisti, Caughlin, & Timmerman, 2001). In contrast, individuals who become part of a stepfamily often share secrets with their original family members that they conceal from new stepparents and stepsiblings (Caughlin, Golish, Olson, Sargent, Cook, & Petronio, 2000). Such restrictions of private information from new family members can signal who is accepted as part of a family subsystem and who is considered outside that group (Golish & Caughlin, 2002; Petronio, Ellemers,

Giles, & Gallois, 1998). Afifi's (2003) research makes the difficulty stepfamilies have in managing boundary lines for privacy more obvious. She found that stepfamilies often face dialectical tensions of loyalty-disloyalty and revealing-concealing among the custodial parents, non-custodial parents, and stepparents. These tensions make all members of the stepfamily feel caught in dilemmatic struggles between levels of loyalties and levels of revealing and concealing. Stepfamilies may go through very rocky times, thus experiencing boundary turbulence because the rules for privacy management unavoidably must change to accommodate new alliances and changed privacy needs in the new family. Those individuals who are used to being part of a family's interior privacy boundary may have to shift to being an outsider and excluded from receiving private disclosures.

Defining who is considered part of an interior family privacy boundary and who is not obviously has import for judgments members make about disclosure. Although it is not clear whether stepfamilies follow the same rules as first-time marriages, the type of rules used to govern the interior privacy orientation, or the way they regulate private disclosures with each other, tends to affect the amount of disclosure from the family to a new member (Morr, 2002). In a sense, stepfamilies may use the rules they have for each other when they interact with engaged or new members because they have redefined them as insiders and they are no longer considered outside of the family.

As individuals join families and become recognized as members, they experience a training period during which they learn acceptable privacy rules (Morr, 2002). This kind of rule socialization is not limited to new members who join a family. For example, when individuals become parents, they teach children their agreed-upon privacy rules. From a young age, children learn family privacy rules about how to protect their world. Interestingly, because the idea of ownership is prominent in CPM theory, the development of "mine" or what belongs to the child may serve as preliminary grounding to cognitively comprehend the more sophisticated notion of privacy, and a child moves from understanding what is "my toy" to what is private information in the family. Because management of privacy requires a complex array of rules and choices, children may not be able to navigate adeptly. Many children, for example, misapply rules about being open and candid inside the family when they interact with outsiders. Such incidents often result in embarrassment for parents, as in the movie *Broadcast News* when Aaron introduces his son Cliff to a former colleague and asks, "Do you know who this is, Cliff?" When Cliff replies, "The big joke," Aaron is obviously uncomfortable and he nudges his son to indicate that a lesson in discretion will be forthcoming.

Even if children are not always skillfully able to negotiate choices regarding privacy, childhood is a training ground to begin the process of understanding control over information. Especially in our world today, children need to be equipped with the ability to determine how to regulate their boundaries. Parents help their children by recognizing their claims on space and territory and desire to keep secrets. Because secrets tend to be defined in more simple terms (either you have one or you do not), parents often use this vehicle to illustrate the larger domain of privacy. Practicing with keeping or telling secrets and witnessing the ramifications of revealing or concealing is a good instructional way for parents to move to schemes that are more complex (Youniss & Smollar, 1985).

By the time children enter adolescence; they have acquired the need for more privacy and concomitantly have advanced cognitively to manage a more complex set of decision criteria. Some scholars have argued that the concept of privacy is a good measure of the deindividuation process in which adolescents move away from their parents and establish their own independent identity (Wolfe & Laufer, 1974; Youniss & Smollar, 1985). When parents respect a child's need to "own" private information, space, possessions, and territory, they are able to have a more satisfying relationship with their children (Petronio, 1994). Consequently, the part that privacy management plays developmentally seems critical for children and parents alike.

Although synchronization of privacy rules is important and helps to keep the systems running easily, CPM argues that the complexity of the process means that there are necessarily breaches of privacy rules. In some cases, this may not be problematic, especially if family members are unaware or do not recognize that privacy rules have been violated. For example, someone in the family may be aware that another family member is breaking a family privacy rule (e.g., an adolescent keeping her dating activities secret when the family has a rule against such secrecy) but chooses to act as if the rule were not being broken. Such instances are examples of pretense awareness (Glaser & Strauss, 1967; Petronio, 2002), in which the parties involved are aware of the secret information, but avoid acknowledging it, perhaps to dodge a conflict that might be involved with renegotiating privacy rules.

In other instances, family members may be unaware that others are breaking rules. Consider, for example, families in which the parents and their daughter have agreed that she should let her parents become acquainted with her friends. As the daughter moves into adolescence, she makes new friends at school and decides not to introduce her parents to these new friends because she is afraid that her parents would disapprove. Assuming that these friends do not lead the daughter into trouble and that the parents do not find out about the new friends, this violation of the previously negotiated rule may cause little trouble for the family and might even be useful in some cases. Keeping such information from parents can be a useful way for adolescents to establish their own autonomy (Finenauer, Engels, & Meeus, 2002; Petronio, 1994). Moreover, Caughlin and Golish (2002) found that parents of college students were only somewhat better than chance at knowing the extent to which their children avoided topics with them. That is, although there would be a risk of the parents finding out about the friends, adolescent children often can successfully hide information from their parents. If the parents never find out about this rule violation, there would be no need to renegotiate the current privacy rules regarding friends. However, if the parents do discover that a previously-agreed-upon rule has been violated, it would lead to boundary turbulence unless they shift to a strategy of pretense awareness. Pretense awareness allows parents to act as if they do not know about (but actually are aware of) the violation. Sometimes this strategy is a good temporary approach that lets the parents "buy time" to decide what they want to do about the violation.

These turbulent moments are both problematic and productive for families. The disturbances can make people feel uncomfortable and uneasy because they disrupt the equilibrium that family members count on when they use privacy rules. However, at the same time, feelings of discomfort resulting from privacy rule violations motivate us to give some attention to the way the rules function (or do not function) in the family. When rules break down, family members are forced to examine the reasons and adjust privacy rules to better fit the needs of the situation.

Boundary turbulence can be particularly salient when family members experience privacy dilemmas. Privacy dilemmas represent another form of privacy rule violations that family members encounter (Petronio, Jones, & Morr, 2003; Petronio, 2002). Research on family privacy dilemmas illustrates a particular way in which privacy rules are compromised. The predicaments are "conversational hot potatoes," and research has identified at least four types of predicaments: confidant dilemmas, accidental dilemmas, illicit dilemmas, and interdependence dilemmas. First, confidant dilemmas illustrate the times when a family member discloses unexpected private information and asks the confidant to keep the information classified. The dilemma arises because keeping it restricted means that the confidant may allow the discloser, the confidant, or others to be harmed. Petronio et al. (2003) described such a dilemma faced by an individual whose uncle revealed that he had a drug problem but asked the family member to keep this information secret. Such cases force family members to choose between two uncomfortable options: betraying the confidence of a family member by revealing or failing to help a family member who may desperately need it by concealing.

Second, an accidental dilemma occurs when a person inadvertently finds out about private information concerning a family member; however, telling someone else would cause that member or another person potential harm (Petronio, et al. 2003). Advice columns are rife with examples of people who inadvertently discover information about other family members that causes accidental dilemmas. In one recent column (Savage, 2004), a college student was visiting home and, while borrowing the parents' computer, noticed that the father had been viewing various adult web pages. Knowing that the mother would be deeply hurt and offended by this material, this person faced unenviable choices. Given that the father did not try to hide the history of viewing these web pages, not saying anything risked allowing the mother to be hurt, but telling either the father or the mother of the discovery involved obvious risks (e.g., causing embarrassment or instigating damage to the parents' relationship).

Third, illicit family privacy dilemmas occur when a member snoops and finds out something that is harmful for that person and/or another family member. Such dilemmas often result from successful "spying," as in cases when a parent listens in to an adolescent's private phone conversations and finds out that the adolescent has been drinking alcohol. Without revealing this information, the parent cannot discipline the child, but revealing the information may require the potentially damaging revelation that the parent has been monitoring the adolescent's phone conversations.

Fourth, an interdependence dilemma is one in which a family member must choose between what is best for the self versus best for another family member or one's relationship with another family member. In such cases, the decision to reveal private information would be straightforward if one is concerned only about oneself. However, the interdependent nature of families means that in addition to the risks and benefits directly affecting the individuals, family members become disturbed about the risks and benefits for other family members and their relationships with those other family members. Somebody keeping a secret from another family member, for instance, may incur psychological costs such as becoming preoccupied and anxious with the secret (Lane & Wegner, 1995; Wegner & Lane, 1995). Revealing the secret, on the other hand, might lead to conflicts with that other family member that are best avoided (Roloff & Ifert, 2000) or could be distressing to another family member (Brown-Smith, 1998; Papp, 1993). However, for family members dealing with them, interdependence dilemmas can have important consequences. For instance, parents who have HIV may go through undeniably stressful measures to hide their viral status from their children to buffer them from worry (Schrimshaw & Siegel, 2002).

All four dilemmatic situations illustrate boundary turbulence because the existing privacy rules are breached in each situation. As we see from the research, there is no right answer in all cases, so there is no one viable solution available. Instead, there are only options available to manage the boundary turbulence (Petronio et al., 2003). Consequently, families experiencing privacy dilemmas must call into question the privacy rules used, and seek adjustments or develop new rules.

Family privacy dilemmas are just one example of boundary turbulence; there are many others (see Petronio, 2002). For each type of privacy dilemma, we witness the way boundary systems regulate after disruption. CPM argues that disruption is inevitable and necessary because it reflects how the management process is self-correcting. Boundary coordination may be compromised when rule expectations are fuzzy to one of the shareholders, when the context of the situation is defined differently by one or more family members, or when assumptions about informational ownership are dissimilar. In each case, the breach resulting in boundary turbulence calls into question the viability of the privacy rules. As that process takes place, families will need to change the rules to accommodate the rift in the system. Once the asynchronous situation is addressed, the modification in rules allows the privacy system to function again in the family to regulate the flow of private disclosures (Petronio, 2002).

In general, Communication Privacy Management theory is designed to understand everyday privacy issues that families face. As such, it is our challenge to test the utility of CPM theory so that we can understand the way families in different contexts manage their privacy. CPM is especially useful to help grasp the way families navigate private disclosures and determine what happens when family rules for disclosure are challenged or inadequate. Theories can live on only if we are brave enough to seek change when change is clearly warranted. Theories die when people are not willing to acknowledge that adjustments in the basic thesis are needed. CPM has benefited from an evolutionary process of development that we hope continues to progress. CPM theory gives us a heuristic to capture the way people in families understand privacy management. We hope that you find new ways to use CPM and contribute to its development.

REFERENCES

Afifi, T. D. (2003). "Feeling caught'" in stepfamilies: Managing boundary turbulence through appropriate communication privacy rules. *Journal of Social and Personal Relationships, 20,* 729–755.

Altman, I., Vinsel, A., & Brown, B. (1981). Dialectic conceptions in social psychology: An application to social penetration and privacy regulation. *Advances in Experimental Social Psychology, 14,* 107–160.

Berardo, F. (1974). Marital invisibility and family privacy. In S. Margulis (Ed.), *Privacy.* Stony Brook, NY: Environmental Design Research Association.

Brown-Smith, N. (1998). Family secrets. *Journal of Family Issues, 19,* 20–42.

Caughlin, J. P., & Afifi, T. D. (2004). When is topic avoidance unsatisfying?: Examining moderators of the association between avoidance and dissatisfaction. *Human Communication Research, 30,* 479–513.

Caughlin, J. P., & Golish, T. D. (2002). An analysis of the association between topic avoidance and dissatisfaction: Comparing perceptual and interpersonal explanations. *Communication Monographs, 69,* 275–295.

Caughlin, J. P., Golish, T. D., Olson, L. N., Sargent, J. E., Cook, J. S., & Petronio, S. (2000). Family secrets in various family configurations: A Communication Boundary Management perspective. *Communication Studies, 51,* 116–134.

Caughlin, J. P., & Petronio, S. (2004). Privacy in families. In A. Vangelisti (Ed.). *Handbook of family communication* (pp. 379–412).

Finenauer, C., Engels, R. C., & Meeus, W. (2002). Keeping secrets from parents: Advantages and disadvantages of secrecy in adolescence. *Journal of Youth and Adolescence, 31,* 123–136.

Glaser, B., & Strauss, A. (1967). Awareness contexts and social interaction. *American Sociological Review, 19,* 669–679.

Golish, T. D., & Caughlin, J. P. (2002). "I'd rather not talk about it." Adolescents' and young adults' use of topic avoidance in stepfamilies. *Journal of Applied Communication Research, 30,* 78–106.

Lane, J. D., & Wegner, D. M. (1995). The cognitive consequences of secrecy. *Journal of Personality and Social Psychology, 69,* 237–253.

Morr, M. C. (2002). Private disclosure in a family membership transition: In-laws' disclosures to newlyweds. *Dissertation Abstracts International, 63(5),* 1627. (UMI No. AAT3054643)

Papp, P. (1993). The worm in the bud: Secrets between parents and children. In E. Imber-Black (Ed.), *Secrets in families and family therapy* (pp. 66–85). New York: Norton.

Petronio, S. (1991). Communication boundary management: A theoretical model of managing disclosure of private information between marital couples. *Communication Theory, 1,* 311–335.

Petronio, S. (1994). Privacy binds in family interactions: The case of parental privacy invasion. In W. R. Cupach & B. H. Spitzberg (Eds.), *The dark side of interpersonal communication* (pp. 241–257). Mahwah, NJ: Lawrence Erlbaum.

Petronio, S. (2002). *Boundaries of privacy: Dialectics of disclosure.* Albany, NY: SUNY Press.

Petronio, S., & Bantz, C. (1991). Controlling the ramifications of disclosure: "Don't tell anybody but . . ." *Journal of Language and Social Psychology, 10,* 263–269.

Petronio, S., Ellemers, N., Giles, H., & Gallois, C. (1998). (Mis) communicating across boundaries: Interpersonal and intergroup considerations. *Communication Research, 25,* 571–595.

Petronio, S., Jones, S., & Morr, M. C. (2003). Family privacy dilemmas: Managing communication boundaries within family groups. In L. R. Frey (Ed.), *Group communication in context: Studies of bona fide groups* (2nd ed., pp. 23–55). Mahwah, NJ: Lawrence Erlbaum.

Roloff, M. E., & Ifert, D. E. (2000). Conflict management through avoidance: Withholding complaints, suppressing arguments, and declaring topics taboo. In S. Petronio (Ed.), *Balancing the secrets of private disclosures* (pp. 151–179). Mahwah, NJ: Lawrence Erlbaum.

Savage, D. (2004, March 30). Save love. [Electronic version.] *The Village Voice.* Retrieved from http://www.villagevoice.com/issues/0413/savage.php

Schrimshaw, E. W., & Siegel, K. (2002). HIV-infected mothers' disclosure to their uninfected children: Rates, reasons, and reactions. *Journal of Social and Personal Relationships, 19,* 19–43.

Vangelisti, A. L. (1994). Family secrets: Forms, functions, and correlates. *Journal of Social and Personal Relationships, 11,* 113–135.

Vangelisti, A. L., & Caughlin J. P. (1997). Revealing family secrets: The influence of topic, function, and relationships. *Journal of Social and Personal Relationships, 14,* 679–705.

Vangelisti, A. L., Caughlin, J. P., & Timmerman, L. M. (2001). Criteria for revealing family secrets. *Communication Monographs, 68,* 1–27.

Wegner, D. M., & Lane, J. D. (1995). From secrecy to psychopathology. In J. W. Pennebaker (Ed.), *Emotion, disclosure, and health* (pp. 25–46). Washington, DC: American Psychological Association.

Wolfe, M., & Laufer, R. (1974). The concept of privacy in childhood and adolescence. In S. Margulis (Ed.), *Privacy.* Stony Brook, NY: Environmental Design Research Association.

Youniss, J., & Smollar, J. (1985). *Adolescent relations with mothers, fathers and friends.* Chicago: University of Chicago Press.

4

Family Communication Patterns Theory: A Social Cognitive Approach

Ascan F. Koerner

Mary Anne Fitzpatrick

Editors' Note: Family Communication Patterns Theory takes a view of communication that is both cognitive and interpersonal. The theory grows out of mass media research, built on earlier work from cognitive psychology. We place Family Communication Patterns Theory in the logical empirical paradigm because it is concerned with causal explanation of why people communicate the way they do based on cognitive orientations in family relationships.

Family communication is a challenging phenomenon to theorize about because it simultaneously depends on *intrapersonal* and on *interpersonal* processes. In other words, the variables that explain family communication reside within each individual as well as within the family system. Thus, "a complete explication of family communication needs to consider both *intersubjectivity* and *interactivity* (Koerner & Fitzpatrick, 2002a, p. 73). Intersubjectivity refers to the similarity of meaning that family members assign to their communicative behaviors and is best understood in terms of relational cognition. In contrast, interactivity refers to the degree to which family members' creation, use, and interpretation of symbols are interdependent and is best understood at the level of interpersonal behavior. Consequently, a comprehensive theory of family communication must consider both relational cognition and interpersonal behavior and explicate how these two are interdependent.

In this chapter, we will present Family Communication Patterns Theory as a comprehensive theory of family communication that operates at the levels of both relational cognition and interpersonal behavior. First, we consider the origin of Family Communication Patterns Theory as a model of how families create a shared social reality through the process of coorientation and the subsequent reformulation of the model as a theory of interpersonal behavior. After describing the underlying cognitive processes, we then describe the resulting communication behaviors in terms of the two dimensions of conversation orientation and conformity orientation and four resulting family types. Then, we discuss what we see as the strengths of Family Communication Patterns Theory and conclude with an outlook on the role that the theory could play in future research on family communication.

DEVELOPMENT OF FAMILY COMMUNICATION PATTERNS THEORY

Family Communication Patterns and the Sharing of Social Reality

McLeod and Chaffee (1972, 1973) developed the original model of family communication patterns to describe families' tendencies to develop fairly stable and predictable ways of communicating with one another. As mass media researchers, McLeod and Chaffee were not interested in family communication as an end in itself. Rather, they wanted to explain how families create and share social reality. Specifically, they were interested in explaining how parents socialize their children to process information stemming from outside the family; in particular, information in the form of mass media messages. At that time, psychology and allied fields experienced a renewed interest in cognitive processes as they turned away from behaviorism and an almost exclusive interest in message properties to explain communication outcomes (Reeves, Chaffee, & Tims, 1982). Thus, it is no surprise that McLeod and Chaffee based their explanation of family communication on the cognitive theory of coorientation.

Coorientation is one of the fundamental concepts of social cognition initially described by Heider (1946, 1958) and Newcomb (1953) and refers to two or more persons focusing on and evaluating the same object in their social or material environment. In dyads that are aware of their shared focus, coorientation leads to two different cognitions for each person. The first cognition is a person's own evaluation of the object and the second cognition is the person's perception of the other persons' evaluation of the object. Combined, these cognitions determine three attributes of coorientation: agreement, accuracy, and congruence. *Agreement* refers to equivalence of the two persons' evaluations of the object. For example, if Chris and Pat are cooriented toward a movie and they both like the movie, they have agreement. *Accuracy* refers to the similarity between a person's perception of the other person's evaluation and the other person's actual evaluation. Thus, if Chris likes the movie and Pat thinks that Chris likes the movie, Pat has accuracy. Finally, *congruence* refers to the similarity between a person's own evaluation of the object and the person's perception of the other person's evaluation of the object. Thus, if Pat likes the movie and thinks that Chris likes the movie, Pat has congruence. Unlike agreement, which is a property of the dyad and necessarily is the same for both persons, accuracy and congruence are properties of the individuals and are not necessarily the same for both individuals. That is, Pat might have accuracy and congruence, whereas Chris has not.

Within individuals, the three attributes of coorientation are linearly dependent on one another. That is, the state of any two determines the state of the third according to the same rules governing multiplication of positive and negative numbers. For example, accuracy and congruence require that there is agreement ($+ * + = +$), congruence and disagreement require there is inaccuracy ($+ * - = -$), inaccuracy and disagreement require that there is congruence ($- * - = +$), and so forth. Although coorientation and its attributes are described here in the dyadic context, it also applies to larger groups such as families.

Dyads and families that are in the process of coorientation do not necessarily share social reality, whereas social reality is defined as a shared perception and evaluation of the social world; that is, as agreement defined previously. The psychological desire for balanced cognition and the pragmatic need to understand the other, however, favor congruence and accuracy, respectively; and because of the linear dependency of congruence, accuracy, and agreement, ultimately also agreement. Because of this, coorientation in dyads and families usually leads to shared social reality (for a detailed explanation of these processes, see Koerner & Fitzpatrick, 2004).

According to McLeod and Chaffee (1972, 1973), dyads and family members can achieve agreement in two distinct ways. First, family members can focus on other family members' evaluations of an object and adopt that evaluation. In other words, they can conform to other family members. Because this process emphasizes the relationships between family members, McLeod and Chaffee called this process *socio-orientation*. The other way to achieve agreement is for families to focus on the object in the environment by discussing it and its attributes and arrive at a shared perception of the object. Because this process emphasizes how family members conceptualize the object, McLeod and Chaffee called this process *concept-orientation*.

McLeod and Chaffee (1972) proposed that families vary in their preferences for and uses of these two strategies to achieve agreement, and consequently children are socialized differently in regard to the processing of information contained in media messages. Children of families that tend to use socio-orientation rely on others to interpret the meaning of media messages to them, mainly their parents or peers. Conversely, children of families that tend to use concept-orientation elaborate on the concepts and ideas contained in the messages to determine their meanings. In other words, the two strategies to achieve agreement in families are associated with different communication behaviors. McLeod and Chaffee realized that the processes families use to share social reality affect the communication behaviors and practices of families, and they used this insight to construct a behavioral measurement of the underlying strategies of information processing. The instrument they developed is the Family Communication Patterns (FCP) instrument, which has been widely used in media effects research. Its relevance to family communication more generally, however, went largely unnoticed until Fitzpatrick and her colleagues started using the instrument in the late 1980s and early 1990s in their research of family communication.

Family Communication
Patterns as Behavioral Tendencies

Although social reality ultimately takes shape and resides in the minds of individual family members, the two strategies of socio-orientation and concept-orientation have direct effects on the communication behavior of family members. Sharing a social reality, however, is an ongoing process in families and not limited to the processing of mass media messages. Recognizing this, Fitzpatrick and Ritchie (1993, 1994; Ritchie, 1991, 1997; Ritchie & Fitzpatrick, 1990) refined and reconceptualized McLeod and Chaffee's (1972) FCP to construct an instrument to measure family communication patterns more generally.

Thus, in the Revised Family Communication Patterns (RFCP) instrument, socio-orientation was reconceptualized as *conformity orientation* because the communication behavior typical of socio-orientation is one that emphasizes conformity within families, particularly that of children to parents. In other words, families that socialize their children to look to others to assign meaning to things are usually headed by parents who encourage children to conform to their views and discourage discussions and divergent opinions. Similarly, concept-orientation was reconceptualized as *conversation orientation* because the communication behavior typical of concept-orientation is one of lengthy and involving family discussions. In other words, parents in these families encourage their children to look at the things themselves when assigning meaning and to explore potential meanings by discussing them with others, paying attention to the strengths of their arguments rather their social position within the family. In addition to the greater emphasis on communication behaviors, the RFCP instrument was also expanded to include additional items to produce more reliable measurements of the two dimensions of family communication (Ritchie & Fitzpatrick, 1990).

DIMENSIONS OF FAMILY COMMUNICATION

Conversation Orientation

The first dimension of family communication, conversation orientation, is defined as the degree to which families create a climate in which all family members are encouraged to participate in unrestrained interaction about a wide array of topics. In families on the high end of this dimension, family members freely, frequently, and spontaneously interact with each other without many limitations in regard to time spent in interaction and topics discussed (Koerner & Fitzpatrick, 2002b). These families spend a lot of time interacting with each other, and family members share their individual activities, thoughts, and feelings with each other. In these families, actions or activities that the family plan to engage in as a unit are discussed within the family, as are other family decisions. Conversely, in families at the low end of the conversation orientation dimension, members interact less frequently with each other, and there are only a few topics that are openly discussed with all family members. There is less exchange of private thoughts, feelings, and activities. In these families, activities that family members engage in as a unit are not usually discussed in great detail, nor is everybody's input sought after for family decisions (Koerner & Fitzpatrick, 2002b).

Associated with high conversation orientation is the belief that open and frequent communication is essential to an enjoyable and rewarding family life. Families holding this view value the exchange of ideas, and parents holding this belief see frequent communication with their children as the main means to educate and to socialize them. Conversely, families low in conversation orientation believe that open and frequent exchanges of ideas, opinion, and values are not necessary for the function of the family in general—and for the children's education and socialization in particular (Koerner & Fitzpatrick, 2002a).

Conformity Orientation

The second dimension of family communication is conformity orientation. Conformity orientation refers to the degree to which family communication stresses a climate of homogeneity of attitudes, values, and beliefs. Families on the high end of this dimension are characterized by interactions that emphasize a uniformity of beliefs and attitudes. Their interactions typically focus on harmony, conflict avoidance, and the interdependence of family members (Koerner & Fitzpatrick, 2002b). In intergenerational exchanges, communication in these families reflects obedience to parents and other adults. Families on the low end of the conformity-orientation dimension are characterized by interactions that focus on heterogeneous attitudes and beliefs, as well as on the individuality of family members and their independence from their family. In intergenerational exchanges, communication reflects the equality of all family members; for example, children are usually involved in decision making (Koerner & Fitzpatrick, 2002b).

Associated with high conformity orientation is the belief in what might be called a traditional family structure. In this view, families are cohesive and hierarchical. That is, family members favor their family relationships over relationships external to the family, and they expect that resources such as space and money will be shared among family members. Families high in conformity orientation believe that individual schedules should be coordinated among family members to maximize family time, and they expect family members to subordinate personal interests to those of the family. Parents in these families expect to make the decisions for the family and children are expected to act according to their parents' wishes. Conversely, families low in conformity orientation do not believe in a traditional family structure. Instead, they believe in less cohesive and hierarchically organized families. Families on the low end of the conformity-orientation dimension believe that relationships outside the family are equally as important as family relationships, and that families should encourage the personal growth of individual family members, even if that leads to a weakening of the family structure. They believe in the independence of family members, value personal space, and subordinate family interests to personal interests (Koerner & Fitzpatrick, 2002b).

The effects that these two core dimensions of communication in families have on actual family communication are often dependent on one another. That is, rather than having simple main effects on family communication, these two dimensions often interact with one another such that the impact of conversation orientation on family outcomes is moderated by the degree of conformity orientation of the family, and vice versa. Therefore, to predict the influence of family communication patterns on family outcomes, it is rarely sufficient to investigate only one dimension without assessing the other dimension as well (Koerner & Fitzpatrick, 2002b, 2004). Because the two dimensions of conformity orientation and conversation orientation interact consistently with one another, in effect they create four family types that are qualitatively different: *consensual, pluralistic, protective,* and *laissez-faire.* To distinguish these types is therefore of theoretical significance and not just a convenient way of describing four family types that are created by crossing these two dimensions (see Figure 4.1).

COMMUNICATION IN DIFFERENT FAMILY TYPES

Consensual Families

Families high in both conversation and conformity orientation are labeled *consensual.* Their communication is characterized by a tension between pressure to agree and to preserve the existing hierarchy

Figure 4.1   Family Types determined by Conversation Orientation and
Conformity Orientation

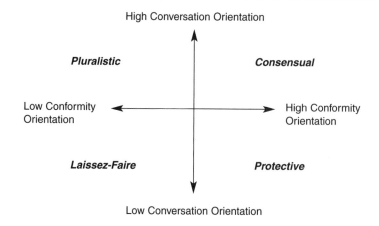

within the family on the one hand, and an interest in open communication and in exploring new ideas on the other hand. That is, parents
in these families are very interested in their children and what the
children have to say, but at the same time also believe that they, as the
parents, should make decisions for the family and for the children.
They resolve this tension by listening to their children and by spending
time and energy in explaining their decisions, as well as their values
and beliefs, to their children in the hope that their children will understand the reasoning behind the parents' decisions and adopt the
parents' belief system. Children in these families usually learn to value
family conversations and tend to adopt their parents' values and
beliefs. In these families, volatile conflict is generally regarded as
negative and harmful to the family, but because unresolved conflict is
perceived as potentially threatening to the relationships within the
family, these families also value and engage in problem solving and
conflict resolution (Koerner & Fitzpatrick, 1997).

Pluralistic Families

Families high in conversation orientation and low in conformity
orientation are labeled *pluralistic.* Communication in pluralistic families is characterized by open, unconstrained discussions that involve all
family members and a wide range of topics. Parents in these families

do not feel the need to be in control of their children by making decisions for them, nor do they feel the need to agree with their children's decisions. This parental attitude leads to family discussions in which opinions are evaluated based on the merit of arguments in their support rather than on which family members espouse them. That is, parents are willing to accept their children's opinions and allow them to participate in family decision making. Because of their emphasis on the free exchange of ideas and the absence of overt pressure to conform or to obey, these families are low in conflict avoidance and openly address their conflicts with one another, engage in positive conflict-resolution strategies, and usually are able to resolve their conflicts. Children of these families learn to value family conversations and learn to be independent and autonomous at the same time, which fosters their communication competence and their confidence in their ability to make their own decisions. (Koerner & Fitzpatrick, 1997).

Protective Families

Families low on conversation orientation and high on conformity orientation are labeled *protective*. Communication in protective families is characterized by an emphasis on obedience to parental authority and by little concern for conceptual matters or for open communication within the family. Parents in these families believe that they should be making the decisions for their family and their children, and they see little value in explaining their reasoning to their children. Conflict in protective families is perceived negatively because of the great emphasis placed on conformity (Koerner & Fitzpatrick, 1997). Family members are expected not to have conflicts with one another and to behave according to the interests and norms of the family. Because communication skills are not valued and not practiced much, these families often lack the necessary skills to engage productively in conflict resolution should it come to open disagreements. Children in protective families learn that there is little value in family conversations and to distrust their own decision-making ability.

Laissez-Faire Families

Families low in both conversation orientation and conformity orientation are labeled *laissez-faire*. Their communication is characterized by few and often lifeless interactions between family members that

Kantor and Lehr (1975) distinguished between open, closed, and random families based both on their communication behavior and on how well these families function. Open families employ the most functional behaviors, closed families are moderately functional, and random families are the least functional families in this typology. Similarly, Olson's (1981, 1993; Olson, Russell, & Sprenkle, 1983; Olson, Sprenkle, & Russell, 1979) Circumplex Model of Family Functioning, which is based on the two underlying dimensions of family cohesion and family flexibility, distinguishes between family types that function well (balanced families = moderate on both dimensions), moderately well (midrange families = extreme on one dimension, moderate on the other), and poorly (unbalanced families = extreme on both dimensions). Communication in Olson's model is a third facilitating dimension that allows families to move along the two other dimensions and is of particular relevance for family counseling that has as its goal to achieve more balanced families.

The problem with typologies that distinguish between families based on functioning is that they are based on two implicit but problematic assumptions. The first implicit assumption is that a behavior or structural property of the family is either consistently functional or consistently dysfunctional. This assumption is problematic because it ignores the context in which behavior occurs, which can be radically different and lead to very different outcomes of the behavior. For example, in many contexts, children benefit from strong and positive relationships with both parents. Should the parents divorce, however, these children are more likely to experience loyalty conflicts and to suffer psychologically from the divorce than children who have formed a strong relationship with only one parent who retains custody. Thus, family characteristics or behaviors that are functional in one context might be dysfunctional in another, and vice versa. It therefore makes little sense to view functionality as a permanent attribute of families or behaviors.

The second implicit and problematic assumption is that family functioning is a unidimensional variable in which all functional behaviors are correlated with one another. Not only is that assumption untenable considering that no behavior is always functional as just discussed, but it also ignores that often very different behaviors are functional even in the same context. Very different behaviors, however, are unlikely to correlate consistently and therefore it is unlikely that all functional behaviors are correlated with one another, which would be necessary if functionality was unidimensional. For example, most communication scholars would agree that being outgoing and spontaneous are generally functional communication behaviors for children. The same scholars, however, would probably also agree that being quiet and deliberate are generally functional behaviors as well. That these two sets of behaviors correlate, however, is highly unlikely because they are on opposing ends of the introversion-extroversion dimension, clearly showing that functionality simply cannot be a unidimensional variable.

A second important difference between Family Communication Patterns Theory and other typologies is that the family types are not just a convenient way to describe different types of observable behaviors. Rather, they are based on a sound theoretical model that explains how different strategies families use to create shared social reality result in differences in the communication behavior of families. Thus, Family Communication Patterns Theory provides a satisfactory answer to the question of the etiology of the different family types that is grounded in established cognitive research rather than just having to refer to the behavioral definitions of family types as a means to edify their existence.

STRENGTHS OF FAMILY COMMUNICATION PATTERNS THEORY

The attributes that make Family Communication Patterns Theory unique are also the attributes that make the theory strong. Thus, one of the great strengths of the Family Communication Patterns Theory is that it is not based on the assumption that there is only one functional way to communicate. Rather, similar to Fitzpatrick's (1988) marital typology and Gottman's (1994) typology of conflict styles, Family Communication Patterns Theory recognizes that different families function well by employing different types of behaviors. In this theory, certain behaviors contribute or detract from family functioning not because they are inherently functional or dysfunctional but because of the way they operate within the different communication contexts created by the family types. Thus, this Family Communication Patterns Theory directs researchers to focus on how behaviors interact with specific communication environments to explain the effects they have on family functioning rather than trying to find behaviors that are functional for all families.

effects on family functioning, not behaviors that are functional

A second great strength of Family Communication Patterns Theory not necessarily shared by other family typologies is that it is based on a well-established cognitive model explaining how families create a shared social reality through the process of coorientation. As a result, it is not only based on observable differences of the behavior of the different family types but also explains the source of these differences. Other typologies that are based solely on observable differences in the behavior of different types they describe can justly be criticized that they essentially reify themselves with the argument that the types they describe are different because they behave differently and that they behave differently because they are different. Obviously, a typology that is based on a less tautological claim is theoretically stronger. In addition, the cognitive bases of Family Communication Pattern Theory provide a natural link to other cognitively based theories of communication, dramatically enhancing the chance that it becomes integrated with these other theories of communication to form a more comprehensive model of human communication.

A final strength of the family typology-based communication patterns is that it is associated with a strong empirical measure of the underlying dimensions and the resulting family types. The 26-item RFCP is an easily administered questionnaire with robust psychometric properties (Koerner & Fitzpatrick, 2002b). It and its predecessor, McLeod and Chaffee's (1972) FCP have been used in countless studies and have proved to be both reliable and valid (Koerner & Fitzpatrick, 2002b). Thus, the RFCP offers researchers interested in family communication a convenient and powerful measure of family communication behaviors.

CONCLUSION

Family Communication Patterns Theory is a powerful theory of family communication that is based on a sophisticated model of social cognition and has showed to be relevant to a number of important family processes, such as communication apprehension (Elwood & Schrader, 1998), conflict and conflict resolution (Koerner & Fitzpatrick, 1997, 2002c), resiliency of children (Fitzpatrick & Koerner, in press), social self-restraint and social withdrawal (Fitzpatrick, Marshall, Leutwiler, & Krcmar, 1996), enactment of family rituals (Baxter & Clark, 1996), effects of parents' work environments on family communication (Ritchie,

1997), children's influence on family political discussions (Saphir & Chaffee, 2002), and self-orientation in family conversation (Koerner & Cvancara, 2002). Although impressive in its scope, this research has barely scratched the surface of the proverbial iceberg, and we expect the Family Communication Patterns Theory to play an important role in our and our colleagues' investigation and understanding of family communication and family processes in the future.

In our opinion, the most promising direction that research on Family Communication Patterns Theory can take involves the integration of family communication patterns with family communication schemata. Like other relationship type schemata, family communication schemata involve complex, hierarchically integrated mental representations that family members have of themselves, their family members and their family relationships. Included in family communication schemata is the procedural knowledge of how to achieve agreement and a shared social reality that determines family conversation and conformity orientation (Koerner & Fitzpatrick, 2002a). As such, family communication schemata have the potential to provide an integrative framework not only for research on family communication patterns but also for other research on family communication behaviors, such as communication standards, attachment, and parenting styles. It is our hope that such research will allow family communication scholars to develop a comprehensive model of family communication that goes far beyond just family communication patterns.

REFERENCES

Baxter, L. A., & Clark, C. L. (1996). Perceptions of family communication patterns and the enactment of family rituals. *Western Journal of Communication, 60,* 254–268.

Elwood, T. D., & Schrader, D. C. (1998). Family communication patterns and communication apprehension. *Journal of Social Behavior and Personality, 13,* 493–502.

Fitzpatrick, M. A. (1988). *Between husbands and wives: Communication in marriage.* Newbury Park, CA: Sage.

Fitzpatrick, M. A., & Koerner, A. F. (in press). Family communication schemata: Effects in children's resiliency. In S. Dunwoody, L B. Becker, D. McLeod, & G. Kosicki (Eds.), *The evolution of key mass communication concepts: Honoring Jack M. McLeod.* Cresskill, NJ: Hampton Press.

Fitzpatrick, M. A., Marshall, L. J., Leutwiler, T. J., & Krcmar, M. (1996). The effect of family communication environments on children's social behavior during middle childhood. *Communication Research, 23,* 379–406.

Fitzpatrick, M. A., & Ritchie, L. D. (1993). Communication theory and the family. In P. G. Boss, W. J. Doherty, W. R. Schumm, & S. K. Steinmetz (Eds.), *Sourcebook of family theories and methods: A contextual approach* (pp. 565–585). New York: Plenum Press.

Fitzpatrick, M. A., & Ritchie, L. D. (1994). Communication schemata within the family: Multiple perspectives on family interaction. *Human Communication Research, 20,* 275–301.

Gottman, J. (1994). *Why marriages succeed or fail . . . and how you can make yours last.* New York: Simon & Schuster.

Heider, F. (1946). Attitudes and cognitive organization. *Journal of Psychology, 21,* 107–112.

Heider, F. (1958). *The psychology of interpersonal relations.* New York: Wiley.

Kantor, D., & Lehr, W. (1975). *Inside the family.* San Francisco: Jossey-Bass.

Koerner, A. F., & Cvancara, K. E. (2002). The influence of conformity orientation on communication patterns in family conversations. *The Journal of Family Communication 2,* 132–152.

Koerner, A. F., & Fitzpatrick, M. A. (1997). Family type and conflict: The impact of conversation orientation and conformity orientation on conflict in the family. *Communication Studies, 48,* 59–75.

Koerner, A. F., & Fitzpatrick, M. A. (2002a). Toward a theory of family communication. *Communication Theory, 12,* 70–91.

Koerner, A. F., & Fitzpatrick, M. A. (2002b). Understanding family communication patterns and family functioning: The roles of conversation orientation and conformity orientation. *Communication Yearbook, 26,* 37–69.

Koerner, A. F., & Fitzpatrick, M. A. (2002c). You never leave your family in a fight: The impact of families of origins on conflict-behavior in romantic relationships. *Communication Studies, 53,* 234–251.

Koerner, A. F., & Fitzpatrick, M. A. (2004). Communication in intact families. In A. L. Vangelisti (Ed.), *The handbook of family communication* (pp. 177–195). Mahwah, NJ: Lawrence Erlbaum.

McLeod, J. M., & Chaffee, S. H. (1972). The construction of social reality. In J. Tedeschi (Ed.), *The social influence process* (pp. 50–59). Chicago: Aldine-Atherton.

McLeod, J. M., & Chaffee, S. H. (1973). Interpersonal approaches to communication research. *American Behavioral Scientist, 16,* 469–499.

Newcomb, T. M. (1953). An approach to the study of communicative acts. *Psychological Review, 60,* 393–404.

Olson, D. H. (1981). Family typologies: Bridging family research and family therapy. In E. E. Filsinger & R. A. Lewis (Eds.), *Assessing marriage: New behavioral approaches* (pp. 74–89). Beverly Hills, CA: Sage.

Olson, D. H. (1993). Circumplex model of marital and family systems. In F. Walsh (Ed.), *Normal family processes* (2nd ed.). New York: Guilford Press.

Olson, D. H., Russell, C. S., & Sprenkle, D. H. (1983). Circumplex model of marital and family systems, VI: Theoretical update. *Family Process, 22,* 69–83.

Olson, D. H., Sprenkle, D. H., & Russell, C. S. (1979). Circumplex model of marital and family systems: Cohesion and adaptability dimensions, family types, and clinical applications. *Family Process, 18,* 3–28.

Reeves, B., Chaffee, S. H., & Tims, A. (1982). Social cognition and mass communication research. In M. E. Roloff & C. R. Berger (Eds.), *Social cognition and communication* (pp. 33–72). Beverly Hills, CA: Sage.

Ritchie, L. D. (1991). Family communication patterns: An epistemic analysis and conceptual reinterpretation. *Communication Research, 18,* 548–565.

Ritchie, L. D. (1997). Parents' workplace experiences and family communication patterns. *Communication Research, 24,* 175–187.

Ritchie, L. D., & Fitzpatrick, M. A. (1990). Family communication patterns: Measuring interpersonal perceptions of interpersonal relationships. *Communication Research, 17,* 523–544.

Saphir, M. N., & Chaffee, S. H. (2002). Adolescents' contributions to family communication patterns. *Human Communication Research, 28,* 86–108.

VanLear, A., Koerner, A. F., & Allen, D. (in press). Relationship typologies. In A. L. Vangelisti & D. Perlmann (Eds.), *Handbook of personal relationships.* Cambridge, UK: Cambridge University Press.

5

Goals-Plans-Action Theories: Theories of Goals, Plans, and Planning Processes in Families

Steven R. Wilson

Wendy M. Morgan

Editors' Note: In this chapter the authors present theories that cohere around the issue of how family members use communication to pursue goals and enact plans to achieve desired future states. Originating in psychology, goals-plans-action (GPA) represents a group of theories from the logical-empirical tradition representing generalizable cause-effect relationships of goals and plans to communication outcomes.

"Goals" and "plans" are concepts we use to make sense of and navigate everyday interactions (Berger, 2002). To illustrate how we do so, consider an example from Steve's (the first author's) life. Steve is married to Patrice, and together they have six (step) children, who range in age from 10–24 years. Their two youngest daughters are Robyn and Annie. The example took place in February 2004, two months before Robyn's tenth birthday.

Example 1

01 Robyn: Dad, I want to get my ears pierced.

02 Steve: What does Mom say?

03 Robyn: She says I'm too young. But Annie got hers pierced when she was 8.

04 Steve: And Annie didn't clean her ears regularly, and they got infected.

05 Robyn: But Dad, I'll clean mine—I promise.

06 Steve: Wouldn't this be a good thing to get done around your birthday?

07 Robyn: But what if Mom won't let me?

08 Steve: I'll talk to Mom. I can't promise she'll say yes, but I'll talk to her. Maybe she'll think that 10 is old enough.

09 Robyn: Please Dad—I really want to get my ears pierced.

What is going on in this example? Would you agree that Robyn is trying to convince Steve that she should be able to get her ears pierced? Notice that the conversation seems coherent because we infer getting her ears pierced to be Robyn's goal. Seeing this as Robyn's goal explains why she states her desire to have her ears pierced in line 01 and why she responds to potential obstacles to getting her ears pierced in lines 03–05. Robyn also appears to have a plan for pursuing her goal, which might be characterized as "talk to Dad." In lines 06–08, Steve proposes a plan of his own—Robyn will wait until she is 10 to get her ears pierced and in the meantime Steve offers to talk with Patrice about the issue. Steve and Robyn discuss the workability and acceptability of this new plan (lines 06–09).

People rely on goals and plans whenever they communicate (Kellermann, 1992); hence, it is not surprising that communication theories often include a focus upon goals or plans. The idea that messages need to be analyzed in light of the goals they are designed to achieve has a long history in the field of speech communication (Clark & Delia, 1979) just as the concepts of goals and plans have a long history in psychology (Austin & Vancouver, 1996). We use the term "goals-plans-action" (GPA) when referring to a group of theories that shed light on how individuals form and pursue goals during face-to-face interaction, make inferences about each others' goals, and manage conflicting goals (see Dillard, 2004; Wilson, 2002).

Although GPA theories address general questions about communication rather than issues unique to families, there are good reasons for thinking that families are an important social context in which to study goals and plans. Family members are interdependent; therefore, each member influences the others' goals and plans (Berscheid & Peplau, 1983). For example, Robyn cannot get her ears pierced without her parents' consent, and Steve cannot grant Robyn permission unilaterally (at least not without starting a major conflict with Patrice). Families also differ in the degree to which members openly discuss plans and expect children to conform to adults' plans (Koerner & Fitzpatrick, 2004). It is from within families that children first pursue goals and enact plans, and they remain an important context in which goals and plans are negotiated across the lifespan. By applying GPA theories to families, we attempt to offer insights about family communication *and* to extend GPA theories in new directions. We begin by defining the terms *goals*, *plans*, and *planning processes* and then offer two examples concerning how GPA theories and research about family communication may be usefully combined.

GPA THEORIES: KEY CONCEPTS AND ASSUMPTIONS

Interaction Goals

Goals are future states of affairs that individuals desire to attain or maintain. Desired states become *interaction goals* when individuals must communicate and coordinate with others to achieve those states (Wilson, 2002). If Steve's daughter Robyn were 18 years old, she could accomplish her goal of getting her ears pierced without talking with her parents. Because Robyn is 9 years old at the time of Example 1, she forms the interaction goal of convincing Steve that she should be able to get her ears pierced. "Convincing my parents to let me get my ears pierced," "comforting my child after her first pet has died," or "gaining my parents' support for my career choices" are examples of goals that necessitate interaction and negotiation.

Many situations give rise to multiple interaction goals (O'Keefe, 1988). In Example 1, Steve has several goals: to avoid making a unilateral decision that would alienate Patrice (Robyn's mother), to seem responsive to Robyn's desires, and to avoid having Robyn repeatedly beg to get her ears pierced. These goals arise from Steve's understanding of what it means to be a "spouse" and a "parent," his relationships with Patrice and Robyn, and his understanding of what Robyn is doing (asking for permission). Multiple goals may be difficult to accomplish at the same time. For example, if Steve is too responsive to Robyn's desires he may appear to already have made the decision before talking with Patrice. Individuals differ in how likely they are to recognize and form multiple goals (O'Keefe, 1988). People find it mentally taxing to pursue multiple conflicting goals (Greene, 1995), yet being perceived as communicatively competent often depends on one's ability to manage multiple goals (Wilson & Sabee, 2003).

Among the range of interaction goals individuals might pursue, Dillard (1990, 2004) distinguishes primary and secondary goals. At any point in a conversation, the *primary goal* is the objective that defines the situation or answers the question "what is going on here?" In Example 1, Robyn's goal of convincing Steve that she should be able to get her ears pierced is the primary goal; both parties orient to this as the implicitly understood purpose of their conversation for the moment. The primary goal "brackets the situation" and "helps segment the flow of behavior into a meaningful unit; it says what the interaction is about" (Dillard, Segrin, & Harden, 1989, p. 21). The primary goal exerts a "push" force and motivates Robyn to speak.

Secondary goals are concerns that arise in a wide range of situations and shape how individuals pursue primary goals. Based on a series of studies, Dillard et al. (1989) propose five categories of secondary goals: (a) identity goals, or desires to act consistently with one's beliefs, morals and values; (b) interaction goals, or desires to maintain a positive self image, to avoid other people losing "face," and to say things that are relevant and coherent in light of the larger conversation; (c) relational resource goals, or desires to maintain valued relationships; (d) personal resource goals, or desires to avoid unnecessarily risking or wasting one's time, money, or safety; and (e) arousal-management goals, or desires to avoid or reduce anxiety or nervousness. In contrast with the primary goal, secondary goals exert a "pull" force in that they shape and constrain what individuals say. Steve's desires to not alienate Patrice (relational resource) and to seem responsive to Robyn (interaction) are examples of secondary goals.

Researchers have investigated types of primary goals that individuals pursue in their close relationships, including the family (Cody, Canary, & Smith, 1994; Rule, Bisanz, & Kohn, 1985). Aside from obtaining permission, primary goals that frame family interaction include giving advice, obtaining assistance, convincing others to share an activity, and eliciting support for a third party. Each of these goals is meaningful, in part, because it is associated with a unique set of potential identity concerns (Wilson, Aleman, & Leatham, 1998). For example, Goldsmith and Fitch (1997) interviewed young adults regarding advice-giving episodes. Although advice could be helpful and often was seen as a sign of caring, interviewees sometimes refrained from giving advice to their spouses or adult siblings out of fear that they would "sound parental" or appear to be "butting in." Asking for assistance is associated with its own set of identity concerns. Older adults typically turn to family rather than friends when they need long-term help or instrumental assistance, but older adults sometimes refrain from asking for help for fear of looking like they can't handle their own affairs or losing their independence (Morgan & Hummert, 2000). As these examples show, the labels "primary" and "secondary" refer to goal function (what goals do) rather than goal importance. Spouses may not offer advice (primary goal) because they place more importance on avoiding making their partner defensive (secondary goal), just as aging parents may not ask their family for assistance (primary goal) because they place greater importance on appearing self-sufficient (secondary goal).

Plans and Planning

Plans are people's mental representations of actions that can be taken to pursue a goal (Berger, 1997). Plans are not actions themselves but are instead people's knowledge of goal-relevant actions; in fact, people may develop plans but choose not to enact them. Plans represent knowledge about one or more goals, obstacles to accomplishing those goals, and actions and preconditions for pursuing those goals. In Example 1, Robyn recognizes that her mother's (Patrice's) resistance is a potential obstacle to getting her ears pierced (see lines 03 and 07), and she appears to be enacting a plan of talking to her father (Steve) as a way of overcoming this obstacle to her goal. People draw on many sources of knowledge to develop plans, including recalling a similar situation(s) from the past, imagining hypothetical interactions, observing role models, and following or adapting instructions from others (Berger, 1997).

Just as there are different types of goals, there are also different types of plans, and they vary in complexity. Complex plans include more actions, more diverse actions, and more contingent actions than simple plans (Berger & Bell, 1988). For example, Berger and Bell had college students write plans for making a good first impression with a new roommate as well as for asking someone out on a first date. A plan for the former goal that included "help the new roommate unpack" and "ask if the new roommate has picked a major yet" demonstrates two different actions. A plan that includes "ask if the new roommate has picked a major yet, and if not, ask what type of music s/he likes" demonstrates a contingency in case an initial planned action fails. In the study, complex plans were rated by other students as more likely to succeed compared to simple plans.

Plans also vary in specificity, or the degree to which the plan is fully articulated. In Example 1, Robyn might have approached Steve with only an abstract plan such as "talk to Dad." However, it also is possible that Robyn planned some of her arguments (e.g., given the stories she had heard about her sister Annie, Robyn might have anticipated her Dad's objection and planned to say that she'd clean her ears regularly). In their study, Waldron and Lavitt (2000) assessed 101 adults in an urban area during their first week of participation in a "Welfare-to-Work" program. Participants described their plans for a hypothetical job search, including what type of job they hoped to obtain after the training program and what their qualifications were for such a job. Adults who eventually found full-time employment 2–3 months later had articulated more specific job search plans during their first week in the program compared with those adults who did not find work, found part-time work, or found but then lost a job. Although not specific to families, these studies suggest that individuals at times benefit from developing complex and specific plans for pursuing interaction goals. Future research might investigate how parents socialize their children to plan (Friedman & Scholnick, 1997), how children learn to anticipate and plan for potential obstacles as they mature (Marshall & Levy, 2000), and when parents themselves might benefit from developing more complex or specific plans (Wilson, 2000).

Planning refers to the psychological and communication processes involved in recalling, generating, selecting, implementing, monitoring, modifying, and negotiating plans (Wilson, 2002). Planning involves both intra-individual and interpersonal processes. At an intraindividual level, planning occurs in advance of many interactions, but a good deal of planning occurs "online" or during conversation. Even if Robyn had planned some arguments before approaching Steve about getting her ears pierced, she still must adapt her plan as their conversation unfolds to be able to say things that are relevant to what Steve says and/or to react to unexpected responses from Steve.

To assess whether individuals actually think about goals and plans during conversation, Waldron (1990) videotaped pairs of undergraduates meeting for the first time. Afterward, students were separated to watch a videotape of their conversation. Each student wrote down all the thoughts and feelings he or she recalled from the get-acquainted conversation. Of the 2,273 thoughts and feelings recalled by students, 44% involved plans for accomplishing goals such as finding out information about the other person without embarrassing either party.

Examining planning in a family context, we adapted this stimulated recall method to study online planning during mother-child interactions (Wilson, Bylund, Hayes, Morgan, & Herman, 2002). Forty-two mothers were videotaped while completing a 10-minute play-period with one of their children (3–8 years old). Each mother then watched a videotape of her play period and described aloud everything she remembered thinking or feeling. Of the 2,192 thoughts and feelings recalled by mothers, 21% involved goals, plans, or obstacles such as "I was thinking about what would be appropriate for her" and "I wanted him to play with the other toys." Adults appear to have frequent, albeit momentary and fleeting awareness of their goals and plans during conversation (Greene, 2000).

In addition to monitoring their own goals and plans, conversationalists also make inferences about their partner's goals and plans (Berger, 2002). Sillars, Roberts, Leonard, and Dun (2000) videotaped 118 couples who had been married three years or less as they spent 15 minutes discussing a current disagreement in their marriage. Afterward, husbands and wives were taken to separate rooms. Each spouse watched a copy of their videotape and recalled their thoughts at various points during the conversation. Although the researchers did not specifically measure goals and plans, they did code "process" thoughts, which refer to "inferences about the pragmatic intentions and communicative strategies (e.g., inferences that the partner was exaggerating, criticizing, or changing the topic) as well as general evaluations of communication or interaction behavior" (p. 487). Examples of process inferences included "He wanted to change the subject" and "[She's] trying to think of something to say" (p. 488). Of the 18,724 recalled thoughts and feelings, 34% fell into the process category.

How much similarity actually exists between family members' streams of thought during interaction? Empathic accuracy refers to the degree to which people's inferences about what their conversational partner is thinking corresponds with the partner's reports of his/her thoughts (Ickes, 1997). Simpson, Orina, and Ickes (2003) argue that "empathic accuracy can sometimes help, but at others times hurt, close relationships" (p. 882). Using methods similar to Sillars et al. (2000), Simpson and colleagues had married individuals recall what they had been thinking during a conversation with their spouse and also infer what their spouse had been thinking. The authors found that married individuals' levels of empathic accuracy were positively associated with their feelings of closeness to their spouse when their spouse reported primarily nonthreatening thoughts, but inversely associated with feelings of closeness when their spouse reported thoughts threatening to the marriage (e.g., feelings of anger or jealousy).

Aside from intraindividual processes, planning also occurs interpersonally as people develop, negotiate, and evaluate plans together (Waldron, 1997). Consider an example from the life of this chapter's second author. Wendy, who is married to Chris, recently gave birth to their first child, Isabella. Although "Izzie" initially seemed like she was going to be a great sleeper, by the time she was 4–5 months old she started waking up frequently, both overnight and during the day, thereby getting less and less sleep. After trying everything else, Wendy and Chris agreed that they were going to have to let Izzie "cry it out." Specifically, they agreed that when Izzie awoke and started crying, they would wait at least 10 minutes to see whether she would go back to sleep before going in to comfort her. In an e-mail to Steve, Wendy described this plan as having the goal of Izzie "being able to get herself to sleep so that she can get herself back to sleep when she wakes up between sleep cycles but still needs more sleep." Despite agreeing to the plan, Wendy and Chris continue to discuss it over time, especially when Izzie is crying.

Example 2

01 Wendy: She's crying so hard.

02 Chris: Just 10 minutes.

03 Wendy: You're sure that won't do any harm?

04 Chris: She won't remember it.

05 Wendy: Emotionally, though. We don't know about that.

06: Chris: Well, we do know she needs more sleep.

((pause while baby continues to cry))

07 Wendy: I think I'm going to be sick

((longer pause; baby gradually quiets))

08 Wendy: Is she actually asleep?

09 Chris: I think so.

10 Wendy: Thank God.

((pause))

11 Wendy: Are you *sure* we didn't do any damage?

Just as in Example 1, we can ask, "What is going on?" in this second example. Although Wendy and Chris have developed a joint plan for pursuing their goal of getting Izzie to sleep more regularly, it appears as if they may have different levels of confidence in the plan, time frames for evaluating the plan's success, or concerns about possible unintended consequences of the plan. Given that such differences likely are common among family members, it is surprising that so little research to date has investigated planning as an interpersonal process in families. Having defined key concepts in GPA theories, we sketch two directions for future research.

GPA THEORIES: RESEARCH QUESTIONS ABOUT GOALS, PLANS, AND FAMILIES

Goal and Plan Dynamics: Negotiating Primary Goals and Plans

From our discussion so far, it might appear that the primary goal defining an interaction is clear to all family members and that goals and plans remain relatively stable during family interactions. A more realistic view is that family members may disagree about what the primary goal is, or should be, that defines their current interaction. Wendy might define the preceding interaction as one in which she was seeking support, whereas Chris might define it as one in which Wendy was questioning their plan. To illustrate how individuals might frame interactions differently, Sabee and Wilson (2004) asked 234 undergraduate students to recall a recent conversation in which they had discussed a disappointing grade with a course instructor and describe why they had talked with their instructor. Students were classified as having one of four primary goals: (a) learning, where the student viewed the point of the interaction to be better understanding the material on which the disappointing grade was received; (b) persuading, where the student viewed the interaction to be about negotiating a higher grade on the assignment in question; (c) fighting, where the student saw the interaction as an opportunity to vent anger and raise complaints about unfair treatment; and (d) impressing, where the student's primary goal was convincing the instructor that the disappointing grade was not reflective of the student's real ability. Although all students described a conversation about a disappointing grade, students with different primary goals had different ideas about what really was "going on."

Because only students recalled interactions, Sabee and Wilson (2004) could not verify whether students and instructors agreed on what primary goal defined their interaction or whether more than one primary goal defined the interaction over time. What occurs when students and instructors disagree about what ought to be the purpose of their interaction, such as when a student wants her grade changed (persuading) and her instructor wants to focus on clarifying course concepts (learning)? Are there predictable patterns of primary goal shifts such as from persuading to learning or persuading to fighting? Do secondary goals change in importance with shifts in primary goals (Waldron, 1997)?

Similar goal dynamics can occur within families. For example, when parents attempt to regulate their children's computer use (e.g., chat rooms, instant messaging, websites, or video games), parents may view such interactions to be about protecting their children from possible exploitation and unhealthy activities (Jennings & Wartella, 2004). Children and adolescents may view such interactions to be about parents attempting to limit their autonomy and interaction with peers. What occurs when parents and children disagree about what is going on? How do children resist their parent's framing of interactions? Do children attempt to negotiate what primary goals their parents ought to pursue? If so, are there developmental patterns to such interactions? Does a family's conversation or conformity orientation influence the likelihood or nature of such interactions (Koerner & Fitzpatrick, 2004)? How are such interactions influenced when families are embedded in collectivistic as opposed to individualistic cultures (Kim & Wilson, 1994)?

These are the types of questions researchers can answer about family communication by using GPA theories.

Although our focus so far has been on primary goals, family members also may negotiate what plan they are, or should be, enacting. Example 2 with Wendy and Chris illustrates how parents may co-construct and evaluate plans for interacting with their children. For example, studies of how parents support or undermine each other's child-rearing plans, and negotiate joint plans, would complement the growing literature on "co-parenting" (Doherty & Beaton, 2004).

Parenting, Children's Plan Development, and Children's Well-Being

Although parents and children are interdependent, parents exert considerable influence on their children's goals and plans. Different parenting styles may teach different lessons about *what* goals children should pursue or *how* to go about achieving those goals. Considerable research has explored associations between parenting styles and children's social and moral development (see Hart, Newell, & Olsen, 2003; Wilson & Morgan, 2004). Aside from influencing how children pursue their goals, parents may help to determine *whether* children feel it is possible to achieve goals at all. In a sense, parents may socialize their children not only in terms of how to get what they want but also in terms of what they can possibly achieve.

This chapter's second author recently proposed a theory of "safe ground" that posits relationships between patterns of parental behavior, children's plans for positive self-presentation, and children's self-esteem and behavioral competence (Morgan, 2004). "Safe ground" connotes a place free from harm, in which one can enjoy secure well-being. Children develop a sense of safe ground in the parent-child relationship when they learn that certain types of interactions, namely positive ones, can be relied upon and elicited at will.

According to safe ground theory, a crucial feature of healthy parent-child relationships is that children are able to develop reliably successful plans for positive self-presentation. Such plans enable children to act in ways that predictably elicit positive parental evaluation and avoid negative evaluation when they so choose (Abramson, Seligman, & Teasdale, 1978). Developing successful plans requires an understanding of the meanings of particular behaviors and a sense of control over those behaviors (the choice to enact the behaviors or not). Consistent parental responses to child behaviors impart clear meaning of those behaviors and allow predictability of future parental responses. But predictability is useful only as it pertains to controllable child behaviors; children must understand which behaviors might elicit (un)desired parental responses but also feel capable of performing or avoiding such behaviors. According to the theory, children are able to develop safe ground when they perceive that their parent provides (a) predictably positive responses to controllable positive child behaviors (e.g., a child who receives a good grade at school is confident that her parent will be pleased and will attribute the good grade to the child's own ability and effort); (b) predictably negative, but focused, parental responses to controllable negative child behaviors (e.g., a child who chooses to watch TV rather than doing homework is confident that her parent, upon discovering this, will be disappointed with her behavior but not with her character); and (c) parental responses to uncontrollable negative child behaviors that avoid blame (e.g., a child who accidentally slips on a wet floor and breaks a plate is confident that her parent, although not happy that the plate is broken, will not view the act as intentional). These patterns of parental responses teach children not only how to achieve their goals but also that they can accomplish goals in the parent-child relationship.

Because physically and emotionally abused children clearly lack safe ground, research on parenting and child abuse offers insight into patterns of parental behavior that may prevent children from developing reliably successful plans for positive self-presentation. Abusive parents are less likely than nonabusive parents to distinguish between their children's mistakes and intentional behaviors (Milner & Foody, 1994) and more likely to make global negative evaluations of their child rather than focusing on specific child misbehaviors (Bugental & Happaney, 2000). Abusive parents also are more likely than nonabusive parents to attribute positive child behaviors to chance or circumstances rather than giving their children credit for behaving well (Larrance & Twentyman, 1983). Furthermore, more abusive parents respond inconsistently to both positive and negative child behaviors (Oldershaw, Walters, & Hall, 1986), which limits their children's ability to predict future parental responses.

Safe ground theory predicts that the aforementioned patterns of parental behavior prevent a child from developing reliably successful plans for positive self-presentation, and thereby undermine the child's sense of having a place safe from harm. Harm in this context refers to the deterioration of a child's self-worth and competence through the inability to avoid unwanted reactions and/or to elicit desired reactions regardless of what the child does. Consistent with this prediction, physically abused children display lower self-esteem (Gross & Keller, 1992) as well as more noncompliance (Oldershaw et al., 1986) and aggressive transgressions (Trickett & Kuczynski, 1986) than nonabused children. Within abusive parent-child relationships, children may be socialized to believe that positive outcomes simply are beyond their reach.

Safe ground theory suggests several future research questions. What types of parental communication patterns (e.g., being consistent, providing credit, avoiding overly global attributions) enable children to develop reliable plans for eliciting positive and avoiding negative parental responses when they wish? Is a certain level of perceived plan efficacy necessary for children to sustain feelings of self-worth and competence? Researching these questions might suggest interventions in families in which children currently do not have a sense of safe ground.

CONCLUSION

This chapter argues that theories of goals, plans, and planning processes offer one useful lens for investigating family communication. Although goals-plans-action (GPA) theories focus on individuals as the locus of sense-making and action, these theories offer insights into how family members jointly negotiate what is (or ought to be) going on as they talk. Applying GPA theories to families highlights the dynamic, interdependent nature of family members' goals and plans. Finally, GPA theories can suggest pragmatic insights, such as clarifying patterns of parental behavior that enable children to have confidence in their own abilities to develop successful plans for self-presentation.

REFERENCES

Abramson, L. Y., Seligman, M. E. P., & Teasdale, J. D. (1978). Learned helplessness in humans: Critique and reformulation. *Journal of Abnormal Psychology, 887*, 49–74.

Austin, J. T., & Vancouver, J. B. (1996). Goal constructs in psychology: Structure, process, and content. *Psychological Bulletin, 120*, 338–375.

Berger, C. R. (1997). *Planning strategic interaction: Attaining goals through communicative action.* Mahwah, NJ: Lawrence Erlbaum.

Berger, C. R. (2002). Goals and knowledge structures in social interaction. In
    M. L. Knapp & J. A. Daly (Eds.), *Handbook of interpersonal communication*
    (pp. 181–212). Thousand Oaks, CA: Sage.

Berger, C. R., & Bell, R. A. (1988). Plans and the initiation of social relationships.
    Human Communication Research, 15, 217–235.

Berscheid, E., & Peplau, L. A. (1983). The emerging science of relationships. In
    H. H. Kelley et al. (Eds.), *Close relationships* (pp. 1–19). New York: W. W.
    Freeman.

Bugental, D. B., & Happaney, K. (2000). Parent-child interaction as a power
    contest. *Journal of Applied Developmental Psychology, 21,* 267–282.

Clark, R. A., & Delia, J. G. (1979). *Topoi* and rhetorical competence. *Quarterly
    Journal of Speech, 65,* 187–206.

Cody, M. J., Canary, D. J., & Smith, S. W. (1994). Compliance-gaining goals:
    An inductive analysis of actors' goal types, strategies, and successes. In
    J. A. Daly & J. M. Wiemann (Eds.), *Strategic interpersonal communication*
    (pp. 33–90). Hillsdale, NJ: Lawrence Erlbaum.

Dillard, J. P. (1990). A goal-driven model of interpersonal influence. In J. P.
    Dillard (Ed.), *Seeking compliance: The production of interpersonal influence
    messages* (pp. 41–56). Scottsdale, AZ: Gorsuch Scarisbrick.

Dillard, J. P. (2004). The goals-plans-action model of interpersonal influence. In
    J. S. Seiter & R. H. Gass (Eds.), *Perspectives on persuasion, social influence, and
    compliance gaining* (pp. 185–206). Boston: Allyn & Bacon.

Dillard, J. P., Segrin, C., & Harden, J. M. (1989). Primary and secondary goals in
    the production of interpersonal influence messages. *Communication
    Monographs, 56,* 19–38.

Doherty, W. J., & Beaton, J. M. (2004). Mothers and fathers parenting together.
    In A. Vangelisti (Ed.), *Handbook of family communication* (pp. 269–286).
    Mahwah, NJ: Lawrence Erlbaum.

Friedman, S. L., & Scholnick, E. K. (Eds.). (1997). *The developmental psychology
    of planning: Why, how, and when do we plan?* Mahwah, NJ: Lawrence
    Erlbaum.

Goldsmith, D. J., & Fitch, K. (1997). The normative context of advice as social
    support. *Human Communication Research, 23,* 454–476.

Greene, J. O. (1995). Production of messages in pursuit of multiple social goals:
    Action assembly theory contributions to the study of cognitive encoding
    processes. In B. R. Burleson (Ed.), *Communication yearbook 18* (pp. 26–53).
    Thousand Oaks, CA: Sage.

Greene, J. O. (2000). Evanescent mentation: An ameliorative conceptual foun-
    dation for research and theory on message production. *Communication
    Theory, 10,* 139–155.

Gross, A. B., & Keller, H. R. (1992). Long-term consequences of childhood phys-
    ical and psychological maltreatment. *Aggressive Behavior, 18,* 171–185.

Hart, C. H., Newell, L. D., & Olsen, S. F. (2003). Parenting skills and social-
    communicative competence in children. In J. O. Greene & B. R. Burleson

(Eds.), *Handbook of communication and social interaction skills* (pp 753–800). Mahwah, NJ: Lawrence Erlbaum.

Ickes, W. (1997). *Empathic accuracy.* New York: Guilford Press.

Jennings, N., & Wartella, E. (2004). Technology and the family. In A. L. Vangelisti (Ed.), *Handbook of family communication* (pp. 593–608). Mahwah, NJ: Lawrence Erlbaum.

Kellermann, K. (1992). Communication: Inherently strategic and primarily automatic. *Communication Monographs, 59,* 288–300.

Kim, M.-S. & Wilson, S. R. (1994). A cross-cultural comparison of implicit theories of requesting. *Communication Monographs, 61,* 210–235.

Koerner, A. F., & Fitzpatrick, M. A. (2004). Communication in intact families. In A. Vangelisti (Ed.), *Handbook of family communication* (pp. 177–196). Mahwah, NJ: Lawrence Erlbaum.

Larrance, D. T., & Twentyman, C.T. (1983). Maternal attributions and child abuse. *Journal of Abnormal Psychology, 92,* 449–457.

Marshall, L. J., & Levy, V. M. (2000). The development of children's perceptions of obstacles in compliance-gaining situations. *Communication Studies, 49,* 342–357.

Milner, J. S., & Foody, R. (1994). The impact of mitigating information on attributions for positive and negative child behaviors by adults at low- and high-risk for child-abusive behavior. *Journal of Social and Clinical Psychology, 13,* 335–351.

Morgan, M., & Hummert, M. L. (2000). Perceptions of communicative control strategies in mother-daughter dyads across the lifespan. *Journal of Communication, 50,* 48–64.

Morgan, W. M. (2004). *Safe ground theory: How parenting patterns shape children's self esteem and competence.* Unpublished manuscript.

O'Keefe, B. J. (1988). The logic of message design: Individual differences in reasoning about communication. *Communication Monographs, 55,* 80–103.

Oldershaw, L., Walters, G. C., & Hall, D. K. (1986). Control strategies and non-compliance in abusive mother-child dyads. *Developmental Psychology, 57,* 722–732.

Rule, B. G., Bisanz, G. L., & Kohn, M. (1985). Anatomy of a persuasion schema: Targets, goals, and strategies. *Journal of Personality and Social Psychology, 48,* 1127–1140.

Sabee, C. M, & Wilson, S. R. (2004). *Understanding students' primary goals during conversations about disappointing grades: Explication, precursors, and consequences.* Manuscript under review.

Sillars, A., Roberts, L. J., Leonard, K. E., & Dun, T. (2000). Cognition during marital conflict: The relationship of thought and talk. *Journal of Social and Personal Relationships, 17,* 479–502.

Simpson, J. A., Orina, M. M., & Ickes, W. (2003). When accuracy hurts, and when it helps: A test of the empathic accuracy model in marital interactions. *Journal of Personality and Social Psychology, 85,* 881–893.

Trickett, P. K., & Kuczynski, L. (1986). Children's misbehaviors and parental discipline strategies in abusive and nonabusive families. *Developmental Psychology, 22,* 115–123.

Waldron, V. R. (1990). Constrained rationality: Situational influences on information acquisition plans and tactics. *Communication Monographs, 57,* 184–201.

Waldron, V. R. (1997). Toward a theory of interactive conversational planning. In J. O. Greene (Ed.), *Message production: Advances in communication theory* (pp. 195–220). Mahwah, NJ: Lawrence Erlbaum.

Waldron, V. R., & Lavitt, M. R. (2000). "Welfare-to-work:" Assessing communication competencies and client outcomes in a job training program. *Southern Communication Journal, 66,* 1–15.

Wilson, S. R. (2000). Developing planning perspectives to explain parent-child interaction patterns in physically abusive families. *Communication Theory, 10,* 200–209.

Wilson, S. R. (2002). *Seeking and resisting compliance: Why individuals say what they do when trying to influence others.* Thousand Oaks, CA: Sage.

Wilson, S. R., Aleman, C. G., & Leatham, G. B. (1998). Identity implications of influence goals: A revised analysis of face-threatening acts and application to seeking compliance with same-sex friends. *Human Communication Research, 25,* 64–96.

Wilson, S. R., Bylund, C., Hayes, J., Morgan, W. M., & Herman, A. (2002, July). *Mothers' child abuse potential and trait verbal aggressiveness as predictors of their on-line thoughts and feelings during mother-child playtime interactions.* Presented at the International Conference on Personal Relationships, Halifax, Nova Scotia, Canada

Wilson, S. R., & Morgan, W. M. (2004). Persuasion and families. In A. Vangelisti (Ed.), *Handbook of family communication* (pp. 447–472). Mahwah, NJ: Lawrence Erlbaum.

Wilson, S. R., & Sabee, C. M. (2003). Explicating communicative competence as a theoretical term. In J. O. Greene & B. R. Burleson (Eds.), *Handbook of communication and social interaction skills* (pp. 3–50). Mahwah, NJ: Lawrence Erlbaum.

6

Inconsistent Nurturing as Control Theory: A New Theory in Family Communication

Beth A. Le Poire

René M. Dailey

Editors' Note: Inconsistent Nurturing as Control (INC) theory comes out of communication studies from the work of the first author. With its roots in learning theory from psychology, the focus is on how the behavior of people who are functional and people who are substance abusers reinforce each other and how the unique dynamics of this pairing create paradoxes that make it very difficult for the functioning partner to positively influence the afflicted partner's behavior. As the theory focuses on generalizable cause-effect relationships, we place it with other logical-empirical theories.

The family system has increasingly become a context in which individuals' compulsive behaviors are examined. Clearly, compulsive and other undesired behaviors (e.g., substance abuse, depression, eating disorders, gambling) affect more than the afflicted member of the family. Indeed, compulsive behaviors result in negative communication patterns. For example, research has shown that drug abuse is related to more communication problems between partners (Fals-Stewart & Birchler, 1998; Kelly, Halford, & Young, 2002), increased detachment and less desire for intimacy (Carroll, Robinson, & Flowers, 2002) as well as increased partner verbal aggressiveness (Straus & Sweet, 1992) and physical abuse or violence (Quigley & Leonard, 2000; Rodriguez, Lasch, Chandra, & Lee, 2001; Testa, Quigley, & Leonard, 2003; Wekerle & Wall, 2002). Additionally, adult children of alcoholics (ACOAs) perceive their families to be less healthy than non-ACOAs (Deming, Chase, & Karesh, 1996) and are more susceptible to psychological, cognitive, and behavioral problems (Johnson & Leff, 1999). Furthermore, research supports the negative effects of compulsive behavior in families, including those with eating disorders or a depressed member. Specifically, in families with an anorexic member, research also suggests greater enmeshment (dependence and entanglement; Kog & Vandereycken, 1989), greater incongruent communication (Humphrey, Apple & Kirschenbaum, 1986), and greater hostility and withholding among members (Humphrey & Stern, 1988). In families with a depressed member, research shows more negative communication (Sher & Baucom, 1993), greater marital distress, less affection, and more destructive conflict strategies (Coyne, Thompson, & Palmer, 2002).

With undesired behaviors such as substance abuse (SAMHSA, 2003), eating disorders (Steiner & Lock, 1998), and depression (National Institute of Mental Health, 2003) on the rise, it is important to understand how the confluence of family members' actions affects the continuation of these behaviors. Though the interdependence between family members allows the afflicted person's behaviors to negatively impact other members, this interdependence may also allow functional members to influence the undesired behavior of the afflicted (e.g., Amey & Albrecht, 1998; Friedman, & Utada, 1992; Rotunda, Scherer, & Imm, 1995). As such, recovery programs are now finding more success by incorporating family members in therapy and treatment (e.g., Mann, 2003; O'Farrell & Feehan, 1999; Osterman & Grubic, 2000; Sher, Baucom, & Larus, 1990), and involving the family system provides greater recovery for the individual as well as improved family functioning.

Thus, research pertaining to substance abuse and other equally compulsive behavioral problems needs to employ theoretical perspectives that incorporate the relational context of, and communication behaviors related to, substance-abusive individuals. Inconsistent

Nurturing as Control (INC) theory aims to provide a theoretical framework for examining communication strategies used in both the long-term relationship as well as during specific interactions about the undesired behavior (Le Poire, 1992, 1995). This theory suggests that functional members may unknowingly perpetuate the undesired behavior in their attempts to decrease this same behavior. INC theory's primary assumption is that functional members have competing goals; they want to control the afflicted partner's behavior, yet they feel the need to nurture the other in order to maintain the relationship (Le Poire, 1992). These competing goals may lead to inconsistent use of reinforcement and punishment strategies, thereby undermining the functional member's attempts to decrease the behavior. This chapter will review the central propositions of the theory as well as the paradoxes associated with the theory. Next, the theory will be examined with regard to how it has guided (and can guide) research. Finally, the theory will be analyzed with regard to its epistemological (the nature of knowledge) and ontological (the nature of human action) underpinnings and Littlejohn's (2002) criteria for evaluating a theory (scope, validity, parsimony, heurism, openness, and appropriateness).

INCONSISTENT NURTURING AS CONTROL THEORY

Initial versions of INC theory address issues of nurturing and control in relationships that include substance abusers (e.g., Le Poire, 1992). Currently, it extends to include all relationships in which one family member tries to influence or diminish the unhealthy behavior of another family member (Le Poire, 1995). The central thesis of the theory is that the unique dynamics of this pairing create several paradoxes that make it very difficult for the functioning partner (the partner with no compulsive behavioral tendencies) to influence the afflicted (e.g., substance abuser, eating-disordered individual, gambling addict) partner's obsessive behavior.

Paradoxical Communication

As identified earlier, the functional-afflicted relationship consists of a functional partner (more commonly known as a codependent), who is without interference with daily functioning, and an afflicted partner, who has a behavioral compulsion that inhibits daily functioning.

Although it is possible that this dynamic extends to full family functioning, the theory focuses on the unique dynamics of the primary couple unit in the family. The relational dynamics of this functional-afflicted relationship produce a power structure that is paradoxical. In the first treatment of the theory, referencing Watzlawick, Beavin, and Jackson's (1967) delineation of paradoxes, Le Poire (1992) argued that there are several paradoxical injunctions in relationships that include afflicted partners and that these paradoxes ultimately impact expressions of control by the functional family member in the relationship. The most deleterious effects of these paradoxes result from the contradictory nature of the functional family member's nurturing and subsequently controlling behavior. Le Poire delineates three primary paradoxes in this relationship.

The first paradox involves issues of control. In the codependent relationship, an outside observer might assume that the functional partner is in control. This is because the afflicted partner is out of control as a result of substance abuse or some other compulsive behavioral problem, and thus lacks control in the relationship. However, because the afflicted's behavior restricts the choices available to the functional partner, the afflicted partner is actually in control. Le Poire (1992) asserted that "[t]his paradox ultimately indicates that the 'helpless' out-of-control behavior of the dependent person ultimately places limitations on the behavioral options of the codependent, or 'in-control' partner" (p. 1467).

The second paradox in the functional-afflicted relationship is about sacrifice and dependency. Because the afflicted's out-of-control behavior results in times of crisis, the functional must nurture the partner through these difficult situations. This requires the functional to sacrifice personal needs to take care of the partner. The abdication invokes a need for reciprocity whereby the afflicted partner feels obligated to the functional; in other words, the afflicted person believes s/he "owes" the functional partner. Therefore, the afflicted person alters their deviant behavior to compensate for the obligation. In this regard, the functional person is placed in a position of control and achieves it through behavior that would normally be indicative of a lack of control. For example, Danny Bonaducci (formerly known as "Danny" from the Partridge family) frequently laments on his radio show in Los Angeles that his wife (Gretchen) is a much better person than he is, primarily because she puts up with his substance-abusive ways. He also claims that his attempts at sobriety are, in fact, a tribute and testament to the selfless behavior she exhibits toward him. Thus, by Gretchen subordinating her needs to Danny's substance-abusive behavior, she has actually succeeded at controlling his substance abuse. She, therefore, controls Danny's substance abuse through submission.

The final paradox concerns the status of the relationship. The functional partner wants to maintain a relationship with the afflicted partner. At the same time, the functional desires to eliminate the abuse of substances by the afflicted. However, because the codependent nurtures the dependent during times of crisis, this caretaking behavior is very rewarding for the dependent. In general, the caregiving behavior of the functional partner provides the support necessary for the afflicted to be substance-abusive. Thus, extinguishing the substance abuse would result in an elimination of this rewarding caretaking behavior. As a result, this paradox suggests that by accomplishing the goal of stopping the substance abuse, the functional partner may actually destroy the relationship.

Propositions Regarding Outcomes of Paradoxes

The paradoxes inherent in the power structure of the codependent relationship have certain consequences for relational interaction. INC theory articulates the proposition that in learning theory terms (Skinner, 1974), the functionals' nurturing behavior may actually *reinforce* the substance-dependents' drug-dependent behavior, and thus increase the likelihood that the behavior will happen again (Le Poire, 1995). More problematically, nonaddicted partners may *intermittently* reinforce behaviors they actually want to extinguish. Specifically, if the nonaddicted partner nurtures the substance-dependent when they are in "crisis," this caretaking behavior may ultimately reinforce the behavior. However, when the caregiver becomes resentful, as is likely to happen (Asher, 1992; Steiner, 1974; Wiseman, 1991), they may not reinforce the behavior and may in fact fail to nurture the dependent in times of crisis. The theory proposes that this inconsistent nurturing behavior may be an example of intermittent reinforcement of behavior and may ultimately strengthen the "helpless" behavior of the afflicted person because intermittent reinforcement produces more long-term, nonextinguishable behavior than continuous reinforcement (e.g., Burgoon, Burgoon, Miller, & Sunnafrank, 1981).

INC theory also proposes that the functional's lack of caregiving is likely an attempt to extinguish the undesirable behavior of the dependent partner. In other words, this behavior may ultimately be an attempt to *punish* the dependent partner or serve to remove the behavior from the partner's repertoire. Thus, the functional partner may be attempting to get the substance-dependent to avoid punishment in the future by discontinuing the helpless behavior. If this is the case, then this punishing behavior should serve to extinguish the helpless behavior on the part of the substance-dependent individual. However, INC theory argues that the intermittent nature of this punishing behavior should actually *increase* the likelihood of the helpless behavior (Le Poire, 1995). Thus, not only do functional partners unwittingly strengthen the likelihood of substance-abusive behavior through intermittent reinforcement, they strengthen the behavior even more through the intermittent nature of the punishing behavior that is interspersed with the reinforcing behavior. Thus, similar to inconsistent parents that increase the likelihood of undesirable behavior in their children (Baumrind, 1978), functional partners strengthen the likelihood of compulsive behavior through the very means by which they attempt to extinguish the compulsive behavior.

RESEARCH EXTENDED FROM INC THEORY

Evidence of Inconsistent Nurturing as Control

Le Poire (1995) and colleagues use INC theory to examine how partners of substance abusers attempted to discourage the ongoing substance abuse of their partners. Given INC theory assumptions and propositions, this work hypothesizes that family members of substance-abusive individuals would be inconsistent in their use of reinforcement and punishment. To consider how this inconsistency manifested itself within communication behavior over the life span of the relationship, it is useful to consider behaviors that are self-reported by significant others of substance abusers (Le Poire, Addis, Duggan, & Dailey, 2003; Le Poire & Cope, 1999; Le Poire, Erlandson, & Hallett, 1998; Le Poire, Hallett, & Erlandson, 2000). Using a time line procedure, substance abusers and their partners reported during interviews in their homes and described behaviors that the partners of substance abusers used surrounding the substance abuse prior to labeling it a problem, subsequent to labeling the substance abuse a problem, and after they became frustrated with their initial attempts to curtail the behavior. Analyses show that partners typically cycle from reinforcing to punishing communication strategies following labeling their partners as substance-abusive. In fact, the first test of INC theory logic hypothesizes and finds that functional partners change their strategy usage over time, such that (a) they reinforce substance-dependent behavior more before their determination that the behavior was problematic than after, (b) they punish substance-dependent behavior more after they labeled the drinking/drugging behavior as being problematic than before, and (c) in a postfrustration period, they employ a mix of reinforcing and punishing strategies, resulting in an overall pattern of inconsistent reinforcement and punishment (Le Poire et al., 1998). This cycling is central to the inconsistent nature of reinforcing or punishing communication strategies as postulated by INC theory. Such cycling clearly supports the expected inconsistent nurturing pattern.

Cycling is also supported by a qualitative analysis of the strategies used by functional partners of substance abusers (Le Poire et al., 2003). They find that functional partners use several macro-level strategies that included both reinforcement and punishment. Specifically, functional partners report using verbal abuse, making rules pertaining to the addiction, punishing, getting a third party involved, threatening, avoiding, ending the relationship, expressing personal feelings, withholding something from the partner as a punishment, supporting abuse by participation, demanding that the partner stop/active involvement, and confronting. The use of these strategies approximates the hypothesized inconsistent and intermittent use of reinforcement and punishment of the substance-abusive behavior.

This theoretical application also successfully applies to mothers with eating-disordered daughters in another study. For instance, Prescott and Le Poire (2002) found that mothers of eating-disordered daughters display similar patterns of reinforcement and punishment. They found that mothers reinforce eating disorders more before they label the behavior problematic, whereas they punish the eating disorders more after labeling the behaviors. Furthermore, results indicate that consistently reinforcing alternative behavior immediately following labeling of the eating disorder significantly predicts higher perceptions of the mothers' persuasive effectiveness. Finally, reinforcing the eating disorder predicts greater amounts of relapse. Thus, for example, a mother might compliment a daughter on her thinness and her ability to wear trendy clothing as she continues to lose weight (inadvertently reinforcing the eating disorder). Following the labeling of the eating disorder, however, the mother might try to encourage the daughter to join a singing group or some such activity that does not revolve around food (reinforcing alternative behavior). The most important implication of these findings is that significant family members (in this case, mothers) used similar patterns of inconsistent reinforcement and punishment as did partners of substance abusers.

Finally, INC theory can guide research on functional partners living with depressed partners (Duggan, 2003). Similar to the previous studies, Duggan found that functional partners of depressed individuals changed their strategy use over time, such that they reinforce the depression more before labeling it as problematic, punish the depression more after labeling it as problematic, and revert to a mix of punishing and reinforcing following frustration with their earlier attempts at diminishing the depressed behaviors. The depressed partners also report that when their partners used positive consistency (using positive reinforcement consistently) throughout the life span of their relationship, they are less depressed. Thus, inconsistency of the functional partner relates to poorer mental health outcomes for the depressed individual as well as for the functional partner.

Evidence of the Effectiveness of Inconsistent Nurturing as Control

Evidence of this patterning of strategy usage supports the contention that family members may intermittently reinforce and punish the behavior they are trying to extinguish. Of further interest is the effectiveness of the strategies exhibited. Learning theory (Skinner, 1974) suggests that more consistent family members should be more effective in their influence attempts. Additionally, greater family involvement in treatment is associated with abstinence, better family relations, and positive feelings about self (e.g., McCrady et al., 1986). Le Poire et al. (2000) found that consistently punishing substance abuse, combined with consistently reinforcing alternative behavior, is predictive of lesser relapse in a substance-abusing sample, whereas Prescott and Le Poire (2002) found that consistently reinforcing alternative behavior predicted significantly higher perceptions of mothers' persuasive effectiveness in an eating-disordered sample. In other words, consistently encouraging both substance abusers and eating-disordered daughters to engage in behaviors that do not include substance use or eating is effective in diminishing both substance abuse and an eating-disordered daughters' perception of her mothers' persuasive effectiveness at getting her to diminish her eating-disordered behavior. Consistently punishing substance-abusive behavior (e.g., withholding sex, threatening to leave) is additionally helpful in reducing recidivism among the substance abusers. Furthermore, Duggan (2003) found that lesser reports of depression are related to greater positive consistency on the part of the functional partner. In other words, more reinforcement and less punishment relate to less depression in the depressed partner.

Le Poire and Cope (1999) studied the subset of the substance-abusing sample dealing with alcoholics only. Given the research findings that steady drinking may provide more positive functioning for the family unit than the less predictable episodic drinking (e.g., Jacob & Leonard, 1988), they predicted that partners of episodic drinkers (drinkers who binge drink in unpredictable patterns) may be more motivated to stop the alcoholic behavior and thus may use more effective strategies than partners of steady drinkers (drinkers who consistently overindulge in alcohol on a daily basis). Contrary to the prediction, partners of episodic drinkers use less effective strategies (less consistency), whereas partners of steady drinkers use more effective strategies (greater reinforcement of alternative behavior) immediately following the alcoholism labeling. Following frustration with initially unsuccessful persuasive attempts, however, alcoholism subtype operates as expected, in that functional partners of episodic drinkers (afflicteds) use more effective strategies (greater consistency combined with more punishment of drinking behavior) than do partners of steady drinkers.

Evidence of the Influence of Inconsistent Nurturing as Control on Mental Health

These patterns of strategy use and effectiveness should also have implications for the mental health of functional family members continuing to live with partners with compulsive behavior. Consistent with research cited previously, Le Poire et al. (2000) found that partners/ spouses of substance abusers are less depressed when their partners relapse less, whereas Duggan (2003) found greater mental health outcomes for both depressed and functional partners when functional partners use greater positive consistency. This is important for two reasons. First, partners of substance abusers (and partners with other compulsive behavioral issues) can assist their partners through consistent punishment of undesired behavior and reinforcement of alternative behavior. Second, partners can aid their own mental health in the process because partners of more successfully recovering substance abusers and depressed individuals were less depressed.

THEORETICAL ANALYSIS AND CRITIQUE OF INC THEORY

Consideration of any theory within the communication discipline requires that it fulfill certain criteria. Littlejohn (2002) asserted that an explanatory, logical, positivistic theory is useful to the extent that it can (a) describe, (b) predict, (c) explain, and (d) control a phenomenon. Given that INC theory is a covering law-like theory (a theory that attempts to explain phenomena in general patterns), it can be argued here that it fulfills all the functions of a theory. First, it describes the communicative processes that functional partners use in order to deter further compulsive behavior on the part of their afflicted partners. Second, the theory predicts the types, nature, and sequencing of the communicative strategies used. Additionally, based on the types of strategies predicted, it also predicts effectiveness outcomes in terms of recidivism, persuasive effectiveness, and mental health outcomes. Third, the theory explains the nature of the strategies and the outcomes based on the paradoxical nature of the functional-afflicted relationship. Finally, the theory offers the capability to control the outcomes through policy implications of increased punishment of problematic behavior and increased reinforcement of alternative behavior.

Epistemological and Ontological Underpinnings

Epistemologically, INC theory operates from the assumption of World View I (Littlejohn, 2002); that there is a physical, knowable reality that is observable by the trained social scientist. In other words, functional and afflicted partners exist in the discoverable world and their behavioral and communicative behavior is observable. Thus, one can observe the types of strategies that partners of afflicted individuals use and can make predictions about their effects in an observable world.

Operationalizations are very important from this perspective and allow the researcher to observe the phenomenon of inconsistent nurturing in more objective ways. In other words, careful systems of measurement allow INC theory to intersubjectively measure reinforcement and punishment by defining certain strategies as punishing and other strategies as reinforcing. INC researchers also attempt to make law-like statements that hold true across situations and over time as they attempt to establish the existence of patterns of reinforcement and punishment in the functional-afflicted relationship that hold true across differing types of functional-afflicted relationships (e.g., those including substance abusers, eating-disordered individuals, depressed individuals, gamblers). Thus, the paradoxes and their predicted impacts are expected to hold true regardless of *type* of relationship.

Ontologically, INC theory takes the determinist standpoint that behavior is caused by a multitude of prior conditions (e.g., being in a relationship with an afflicted partner) and that these predetermined conditions restrict the types of responses that are available in any given situation. INC theory can best be thought of as a *nonactional* theory (Littlejohn, 2002), in that a functional partner might want to do the best they can to diminish the undesirable behavior of the afflicted partner, but the strategies they choose to execute are limited by the nature of the paradoxical power structure in the relationship. Thus, INC theory can best be thought of as a midlevel determinist theory, in that individuals are assumed to choose to enact strategies within a narrow bandwidth of opportunities available to them based on the preexisting conditions of the paradoxical nature of the relationship.

Criteria for Evaluation

It is similarly important that a theory be evaluated to determine its general usefulness to communication researchers. Therefore, Littlejohn's (2002) criteria for evaluating a communication theory are adopted. INC theory will be critiqued for its scope, validity, heurism, parsimony, openness, and appropriateness.

Scope. The criterion of theoretical scope refers to a theory's comprehensiveness or inclusiveness (Littlejohn, 2002). According to Littlejohn, scope can be general, in that the theory deals with many phenomena, or a theory can be narrow but apply to a number of different situations. INC theory is certainly not broad, in that not all relationships include one afflicted and one functional partner. Therefore, INC theory can be evaluated according to the second type of scope that is narrow in nature, yet applies across a variety of different situations. Thus, it can be said that INC theory is narrow, in that it applies only to functional-afflicted relationships. However, we also claim that INC theory can be applied to *any* type of functional-afflicted relationship, and therefore, its scope is quite good. Because INC assumes that paradoxes exist in any type of functional-afflicted relationship, it should apply to any relationship in which one partner has out-of-control behavioral tendencies. In other words, although INC theory applies only to functional-afflicted relationships, it can describe, predict, explain, and control across various types of functional-afflicted relationships. We have already seen examples of research in couples, including substance abusers and depressed individuals, and with mothers with eating-disordered daughters. It is also possible that INC theory may apply to couples that include gamblers, overly aggressive individuals, overeaters, and any other type of individual with some sort of compulsive behavioral tendencies. Furthermore, it is also possible that INC theory may apply to any type of functional partner (e.g., spouse, mother, sibling) and is not limited to spouses.

Validity. Littlejohn (2002) refers to validity as the truth value of theory. The first type of validity that Littlejohn introduces is the value or worth. This work makes the claim that the value of INC theory lies in its capability to describe, predict, explain, and control. Further, INC theory has the second type of validity, in that it has correspondence or fit. In other words, it is possible to observe functional partners using reinforcement and punishment in real world examples. Although some would argue that these learning-theory concepts are difficult to operationalize in the real world, it is possible to interpret calling the police, threatening to leave the partner, and sexual withdrawal as punishing while drinking together, taking care of the children, and calling in sick to work as reinforcing of substance abuse. Furthermore, INC theory can claim to have the third type of validity, or generalizability, to a variety of relationships including one functional and one afflicted (e.g., substance abuser, eating-disordered individual, or depressed individual). Thus, it is possible to argue that INC theory has strong validity, in that it has value, correspondence with observable phenomena, and generalizability.

Heurism. Heurism is the capability to generate new ideas for research and additional theory (Littlejohn, 2002). Although no competing theories have been offered to date, from the review provided here, it can be evidenced that INC theory has generated research across various relationships including substance abusing, eating-disordered, and depressed individuals. Thus it can be claimed that INC theory is heuristic.

Parsimony. Parsimony refers to logical simplicity (Littlejohn, 2002). Although some might argue that INC theory's use of the concepts of paradoxes and reinforcement, punishment, and consistency make the theory cumbersome, it is argued here that this type of complexity is necessary to build the explanatory calculus of the theory. Thus, what INC theory might lack in terms of elegance, it makes up for in the criterion of worth validity, in that it provides a full explanatory calculus.

Openness. Openness refers to the theory's openness to alternative possibilities. Although INC theory can be criticized for being overly deterministic (as can most law-like theories), it does advance openness, in that it is built on the empirical findings of qualitative and quantitative approaches to research. Its strength lies in providing an interpretation that does not blame the spouse of the afflicted person but explains the phenomenon in terms of the unique characteristics of the relationship. As such, it provides an alternative interpretation to other approaches.

Appropriateness. Finally, a theory can be evaluated in terms of its appropriateness for the theoretical questions addressed and research methods used (Littlejohn, 2002). While certainly the social science methods used by INC theory researchers are appropriate for the law-like assumptions proffered by the theory, some might argue that by their very nature, the theory and methods are overly reductionistic and do not allow for individual choice or variation. Alternatively, the initiators of the theory would argue that functionals operate with choice; however, it is likely that they will choose a pattern of strategies unlikely to fulfill their purposes. Additionally, reducing strategies to the more manageable categories of reinforcement and punishment may allow a richer understanding of the effectiveness or ineffectiveness of such strategies. This greater understanding will allow for greater predictive abilities and the all-too-important practical policy implications that individuals working with functional-afflicted couples can now make.

SUMMARY

In sum, INC theory is a uniquely family communication theory that proffers that functional partners, through their efforts to both nurture and control their afflicted partners, can inadvertently strengthen the very behavior they are trying to extinguish. As such, this theory guides research in couples including substance abusing and depressed individuals, as well as research on mothers with eating-disordered daughters. In terms of theoretical analysis, it is argued that INC is a deterministic theory operating from the assumption of an observable world. Finally, INC has narrow yet acceptable scope (it cannot apply to all families but yet can apply to all families in which there is a functional-afflicted pairing), strong validity, good and potential heurism, acceptable parsimony, acceptable openness to alternative perspectives, and appropriateness within the law-like framework.

REFERENCES

Amey, C. H., & Albrecht, S. L. (1998). Race and ethnic differences in adolescent drug use: The impact of family structure and the quantity and quality of parental interaction. *Journal of Drug Issues, 28,* 283–298.

Asher, R. M. (1992). *Women with alcoholic husbands.* Chapel Hill: University of North Carolina Press.

Baumrind, D. (1978). Parental disciplinary patterns and social competence in children. *Youth and Society, 9,* 239–276.

Burgoon, J. K., Burgoon, M., Miller, G. R., & Sunnafrank, M. (1981). Learning theory approaches to persuasion. *Human Communication Research, 13,* 463–494.

Carroll, J. J, Robinson, B. E., & Flowers, C. (2002). Marital estrangement, positive feelings toward partners and locus of control: Female counselors married to alcohol-abusing and non-alcohol-abusing spouses. *Journal of Addictions and Offender Counseling, 23,* 30–40.

Coyne, J. C., Thompson, R. & Palmer, S. C. (2002). Marital quality, coping with conflict, marital complaints, and affection in couples with a depressed wife. *Journal of Family Psychology, 16,* 26–37.

Deming, M. P., Chase, N. D., & Karesh, D. (1996). Parental alcoholism and perceived levels of family health among college freshmen. *Alcoholism Treatment Quarterly, 14,* 47–57.

Duggan, A. (2003). *One-up two-down: An application of inconsistent nurturing as control theory to depressed individuals and their partners.* Unpublished doctoral dissertation, University of California, Santa Barbara.

Fals-Stewart, W., & Birchler, G. R. (1998). Marital interactions of drug-abusing patients and their partners: Comparisons with distressed couples and relationship to drug-using behavior. *Psychology of Addictive Behaviors, 12,* 28–38.

Friedman, A. S., & Utada, A. T. (1992). The family environments of adolescent drug abusers. *Family Dynamics of Addiction Quarterly, 2,* 32–45.

Humphrey, L. L., Apple, R. F., & Kirschenbaum, D. S. (1986). Differentiating bulimic-anorexic from normal families using interpersonal and behavioral observational systems. *Journal of Consulting and Clinical Psychology, 54,* 190–195.

Humphrey, L. L., & Stern, S. (1988). Objection relations and the family system in bulimia. *Journal of Marital and Family Therapy, 14,* 337–350.

Jacob, T., & Leonard, K. E. (1988). Alcoholic-spouse interaction as a function of alcoholism subtype and alcohol consumption interaction. *Journal of Abnormal Psychology, 97,* 231–237.

Johnson, J. L., & Leff, M. (1999). Children of substance abusers: Overview of research findings. *Pediatrics, 103,* 1085–1099.

Kelly, A. B., Halford, W. K., & Young, R. M. (2002). Couple communication and female problem drinking: A behavioral observation study. *Psychology of Addictive Behaviors, 16,* 269–271.

Kog, E., & Vandereycken, W. (1989). Family interaction in eating disorder patients and normal controls. *International Journal of Eating Disorders, 8,* 11–23.

Le Poire, B. A. (1992). Does the codependent encourage substance dependent behavior? Paradoxical injunctions in the codependent relationship. *The International Journal of Addictions, 27,* 1465–1474.

Le Poire, B. A. (1995). Inconsistent nurturing as control theory: Implications for communication-based research and treatment programs. *Journal of Applied Communication Research, 23,* 1–15.

Le Poire, B. A., Addis, K. A., Duggan, A. P., & Dailey, R. M. (2003). *Communicative strategies used by partners of drug abusers.* Manuscript submitted for publication.

Le Poire, B. A., & Cope, K. (1999). Episodic versus steady state drinkers: Evidence of differential reinforcement patterns. *Alcoholism Treatment Quarterly, 17,* 79–90.

Le Poire, B. A., Erlandson, K. T., & Hallett, J. S. (1998). Punishing versus reinforcing strategies of drug discontinuance: Effect of persuaders' drug use. *Health Communication, 10,* 293–316.

Le Poire, B. A., Hallett, J. S., & Erlandson, K. T. (2000). An initial test of inconsistent nurturing as control theory: How partners of drug abusers assist their partners' sobriety. *Human Communication Research, 26,* 432–457.

Littlejohn, S. W. (2002). *Theories of human communication* (7th ed.). Belmont, CA: Wadsworth.

Mann, A. (2003). *Relationships matter: Impact of parental, peer factors on teen, young adult substance abuse.* National Institute on Drug Abuse, *18*(2). Retrieved December, 2003 from http://www.drugabuse.gov/NIDA_notes/NNV0118N2/Relationships.html.

McCrady, B. S., Noel, N. E., Abrams, D. B., Stout, R. L., Nelson, H. F., & Hay, W. M. (1986). Comparative effectiveness of three types of spouse involvement in outpatient behavioral alcoholism treatment. *Journal of Studies on Alcohol, 47*, 459–465.

National Institute of Mental Health. (2003). *The invisible disease: Depression.* Retrieved December, 2003 from *http://www.nimh.nih.gov/publicat/depresfact.cfm.*

O'Farrell, T. J., & Feehan, M. (1999). Alcoholism treatment and the family: Do family and individual treatments for alcoholic adults have preventive effects for children? *Journal of Studies on Alcohol, 13*, 125–129.

Osterman, F., & Grubic, V. N. (2000). Family functioning of recovered alcohol-addicted patients: A comparative study. *Journal of Substance Abuse Treatment, 19*, 475–479.

Prescott, M. E., & Le Poire, B. A. (2002). Eating disorders and mother-daughter communication: A test of inconsistent nurturing as control theory. *Journal of Family Communication, 2*, 59–78.

Quigley, B. M., & Leonard, K. E. (2000). Alcohol, drugs, and violence. In V. B. Van Hasselt & M. Hersen (Eds.), *Aggression and violence: An introductory text* (pp. 259–283). Boston: Allyn & Bacon.

Rodriguez, E., Lasch, K. E., Chandra, J., & Lee, P. (2001). Family violence, employment status, welfare benefits, and alcohol drinking in the United States: What is the relation? *Journal of Epidemiology and Community Health, 55*, 172–178.

Rotunda, R. J., Scherer, D. G., & Imm, P. S. (1995). Family systems and alcohol misuse—Research on the effects of alcoholism and family functioning and effective family interventions. *Professional Psychology-Research and Practice, 26*, 95–104.

Substance Abuse and Mental Health Services Administration (SAMHSA). (2003). *Overview of findings from the 2002 national survey on drug use and health.* Retrieved December, 2003 from *http://www.oas.samhsa.gov/nhsda/ 2k2nsduh/ Overview/2k2Overview.htm#toc.*

Sher, T. G., & Baucom, D. H. (1993). Marital communication: Differences among maritally distressed, depressed, and nondistressed on depressed couples. *Journal of Family Psychology, 7*, 148–153.

Sher, T. G., Baucom, D. H., & Larus, J. M. (1990). Communication patterns and response to treatment among depressed and nondepressed maritally distressed couples. *Journal of Family Psychology, 4*, 63–79.

Skinner, B. F. (1974). *About behaviorism.* New York: Alfred A. Knopf.

Steiner, C. M. (1974). *Scripts people live: Transactional analysis of life scripts.* New York: Bantam Books.

Steiner, H., & Lock, L. (1998). Anorexia nervosa and bulimia nervosa in children and adolescents: A review of the past 10 years. *Journal of the American Academy of Child and Adolescent Psychiatry, 37*, 352–359.

Straus, M. A., & Sweet, S. (1992). Verbal/symbolic aggression in couples: Incidence rates and relationships to personal characteristics. *Journal of Marriage and the Family, 54,* 346–357.

Testa, M., Quigley, B. M., & Leonard, K. E. (2003). Does alcohol make a difference? Within-participants comparison of incidents of partner violence. *Journal of Interpersonal Violence, 18,* 735–743.

Watzlawick, P., Beavin, J., & Jackson, D. D. (1967). *Pragmatics of human communication.* New York: Norton.

Wekerle, C., & Wall, A. M. (Eds.). (2002). *The violence and addiction equation: Theoretical and clinical issues in substance abuse and relationship violence.* New York: Brunner-Routledge.

Wiseman, J. P. (1991). *The other half: Wives of alcoholics and their social-psychology.* New York: de Gruyter.

7

Narrative Performance Theory: Telling Stories, Doing Family

Kristin M. Langellier

Eric E. Peterson

Editors' Note: As discussed in the book's Introduction, critical theories are the least frequently encountered metatheoretical discourse. Narrative performance theory is an exception, providing us with a useful exemplar of critical theory in the study of family communication.

Families tell stories. "Tell about Mother laying under the car," someone calls out at the dinner table. Such family storytelling is a routine and ubiquitous aspect of daily life and is generally accepted as such throughout family communication scholarship. Considered theoretically, this normative observation conceptualizes family storytelling as something that happens in families; that is, as a product of family interaction, as a way of making sense of experience, as a means to encode familial images and abstractions in stories, and as part of an ongoing struggle to create and maintain a coherent system of meanings through narrative.

Certainly families do tell stories; they engage in storytelling. However, in this essay we advance the reverse—and more comprehensive—theoretical claim: In short, not only do families *tell* stories, but storytelling is one way of *doing* family.

Although the existence of family storytelling may be readily reeognized, its function is less obvious. Part of the difficulty in specifying its function arises because family storytelling rarely occurs in a consistent, coherent, or unified fashion. Instead, family storytelling is performed by multiple and changing participants in temporally and spatially dispersed performances that are partial, fragmentary, contradictory, conflicted, and sometimes incoherent. Narrative performance theory provides a way to understand both the empirical and the eidetic variability of family communication practices. Empirical descriptions of family storytelling locate variations in what particular stories are told, how they are told, and what identities they constitute. Eidetic descriptions of family storytelling locate variations in the normative and normalizing context that regulates what kinds of stories, types of storytelling, and possibilities for identity and agency can be realized in a particular situation.

Theories of narrative performance typically address the empirical and eidetic variability of storytelling in the distinction between performance and performativity (Butler, 1993; Langellier, 1999; Pollock, 1999). The focus on *performance* is illustrated by the growing research on family stories (e.g., Jorgensen & Bochner, 2004), on interaction and the joint behavior by which stories are told (e.g., Ochs & Capps, 2001), and on the meanings and identities constituted in family storytelling. In these instances, family storytellers perform narrative not by representing their experiences but by living them and by occasioning them for a particular audience in the present situation (Young, 1987, 2000). Families, in other words, perform stories—they have something to say or to figure out how to say, stories old and new to tell, and habitual and innovative ways of working together to tell these stories. The focus on *performance* brings forth the varieties of stories families tell and the varieties of ways in which they tell them. Such performances also are "telling" in the sense that they reveal the family in operation as family. Storytelling constitutes or performs family identity. Storytelling is a way of doing family, of routinely functioning as a family, in daily life.

The focus on *performativity* draws upon Butler's (1993) critical revisions of speech act theory. Speech act theory emphasizes the meaning of performance as the fulfillment of a promise or expectation. Strine

(1998) remarks that in contrast to performance, "performativity refers more specifically to the complexities of discursive practices, to the often unconscious investments and desires that circulate in all discourses, and to the decisive effects that various modes of discursive action have on individual and group subjectivities and identity formations" (p. 313). Rather than seeing storytelling as the result of an extralinguistic social entity called "family," the focus on performativity asks what behaviors, habits, practices, and conventions produce the very idea of family (as well as this particular family). Family storytelling draws upon ideas, circulating in discourse, of what constitutes "family" and "telling" and "story" for a particular family to tell a particular story in this particular way. The focus on *performativity* explores the variety of ideas, investments, desires, and expectations that storytelling mobilizes or re-cites in order to produce "family" in an ongoing struggle over meanings, bodies, and identities.

NARRATIVE PERFORMANCE THEORY: A COMMUNICATION PERSPECTIVE

Just as family storytelling is characterized in part by empirical and eidetic variability, so too are narrative performance theories. In this chapter, we explicate a narrative performance theory based in phenomenological and semiotic traditions of studying human communication (Lanigan, 1992). This theory draws upon the work of Merleau-Ponty (e.g., 1964) and Foucault (e.g., 1980) and is described elsewhere in greater detail (Langellier & Peterson, 2004). In brief, narrative performance theory interrogates family as the intersection of experience and discourse, of the existential and the institutional, of lived bodies and inscribed bodies. Family storytelling is embodied in particular material conditions and ordered by discursive practices. When the focus turns from doing household chores or having coffee or complaining about work to storytelling, participants put aside other communication practices and recapture their corporeal existence to perform narrative in the present situation. Just as families are not collections of individuals, neither is family storytelling a collection of stories. For that reason, family storytelling is inadequately conceptualized by theories that describe it as a collection of ritual practices shared by a group of individuals or as a collection of stories to be shared. Neither formulation explicates what is meant by "sharing," by the intersubjective and social relations in which family storytelling is embedded and that make it possible. Storytelling is participatory. In performance terms, family storytelling forms a system of shifting relationships among audiences and storytellers, narrators and characters. Family storytelling is a bodily practice that occurs with others and within a field of other possible bodily practices.

To theorize family communication as narrative performance is to take seriously how storytelling is radically contextual and situated not only in bodies but in history and culture. Embodiment is not somehow separate from a particular material and social context but assumes all its meanings. Family storytelling is constrained by these material conditions. Constraints are boundaries that define the conditions of what is possible. Constraints both facilitate and restrict possibilities for who can tell or listen to stories, what counts as a story, what kinds of stories can be told, how stories can be told and listened to, and which meanings and identities matter. Habitual forms of behavior and interaction as well as institutionalized practices and cultural formations (such as those formulated around ethnicity and race, sexuality and gender, class and generation) are resources for ordering content, tasks, and identities in family storytelling. Participants in storytelling mobilize these shared resources to create, recall, refashion, and discover possible narrative performances.

Family storytelling, embodied and constrained by material conditions, is known through the discursive practices in which it participates. These discursive practices operate according to rules of power and knowledge. External rules prohibit or exclude particular forms of discourse, divide and reject some discourses as meaningful or meaningless, and attempt to fix truth and falsity. The effort to define family storytelling as the creative expression of an individual ("that Pauline is such a funny storyteller") or an individual family, for example, is an attempt to separate storytelling from an exercise of power by defining it as an entertaining fiction or artistic creation of family interaction. Discursive practices also operate according to internal rules or regularities in repetition, in types of coherence, and in disciplinary actions. The definition of family storytelling according to types of major narratives (e.g., the family genesis story) or as ritualized forms of symbolic action (e.g., at anniversaries, funerals, weddings) illustrates the operation of internal rules as a regulatory principle. Another type of principle concerns speaking subjects—both as a subject of discourse and as subject to discursive power—as regularities in discourse. These rules order who can speak and listen on a particular subject, how such roles are distributed, and the types of adherence demanded of subjects. The analysis of these rules and regularities locates family as a narrative formation in discourse.

Family is a narrative formation organized by discursive rules and regulations embodied in a particular material context. As a narrative formation, family storytelling recaptures, reproduces, and reinscribes power relations. At the same time, this participation in power relations makes it possible to alter, thwart, or rupture them. Family storytelling functions to both legitimate and critique the normative and normalizing functions of narratives it performs. The question is not what motivates an individual or an individual family to tell this particular story in this way to this audience. Rather, the question is one of the efficacy of family storytelling, of how narrative functions strategically (Patterson, 2002). Strategy concerns the interests and goals around which family storytelling is organized. What interests are served by family storytelling? How does family storytelling intervene in what stories, what bodies, and what meanings matter? A strategy is put into practice by the tactics that make it work (Wilden, 1987). Therefore, any theory of family communication must account for how power relations are distributed in strategy and tactics. Next, we consider how family storytelling strategically orders content and meanings in stories and how these stories are enacted tactically by storytelling tasks that serve, in turn, to locate possibilities for group and personal identity.

Storytelling functions strategically to form and perform family in what McFeat (1974) describes as a small-group culture. We reinterpret McFeat's analysis according to a strategic model that locates family storytelling in a semidependent hierarchy of content-, task-, and group-ordering (Langellier & Peterson, 1993, 2004; Peterson, 1987). Each level of this hierarchy can be distinguished by its complexity and the generality of the constraints that govern its operation (Wilden, 1987). For example, the ordering of cultural "content" in storytelling— lived-meanings, sensibilities and experiences, information—takes place at the most general level of constraint. A group culture that fails to order content so that it survives in an environment to be passed along to succeeding generations ceases to exist as a culture. Any tasks or identities that a family innovates depend upon the success of this overall strategy for survival as a small-group culture.

Content-ordering concerns how information, experiences, and lived meanings are organized so they can be stored, retrieved, and transmitted. The choice of the term *family storytelling* rather than family stories has the advantage of emphasizing the performative sense of narrative as a communication practice engaged in ordering content over other senses that would limit narrative to a static text or cultural artifact. Content is formed in the struggle over sensibilities and meanings for particular events, activities, and identities; and such content is performed as it is told and retold over time. Families make sense of events and innovate meanings; they remember and forget stories; they reinterpret and empha-size what has been marginal or muted; they relocate and reject what has been formative. Ordering content works to ensure transmission across generations, for example, by diffusing content among multiple partici-pants through collective practices of remembering, by timing the distrib-ution of content so that stories are told when they are most salient and likely to be perpetuated, by sedimenting content in family classics according to canonical or socially available genres, and by maintaining family secrets that preserve meanings through exclusionary practices.

To illustrate each level of the strategic model, we briefly describe a session of storytelling around "the sewing sandwiches" analyzed else-where in greater detail (Langellier & Peterson, 2004). In this session, two male cousins in their 70s sit at a kitchen table with Kristin, the researcher, as the wife of one of the cousins moves about the kitchen in the background. The three participants describe for Kristin a family sewing circle that brought together women in the family (and "wives of the men in the family") on Monday nights to sew, "talk a lot of French," and have a little lunch. The older generation collectively remembers—with some disagreements, ongoing modifications, and innovations—who participated, who was excluded by the use of French language (the children trying to listen in from upstairs), when new members joined the circle, and the chopped bologna and eggs and onions that made up the "sewing sandwiches" served for the lunch. At the level of content-ordering, the participants work to recall events, activities, and identities; and order that information so that it survives over time ("I remember sewing sandwiches before the grandchildren started getting into it").

Task-ordering takes place within the context of content-ordering and focuses on creating and maintaining a productive relationship with the overall environment. A group acquires a structure when taking on and articulating the specialized tasks required to survive that environment: Someone must do the labor of listening and telling, of remembering and reflecting, of innovating and interpreting, and of sorting and saving. Typically, the interactional work of storytelling is ordered in families according to generation and gender. McFeat (1974) identifies a three-generational structure in which the middle generation transmits and interprets basic information for the younger generation, subject to correction by the senior generation. This structure may be favored by nuclear families insofar as it requires only intermittent contact with the senior generation. Other generational structures might emphasize the interpretation and innovation of younger members or they might collapse tasks to two generations. In addition to generation, families reflect gendered divisions of labor. For example, women may be responsible for the conversational and relational work that is required if storytelling is to happen at family meals, holidays, and celebrations. Although storytelling tasks may be distributed in a variety of ways, this distribution is regularized and routinized in particular patterns of collaboration, competition, and specialization among family members. In this allocation of storytelling tasks, families adapt and survive environmental changes and thereby form group and individual identities.

In the example of the "sewing sandwiches" storytelling session, the three participants take on the task of recalling content for Kristin, who stands in for a younger generation. Some elements of the storytelling work are distributed across all participants, such as discussion about who belonged to the sewing circle and who did not, or how the children tried to listen in on the discussions in French from upstairs. Other elements are differentiated by gender, such as when talk turns to the "lunches," and it is the wife who contributes how a special dessert was made and lists the ingredients for it. Such patterns of task allocation suggest divisions of labor that mark internal boundaries by generation (older women—grandparents and parents—downstairs, children upstairs) and gender (who makes the food), and external boundaries for who can participate in family work (such as the work of the sewing circle) and who can tell or hear family secrets (the "inside" information spoken in French).

Group-ordering is the most complex and least general level in that it depends upon successful content- and task-ordering. A group culture innovates identities for itself and its members as it successfully adapts to an environment and passes along its culture to a new generation. Group-ordering constitutes identities and regulates interests that distinguish individuals and individual families. In storytelling, families and family members become visible and audible to themselves and to others. Family storytelling constitutes particular identities by drawing upon and distinguishing social and cultural resources such as class, race, and ethnicity embodied in myths of, for example, individualism, motherhood, fatherhood, cultural heritage, and nation (the "American" family). Families negotiate these identities in storytelling as a way to adapt to conflicting internal and external demands. The fluctuating boundaries that define "you" and "me," as well as "our family" and "their family," evolve within the larger context of content- and task-ordering. For example, a family may employ ethnicity as a minor tactic to maintain family identity (group-ordering through family storytelling about ethnic foods) while following a larger grand tactic of assimilation to survive in a mainstream U. S. community (task-ordering by elders who tell how they immigrated and flourished through hard work), and that embodies an overall strategy of white ethnicity obscuring real political and material differences (content-ordering in constructing "the American Dream"). In group-ordering, families articulate who they are for themselves, for others, for the diverse communities they comprise, and for society and future generations.

In the example of the sewing sandwiches, the participants work within the larger context of content- and task-ordering to locate themselves as members of a particular Franco-American family in a specific community and geographic location. The ordering of identities can be explicit, such as when the participants review who belonged and did not belong to the sewing circle. Or the ordering of identities can be implicit, such as defining sewing and cooking as women's work in the family. The ordering of the group into a specific family identity participates in larger cultural resources; in this case, the cousin's generation locates family identity in a Franco-American community in which "most every family" had a large number of children, went to school and church, worked at the mill, and so on. The ordering of group and personal identity may be repunctuated or change over time; for example, when one of the participants describes how he now makes the sewing sandwiches for his children who call them "daddy sandwiches." The shift in the label from communally based "sewing sandwiches" to individual or nuclear family-based "daddy sandwiches" suggests a change in family identity that moves from an ethnically oriented to an assimilated "American" identity.

READING RESEARCH THROUGH
NARRATIVE PERFORMANCE THEORY

Now that we have outlined how family storytelling orders content, tasks, and identities in a strategic hierarchy, let us consider how existing research on narrative performance can be interpreted or read according to this theoretical perspective. This brief and partial review is meant to suggest how existing narrative performance research can be mobilized to understand communication practices of doing family.

From the perspective of narrative performance theory, existing research emphasizes content-ordering when it focuses on what makes memorable stories or memorable performances. One reason why family storytelling is memorable is that it draws upon existing genres to organize meanings and frame information (Briggs, 1993; Bruner & Weisser, 1991). Existing genres serve as a readily available and generally dispersed resource for generating and perpetuating family classics (Stone, 1988) and the family canon (Yerby, Buerkel-Rothfuss, & Bochner, 1995) around stories of, for example, family fortune and misfortune, childhood antics, courtship, birth, death, and divorce. And just as there are generic conventions for memorable stories, there are generic conventions for memorable tellings. Content is easier to perform, remember, transmit, and store when it uses poetic forms and features within an aesthetic or performance frame (Bauman, 1986). But just as these widely dispersed genres and generic conventions facilitate some forms of content-ordering, they restrict others. For example, Pollock (1999) explores how birth stories and the timing of their performances may privilege biological parenting and thus marginalize adoption, technologically assisted childbirth, pain, and childlessness through active forgetting and secrecy. Indeed, what comes to constitute content is as much a matter of what counts as a narrative performance in the first place—that is, what narrative forms are understood as narratives; what performances are acknowledged and credited. Content-ordering in narrative performance is not natural or neutral but inflected by class (Heath, 1983); gender (Sawin, 1999); sexuality (Roof, 1996); and ethnicity, race, and culture (Alexander & Leblanc, 1999; Georgakapoulou, 1997; Johnson, 2003; Scollon & Scollon, 1981).

The larger context of content-ordering is put into practice by a variety of tactics. Someone must do the work to create opportunities and situations in which storytelling can take place, to retrieve basic information, and to innovate and interpret information. There are many ways to order the tasks of family storytelling. Family storytelling may be invited, invoked, or demanded by audiences whose participation may be voluntary, partial, or enforced. Storytelling may be performed by a single person or by a group of participants working together. Researchers detail the work accomplished by solo storytellers (e.g., Bauman, 1986; Johnson, 2003) and by group collaboration and corroboration (Baldwin, 1985; Langellier & Peterson, 1992; Yocum, 1985). Families form shifting and stable alliances, alignments, and sub-units (e.g., Mandelbaum, 1987) while distributing these tasks differentially by generation and gender (Blum-Kulka, 1997; Ochs & Capps, 2001). Following Ochs and Capps (2001, p. 8), we conclude that "active narrative involvement" in the shifting relations of communication among tellers, listeners, narrators, and characters defines what it means to participate in family.

The work of surviving in an environment forms the basis for ordering group and personal identities. Researchers argue that identity is intrinsic to narrative performance (Brockmeier & Carbaugh, 2001; Mishler, 1999; Smith & Watson, 1996). In storytelling, a family "explains itself to itself" (McFeat, 1974, p. 61); a family performs and struggles over identities that are always being destabilized, challenged, and deferred. An example of research that investigates the narrative performance of identity in family storytelling is Trujillo's (2002) study of more than 50 family members' stories about Naunny, his grandmother. He interrogates how ethnicity and patriarchy function normatively to frame family history and identities. Such narratives work to distinguish identities—however contingent or conventional—within the family (Dills, 1998; Patton, 1996; Schely-Newman, 1999) and to distinguish a family identity within a larger community or network of social relations (Langellier, 2002; Watson, 1996; Weston, 1991).

As is evident in the preceding discussion, consideration of any one level in the hierarchical ordering of content, tasks, and identities entails consideration of the remaining levels of narrative performance. The focus on the interaction among these levels is emphasized when researchers turn explicitly to consider ideological and strategic functions (Nelson, 2001; Patterson, 2002). For example, Riessman (2002) revisits her earlier analysis (1990) of Tessa's divorce narrative to make explicit the unconscious investments and desires that narrative researchers inscribe in conventional research practices on family storytelling. Riessman's reexamination is initiated by issues of group-ordering, in particular, her ongoing exploration of narrative positioning and subjectivity in research. She argues that the narrative "is not 'Tessa's story,' as some suggest about personal narratives—it does not reveal an essential self" (p. 198). Rather, the ordering of identities (multiple and dynamic senses of "Tessa" and "Cathy") must be situated as narrative tactics within a dialogic context (task-ordering) in which storytelling develops collaboratively in the interview setting and in analysis. Riessman then moves to contextualize these forms of collaboration and dialogue within a larger strategy (content-ordering). She reinterprets her reading of Tessa's divorce by complicating the initial emphasis on generic conventions that framed Tessa as a survivor of a violent marriage. This reinterpretation focuses on understanding the complexities of a harsh life, loneliness, and complicity in violence that were marginalized by ordering Tessa's divorce as survivor discourse. As Riessman points out, "I had difficulty even seeing" these complexities at the time because of "theoretical, political, and personal commitments" (p. 203). In brief, Riessman's concern to "do justice" ruptures her earlier account and its transcription of "perfectly formed" stories. By shifting focus to what had been peripheral—the conventions of narrative performance and research on narrative performance—she repunctuates and reorders narrative content, tasks, and identities.

THEORETICAL AND METHODOLOGICAL ISSUES

The brief review of existing research illustrates three advantages that narrative performance theory offers for understanding family communication: narrative performance theory emphasizes family as a production of communication practices, as performance and performativity, and as a hierarchy of strategy and tactics. First, narrative performance theory has the advantage of emphasizing family as a production of communication practices rather than an extralinguistic, ahistorical, decontextualized, or natural entity. Family storytelling is an embodied struggle in specific material conditions, under multiple discursive conventions, and with complex political consequences. The focus on narrative performance makes it possible to investigate family communication—rather than assume its existence—as it emerges in particular behaviors, in habitual and habituating patterns, according to conventional and unconventional practices that reproduce and challenge institutional arrangements. Storytelling is one way to produce and reproduce particular families as well as ideological constructions of "the family." Narrative performance theory locates family storytelling as an object of analysis that involves both situated events and their social and cultural contexts of power and knowledge.

Second, narrative performance theory has the advantage of emphasizing family as both a performance and a performative accomplishment.

The study of family storytelling performance is the access to under-standing performativity and the circulation of investments, desires, and subjectivities inscribed in particular performances. At the same time, the study of performativity in family storytelling is the access to under-standing particular performances and the interests they mobilize and serve. The reflexive combination of performance and performativity serves an important theory construction function (Lanigan, 1992, pp. 212–213) in family communication research. That is, the empirical study of performance in all its varieties provides a test for how family and family storytelling is conceptualized (eidetic theory construction). Similarly, the eidetic study of variations in performative constraints provides a test for how family and family storytelling are actually practiced and performed (empirical theory construction). Narrative performance theory locates both performance and performativity as a combined unit of analysis in family storytelling.

Third, narrative performance theory utilizes a strategic model that provides a way to explore the complexities of family and family story-telling without collapsing or reducing narrative discourse to opposi-tions between dominant or resistant discourses. Discourse, whether described as a narrative or counternarrative, functions differently at different levels in a hierarchy of strategy and tactics. For example, family storytelling might function to restructure individual identities as part of a rupture in group-ordering. Changes in group-ordering, however, might not affect the larger strategic context of content- and task-ordering. A "resistant" identity (a tactic of group-ordering) may do little to alter existing allocations of labor (task-ordering) or the larger strategic context of institutional and ideological arrangements (content-ordering). A strategic model, therefore, can help researchers explore how any particular storytelling performance can work to both resist and reinscribe existing conventions and institutional practices.

Finally, we suggest three related areas of caution or concern that narrative performance theory raises for family communication research. Research may overemphasize experience, the family as a group, and communication practices to the exclusion of other phenomena. First, the emphasis in research on studying "experience" may obscure conscious-ness and how experience is constituted in consciousness. This neglect of conscious experience can be seen in studies of family storytelling that articulate the research process as one of gathering family stories. Such research tends to privilege individuals and individual families as the origin or source of storytelling. Experience, in this instance, is decontextualized and taken to be self-evident and authentic. For that reason, narrative performance theory begins with storytelling as an intersubjective phenomenon and with conscious experience in the phenomenological sense rather than with the individual or individual family. The uncritical use of experience can be offset by research that explores differences and the variability of family storytelling and family communication. This shift in emphasis requires an ongoing and continuous effort to critique rather than naturalize experience and conventions for understanding experience.

Second, research may overemphasize the family as a homogeneous group or system (Yerby, 1995). This focus on family as a group may overstate group stability and interests at the expense of social structures, intragroup conflicts, and participants and participant subjectivity. This overemphasis on group homogeneity can be seen in the way power is conceptualized in two types of research. One type of research conceptualizes power as "power over" and finds evidence for it in asymmetrical relations among participants that place, for example, the father over the mother and parents over children. In this instance, variable practices that constitute the family as a group are de-emphasized to focus on the "amount" of power "held" by family members or by the family itself. The second type of research explains the operation of power by attributing it to external sources beyond and unaffected by family communication practices. In this instance, social structures such as classism, racism, heterosexism, and sexism function as undifferentiated and uniform explanations for asymmetrical power relations upon and within the family. The overemphasis on group homogeneity in both types of research can be countered by investigating the multiple, contingent, and contradictory ways communication practices circulate and participate in power relations to form families and perform storytelling.

Third, although we have emphasized the importance of storytelling as a way of doing family, it is not an exclusive practice. Storytelling does work in ways other than to form families, and storytelling is not the only practice—and certainly not the only communication practice—that functions to form and perform families. The challenge for family communication theory is to develop ways to understand and explore the variety of behaviors, habits, practices, and conventions that form families and that families perform. Narrative performance theory offers a productive approach to understand and explore the empirical and eidetic variability of family communication.

REFERENCES

Alexander, B. K., & LeBlanc, H. P. (1999). Cooking gumbo—examining cultural dialogue about family: A black-white narrativization of lived experience in Southern Louisiana. In T. J. Socha & R. C. Diggs (Eds.), *Communication, race, and family* (pp. 181–208). Mahwah, NJ: Lawrence Erlbaum.

Baldwin, K. (1985). "Woof!" A word on women's roles in family storytelling. In R. A. Jordon & S. J. Kalčik (Eds.), *Women's folklore, women's culture* (pp. 149–162). Philadelphia: University of Pennsylvania Press.

Bauman, R. (1986). *Story, performance, and event: Contextual studies of oral narratives.* Cambridge, UK: Cambridge University Press.

Blum-Kulka, S. (1997). *Dinner talk: Cultural patterns of sociability and socialization in family discourse.* Mahwah, NJ: Lawrence Erlbaum.

Briggs, C. L. (1993). "I'm not just talking to the victims of oppression tonight—I'm talking to everybody": Rhetorical authority and narrative authenticity in an African-American poetics of political engagement. *Journal of Narrative and Life History, 3,* 33–78.

Brockmeier, J., & Carbaugh, D. (2001). *Narrative and identity: Studies in autobiography, self and culture.* Amsterdam and Philadelphia: John Benjamins.

Bruner, J., & Weisser, S. (1991). The invention of self: Autobiography and its forms. In D. R. Olson & N. Torrance (Eds.), *Literacy and orality* (pp. 129–148). Cambridge, UK: Cambridge University Press.

Butler, J. (1993). *Bodies that matter: On the discursive limits of "sex."* New York: Routledge.

Dills, V. L. (1998). Transferring and transforming cultural norms: A mother-daughter-son lifestory in process. *Narrative Inquiry, 8,* 213–222.

Foucault, M. (1980). *The history of sexuality, Vol. 1: An introduction* (R. Hurley, Trans.). New York: Vintage Books.

Georgakopoulou, A. (1997). *Narrative performances: A study of modern Greek storytelling.* Amsterdam and Philadelphia: John Benjamins.

Heath, S. B. (1983). *Ways with words: Language, life and work in communities and classroom.* Cambridge, UK: Cambridge University Press.

Johnson, E. P. (2003). *Appropriating blackness: Performance and the politics of authenticity.* Durham, NC: Duke University Press.

Jorgenson, J., & Bochner, A. P. (2004). Imagining families through stories and rituals. In A. L. Vangelisti (Ed.), *Handbook of family communication* (pp. 513–538). Mahwah, NJ: Lawrence Erlbaum.

Langellier, K. M. (1999). Personal narrative, performance, performativity: Two or three things I know for sure. *Text and Performance Quarterly, 19,* 125–144.

Langellier, K. M. (2002). Performing family stories, forming cultural identity: Franco American *Mémère* stories. *Communication Studies, 53,* 56–73.

Langellier, K. M., & Peterson, E. E. (1992). Spinstorying: An analysis of women storytelling. In E. C. Fine & J. H. Speer (Eds.), *Performance, culture, and identity* (pp. 157–180). Westport, CT: Praeger.

Langellier, K. M., & Peterson, E. E. (1993). Family storytelling as a strategy of social control. In D. Mumby (Ed.), *Narrative and social control* (pp. 49–76). Newbury Park, CA: Sage.

Langellier, K. M., & Peterson, E. E. (2004). *Storytelling in daily life: Performing narrative.* Philadelphia: Temple University Press.

Lanigan, R. L. (1992). *The human science of communicology: A phenomenology of discourse in Foucault and Merleau-Ponty.* Pittsburgh, PA: Duquesne University Press.

Mandelbaum, J. (1987). Couples sharing stories. *Communication Quarterly, 35,* 144–170.

McFeat, T. (1974). *Small group cultures.* New York: Pergamon.

Merleau-Ponty, M. (1964). *Signs* (R. C. McLeary, Trans.). Evanston, IL: Northwestern University Press.

Mishler, E. G. (1999). *Storylines: Craftartists' narratives of identity.* Cambridge, MA: Harvard University Press.

Nelson, H. L. (2001). *Damaged identities: Narrative repair.* Ithaca, NY: Cornell University Press.

Ochs, E., & Capps, L. (2001). *Living narrative: Creating lives in everyday storytelling.* Cambridge, MA: Harvard University Press.

Patterson, W. (Ed.). (2002). *Strategic narrative: New perspectives on the power of personal and cultural stories.* Lanham, MD: Lexington.

Patton, S. (1996). Race/identity/culture/kin: Constructions of African American identity in transracial adoption. In S. Smith & J. Watson (Eds.), *Getting a life: Everyday uses of autobiography* (pp. 271–296). Minneapolis: University of Minnesota Press.

Peterson, E. E. (1987). The stories of pregnancy: On interpretation of small-group cultures. *Communication Quarterly, 35,* 39–47.

Pollock, D. (1999). *Telling bodies, performing birth: Everyday narratives of childbirth.* ⌉ ?
New York: Columbia University Press.

Riessman, C. K. (1990). *Divorce talk: Women and men make sense of personal relationships.* New Brunswick, NJ: Rutgers University Press.

Riessman, C. K. (2002). Doing justice: Positioning the interpreter in narrative work. In W. Patterson (Ed.), *Strategic narrative: New perspectives on the power of personal and cultural stories* (pp. 193–214). Lanham, MD: Lexington.

Roof, J. (1996). *Come as you are: Sexuality and narrative.* New York: Columbia University Press.

Sawin, P. E. (1999). Gender context, and the narrative construction of identity: Rethinking models of "women's narrative." In M. Bucholtz, A. C. Lieng, & L. A. Sutton (Eds.), *Reinventing identities: The gendered self in discourse* (pp. 241–258). New York: Oxford University Press.

Schely-Newman, E. (1999). Mothers know best: Constructing meaning in a narrative event. *Quarterly Journal of Speech, 85,* 285–302.

Scollon, R., & Scollon, S. B. K. (1981). *Narrative, literacy, and face in interethnic communication.* Norwood, NJ: Ablex.

Smith, S., & Watson, J. (Eds.). (1996). *Getting a life: Everyday uses of autobiography.* Minneapolis: University of Minnesota Press.

Stone, E. (1988). *Black sheep and kissing cousins: How our family stories shape us.* New York: Times Books.

Strine, M. S. (1998). Articulating performance/performativity: Disciplinary tasks and the contingencies of practice. In J. S. Trent (Ed.), *Communication: Views from the helm for the 21st century* (pp. 312–317). Boston, MA: Allyn and Bacon.

Trujillo, N. (2002). In search of Naunny's history: Reproducing gender ideology in family stories. *Women's Studies in Communication, 25,* 88–118.

Watson, J. (1996). Ordering the family: Genealogy as autobiographical pedigree. In S. Smith & J. Watson (Eds.), *Getting a life: Everyday uses of autobiography* (pp. 297–323). Minneapolis: University of Minnesota Press.

Weston, K. (1991). *Families we choose: Lesbians and gays kinship.* New York: Columbia University Press.

Wilden, A. (1987). *The rules are no game: The strategy of communication.* London: Routledge.

Yerby, J. (1995). Family systems theory reconsidered: Integrating social construction theory and dialectical process. *Communication Theory, 5,* 339–365.

Yerby, J., Buerkel-Rothfuss, N., & Bochner, A. (1995). *Understanding family communication* (2nd ed.). Scottsdale, AZ: Gorsuch Scarisbrick.

Yocum, M. R. (1985). Woman to woman: Fieldwork and the private sphere. In R. A. Jordan & S. J. Kalčik (Eds.), *Women's folklore, women's culture* (pp. 54–64). Philadelphia: University of Pennsylvania Press.

Young, K. (1987). *Taleworlds and storyrealms: The phenomenology of narrative.* Dordrecht, Holland: Martinus Nijhoff.

Young, K. (2000). Gestures and the phenomenology of emotion in narrative. *Semiotica, 131,* 79–112.

8

Relational Communication Theory: An Interactional Family Theory

L. Edna Rogers

Editors' Note: Relational communication is one of the earliest theories coming out of family communication. With roots in studies of culture and systems theory, the theory falls into the logical-empirical paradigm, focused on what Rogers explains as interactional patterns that characterize relational types and the outcome of these patterns.

The metaphor of the dance has often been used as a way of visualizing the theoretical perspective of relational communication toward understanding family relationships. Just as a dance unfolds in the movement of the dancers, relational communication focuses on the interactive movements of relational members' communication behaviors as they interrelate with one another. When we think of dance, we think of movement, rhythm, coming together, moving away, with different dance forms emerging from the combination of the partners' different dance steps. Analogous to dance steps, different message behaviors combine into patterned interactions descriptive of different types of relations. Whether you view a particular relationship as akin to a formal waltz, a dramatic tango, an energetic folk dance, or a sensual slow dance, punctuated occasionally, perhaps, with a bit of slam dancing, or a mix of all these, the relational dance does not rest on the actions of one member, but on the evolving patterns and rhythms created together by the interactors. Lindbergh (1955), in her poetic style, spoke to the potential of these processes:

> A good relationship has a pattern like a dance and is built on some of the same rules. The partners do not need to hold on tightly . . . they move confidently in the same patterns, intricate but gay and swift and free . . . To touch heavily would be to arrest the pattern and freeze the movement, to check the endlessly changing beauty of its unfolding. There is no place here for the possessive clutch, the clinging arm, the heavy hand; only the barest touch in passing . . . creating a pattern together, and being invisibly nourished by it. (p. 104)

In line with the dance metaphor, the theoretical focus of relational communication is centered on the interactive, formative quality of the communicative process, on how members move in relation to one another via their verbal and nonverbal behaviors in the process of jointly constructing the patterns of communication that both characterize and impact family relationships. The goal of this perspective is to provide a theoretical and practical understanding of the interactional dynamics of relationships and the consequences of these processes. One practical implication in taking this view is the recognition that because we create our relationships, we can change them. For better or worse, our relationships are of our own making, and are thus malleable and changeable. Change the dance steps and you change the dance.

Given this view of the interwoven connection between communication and relationship, communication is seen as the process by which relationships are constructed. Through the interchange of message behaviors, relational members reciprocally enact definitions of self in relation to others and simultaneously shape the ongoing nature of their relationship. In this process, each of the members actively influences one another, but the relational impact of their actions resides in the mutually produced patterns of the relationship. The formative and influential nature of our ways of talking was emphasized by Shotter (1993) in the following quote: "to talk in new ways is to construct new

forms of social relation, and, to construct new forms of social relation
. . . is to construct new ways of being" (p. 9). The power of this statement points out that not only our relationships but the very essence of
our being lie within our ways of talking with one another. And perhaps
the poignancy of this process is never as profound as it is in our family
relationships. These introductory thoughts set the scene for an
expanded discussion of the central tenets of the relational communication perspective.

THE THEORETICAL PERSPECTIVE

Relational communication had its beginnings in the cultural studies of
Bateson in the early 1930s. Bateson's (1935) approach for understanding cultural systems was based on the observation of the members' nat-
urally occurring social interactions. In contrast to the more traditional
model of describing cultures in terms of their basic social institutions,
he sought a more grounded approach focused on the pragmatic meaning of everyday enactments of cultural practices. Basic to Bateson's
thinking was that social relationships and the resulting social order
emanated from the reoccurring communicative enactments. This once
novel view of communication as a constitutive, formative social process
has, in more recent times, gained widespread consensus and remains a
basic premise of relational communication theory.

Bateson's (1936) writings and initial theoretical ideas for conceptualizing relational processes remained largely unknown until the 1950s,
when a research project he directed at Menlo Park (California) brought
him into contact with members of the Mental Research Institute (MRI)
in nearby Palo Alto. Through his association with the Palo Alto group
of clinicians and researchers, the significance of his work began to
receive wider attention, especially among family system scholars and
therapists. The growing awareness of Bateson's ideas came largely
through the writings of the members of MRI (e.g., Haley, 1963; Jackson,
1965; Sluzki & Beavin, 1965), and most notably through the 1967 publication of Watzlawick, Beavin and Jackson's *Pragmatics of Human
Communication*. This time period also coincided with the increasing
influence of system theory and cybernetics on the study of communication. The coalescence of these lines of thought formed an interrelated
theoretical foundation for the development of the relational communication perspective. In particular, system theory and cybernetics

provided the general framework, with the more central features of the perspective based on the conceptual work of Bateson.

System theory presents a worldview based on the interrelatedness of events. The organizing principles of this perspective (von Bertalanffy, 1968) focus on the interconnection and integration of the component parts that form a larger systemic whole. With this approach, a social system such as the family represents an integrated, unified whole based on the mutually influencing relationships between the family members. Of the defining characteristics of a system, outlined in the theory, the most central is the concept of interdependency. The interdependence of the member parts is what creates a system. It is also the quality that forms the hierarchical levels or interconnected layers of systems within larger systems. For instance, a husband and wife relationship forms one system within the family; a father and son another; a sibling relationship yet another. Each of these relational systems represent an integrated whole, and at the same time each is a part, or subsystem, of the larger family system.

The "part/whole" nature of systems (Koestler, 1978) speaks to the variety of interrelated relational dynamics occurring in the family and their organizational complexities. The part/whole structuring of systems encompassed within higher-ordered systems is such that each level simultaneously influences and is influenced by the higher level. Thus, each relational subsystem influences the larger family system and is influenced by the larger system. An additional distinguishing feature of multileveled systems is that each level has properties that are not present in other levels. To illustrate this point, a husband-wife relationship, for example, does not represent nor describe the larger family system, just as with the dance steps of one partner do not produce the "whole" of the dance. In related fashion, different levels of analysis offer different forms of insight. Thus, in terms of understanding relational and family systems, studies of the singular, individual parts (as insightful as these might be) do not provide a description of the relational whole. Stated differently, in our personal relationships, you and I each make a difference, but together we are that difference.

The field of cybernetics (Wiener, 1948) complements the system perspective by focusing on how systems are regulated through the flow of feedback information occurring within the system. In other words, the focus is on how systems are maintained, modified, and changed by the circles of influence that emerge from and guide the members' communicative interactions. The cybernetic principles of self-organizing systems are represented in the ongoing dialectic oscillations of continuity and change in the process of maintaining systemic integration. These fluctuating dynamics reflect the cyclic flow of information that is being monitored by the system members. Based on the cybernetic processes of self-regulation, a system is continually informing itself about itself through the feedback loops of message exchange among the system components.

Jackson (1965), in his seminal work on the family, applied these principles by viewing the family as a self-regulating system guided by family rules. Likewise, Kantor and Lehr's (1975) influential model of family process is based on the concept of "distance regulation." In their view, family members are continually informing one another through their communicative behaviors as to what constitutes appropriate distance within as well as outside the family. When system and cybernetic principles are applied to the study of families, interaction, process, and patterns come to the forefront.

From the beginning, system thinking was central to Bateson's interactional view of relationships. In developing this approach, Bateson focused on identifying pattern formations that progressively moved, in his words, toward "knowledge of the larger interactive system" (Bateson, 1972, p. 433). The influence and guidance of Bateson's propositions are clearly visible in shaping the theoretical and analytical stance of relational communication. His conceptualization of the duality of message meaning provides a stepping-off point for describing how patterns of relationship are formed.

Bateson (1951) proposed that messages simultaneously offer two levels of meaning: a content (report) meaning and a relational (command) meaning. The content level provides information based on what the message is about, while the relational level "gives off" information on how the message is to be interpreted. For example, the content of the comment "You're late" refers to time, but at the relational level the comment typically implies a form of criticism of the other's lack of responsibility or concern. If the other responds with "You're always too uptight" or "too self-centered," the initiation of a relational pattern of mutual blaming is put in place. If, however, the other responds with "You're right, I'm really sorry," a different, softer definition of relational meaning is likely to emerge from the partners' interaction. In light of these two levels of message meaning, the content, or what is said, is always contextualized by the higher, meta-level relational meaning of how it is said. Content plays a part, but it is largely at the relational level that interactors indicate how they define their relationship. In the ongoing negotiation of relational meaning, members co-define the patterns that are descriptive of their relationship.

The concepts of symmetry and complementarity, described by Bateson (1935) in his early work, represent two general patterns of communication. Based on the similarity or difference of the relational meaning of the messages exchanged, symmetry refers to interaction sequences in which the participants' behaviors mirror one another, such as responding to a complaint with a complaint or a supportive message with support. In contrast, complementary patterns refer to sequences in which the behaviors are different but fit together, as in giving/receiving or question/answer interacts. Both symmetry and complementarity can take different forms, depending on the type and order of the messages exchanged. To illustrate with a few simple examples, an argument between two siblings over which TV show to watch represents a competitive form of symmetry; submissive symmetry is likely to result when a husband and wife, in planning a night out, both want to do whatever the other wants to do. If one partner initiates a suggestion that the other accepts, one type of complementarity is formed; a different type results if one person's request for assistance is refused by the other.

Bateson's (1979) approach for depicting patterns of relationship moves from the identification of communication patterns that are formed from the combination of messages with messages, as illustrated previously, to successive combinations of patterns with patterns which form larger patterns that provide a more holistic description of the relationship. The following configurations are representative of these larger patterns. For example, interaction episodes that intermix symmetry and complementarity form an overall relatively flexible interaction pattern, what Lederer and Jackson (1968) later referred to as a "parallel" pattern. Bateson's description of reciprocal complementarity represents another relatively flexible pattern. It consists of a series of complementary exchanges in which the members alternate between asserting and accepting each others suggestions or ideas. This type of complementarity represents one of the more harmonious relational patterns, while rigid complementary, as the term suggests, is a highly redundant, potentially stifling form of complementarity. This pattern results when each member repeatedly enacts the same part in an ongoing complementary sequence, for instance, with one person asserting control and the other submitting to their directives. In contrast, patterns of escalating competitive symmetry reflect an ongoing control struggle over who will be in charge of the relationship. With each exchange, the members disagree or reject the other's relational defini- tion. Although brief episodes of this pattern occur in most relationships and certainly in intimate ones, repeated enactments of this pattern are indicative of flawed relations. The prominence of escalating symmetry in troubled relationships has clearly been evidenced by studies of mar- ital and family violence.

Symmetry and complementarity exemplify the process of pattern identification and serve as prototypes for describing relational form. The progressive movement of mapping relationships through the evolving formative process of communication gives meaning to Bateson's (1979) description of his approach as a "dialectic of process and form" (p. 211), with process influencing relational form, and form influencing the ongoing process.

Although presented in an abbreviated form, a defining feature of each of the theoretical perspectives discussed is the movement or shift in attention from an individual-based approach to a systems approach for studying relationships. With this move, attention is given to the interrelatedness of system members as they co-construct their relation- ship. This reframing represents a central feature of the relational com- munication view of relationships (Rogers, Millar & Bavelas, 1985).

PURPOSE AND THEORETICAL PROPOSITIONS

The overall goal of the relational communication perspective is to pro- vide a communication theory of relationships based on an interactional approach to the study of relational process and patterns. More specifi- cally, the purpose is to describe the communication patterns that char- acterize different types of relationships and the ramification of these patterns. In other words, the relational perspective seeks to identify the patterns of communication that work for us, and those that work against us, in our personal and family relationships and offer potential explanations for these differences.

The general theoretical propositions of relational communication are based on the dynamic qualities reflective of the flexibility or rigidity of relational systems. One of the most widely held premises in the family literature is the limited functionality of rigidly enacted family systems. This premise holds that over time, overly redundant (rigid) patterns of interactions constrain system members' negotiation of relational differences and their ability to accommodate or adjust to changing situations. In turn, the narrowed range of options will work against the members' positive resolutions of family difficulties and will be associated with negative relational evaluations and outcomes. For instance, a potential problematic issue of rigidly enacted systems is a continual tension between individual freedom and established patterns of family authority. In contrast, it is proposed that members of viable, well-functioning systems will enact patterns that offer sufficient confirmation and acceptance of their reciprocal relational definitions for maintaining a relatively predicable set of patterns, yet retain a range of flexibility for relational spontaneity and novelty, the negotiation of differences, and pattern modifications to fit changing situations and contexts. Thus, viable family relationships will demonstrate a fluctuating dialectic interplay of continuity and change, autonomy and closeness, and similar pattern alterations associated with positive relational outcomes.

When negotiating problematic issues, members of rigidly structured systems are predicted to be particularly prone to reenacting the same communicative "dance steps," regardless of the ineffectiveness of those patterns. Thus, members will tend to increasingly become entrapped in patterns that work against them and that may, over time, rupture the very system they hope to maintain. Faced with similar issues, the members of flexible systems are not seen as being exempt from engaging in disruptive ineffective patterns, such as rigid complementarity or escalating symmetry, but when they occur, the members will more quickly transition to enacting communication patterns that constrain and alter the continuation of potentially dysfunctional patterns (Watzlawick, Weakland, & Fisch, 1974). Given these proposed differences, well-functioning systems are predicted to evidence a fluidity of self-correcting communicative processes that counter potentially problematic relational tendencies. In the continuing development of the theory, additional propositions have been generated regarding how different patterned forms of flexibility and redundancy influence the relationship.

APPLICATION OF THE THEORY

To move from the theoretical realm to its application, the relational communication coding system was developed to describe interactive patterns of communication (Rogers, 1972; Rogers & Farace, 1975). Based on the relational (command) level of message meaning, the coding system indexes the control aspects of relationships by examining how interactors define and direct the nature of their relationship. The relational implication of each message is coded in terms of its grammatical form (e.g., assertion, question, talkover, etc.) and type of response relative to the previous speakers' message (e.g., support, nonsupport, extension, order, disconfirmation, etc.). Messages that assert a directive or firm definition of the relationship (e.g., talkover/order) represent a one-up control movement (↑); an acceptance or request of the other's relational definition (e.g., question/support) indicates a one-down message (↓); whereas a less constraining, control-leveling maneuver (e.g., assertion/extension) is coded as a one-across move (→).

For describing interaction patterns, the sequential combination of message control codes provides specific transactional descriptions of different types of communication patterns. Based on the definitions given earlier, complementary patterns are represented by opposite control messages of one-up and one-down (↑↓, ↓↑); symmetrical patterns are based on similar control directions (↑↑, ↓↓, →→). An additional set of patterns, referred to as transitory transactions, are formed by the combination of one-across messages with one-up and one-down messages (→↑, ↑→, →↓, ↓→). In turn, these transactional patterns provide the basis for forming larger pattern configurations. For instance, rigid complementarity is represented by a series of one-up/one-down messages with the same speaker consistently in the one-up position. Competitive escalating symmetry results from an ongoing exchange of one-up control messages.

Two examples are given to illustrate the application of the coding system. Each husband (H) and wife (W) interaction represents a small slice of a longer conversation.

Control Code

W: Well, we've got, you know, this list of ours.	→
H: Your list.	↑
W: My list is different from what your list is.	↑
H: I don't have a list. You have a list.	↑
W: I have a list, and your stereo wasn't on it; we needed a kitchen table, and you went and bought a dang stereo.	↑

H: Let me tell you another thing that bugs me: when   ↑
you go charge up all the credit cards.

W: But see, I don't like to charge, but I have to   →
when it's such a good deal and on sale.

H: You don't like to charge! Then how come all of my   ↑
cards are maxed out?

W: This is what bugs me, when you go and buy the   ↑
most expensive thing for your car and it doesn't matter.

H: It does matter; The transmission could drop   ↑
out of your car, and you wouldn't notice it.

As readily observable, this interaction illustrates an escalating pattern of competitive symmetry, with only a single one-across move before a quick return to one-up escalation. In the longer conversation, this marital pair demonstrated that they were "pros" at producing this pattern as they continued to find issue after issue on which to disagree. This example is from a comparative study of physically aggressive and nonaggressive marital couples (Rogers, Castleton, & Lloyd, 1996), and as you might guess, it is of a physically aggressive couple. The second example is from the same study, but of a physically nonaggressive couple.

Control Code

W: I don't think we have any major differences,   →
just minor ones like when to sell the car.

H: Uh huh, I think we're both willing to   ↓
meet halfway.

W: Yeah.   ↓

H: There's times when I'm sort of   →
impulsive, and at the moment I might
be difficult to discuss something with.

W: Oh, maybe like that car.   →

H: Hmmmm.   →

W: I think you're a pretty reasonable person.   ↓

H: You know, I really don't want to buy a new car.   →

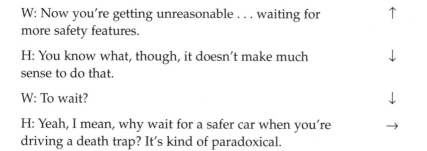

W: Now you're getting unreasonable . . . waiting for   ↑
more safety features.

H: You know what, though, it doesn't make much   ↓
sense to do that.

W: To wait?   ↓

H: Yeah, I mean, why wait for a safer car when you're   →
driving a death trap? It's kind of paradoxical.

This couple's interaction represents a leveling pattern of negotiation, a mix of one-across with one-down moves. The issue of the car
is one of contention, and even though the wife's one-up message
expresses some frustration, it did not lead to a competitive sequence of
one-up exchange. For the first couple, this would likely trigger another
round of escalation. This second example illustrates the one-across/
one-down transitory pattern that has been found across different marital studies to be a distinguishing pattern of satisfied, well-adjusted
couples in comparison with more troubled couples. This communication sequence allows for a continuing discussion facilitated by the supportive one-down moves on the part of each of the partners.

The investigations of marital and family systems based on this
research approach have both supported and refined the theoretical
propositions of relational communication. These investigations have
provided a range of research findings that allow a better understanding of how different types of communication patterns are played out
among family members and the influence of these patterns on the quality of family relationships. For a full review of this program of research,
see Rogers and Escudero (2004).

CONTINUING DEVELOPMENTS

In the development of the relational communication perspective, the
majority of the research focused on the control dimension of dyadic
relationships. This focus, guided by the earlier theoretical work, was
foundational in establishing the perspective and remains an important
line of research. Yet it was clearly recognized that to develop a more
complete study of relationships a broader scope was necessary (Millar
& Rogers, 1987). The directions considered to be most central for
advancing the perspective include moving beyond the dyad, expanding

the relational dimensions investigated, and incorporating the emotional and cognitive aspects of the participants in the research. These developments are presently under way in several recently initiated research efforts.

The first of these initiatives is Heatherington and Friedlander's (1987) adaptation of the relational coding system to the larger family unit. This system is designed to code communicative processes occurring within multiple-member groups that are not present in dyadic interactions. With the interactions of three or more members, messages may have relational implications for more than one member. This occurs when one member's message, given as a direct response to one person, indirectly defines their relation with another member. A central feature of the family communication coding system is the identification of direct and indirect message targets, which provides the basis for tracking different types of triadic patterns of relational control within the family. The relational implications of these triadic interactions are illustrated, for example, when a message that directly disagrees with one member indirectly supports the view of another member, or when one person speaks directly to another person about a third member or ignores another's direct message by speaking to a different member. When members exchange direct messages, the coding procedures are the same as with the original system, but the added ability to detect patterns such as family coalitions or indirect disconfirmation is a particular strength of the family coding system. With the development of this system, the investigation of the relational patterns of multiple family members has moved forward (Heatherington & Friedlander, 2004).

Another direction considered essential for a more fully developed understanding of relationships is the expansion of the relational dimensions included for investigation. Recent research carried out on the combined analysis of relational control and nonverbal affect patterns of interaction has proven to provide a more detailed, integrated description of marital relationships than each dimension alone (Escudero, Rogers, & Gutierrez, 1997). The research, based on a comparison of distressed and nondistressed couples, found the conjoint control-affect analysis resulted in a significantly larger number of specific pattern distinctions between these two couple groups than the separate analysis of each dimension. These patterns gave a sharper contrast of the progressive entrapment of distressed couples in negative affect-control patterns and the more flexible positive or neutral affect-control patterns of the nondistressed couples.

A more inclusive effort for investigating the interrelated dimensions of relationships is the research by Escudero, Heatherington and Friedlander (2001). Based on a longitudinal study of couple interaction, the research includes the combined analysis of three simultaneously occurring aspects of the communication process: relational control, emotional affect, and cognitive meaning. More specifically, these dimensions are identified in terms of the relational control codes, the partners' ongoing emotional response to the messages exchanged, and the constructed meaning of their relationship as expressed in the content of their messages. Although the complexity of this type of investigation is challenging, it moves the research in the direction of taking the participants' views into account and adds an important dimension to the relational perspective.

With the continuing development of these research directions, each of the advances described has expanded the theoretical and research application of the relational perspective toward a more encompassing, comprehensive study of family relationships. In the study of the family, interaction research has received less attention in comparison with other approaches. By taking an interactional approach, relational communication contributes to "filling in" and strengthening this area of family study. In addition to describing more general family system patterns, a particular advantage of this approach, given the use of coded observations, is the ability to identify specific communication behaviors or patterns that lead in directions desired or toward less desired family outcomes. This type of information is not only theoretically important but it has a clear practical value. It allows specific interpretations of the research findings that offer useful and applicable insights for family members, marital and family counselors, and (importantly) family educators.

CONCLUSION

This relatively abbreviated unfolding of relational communication has traversed a considerable distance from the foundational work of Bateson. Yet during this span of time, the fundamental stance of the perspective has remained centered on the "patterns which connect" (Bateson, 1979, p. 11). From the theoretical perspective of relational communication, relationships are viewed as moving art forms, creatively shaped by the interactive connections of the participants. The unfolding movements of the communicative "dance" give meaning and definition to their relationship (Rogers, 1998). For the study of the family, relational communication theory offers a way of understanding these inner workings of family systems.

REFERENCES

Bateson, G. (1935). Culture, contact and schismogenesis, *Man, 35,* 178–183.

Bateson, G. (1936). *Naven.* Cambridge, UK: Cambridge University Press.

Bateson, G. (1951). Information and codification: A philosophical approach. In J. Ruesch & G. Bateson (Eds.), *Communication: The social matrix of psychiatry* (pp.168–211). New York: Norton.

Bateson, G. (1972). *Steps to an ecology of mind.* New York: Ballantine Books.

Bateson, G. (1979). *Mind and nature: A necessary unity.* New York: Bantam Books.

Escudero, V., Heatherington, L., & Friedlander, M. (2001). Observing couples' interaction: Integrative analysis of interpersonal control, cognitive constructions and emotional impact. *Metodologia de las Ciencias del Comportamiento, 3,* 247–265.

Escudero, V., Rogers, L. E., & Gutierrez, E. (1997). Patterns of relational control and nonverbal affect in clinic and nonclinic couples. *Journal of Social and Personal Relationships, 14,* 5–29.

Haley, J. (1963). *Strategies of psychotherapy.* New York: Grune & Stratton.

Heatherington, L., & Friedlander, M. (1987). *Family relational communication control coding system.* Unpublished coding manual, Department of Psychology, Williams College, Williamstown, MA.

Heatherington, L., & Friedlander, M. (2004). From dyads to triads, and beyond: Relational control in individual and family therapy. In L. E. Rogers & V. Escudero (Eds.), *Relational communication: An interactional perspective to the study of process and form* (pp. 103–129). Mahwah, NJ: LawrenceErlbaum.

Jackson, D. (1965). The study of the family. *Family Process, 4,* 1–20.

Kantor, D., & Lehr, W. (1975). *Inside the family: Toward a theory of family process.* San Francisco: Jossey-Bass.

Koestler, A. (1978). *Janus: A summing up.* New York: Vintage Books.

Lederer, W., & Jackson, D. (1968). *The mirages of marriage.* New York: Norton.

Lindbergh, A. M. (1955). *Gift from the sea.* New York: Random House.

Millar, F., & Rogers, L. E. (1987). Relational dimensions of interpersonal dynamics. In M. Roloff & G. Miller (Eds.), *Explorations in interpersonal processes: New directions in communication research* (pp. 117–139). Newbury Park, CA: Sage.

Rogers, L. E. (1972). *Dyadic systems and transactional communication in a family context.* Unpublished doctoral dissertation, Michigan State University.

Rogers, L. E. (1998). The meaning of relationship in relational communication. In R. Conville & L. E. Rogers (Eds.), *The meaning of 'relationship' in interpersonal communication* (pp. 69–82). Westport, CT: Praeger.

Rogers, L. E., Castleton, A., & Lloyd, S. A. (1996). Relational control and physical aggression in satisfying marital relationships. In D. Cahn & S. Lloyd (Eds.), *Family violence from a communication perspective* (pp. 218–239). Thousand Oaks, CA: Sage.

Rogers, L. E., & Escudero, V. (Eds.). (2004). *Relational communication: An interactional perspective to the study of process and form.* Mahwah, NJ: Lawrence Erlbaum.

Rogers, L. E., & Farace, R. (1975). Analysis of relational communication in dyads: New measurement procedures. *Human Communication Research, 1,* 222–239.

Rogers, L. E., Millar, F., & Bavelas, J. B. (1985). Methods for analyzing marital conflict discourse: Implications of a systems approach. *Family Process, 24,* 53–72.

Shotter, J. (1993). *Conversational realities: Constructing life through language.* Thousand Oaks, CA: Sage.

Sluzki, C., & Beavin, J. (1965). Simetria y complementaridad: Una definicion operacional y una tipologia de parejas. *Acta psiquiatrica y psicologica de America Latina, 11,* 321–330.

von Bertalanffy, L. (1968). *General systems theory: Foundations, development, applications.* New York: Braziller.

Watzlawick, P., Beavin, J., & Jackson, D. (1967). *Pragmatics of human communication.* New York: Norton.

Watzlawick, P., Weakland, J., & Fisch, R. (1974). *Change: Principles of problem formation and problem resolution.* New York: Norton.

Wiener, N. (1948). *Cybernetics.* Cambridge, MA: MIT Press.

9

Relational Dialectics Theory: Multivocal Dialogues of Family Communication

Leslie A. Baxter

Editors' Note: Relational dialectics provides us with an interpretive theory of family communication in its focus on meaning-making through the interplay of competing perspectives, or discourses. Although this theory originates in communication studies, it is based on the more general theoretical works of Russian social theorist Mikhail Bakhtin.

Relational dialectics (Baxter, 2004a, 2004b; Baxter & Montgomery, 1996) is a theory whose purpose is to render intelligible the communicative processes of relating, whether familial or nonfamilial. The theory is amenable to both quantitative and qualitative methods directed toward a goal of understanding. Because relational dialectics is predicated on the assumption that relating is a complex and indeterminate process of meaning-making, the positivist goals of prediction, explanation, and control are not the appropriate benchmarks by which the theory should be evaluated. Instead, the theory should be assessed against the benchmarks of insight and heurism: Does the theory shed rich insight into how family members constitute and experience their communicative lives? Is the theory useful in generating new and interesting questions about family communication?

Relational dialectics is grounded in the theory of dialogism developed by Russian social theorist Mikhail Bakhtin (1981, 1984, 1986, 1990). Holquist (1990) invoked the term "dialogism" to label Bakhtin's body of work based on his view that "dialogue" is the concept that brings coherence to it. Bakhtin's lifelong intellectual purpose was to critique theories and practices that reduced the unfinalizable, open, and varied nature of social life in determinate, closed, totalizing ways. To Bakhtin, social life was not a closed, univocal "monologue" in which only a single voice could be heard; instead, social life was an open "dialogue" characterized by multivocality and the indeterminacy inherent when those multiple voices came together.

At its most general level, relational dialectics provides a dialogic complement to more monologic theoretical approaches. For example, nondialogic approaches tend to position "closeness" as positive, whereas "distance" is viewed as negative, a symptom of problems. By contrast, the dialogic move is one of recognizing that family life is a both/and experience—families gain their meanings from the give-and-take interplay of multiple, competing themes or perspectives, for example, the discourse of "intimacy" and the discourse of "independence." No theme or perspective is better or worse than its opposites—their interplay is what is important.

However, a careful reading of Bakhtin suggests several related meanings of dialogue. In the remainder of this chapter I will discuss four of these conceptions of dialogue integral to relational dialectics theory: (a) dialectical flux, (b) constitutive process, (c) utterance, and (d) aesthetic moment. However, the bulk of my attention will be devoted to the first conception because most of the research attention in family communication has been placed there. A fifth conception—dialogue as a critical sensibility—is the least developed in relational dialectics and thus I will not present it here because of space limitations (see Baxter, 2004, for a discussion of it).

DIALOGUE AS DIALECTICAL FLUX

To Bakhtin (1984), the essence of dialogue is its simultaneous fusion with, yet differentiation from, another. To engage in dialogue, participants must fuse their perspectives to some extent while sustaining the uniqueness of their individual perspectives. Just as dialogue is simultaneously fusion and differentiation, Bakhtin (1981, p. 272) regarded all of social life as the product of "a contradiction-ridden, tension-filled unity of two embattled tendencies," centripetal (i.e., dynamics of unity, homogeneity, centrality) and centrifugal (dynamics of difference, dispersion, decentering). Communicative life in families can be viewed as a dialectic in which different, often opposing, voices interpenetrate—some more dominant and others more marginalized. These united-yet-opposed voices are *dialectical contradictions* (Baxter & Montgomery, 1996). Contradictory voices permeate communication, and it is their interplay that constructs meaning for family members. Dialogue is not a negative factor in relational dialectics theory; rather, the interplay of competing voices is an energizing source of vitality.

In every interaction, multiple opposed voices can be heard, although not necessarily with equal force. Sometimes, this interplay takes the genre form (Bakhtin, 1986) of interpersonal conflict—what Baxter and Montgomery (1996) called an *antagonistic contradiction*—in which each family member is aligned with a different perspective. For example, in a conflict over curfew between an adolescent and parents, the adolescent might give voice to the ideology of independence, arguing for the right to do what he or she wants; whereas the parent might give voice to an opposed perspective of respect for parental authority. However, relational dialectics, following dialogism, asserts that centripetal-centrifugal flux is an undercurrent in all interaction, not just interpersonal conflict. These more prevalent occasions of *nonantagonistic contradiction* (Baxter & Montgomery, 1996) feature the interpenetration of opposed voices, or perspectives, in all family members' utterances. For example, you can hear the centrifugal voices of dependence, affection, and connectedness as shadows in even the most strident and impassioned adolescent assertion of independence, just as you can hear the centrifugal voices of support for child independence in parents' most firmly expressed articulations of a curfew rule. When parents and children talk jointly on the topic of curfew, regardless of whether that talk takes the form of interpersonal conflict, their discourse is a dialectical dance in which the careful listener can hear multiple perspectives in play with and against one another: the discourse of "independence," the discourse of "respect" for family rules, the discourse of "responsibility," the discourse of "trust," and so forth. The meaning of the curfew talk for its participants is located in the interplay of these various discursive perspectives.

It is important to underscore that the contradictions of relational dialectics are not comprised of competing psychological needs. In the end, dialectical flux is a discursive phenomenon, not a psychological one. Family members, particularly in the enactment of nonantagonistic contradictions, may experience ambivalence but the source of such feelings is not psychologically driven but rather discursively driven. From a dialogic perspective, internal psychological thoughts and feelings are conceptualized as inner dialogues in which multiple discourses are at play. Family members exist in webs of meaning spun through communication with others. Thus, scholars committed to a relational dialectics perspective are well served by Bakhtin's conception of *voice* as "verbal-ideological" (Bakhtin, 1981, p. 272) in nature. Bakhtin used the term "ideological" in its broadest sense to mean any idea-system. Thus, the scholar committed to a relational dialectics approach examines family communication with an eye toward identifying the systems of meaning—the discourses, the ideologies, the codes—that are united yet competing. Obviously, these systems of meaning are likely to vary by culture, not only in reference to the unique worldview constructed by each family but additionally in reference to larger socio-historical units such as nationalities and ethnic heritages.

This first meaning of dialogue, dialectical flux, was given a prominent place in Baxter and Montgomery's (1996) articulation of relational dialectics. Space limitations allow little more than bibliographic pointing to the family communication research in which relational dialectics has been used to frame the study of a variety of contradictions that animate family life. For example, several scholars have examined the contradictions that organize marital life in general (e.g., Baxter & Braithwaite, 2002; Baxter & Simon, 1993; Braithwaite & Baxter, 1995; Hoppe-Nagao & Ting-Toomey, 2002; Pawlowski, 1998; Wood, Dendy, Dordek, Germany, & Varallo, 1994). For example, marital couples in the United States appear to make sense of marriage as a relationship framed in two competing discourses: a traditional ideology in which obligation, responsibility, and institution feature prominently; and an ideology of individualism in which individual wants and needs are privileged. The particular dialogic dance of these discourses organizes a given couple's meaning of their unique marriage. Researchers also have used relational dialectics as a way to understand marital couples who experience specific challenges such as abuse (e.g., Sabourin & Stamp, 1995), conflict (e.g., Erbert, 2000), and the "married widowhood" that characterizes marriages in which one spouse is living in a nursing home with

Alzheimer's (e.g., Baxter, Braithwaite, Golish, & Olson, 2002). Initiated by the work by Masheter and Harris (1986), subsequent researchers have elaborated our understanding of the contradictory qualities of the postmarital relationship between former spouses (e.g., Graham, 2003; Masheter, 1994). The dialectics of older adult romantic relationships in retirement communities has also received scholarly attention (e.g., Aleman, 2001, 2003; Williams & Guendouzi, 2000).

Dialectical work has also been used increasingly to understand family forms other than the traditional two-parent-plus-biological-offspring structure. Dialectical research on the stepfamily, initiated in the now classic study by Cissna, Cox, and Bochner (1990), has witnessed substantial growth over the past decade. Issues of stepfamily formation (e.g., Braithwaite, Baxter, & Harper, 1998) and (step)parent-child relating (e.g., Baxter, Braithwaite, & Bryant, 2004; Baxter, Braithwaite, Bryant, & Wagner, 2004; Braithwaite & Baxter, 2003; Braithwaite, Toller, Daas, Durham, & Jones, 2004) have received particular focus.

Issues of parenting and parent-child relations outside of the stepfamily context have received surprisingly less attention by dialectically oriented researchers. Some dialectically centered research has examined the process of becoming a parent, whether through the birth (e.g., Stamp, 1994; Stamp & Banski, 1992) or adoption (e.g., Krusiewicz & Wood, 2001) of a child. Researchers have employed relational dialectics to focus on specific problems such as child abuse (e.g., Ford, Ray, & Ellis, 1999), premature birth (e.g., Golish & Powell, 2003), and pregnant mothers' communication with others surrounding alcohol use (e.g., Baxter, Hirokawa, Lowe, Nathan, & Pearce, 2004). Miller-Day (2004) employed dialectical thinking in shedding insight into maternal communication patterns among grandmothers, mothers, and daughters.

I will discuss three broad issues with respect to this corpus of cited research. First, I have limited my attention to work that is explicitly framed in relational dialectics theory. As colleagues and I have argued (e.g., Baxter & Braithwaite, in press; Montgomery & Baxter, 1998), relational dialectics is but one dialectical theory in a much larger family of dialectical approaches that can be identified. For example, Petronio (2002, and Chapter 3 of this volume with Caughlin) has developed a different dialectically oriented family theory, communication privacy management, which focuses on the dialectic of expression from a more positivistic approach. The prolific dialectical program of research undertaken by Altman and his colleagues (e.g., Altman, Vinsel, & Brown, 1981; Brown, Werner, & Altman, 1998) tended to take a social ecological approach in its emphasis on the social environment and its uses. Arguably the best exemplar of the Altman et al. approach is Altman and Ginat's (1996) ethnographic study of how contemporary polygamous families in the United States use space and time to maintain their identities as one-family-but-many-families. Other alternative dialectical approaches emphasize issues or contexts other than family communication. For example, Rawlins's dialectical theory (e.g., 1992) tended to emphasize friendship (for a notable exception, however, see Rawlins & Holl, 1988).

In the interdisciplinary field of family studies, there is a long tradition of dialectically flavored research, particularly from a clinical or therapeutic tradition (for a useful review, see Yerby, 1995). Often grounded in family systems perspectives, these approaches frame contradictions as system functions that are heavily influenced by the structural properties of systems themselves or the psychological needs of family members. These approaches tend to regard families as healthier to the extent that they can balance such competing family needs or functions as integration and differentiation. By contrast, relational dialectics does not view balance as a preferred state; rather, the interplay of competing discourses takes many different forms according to relational dialectics theory (Baxter, 2004a; Baxter & Montgomery, 1996). Furthermore, according to relational dialectics, the contradictory voices are not inherent system features or the psychological states of constituent family members but rather discursive constructions—that is, discourses, ideologies, or codes of meaning.

The second general issue I want to raise is the ongoing tension between generality and particularity. Considered as a whole, the body of work framed by relational dialectics theory repeatedly points to three major families of contradictions: dialectics of integration, certainty, and expression. The dialectic of integration addresses the unity-and-opposition of discourses of autonomy, independence, and separation on the one hand; and discourses of connectedness, interdependence, and integration on the other hand. It is nicely illustrated by a metaphorical image used by one of my former students who referred to her family as a hand: individual fingers whose strength rests in their capacity to function independently yet which unite to form the strength of a single fist. This image illustrates a discourse of unity or integration (the fist) in play with a discourse of differentiation (the fingers). The dialectic of certainty refers to the interplay of discourses of stability, continuity, certainty, predictability, and routine with opposing discourses of change, novelty, surprise, and newness. For example, in writing about his family, one of my former students nicely captured this dialectic when he referred to his multigenerational family in this way: "The [Jones] are the [Jones]: the same from one generation to the next, but different, too." In this statement, my student put a discourse of sameness—intergenerational continuity—in play with a discourse of uniqueness in which each generation is different from the preceding ones. The dialectic of expression refers to the interplay of discourses of openness, disclosure, and candor with the competing discourses of discretion, privacy, and secrecy. Illustrating this dialectic is another statement from one of my former students, who described her family's culture as "Totally open. We're the kind of household where anybody is free to say anything to anybody, except we don't do it." This statement suggests a family that sustains an artful dialectical dance between a culture of openness and a practice of discretion.

Although these three contradictions emerge with some frequency, it is important not to view them as a unitary, "cookie-cutter" template. Instead, scholars of relational dialectics should take seriously Bakhtin's (1986) view that "An utterance is never just a reflection or an expression of something already existing outside it that is given and final. It always creates something that never existed before, something absolutely new and unrepeatable" (pp. 119–120). The implication of Bakhtin's statement is that these three abstract contradictions, as well as others that have emerged in the research, must be examined in their concrete and situated particularities; for example, within different family types and contexts. In doing so, we can appreciate the differences from one situation to another in a contradiction glossed over with the same label by researchers. In addition, we can resist the temptation to view variations in the labels for contradictions as mere synonyms of one another. As Baxter and Montgomery (1996) indicated, a given contradiction is itself multivocal, with many contradictions contained within it. For example, consider the dialectic of expression in stepfamilies (Baxter, 2004a). One discursive construction of this dialectic revolves around privacy, or the right to "own" information and to control others' access to it. But the dialectic of expression cannot be reduced only to privacy management, because it is constructed along other radiants of meaning, as well. For example, this dialectic is often constructed by stepchildren as a loyalty matter: What is said to the residential parent and the stepparent is refracted through the issue of loyalty to the nonresidential parent, and vice versa. Alternatively, the dialectic of expression is often constructed by stepfamily members as a matter of safety; in the unpredictable seas of stepfamily life in which currents are not fully mapped, discretion is a way to avoid embarrassment or hurt. The dialectic of expression can also be constructed as a matter of identity: In the stepfamily, "we" represents the remains of the family of origin; "you" represents the stepparent and stepsiblings who are seen as outsiders. In such an identity construction, expression and its opposite perform boundary work, determining who is an insider and who is an outsider. My point here is that it is important not to lose an understanding of these various radiants of meaning under a single gloss such as "openness-closedness" or "expression-nonexpression." Meaning-making is a multivocal enterprise for family members, even within the parameters of a single, more abstract contradiction.

Additionally, it is important for researchers to identify contradictions other than integration, certainty, and expression that may animate specific family situations. A survey of existing literature reveals a variety of contradictions other than the "big three," including the perceived contradiction between the "old" family of origin and the "new" stepfamily (Braithwaite et al., 1998), the physical presence and emotional/cognitive absence of a spouse with Alzheimer's (Baxter et al., 2002), and misfortune and fortune (Krusiewicz & Wood, 2001), to mention but a few.

A third general issue I want to raise concerns the limitations of the corpus of work that I previously cited. To date, researchers have not dealt very well with the concept of flux. The ongoing interplay of competing voices resists finalized meanings; a dialogic meaning constructed at one moment is likely to unravel, shift, or add additional layers at another point in time. If researchers are going to understand this indeterminate quality of meaning-making, they must gather data from a minimum of two points in time; one cannot capture change with data based on a single point in time. Unfortunately, existing research has a static quality to it, ignoring issues of time. At best, some researchers artificially capture the flow of time by asking informants to provide retrospective accounts. In summarizing this body of work, Baxter (2004a) differentiates synchronic (one point in time) and diachronic (through time) ways in which relating parties constitute their contradictions. However, longitudinal work is needed to validate this analytic approach.

A second limitation of existing research is its collective overreliance on a single kind of data—borrowing from Giddens (1984), what I shall call "discursive-consciousness" data. Discursive-consciousness data are those that rely on people's awareness of, and capacity to talk about, the contradictions that they experience in family life. Generally, such data are derived from interviews with individuals. Future researchers need to complement this kind of data with practical-consciousness data (Giddens, 1984), which are social interactions, not people's reflections on social interactions. Although relational dialectics argues that contradictions are "done" in jointly enacted communication, we have limited insight into how this is done.

A third major limitation of existing research is its emphasis on the opposition component of contradiction to the relative neglect of the unity component. In large measure, unity has been undertheorized and underresearched, typically glossed as simple co-presence. What this gloss ignores is the importance of the interplay of opposing voices. For example, connection between siblings no doubt is meaningful because they may be competing for parental attention. Yet the power of contradiction comes from the interplay, not merely the identification that opposites are co-present. This limitation brings us to the other strands of meaning for dialogue in dialogism and in relational dialectics.

DIALOGUE: THE REST OF THE PICTURE

Grounded in Bakhtin's dialogism, Baxter and Montgomery (1996) weaved together several additional meanings of dialogue in their formal articulation of relational dialectics theory. Because they have not received much scholarly attention among family communication scholars, my discussion of them will be abbreviated. However, they are as important as the concept of contradiction to relational dialectics theory. As a set, they further differentiate relational dialectics from other dialectical approaches that are not grounded in dialogism.

Dialogue as Constitutive Process

Relational dialectics in particular, and dialogism more generally, join a growing list of theories that take a constitutive approach to communication (for a useful discussion, see Penman, 2000). A constitutive approach to communication asks how communication defines, or constructs, the social world, including our notions of "self" and "family." Relational dialectics, based on dialogism, differs from other constitutive perspectives in its focus on multivocality. Multivocality—contradiction—does not exist independent of, or outside of, communication. Rather, contradictions are constructed in communicative practices. Furthermore, meaning is constructed from the unity or interplay of the competing voices that comprise a contradiction. For example, the meaning of "stepfamily" is constructed from the tension, or interpenetration, of the "old" family of origin with the "new" family composition. The meaning of "loyalty" to the nonresidential parent is constructed out of its interplay with competing bids for loyalty in the residential parent and the stepparent. A family's celebration of the individual, unique accomplishments of each of its members is rendered meaningful only when put in play with an opposing discourse of what unites the family as a whole.

When researchers reduce the "unity" component of contradiction to mere co-presence, what they are ignoring is the process of meaning-making and the meanings that result from that tensionality. The interplay of multivocality is akin to jazz (Baxter & Montgomery, 1996); the interplay of competing voices produces emergent meanings that are impossible to conceive from the individual musical instruments playing in parallel.

Dialogue as Utterance

It is important to understand that Bakhtin's concept of the *utterance* does not refer to the individualized act of a single speaker. Utterances are not the product of individual cognitive work, in which speakers assemble messages responsive to preformed goals, needs, or motivations. Instead, as Bakhtin (1986) conceived it, an utterance exists only at the boundary between consciousnesses. As Volosinov (1973; however, many Bakhtin scholars believe that Bakhtin authored this work) expressed it, "Word is a two-sided act. . . . It is precisely the product of the reciprocal relationship between speaker and listener" (p. 86). Relational dialectics emphasizes communication as a social, or joint, enterprise between interlocutors (Baxter & Montgomery, 1996).

Baxter and Montgomery (1996) articulated several basic kinds of joint communicative activity, which, following Bakhtin (1986), are different *genres* by which multivocal meaning-making happens. As noted above, these activities can be loosely grouped into synchronic and diachronic types (Baxter, 2004a). Existing research on these communicative forms comes primarily from the interpersonal work on non-familial relating (Baxter, 2004a), and family communication scholars need to pay closer attention to the communicative practices of multivocality. In nonfamilial contexts, relating parties appear to enact with some frequency two diachronic practices: *spiraling inversion* and *segmentation*. When parties enact spiraling inversion, voices at the margin at one point in time are centered at another point in time, thereby altering meaning. For example, parents and children might move in and out of conversations about sexuality, sometimes open and sometimes closed. When parties enact segmentation, they are discursively determining which voices will be centripetal and which centrifugal for given topical domains at given times. For example, parents and children might be open about the reproductive side of sexuality yet closed on the topic of sexual techniques.

Our understanding of synchronic enactments, in which voices actively interpenetrate at a given point in time, will require more micro-oriented research methods sensitive to the details of talk. Crucial to that enterprise will be the Bakhtin/Volosinov concept of double-voicedness, or reported speech (Bakhtin, 1981; Volosinov, 1973). This concept refers to the discursive ways in which one voice recognizes another voice or perspective in utterances. For example, when a speaker utters two independent clauses joined with the conjunctive "but," this word choice places two contrasting voices into play with one another (Schiffrin, 1987). For example, if a mother says "I respect your right to make decisions, but you aren't old enough to determine your bedtime," she is attempting to give voice to her child's growing autonomy and independence at the same time that she is giving voice to the child's dependence on parental rules. To date, research on reported speech has tended to examine how one *speaker* takes into account another speaker, whereas the emphasis in relational dialectics theory is how *voices*—discourses or systems of meaning—interpenetrate, as illustrated in the mother's statement.

However, one synchronic practice, the ritual, has been examined successfully by dialectically oriented researchers using less micro-oriented research methods. The communication ritual also provides a useful illustration of a fourth way to conceive of dialogue.

Dialogue as Aesthetic Moment

Bakhtin (1981) viewed social life as a fragmented, disorderly, and messy cacophony of opposing discourses, or voices. In such a social world, order is not given; it is a task to be accomplished. Whenever parties construct meaning from the interplay of competing voices, they are constituting order, however fleeting. Sometimes, however, this meaning takes on particular poignancy, and parties experience a fleeting yet intense feeling of consummation or completion. Such a feeling is dialogue in the fourth sense—the aesthetic moment (Bakhtin, 1990). Baxter and DeGooyer (2001) identified five types of aesthetic moments that are experienced in friendships, romantic relationships, and familial relationships. For example, one kind of aesthetic moment is that feeling of wholeness that comes when interaction with another person somehow makes one feel more complete as a human being. Conversational flow, in which parties feel that discrete utterances flow into one another effortlessly and the conversation appears to take on a life of its own, is another type of aesthetic moment. Clearly, dialogue-as-aesthetic-moment resembles the dialogic moment conceived by Buber and by Rogers (Cissna & Anderson, 1998).

Family rituals are likely candidates for aesthetic moments (Baxter, 2004a). I am defining *ritual* not in the pedestrian sense of any routinized pattern but rather in reference to a structured sequence of symbolic acts in which homage is paid to some sacred object such as the family (Goffman, 1967). Several scholars have argued that the power of ritual rests in its symbolic interplay of contradictory discourses (e.g., Turner, 1969). As Baxter and Braithwaite have noted for the ritualized renewal of marriage vows (Baxter & Braithwaite, 2002; Braithwaite & Baxter, 1995), rituals weave together competing voices in powerful ways. For example, marriage renewal vows at once give voice to the couple's marriage as a stable institution that has endured over time; yet at the same time, the couple's marriage is presented as a living organism that has changed over time.

It is important to note that dialogue-as-aesthetic-moment is radically different from the Hegelian concept of synthesis. In Hegelian dialectics, a thesis produces its opposite (the antithesis), which then culminates in a synthesis. The aesthetic moment is not the result of a mechanistic sequence of thesis-antithesis-synthesis. Nor is the aesthetic moment a permanent resolution, or synthesis, of oppositions. Some dialectical approaches (e.g., Conville, 1991) are more Hegelian in nature and thus should not be confused with relational dialectics theory.

CONCLUSION

Relational dialectics, a theory of meaning-making in familial and nonfamilial relationships, employs Bakhtin's multivocal concept of dialogue: as dialectical flux, as constitutive process, as utterance, and as aesthetic moment. This chapter has provided a brief introduction and bibliographic gateway to the research in family communication framed by relational dialectics.

Many facets of the theory have not yet been fully realized in the research to date. The theory is still relatively new, and there's much room at the relational dialectics table for the interested family communication scholar. Directions for future research are several. First, a range of family relationships merit study from a relational dialectics perspective. For example, sibling relationships are often experienced as a dialogic bond of both love and competition. Fictive-kin relationships—those who are "family" in our hearts but are not recognized by either blood or law—occupy an interesting dialogic borderland between "insider" and "outsider" positions. Second, existing research using relational dialectics theory has oversampled middle-class white Americans; dialogic voices are systems of meaning and thus are likely to vary by culture and speech community. Third, research needs to adopt longitudinal methods and additionally needs to examine the dialogic quality of actual family talk. Last, researchers need to examine issues of efficacy. Some families appear to sustain productive and creative interplay of dialogic voices, whereas other families may be paralyzed by the tensionality of competing voices. We need to understand how different families experience dialogue. Join the scholarly conversation and advance relational dialectics theory beyond its promising beginnings.

REFERENCES

Aleman, M. W. (2001). Complaining among the elderly: Examining multiple dialectical oppositions to independence in a retirement community. *Western Journal of Communication, 65,* 89–112.

Aleman, M. W. (2003). "You should get yourself a boyfriend" but "Let's not get serious": Communicating a code of romance in a retirement community. *Qualitative Research Reports in Communication, 4,* 31–37.

Altman, I., & Ginat, J. (1996). *Polygamous families in contemporary society.* New York: Cambridge University Press.

Altman, I., Vinsel, A., & Brown, B. (1981). Dialectic conceptions in social psychology: An application to social penetration and privacy regulation. *Advances in Experimental Social Psychology, 14,* 107–160.

Bakhtin, M. M. (1981). *The dialogic imagination: Four essays by M. M. Bakhtin* (M. Holquist, Ed.; C. Emerson & M. Holquist, Trans.). Austin: University of Texas Press.

Bakhtin, M. M. (1984). *Problems of Dostoevsky's poetics* (C. Emerson, Ed. and Trans.). Minneapolis: University of Minnesota Press.

Bakhtin, M. M. (1986). *Speech genres and other late essays* (C. Emerson & M. Holquist, Eds.; V. McGee, Trans.). Austin: University of Texas Press.

Bakhtin, M. M. (1990). *Art and answerability: Early philosophical essays by M. M. Bakhtin* (M. Holquist & V. Liapunov, Eds.; V. Liapunov & K. Brostrom, Trans.). Austin: University of Texas Press.

Baxter, L. A. (2004a). Distinguished scholar article: Relationships as dialogues. *Personal Relationships, 11*, 1–22.

Baxter, L. A. (2004b). A tale of two voices: Relational dialectics theory. *Journal of Family Communication, 4*, 181–192.

Baxter, L. A., & Braithwaite, D. O. (in press). Social dialectics: The contradictions of relating. In B. Whaley & W. Samter (Eds.), *Contemporary communication theories and exemplars*. Mahwah, NJ: Erlbaum.

Baxter, L. A., & Braithwaite, D. O. (2002). Performing marriage: The marriage renewal ritual as cultural performance. *Southern Communication Journal, 67*, 94–109.

Baxter, L. A., Braithwaite, D. O., & Bryant, L. (2004). *Types of communication triads perceived by young-adult stepchildren in established stepfamilies*. Under review.

Baxter, L. A., Braithwaite, D. O., Bryant, L., & Wagner, A. (2004). Stepchildren's perceptions of the contradictions in communication with stepparents. *Journal of Social and Personal Relationships, 21*, 447–467.

Baxter, L. A., Braithwaite, D. O., Golish, T. D., & Olson, L. N. (2002). Contradictions of interaction for wives of elderly husbands with adult dementia. *Journal of Applied Communication Research, 30*, 1–26.

Baxter, L. A., & DeGooyer, D., Jr. (2001). Perceived aesthetic characteristics of interpersonal conversations. *Southern Communication Journal, 67*, 1–18.

Baxter, L. A., Hirokawa, R., Lowe, J. B., Nathan, P., & Pearce, L. (2004). Dialogic voices in talk about drinking and pregnancy. *Journal of Applied Communication Research, 32*, 224–248.

Baxter, L. A., & Montgomery, B. M. (1996). *Relating: Dialogues and dialectics*. New York: Guilford Press.

Baxter, L. A., & Simon, E. (1993). Relationship maintenance strategies and dialectical contradictions in personal relationships. *Journal of Social and Personal Relationships, 10*, 225–242.

Braithwaite, D. O., & Baxter, L. A. (1995). "I do" again: The relational dialectics of renewing marriage vows. *Journal of Social and Personal Relationships, 12*, 177–198.

Braithwaite, D. O., & Baxter, L. A. (2003). *"You're my parent but you're not my parent": Contradictions of communication between stepchildren and their non-residential parents*. Manuscript under review.

Braithwaite, D. O., Baxter, L. A., & Harper, A. M. (1998). The role of rituals in the management of the dialectical tension of "old" and "new" in blended families. *Communication Studies, 48*, 101–112.

Braithwaite, D. O., Toller, P., Daas, K., Durham, W., & Jones, A. (2004, February). *Centered, but not caught in the middle: Stepchildren's perceptions of the contradictions of communication of co-parents.* Paper presented at the annual meeting of the Western States Communication Association, Albuquerque, NM.

Brown, B. B., Werner, C. M., & Altman, I. (1998). Choice points for dialecticians: A dialectical-transactional perspective on close relationships. In B. M. Montgomery & L. A. Baxter (Eds.), *Dialectical approaches to studying personal relationships* (pp. 137–154). Mahwah, NJ: Erlbaum.

Cissna, K. N., & Anderson, R. (1998). Theorizing about dialogic moments: The Buber-Rogers position and postmodern themes. *Communication Theory, 8,* 63–104.

Cissna, K. N., Cox, D. E., & Bochner, A. P. (1990). The dialectic of marital and parental relationships within the stepfamily. *Communication Monographs, 57,* 44–61.

Conville, R. L. (1991). *Relational transitions: The evolution of personal relationships.* New York: Praeger.

Erbert, L. (2000). Conflict and dialectics: Perceptions of dialectical contradictions in marital conflict. *Journal of Social and Personal Relationships, 17,* 638–659.

Ford, L. A., Ray, E. B., & Ellis, B. H. (1999). Translating scholarship on intrafamilial sexual abuse: The utility of a dialectical perspective for adult survivors. *Journal of Applied Communication Research, 27,* 139–157.

Giddens, A. (1984). *The constitution of society.* Berkeley: University of California Press.

Goffman, I. (1967). *Interaction ritual.* Garden City, NY: Anchor.

Golish, T. D., & Powell, K. A. (2003). "Ambiguous loss": Managing the dialectics of grief associated with premature birth. *Journal of Social and Personal Relationships, 20,* 309–334.

Graham, E. E. (2003). Dialectic contradictions in postmarital relationships. *Journal of Family Communication, 3,* 193–214.

Holquist, M. (1990). *Dialogism: Bakhtin and his world.* New York: Routledge.

Hoppe-Nagao, A., & Ting-Toomey, S. (2002). Relational dialectics and management strategies in marital couples. *Southern Communication Journal, 67,* 142–159.

Krusiewicz, E. S., & Wood, J. T. (2001). "He was our child from the moment we walked in that room": Entrance stories of adoptive parents. *Journal of Social and Personal Relationships, 18,* 785–803.

Masheter, C. (1994). Dialogues between ex-spouses: Evidence of dialectic relationship development. In R. Conville (Ed.), *Uses of structure in communication studies* (pp. 83–101). Westport, CT: Praeger.

Masheter, C., & Harris, L. M. (1986). From divorce to friendship: A study of dialectic relationship development. *Journal of Social and Personal Relationships, 3,* 177–190.

Miller-Day, M. (2004). *Communication among grandmothers, mothers, and adult daughters.* Mahwah, NJ: Lawrence Erlbaum.

Montgomery, B. M., & Baxter, L. A. (Eds.). (1998). *Dialectical approaches to studying personal relationships.* Mahwah, NJ: Erlbaum.

Pawlowski, D. R. (1998). Dialectical tensions in marital partners' accounts of their relationships. *Communication Quarterly, 46,* 396–412.

Penman, R. (2000). *Reconstructing communicating: Looking to a future.* Mahwah, NJ: Erlbaum.

Petronio, S. (2002). *Boundaries of privacy: Dialectics of disclosure.* Albany: State University of New York Press.

Rawlins, W. K. (1992). *Friendship matters: Communication, dialectics, and the life course.* New York: Aldine de Gruyter.

Rawlins, W. K., & Holl, M. (1988). Adolescents' interaction with parents and friends: Dialectics of temporal perspective and evaluation. *Journal of Social and Personal Relationships, 5,* 27–46.

Sabourin, T. C., & Stamp, G. H. (1995). Communication and the experience of dialectical tensions in family life: An examination of abusive and nonabusive families. *Communication Monographs, 62,* 213–242.

Schiffrin, D. (1987). *Discourse markers.* New York: Cambridge University Press.

Stamp, G. H. (1994). The appropriation of the parental role through communication during the transition to parenthood. *Communication Monographs, 61,* 89–112.

Stamp, G. H., & Banski, M. A. (1992). The communicative management of constrained autonomy during the transition to parenthood. *Western Journal of Communication, 56,* 281–300.

Turner, V. (1969). *The ritual process: Structure and anti-structure.* Ithaca, NY: Cornell University Press.

Volosinov, V. N. (1973). *Marxism and the philosophy of language* (L. Matejks & I. R. Titunik, Trans.). Cambridge, MA: Harvard University Press.

Williams, A., & Guendouzi, J. (2000). Adjusting to "the home": Dialectical dilemmas and personal relationships in a retirement community. *Journal of Communication, 50,* 65–82.

Wood, J. T., Dendy, L. L., Dordek, E., Germany, M., & Varallo, S. M. (1994). Dialectic of difference: A thematic analysis of intimates' meanings for differences. In K. Carter & M. Prisnell (Eds.), *Interpretive approaches to interpersonal communication* (pp. 115–136). New York: SUNY Press.

Yerby, J. (1995). Family systems theory reconsidered: Integrating social construction theory and dialectical process. *Communication Theory, 5,* 339–365.

10

Symbolic Convergence Theory: Communication, Dramatizing Messages, and Rhetorical Visions in Families

Dawn O. Braithwaite

Paul Schrodt

Jody Koenig Kellas

Editors' Note: Symbolic Convergence Theory comes from the interpretive perspective, centered on joint meaning-making, or how rhetorical visions are co-constructed via interaction. The theory has its origins in rhetoric and small group communication and has been used largely to analyze group, organizational, and political discourse.

O ne goal of this theory book is to identify existing communication theories that are potentially useful to study communication in families. One place to look is in small group communication theory, since we can think of families as small groups (Poole, 1999; Schrodt & Durham, 2002; Socha, 1999). In fact, in his call for integration between family and group communication approaches, Socha (1999) described families as our "first" group. Symbolic Convergence Theory (SCT) comes out of the small group communication tradition, and we believe it has great potential for understanding how families interact and create a shared vision of their culture, history, traditions, present, and future. To follow, we discuss the history and purpose of SCT, the major features of the theory, applications of SCT research to date, and future applications of SCT for understanding communication in families.

HISTORY AND PURPOSE OF SYMBOLIC CONVERGENCE THEORY

Communication scholar Ernest G. Bormann is the chief author of Symbolic Convergence Theory (SCT). Bormann and his students at the University of Minnesota began working on SCT in the early 1970s, and the theory has yielded a broad array of basic and applied research. Bormann (1985, 1989) argued that SCT is a general theory of communication, a universal theory that spans contexts and cultures. The theory represents a marriage of social science and humanism that was particularly important in the late 1970s, at a time when a number of communication departments were rife with conflict between humanistic (rhetorical) and social scientific (usually positivist) scholars. Bormann (1989) saw this disciplinary division as counterproductive and believed that SCT research provided a place in which "muddle-headed anecdotalists and the hard-headed empiricists" could come together in a cooperative fashion (p. 190).

What was to become SCT began with Bormann's work in small group communication in the late 1950s. In what he called the Minnesota Studies, Bormann and his students worked on content analyses of small task group meetings, complemented by qualitative case studies of groups meeting over time and in process. This stood in contrast to the laboratory approach for studying small groups (i.e., groups artificially created to perform a task in the lab) that was common at the time (Bormann, 1970). In contrast to laboratory studies, Bormann and students studied meetings of ongoing task groups, today called bona-fide small groups (Stohl & Putnam, 1994). The scholars analyzed audio- or videotapes, or word-for-word transcripts of group meetings.

These researchers began to "develop a method of process analysis that would capture some of the richness of case studies and still allow for generalization . . . a rhetorical analysis of the communication in group discussions," or what Bormann (1975) labeled a "rhetorical criticism of small-group communication" (p. 163).

The efforts of the Minnesota team were revolutionized in 1970 when Robert Freed Bales published his work, *Personality and Interpersonal Behavior*. According to Bormann (1990), Bales's work filled in "a key part to the puzzle of how group communication creates cohesion when he discovered the dynamic process of group fantasizing" (p. 163). Bormann explained that Bales "provided the student of small-group communication with an account of how dramatizing communication creates a social reality for a group of people and a way to examine the dramatizing for insights into the group's culture, motivation, emotional style, and cohesion" (p. 163).

Bales (1970) created and validated the "Interaction Process Analysis" (IPA), a coding scheme of 12 categories of positive and negative statements (e.g., "shows agreement" or "seems unfriendly") and questions and answers (e.g., "gives information" or "asks for opinion") in the task and social dimensions of group interaction. IPA became a tool that allowed an observer to follow and code group interaction. Bormann became particularly interested in Bales's category of "shows tension release," which Bales later renamed "dramatizes." Bormann and his colleagues focused on dramatizing messages that occurred when the communication would leave the "here and now" and members would tell stories that had or could happen, and talked about the past or the future. From this point, Bormann and his colleagues began to study the dramatic themes that chained out in small groups and within the larger culture, noting that not all fantasy themes catch on and chain out, "while some of the dramatizing caused a greater or lesser symbolic explosion in the form of a chain reaction" (1985, p. 5). For Bormann (1975), small groups developed their own group history, traditions, culture, and cohesion by participating in fantasy chains, thereby creating a rhetorical vision of a group of people.

Bormann and colleagues also extended the study of rhetorical visions in small groups to communities and larger cultures. In the *Force of Fantasy*, Bormann (1985) explored the rhetorical visions of American culture as reflected in religious and secular speakers in pre-Civil War America, and he analyzed other historical events, such as the release of American hostages held in Iran during Ronald Reagan's presidential inauguration (Bormann, 1982). Scholars applied SCT to analyze group- and community-based fantasies to understand the creation of shared consciousness and meaning via communication. Since 1970 scholars have used SCT to study the sharing of fantasies and rhetorical visions in small groups, organizations, and more recently (although much less frequently) in personal relationships and families.

MAJOR FEATURES OF SYMBOLIC CONVERGENCE THEORY

SCT offers a number of concepts and propositions relevant to the study of family communication. The theory begins by focusing our attention on the relationships among a dramatizing message, a fantasy chain among group members, and the shared group fantasy that emerges out of the convergence process (Bormann, Knutson, & Musolf, 1997). According to Bormann (1985, 1998), a dramatizing message is one that contains any form of imaginative language, including such figures of speech as metaphors, similes, puns, double entendres, and personifications, as well as analogies, anecdotes, allegories, fables, or narratives. The most important element of dramatizing messages is that they are always set in a time and place other than the here-and-now communication of the group (Bormann, Cragan, & Shields, 1994). For example, in a family context, family members may be involved in a conflict that is dramatic and filled with tension, but because the interaction is occurring in the immediate experience of the family members, it would not qualify as a basis for the sharing of a group fantasy. If, however, the family members began talking about disagreements they have had in the past or if they envisioned future disagreements, then such comments would qualify as dramatizing messages (cf., Bormann, 1985, 1998).

The basic communicative dynamic of SCT is the expression of a dramatizing message, which in turn sparks the sharing of group fantasies that facilitate symbolic convergence for group members (Bormann, 1985, 1998). In SCT, the term "fantasy" does not refer to the layperson's interpretation of messages as imaginary, or not grounded in reality. Rather, in SCT, fantasy is the creative and imaginative interpretation of events that fulfills a psychological or rhetorical need. Some fantasies include fanciful and fictitious stories of imaginary characters, yet others deal with events that have actually happened to members of the group (or family) or that are reported in works of history, in media outlets, or in the oral history and folklore of a group (Bormann, 1985).

The dynamic communication process of sharing a group fantasy begins when one member dramatizes, leaving the here and now with the message (Bormann et al., 1994). For example, a parent expecting a first child might talk about what it will be like when the baby is born and imagine the fun times to come playing with the child. The parent may then begin to talk with other family members about what the child will become when grown up. What Bormann observed in the development of SCT is that some dramatizing messages are ignored by other interactants, but other messages lead to a greater or lesser symbolic explosion whereby other group (or family) members begin to share and actively participate in appropriating, modifying, and sharing the drama publicly. "As the members share the fantasy the tempo of the conversations picks up. People grow excited, interrupt one another, laugh, show emotion, and forget their self-consciousness" (Bormann et al., 1994, p. 280). In the case of the new parent, other family members may join in on the dramatizing message at family get-togethers and over electronic mail. For example, grandmother talks about how her grandchild will be a nurse or a doctor, mother-to-be adds that she thinks her daughter is kicking so hard that she will be a star soccer player, and still other family members respond that the child will become the first member of their family to graduate from Harvard University Law School. The result of this family conversation is a symbolic chain reaction, or fantasy chain, that connects family members until they become united in a group fantasy. The family members symbolically create a fantasy chain that enables them to converge on a picture of the potential success and strength of its newest generation. Consequently, group fantasy chains describe those moments of dramatization in which all or most of the members participate, thereby facilitating the development of a shared group consciousness or group identity. Returning to our example, the family members symbolically create a fantasy chain centered on the new child, as their dramatizing messages create a picture of their family as successful and powerful as this next generation is born, even though they may or may not see their family in this way at present.

The content of dramatizing messages, referred to as fantasy themes, represents the fundamental unit of analysis of SCT researchers. Although the content of a dramatizing message and fantasy theme are identical, the difference is that the fantasy theme has become part of the group consciousness through the communication process of chaining and sharing (Bormann et al., 1994). These fantasy themes are interaction patterns that families will return to in subsequent interactions. In contrast to the way in which group members experience the here-and-now, fantasy themes are organized and artistic. They help provide an ordered and interpretive explanation of events, allowing group members to make sense out of what before may have been a confusing state of affairs.

In *The Force of Fantasy*, Bormann (1985) suggested that the researcher's primary task in conducting a fantasy theme analysis is to find evidence that symbolic convergence has taken place. In the family context, this entails looking for evidence that family members have shared a fantasy. When similar dramatizing messages such as word-plays, narratives, puns, figures of speech, and analogies repeatedly surface in a variety of family messages across different family contexts, there is evidence of symbolic convergence (Bormann, 1985). In addition, symbolic cues, which are cryptic allusions to symbolic common ground, provide even further evidence to suggest that people have shared fantasies. Symbolic cues, such as inside jokes, serve as triggers that touch the common group consciousness and stimulate a set of emotions, motives, and meanings around a shared fantasy theme (Bormann et al., 1994). For example, based on the fantasy chain described earlier, family members may start to call the new baby "Miss Harvard," a symbolic cue that will invoke the fantasy theme and will be meaningful to other family members. Consequently, symbolic cues provide "the best evidence available to a scholar that people have shared fantasies" (Bormann et al., 1994, p. 281).

Not all symbolic cues are positive, however, as allusions to previously shared fantasy themes may evoke emotions such as fear, anger, or hatred rather than love and affection. For example, if the aunt and uncle of "Miss Harvard" fail to hear similar references to their own children, they may come to believe that other family members think less of their children. At that point, they may refuse to participate in the fantasy or may try to counter it with a fantasy of their own.

Once group members have shared a number of fantasy themes with similar scenarios or plotlines, the collection of fantasy themes forms a fantasy type. According to Bormann (1985), a fantasy type is a stock scenario that covers several of the more concrete fantasy themes. For example, in his study of leaderless natural groups in the college classroom, Bormann found that group members often shared personal experience fantasies about parties they had recently attended. Rather than detail the specific scenes, characters, and situations of the party, group members would often refer to a stock scenario (such as "frat party"), which conjures a shared image of what typically happens at this type of party. In a similar fashion, family members often refer to family reunions, holidays, and other rituals in terms of what typically happens at these events. The use of symbolic cues would enable other family members to reference previously shared fantasy themes revolving around the stock scenario of "Christmas Eve" or " Sunday Dinner." References to fantasy types, then, provide further evidence to suggest that group or family members have developed symbolic common ground and a shared group consciousness.

In SCT, the culmination of dramatizing messages, fantasy themes, and fantasy types is the emergence of a rhetorical vision. A rhetorical vision is a unified collection of the various themes and types that give group members a broader view of things (Bormann et al., 1994). In other words, rhetorical visions provide a total coherent view of the group's social reality. These visions are often integrated by the sharing of a dramatizing message that contains a master analogy that brings together the various types and themes into a more or less elegant and meaningful whole (Bormann, 1985). For example, when the first author was conducting focus groups with college-aged stepchildren, and a stepchild called her stepmother a "stepmonster," immediately the other stepchildren began laughing and shaking their heads, and several told stories about difficulties with stepparents. While the story each member told about their own family was different, it was clear that they shared a rhetorical vision of difficulties with stepparents that came from media visions of stepfamilies, including fairy tales of "wicked stepmothers," and their own stepfamily experiences.

In explicating the final aspect of SCT, Bormann explained why group members are predisposed to share some fantasies, to respond nonchalantly to others, and to actively reject others. Bormann (1998) suggested that three promising factors may explain why people share fantasies: (a) the extent to which group members bring common symbolic predispositions to the group setting, (b) the common concerns that group members share because of their experiences in the group, and (c) the rhetorical skill with which group members communicate their fantasies. Although SCT was developed primarily in task group settings, we believe these three propositions have important implications for family communication scholars as well. Indeed, the extent to which different family members share common concerns about the family, as well as the different abilities of family members to initiate or share dramatizing messages may explain, in part, the degree to which different family members participate in fantasy chaining and share in the family's group culture. Returning to the "stepmonster" example, we may see biological siblings in a stepfamily weave a narrative about how their stepmonster favors her own children over them. In this fantasy, the siblings might chain out a story of how, like Cinderella, they would be expected to stay at home and scrub the floors while their stepmother takes their stepsiblings to Disneyland. Although they likely know that the actual occurrence of this particular situation is unlikely, this "us" versus "them" fantasy (Bormann, 1975) might emerge whenever the children believe their stepmother is favoring her own children over them. The siblings might even develop an inside joke among themselves and whisper "start scrubbing" to one another, or perhaps use a nonverbal gesture for scrubbing to represent the shared rhetorical vision that they hold. It is likely that the other stepfamily members, and even their own parent, will not participate in these fantasy chains or know what these symbols mean. These siblings likely partake in this fantasy because of their shared symbolic predispositions about their stepfamily, common concerns about their stepmother, and the shared American rhetorical vision surrounding Cinderella's wicked stepmother. Exploring the symbolic meanings present in shared fantasies and larger rhetorical visions can help us further understand interactions and relationships both within and across families.

Overall, then, SCT focuses our attention on the dramatizing messages that are shared by family members and that result in the symbolic convergence process, a process that creates common ground and serves to unite family members (c.f., Bormann et al., 1997). Using key concepts such as fantasy themes, fantasy types, symbolic cues, and rhetorical visions, family communication researchers can analyze the various ways in which different families socially construct a shared group consciousness with its implied shared emotions, values, motives, and meanings. In the next section of this chapter, we briefly explore some of the ways in which previous researchers have used SCT to understand communication processes in the family.

APPLICATIONS OF SYMBOLIC CONVERGENCE THEORY TO FAMILY COMMUNICATION

Scholars have used SCT most frequently for small group research, and only a handful of researchers have used SCT in the family context. Although there are differences between group and families (for example, group membership is often more voluntary than family membership), these differences do not preclude the applicability of SCT to family scholarship. Of the multitude of studies employing SCT, we located 10 situated in families (Bray, 2001; Endres, 1989, 1997; Frazier, 1988; Gaetano, 1994; Hudson, 2003; M. A. Miller, 1997; S. A. Miller, 1998; Schrag, 1982; Shireen, 1990). For example, Gaetano (1994) studied the rhetorical visions of sons concerning communication with their fathers, and Frazier (1988) studied the rhetorical visions in parenting self-help books from 1940–1979.

The published SCT work centering on family communication is by Thomas Endres (1989, 1997). In two separate studies, Endres analyzed the rhetorical visions of unmarried mothers in one study and father-daughter relationships in the other. Endres produced a set of visions and issues (composed of fantasy themes, types, and cues) reflective of the family images portrayed within the popular and academic press. In his study of unmarried mothers, Endres (1989) identified three rhetorical visions of unmarried mothers that emerged from popular and academic press sources: The Down and Out Vision, The Making The Best Vision, and The Yummie (Young Upwardly Mobile Mother) Vision. In his study of father-daughter relationships, Endres (1997) identified four rhetorical visions of fathers from written sources, including The Knight in Shining Armor, The Buddy, The Authoritarian, and The Shadow.

To assess the accuracy of the rhetorical visions that emerged from his fantasy theme analysis of the popular and academic press, Endres used the Q-sort methodology, used by several SCT researchers. Q-sort is a social scientific method that compares the researcher's interpretation of a fantasy theme analysis "against the perceptions of the rhetorical community in question" (Endres, 1997, p. 320). Scholars using Q-sort put descriptions of rhetorical visions and issues into narrative form and copy each onto individual cards that comprise a deck. Members of the rhetorical community are instructed to sort the deck into piles. In Endres's studies, a group of unmarried mothers (Endres, 1989) and a group of daughters (Endres, 1997) were asked to sort a deck into piles according to which narratives were "most like me" and "least like me." The Q-sort methodology allows researchers to identify rhetorical visions that are salient to the members of the community in question. These rhetorical visions are based on, but may also move beyond, the visions found in the fantasy theme analysis. For example, from the Q-sort in the father-daughter drama study Endres (1997) produced four new visions of fathers including The Essential Companion, The Silent Intruder, The Loving Patriarch, and The Storyteller.

Endres's (1989, 1997) research offers insight into the rhetorical and individual perceptions about family communication. Endres suggested that rhetorical visions about certain family forms are best understood when assessed by members of the rhetorical community of which they are a part. In addition, this body of research has the potential to have practical application. Endres (1997) argued that Q-sort decks of rhetorical visions may be useful in applied settings, such as unmarried mother support groups and family therapy sessions, and may provide practitioners with "practical communicative tool[s]" such as icebreakers or discussion starters (p. 335). In this same spirit of speculation, we now turn our attention to future applications of SCT and avenues for SCT research on family communication.

FUTURE APPLICATIONS OF SYMBOLIC CONVERGENCE THEORY TO FAMILY COMMUNICATION

Scholars have only recently begun to call for research examining the intersections of family and group communication and have identified SCT as a promising theoretical perspective for exploring family communication (e.g., Schrodt & Durham, 2002; Socha, 1999). While SCT has the potential to enhance our understanding of fantasy themes about certain family forms (e.g., Endres, 1989, 1997), researchers have yet to examine how families act as small groups, participating in fantasy chains and experiencing symbolic convergence. In this section, we contend that SCT provides a fruitful theoretical lens for examining a variety of family communication processes including, but certainly not limited to, the study of family decision making, family membership, and, in particular, family narratives and storytelling.

Family Decision Making

One area of family communication that may benefit from applications of SCT is family decision-making processes. As part of SCT, Bormann (1998) suggested that sharing group fantasies aids group decision making, motivation, and creativity. When extended to families, SCT may enable family communication scholars to more closely examine the types of dramatizing messages, fantasy chains, and themes that facilitate greater levels of family cohesiveness, and in turn, influence decision making. Family scholars (e.g., Galvin, Bylund, & Brommel,

2004; Turner, 1970) have identified three types of decision-making processes, including consensus, accommodation, and de facto processes, and a fruitful extension of this research using SCT might enable communication scholars to further understand the ways in which different levels of convergence influence the types of processes employed within different types of families. In another potential application, Kieren, Maguire, and Hurlbut (1996) developed a family problem-solving loop that illustrates eight phases of decision making. Researchers might extend their model by using SCT to understand how the convergence process strengthens a shared family consciousness or identity, which in turn strengthens the family's motivation to engage in more creative, participatory decision-making processes. We suggest that scholars consider to what extent symbolic convergence in families is associated with higher motivation, greater creativity, and a more participatory approach to family problem solving. For example, SCT could be used to study convergence as couples make decisions to pursue adoption. We believe SCT holds promise for addressing questions of this nature, as well as others related to factors that influence family decision making.

Family Membership

A second area we believe would benefit from SCT involves examining the intersection of communication behaviors and family membership. Applying SCT, sharing group fantasies and the process of symbolic convergence create a common group identity by identifying who is "in" and "out" of the group. When used to study family interaction, SCT may provide further insight into the communicative construction of family identity, providing a more in-depth understanding of how different types of families construct a collective identity through sharing dramatizing messages and the subsequent development of shared fantasy themes and rhetorical visions. Rather than approach family membership from purely a psychological perspective, SCT provides a theoretical lens allowing researchers to examine how the family collectively creates and sustains a sense of family membership and identity through talk. We envision applications of SCT for exploring family membership with in-laws, in adoptive families, and in stepfamilies. For example, Banker and Gaertner (1998) used an intergroup-relations approach to understanding stepfamily interaction and found that the more the stepfamily was viewed by its members as being like one group, the more stepfamily members perceived their family relationships as cooperative and harmonious. Using SCT, family scholars may extend stepfamily research by examining the ways in which the symbolic convergence process facilitates family cohesiveness, which in turn may increase family satisfaction. Similarly, Koenig Kellas (2003) found that the more families identified as a group in terms of "we-ness" and family identity statements, the more involved, warm, and confirming they were in the joint telling of family identity stories. Building from this research, SCT offers a framework for examining the process of building and sustaining stepfamily membership through interaction, as well as comparing and contrasting different types of families.

Family Narratives and Storytelling

The third area of research that may benefit from adopting SCT as a theoretical framework is the research on family narratives and storytelling. Researchers who study family narratives and storytelling can benefit from using SCT to understand how families make sense of their individual and group identities, teach values, as well as establish and enact family culture through telling family stories. Researchers focusing on joint family storytelling have found that as families tell stories together they work collaboratively to tell the story and negotiate the story morals or meanings. For example, Koenig and Trees (2001) found that during a collaborative storytelling interaction about a difficult family experience, families differed in the ways they engaged, took turns, and attended to the others' perspectives and created a coherent narrative. Some families were much more warm and lively than other families, interrupting and building on others' comments in a way that might suggest symbolic convergence. The researchers found that these behaviors also helped to distinguish the different ways in which families converged (or not) on the meaning of the story. Some families collaboratively created family meaning, some families created individual meaning, and other families did not draw conclusions from the stories either individually or as a group (Koenig & Trees, 2001).

We suggest that future researchers exploring collaborative telling of family narratives would benefit from applications of SCT. For example, researchers could extend Bormann's (1998) explanation for why people share group fantasies (i.e., common symbolic predispositions, shared concerns, and rhetorical skill) by exploring why some stories chain out and become fantasy themes within the family while others do not, and by assessing whether or not these factors apply to families in ways similar to small groups. In addition, researchers may wish to investigate how this chaining-out process differs among various family members. For instance, people entering into in-law relationships may find themselves in a context in which symbolic convergence could be useful and desired for increasing family cohesion and a sense of family identity. Norrick (1997) described collaborative family narratives as particularly useful tools for sons- and daughters-in-law who want to show their understanding of the new family culture. Researchers may investigate how such "marginal" family members use narratives and symbolic material to converge with the existing family members and solidify a stronger sense of the "new" family. Finally, researchers may wish to examine the content of dramatizing messages for the emergence of protagonists and antagonists in family stories and how fantasy themes are used to characterize the identity and culture of the family.

In addition to examining these various types of narratives, future researchers could also contribute to our understanding by investigating the relationships among the degree of symbolic convergence in the collaborative storytelling of family narratives and other relational quality variables, such as family satisfaction, cohesion, adaptability, and conflict. In other words, scholars might explore jointly told family stories for symbolic convergence in families, and examine possible relationships among convergence and a family's satisfaction and functioning. This line of future research has potential implications for family practitioners, such as narrative therapists who attempt to help families re-story the traumatic and undesirable narratives in their lives.

Finally, we encourage future researchers to continue developing new methodologies for observing symbolic convergence in family interaction. Historically, researchers adopting SCT have employed fantasy theme analysis and compared the results of such analyses to Q-sorts in the community of interest. Examining the relationships among symbolic convergence and family relational qualities, however, necessitates the development of new methodologies for coding or rating symbolic convergence. Koenig and Esseln (2001) offered an initial approach to the quantitative coding of symbolic convergence by coding for the rate of initiating, chaining, and cueing dramatizing messages during small group interactions, and this coding system is currently being refined and further developed. In addition, Koenig Kellas and Trees (in press) have developed and used a rating scheme that assesses the verbal and nonverbal interactive family behaviors and collaborative sense-making that emerge in the joint telling of family stories. Although not specifically guided by SCT in its current form, the rating scheme measures the degree of engagement, turn-taking, perspective-taking, and coherence in jointly told stories, and may be used and/or modified to assess aspects of symbolic convergence during family interactions.

Ultimately, we believe that SCT represents a theory with great potential that is currently underused by family communication scholars. The types of studies we have suggested in the preceding discussion will allow scholars to assess the utility of SCT for furthering our understanding of how family messages contribute to, and detract from, the social construction of family identity.

REFERENCES

Bales, R. F. (1970). *Personality and interpersonal behavior.* New York: Holt, Rinehart & Winston.

Banker, B. S., & Gaertner, S. L. (1998). Achieving stepfamily harmony: An intergroup-relations approach. *Journal of Family Psychology, 12,* 310–325.

Bormann, E. G. (1970). The paradox and promise of small group research. *Speech Monographs, 37,* 211–217.

Bormann, E. G. (1975). *Discussion and group methods: Theory and practice* (2nd ed.). New York: Harper & Row.

Bormann, E. G. (1982). A fantasy theme analysis of the television coverage of the hostage release and the Reagan inaugural. *Quarterly Journal of Speech, 68,* 133–144.

Bormann, E. G. (1985). *The force of fantasy: Restoring the American dream.* Carbondale, IL: Southern Illinois University.

Bormann, E. G. (1989). *Communication theory.* Salem, WI: Sheffield.

Bormann, E. G. (1990). *Small group communication: Theory and practice* (3rd ed.). New York: HarperCollins.

Bormann, E. G. (1998). Symbolic convergence theory and the communication in group decision-making. In R. Y. Hirokawa & M. S. Poole (Eds.), *Communication and group decision-making* (pp. 219–236). Thousand Oaks, CA: Sage.

Bormann, E. G., Cragan, J. F., & Shields, D. C. (1994). In defense of symbolic convergence theory: A look at the theory and its criticisms after two decades. *Communication Theory, 4,* 259–294.

Bormann, E. G., Knutson, R. L., & Musolf, K. (1997). Why do people share fantasies? An empirical investigation of a basic tenet of the symbolic convergence communication theory. *Communication Studies, 48,* 254–276.

Bray, S. A. (2001). *Son's remembered communication experiences with their mothers: A fantasy theme analysis and Q-sort investigation.* Unpublished doctoral dissertation, University of Minnesota.

Endres, T. G. (1989). Rhetorical visions of unmarried mothers. *Communication Quarterly, 37,* 134–150.

Endres, T. G. (1997). Father-daughter dramas: A Q-investigation of rhetorical visions. *Journal of Applied Communication Research, 25,* 317–340.

Frazier, L. J. G. (1988). *A contextual, content analysis of the rhetorical visions in parenting self-help books (1940–1979).* Unpublished doctoral dissertation, University of Minnesota.

Gaetano, G. M. (1994). *A fantasy theme analysis of sons' remembered communication experiences with their fathers.* Unpublished doctoral dissertation, University of Minnesota.

Galvin, K. M., Bylund, C. L., & Brommel, B. J. (2004). *Family communication: Cohesion and change* (6th ed.). Boston: Allyn & Bacon.

Hudson, L. (2003, November). *A family that prays together stays together: The religious implications of cohabitation, divorce, and remarriage.* Paper presented at the annual meeting of the National Communication Association, Miami, FL.

Kieren, D. K., Maguire, T. O., & Hurlbut, N. (1996). A marker method to test a phasing hypothesis in family problem-solving interaction. *Journal of Marriage and the Family, 58,* 442–455.

Koenig, J., & Esseln, D. (2001, November). *The complex convergence of communication research: Cognitive complexity and symbolic convergence theory in small group communication.* Paper presented at the annual meeting of the National Communication Association, Atlanta, GA.

Koenig, J., & Trees, A. R. (2001, July). *Finding meaning in difficult family experiences: Sense-making and interaction processes during joint family storytelling.* Paper presented at the annual meeting of the International Network on Personal Relationships, Prescott, AZ.

Koenig Kellas, J. (2003, November). *Family ties: Communicating identity through jointly told family stories.* Paper presented at the annual meeting of the National Communication Association, Miami, FL.

Koenig Kellas, J., & Trees, A. R. (in press). Interactional sense-making in the process of joint storytelling. In V. Manusov (Ed.), *The sourcebook of nonverbal measures: Going beyond words.* Mahwah, NJ: Lawrence Erlbaum.

Miller, M. A. (1997, November). *Intergenerational stories and the co-construction of reality: A fantasy theme analysis.* Paper presented at the annual meeting of the National Communication Association, Louisville, KY.

Miller, S. A. (1998). *Family values and the 1992 Republicans: A fantasy theme analysis.* Unpublished master's thesis, California State University, Chico.

Norrick, N. R. (1997). Twice-told tales: Collaborative narration of familiar stories. *Language in Society, 26,* 199–220.

Poole, M. S. (1999). Group communication theory. In L. R. Frey, D. S. Gouran, & M. S. Poole (Eds.), *The handbook of group communication theory and research* (pp. 37–70). Thousand Oaks, CA: Sage.

Schrag, R. L. (1982). Teach your children well: Method and rationale in the criticism of adolescent oriented television programming. *Western Journal of Speech Communication, 46,* 98–108.

Schrodt, P., & Durham, W. D. (2002, November). *Symbolic convergence theory and the social construction of blended family identity.* Paper presented at the annual meeting of the National Communication Association, New Orleans, LA.

Shireen, M. (1990). *The debate over child care in America: A fantasy theme analysis.* Unpublished master's thesis, California State University, Sacramento.

Socha, T. J. (1999). Communication in family units. In L. R. Frey, D. S. Gouran, & M. S. Poole (Eds.), *The handbook of group communication theory and research* (pp. 475–492). Thousand Oaks, CA: Sage.

Stohl, C., & Putnam, L. L. (1994). Group communication in context: implications for the study of bona fide groups. In L. R. Frey (Ed.), *Group communication in context: Studies of natural groups* (pp. 285–292).

Turner, R. H. (1970). *Family interaction.* New York: John Wiley.

PART II

Theories Originating In Complementary Fields

11

Attachment Theory: The Reciprocal Relationship Between Family Communication and Attachment Patterns

April R. Trees

Editors' Note: Attachment theory has its origins in the fields of psychiatry and psychology. The theory is logical-empirical in nature in its focus on causal explanation of why people communicate the way they do in family relationships.

In the 1940s and 1950s, researchers reported a number of negative developmental outcomes experienced by children separated from their mothers for various reasons (e.g., bereavement, hospitalization). These children engaged in protest, despair, and detachment behaviors when experiencing separation (for a review, see Bowlby, 1969, 1988). This body of research, in conjunction with ethological research being done at the time, provided the impetus for the initial formulation of attachment theory by John Bowlby. A psychiatrist, John Bowlby (1969,

1973), proposed attachment theory to explain why children tend to develop strong bonds with an attachment figure and experience distress when separated from primary caregivers. Taking an ethological perspective, Bowlby argued that children's tendency to seek proximity to caregivers reflects the need for protection as a part of survival.

Given its origins, initial theorizing focused predominantly on infant-parent affective ties; however, attachment bonds impact relationships and interactions across the life span. A positivist theory, scholars use attachment theory to explain and predict cognition, affect, and behavior. This chapter provides an overview of the central assumptions of attachment theory, paying particular attention to three important questions in attachment theory with a direct connection to family communication. First, how does communication shape the initial development of attachment security? Second, how do attachment styles influence interaction in family relationships? Third, how might family interaction contribute to changes in attachment security? The research on attachment theory also covers a number of topics beyond the focus of this chapter that are relevant to family communication interests (i.e., attachment and family therapy; the influence of attachment patterns on children's developmental processes).

OVERVIEW OF ATTACHMENT THEORY

Attachment theory (Bowlby, 1988) suggests that an infant's primary caregiver serves as a *secure base* from which he or she can explore the world, as well as a *safe haven* when the infant experiences distress and the attachment behavioral system is activated. Children initiate attachment behaviors such as crying or seeking when they feel threatened, fearful, or realize they can't easily reach the caregiver. These behaviors ideally help the infant restore equilibrium and gain security. If the caregiver repeatedly is not responsive or available, however, detachment develops. Research on attachment in infancy focuses primarily on the mother-infant bond (i.e., Ainsworth, Blehar, Waters, & Wall, 1978), and several researchers have critiqued the ideological underpinnings of attachment theory and its primary focus on mothers (i.e., Hays, 1998). However, some studies have investigated the father-infant bond (see van IJzendoorn & De Wolff, 1997, for a meta-analysis) and other types of caregiving relationships (see Howes, 1999, for a review of research on multiple caregivers).

The *attachment bond,* a central concept in attachment theory, refers to a very specific type of relationship. Key criteria differentiating attachment bonds from other types of relationships include strong emotional ties and resistance to separation from the attachment figure, along with use of the attachment figure as a source of comfort in times of distress and a secure base from which to explore the world (Feeney, 1999). Individuals may have multiple attachment relationships organized in a hierarchy with a primary relationship at the top (Bretherton, 1985).

Communication within attachment relationships impacts children's psychological development through its influence on children's perception of the attachment figure as a safe haven and secure base. Children develop *working models,* or internal pictures of themselves in relation to others, through their interactions with their attachment figure(s) (Bowlby, 1973). These working models include two major elements: conception of self and conception of the attachment figure. These two dimensions are interdependent and reflect expectations concerning whether or not the self is the sort of person who is valued and competent and likely to receive help from others, and whether the attachment figure is someone who is emotionally available and who can be counted on to respond to calls for help and provide protection. Ongoing interactions that create expectations concerning the availability and responsiveness of the attachment figure contribute to the development of these attachment patterns (Bretherton, 1985), and children's internal representations shape their beliefs and expectations in other relational contexts.

Concurrently with Bowlby's work on attachment bonds and working models, Mary Ainsworth and her colleagues (i.e., Ainsworth, Blehar, Waters, & Wall, 1978) developed the Strange Situation protocol to observe infants' reactions to caregivers' presence, absence, and return. Based upon infants' behaviors toward mothers when they experience distress, Ainsworth et al. identified three primary attachment patterns: avoidant, secure, and anxious-resistant. When faced with the absence of the mother in the strange situation, *avoidant* infants expressed minimal distress and minimal relief at her return. Infants with a *secure* attachment pattern moved to seek physical contact with the mother when she returned, were easily comforted, and then continued to explore and play. Finally, a combination of angry behavior and proximity-seeking characterized *anxious-resistant* infants. Main and Solomon (1990) suggested a fourth pattern, *disorganized,* to describe infants who exhibited less-coherent behavior such as contradictory behavior (i.e., avoidance and proximity-seeking), stillness, or confusion.

HOW DOES FAMILY COMMUNICATION SHAPE
THE DEVELOPMENT OF ATTACHMENT SECURITY?

In attachment theory, parent-infant interaction serves as an important influence in children's development of these attachment patterns. Parental *sensitivity*, which includes both a cognitive awareness of the child's needs and a behavioral response to those needs, shapes children's attachment patterns. Sensitive mothers are able to see things from the baby's point of view, attend to the infant's signals, accurately interpret them, and promptly and appropriately respond to those signals (Ainsworth et al., 1978; Bowlby, 1969, 1973). Interactional sensitivity emphasizes mutual responsiveness, and parental responses can be understood only within the context of the behavior to which they are responding. Ainsworth et al. (1978), for example, found that mothers tended to be inconsistent when responding to anxious-resistant infants' distress signals, consistently responsive toward secure infants' signals, and unresponsive or rejecting toward avoidant infants' signals.

Since Ainsworth and her colleagues' (1978) initial research, a number of studies have confirmed the importance of mothers' responsiveness, appropriateness, and timing or coordination for developing secure attachments. For example, mothers of securely attached children engage in more responsive caregiving, lower levels of rejection, and more appropriate responses (Isabella, 1993; Smith & Pederson, 1988). Mothers of avoidant infants, on the other hand, tend to engage in overly intense or intrusive behaviors, and mothers of anxious-resistant children may respond insufficiently or inconsistently (Smith & Pederson, 1988). In addition to maternal sensitivity, several other qualities have been linked to attachment security, including synchrony, warmth, involvement, positive affect, emotional support, and appropriate stimulation (for reviews, see Belsky, 1999b; De Wolff & van IJzendoorn, 1997). More recently, researchers also have investigated maternal behaviors related to a disorganized attachment. Schuengel, Bakermans-Kranenburg, and van IJzendoorn (1999) found that mothers of disorganized infants had higher scores for frightening (i.e., sudden movements in the facial area, negative vocal tones) and frightened (i.e., backing away) behavior in interactions with their children.

Although the dominant focus has been on maternal sensitivity, some research has also attended to father-infant interaction qualities and father-infant attachment security. For example, Lundy (2002) found that fathers' interactional synchrony predicted infant attachment to fathers. A meta-analysis by van IJzendoorn and De Wolff (1997) of the research in this area indicated a small but significant relationship between infant-father attachment security and paternal sensitivity. The relationship between maternal sensitivity and infant-mother attachment security was stronger (De Wolff & van IJzendoorn, 1997). A comparison of studies, including both father-infant and mother-infant attachment patterns, suggests that attachment patterns are relationship-specific rather than generalized within the infant.

Research indicates that maternal attachment style and infant attachment style frequently correspond. An intergenerational model of transmission proposes that parenting behavior creates a link between parents' attachment representations from their own childhood and their children's development of attachment security (van IJzendoorn, 1995). However, the link is a complex one. Maternal sensitivity accounts for only a small amount of the consistency in parent and infant attachment security. Instead, parent attachment style and interactional sensitivity seem to be largely independent influences on infants' attachment security (Raval, Goldberg, Atkinson, Benoit, Myhal, Poulton, & Zwiers, 2001; van IJzendoorn, 1995). In addition, De Wolff and van IJzendoorn's (1997) meta-analysis suggested that factors other than maternal sensitivity and responsive, coordinated interaction shape infant attachment styles. These findings raise questions concerning what psychological, contextual, and/or interactional qualities might explain the relationship between parent and infant attachment styles and contribute to infant attachment security.

Several answers to these questions, including mothers' psychological health, infant temperament, the quality of the parents' spousal relationship, and family stress and access to social support and resources, have already been proposed by attachment researchers with mixed support (Belsky, 1999a; 1999b; De Wolff & van IJzendoorn, 1997). Additionally, some scholars have suggested that researchers need to look beyond warmth and responsiveness to other important aspects of parent-infant interaction, such as control or discipline behaviors, to gain a complete understanding of the role of parenting behaviors in developing or transmitting attachment security (Cummings & Cummings, 2002; De Wolff & van IJzendoorn, 1997).

Along with additional parenting behaviors, researchers should consider ways in which children contribute to parent-child interaction patterns, particularly as children develop socially. Although some research (i.e., Ravel et al., 2001) suggests that maternal rather than infant behavior is a key determinant of attachment patterns, infant/child behavior impacts processes of mutual influence in interaction. Belsky (1999b), for example, argued that infant temperament may indirectly impact attachment security through its influence on parent-infant interaction.

In contrast with the dyadic focus most typical to discussions of attachment theory, several scholars have advocated for a systemic view of attachment, considering ways in which various parts of the family system influence attachment processes. For example, marital relational quality impacts fathers' interactional sensitivity with infants, and marital quality and conflict relate to children's attachment patterns (Lundy, 2002; Teti, Sakin, Kucera, Corns, & Das Eisen, 1996). In addition, sibling relationships may influence maternal sensitivity and sibling security. For example, maternal sensitivity sometimes decreases from older to younger siblings in the face of competing demands from multiple children (van IJzendoorn, Moran, Belsky, Pederson, Bakermans-Kranenburg, & Kneppers, 2000). Also, Teti et al. (1996) found that firstborn children's attachment security decreased with the birth of a second sibling, although this may reflect a temporary shift as families deal with the changes and stress of a family transition. A systems approach (see Galvin, Dickson, & Ferguson, this volume) would provide clearer insight into the complex processes that contribute to the development and modification of children's internal working models.

HOW DOES ATTACHMENT SECURITY INFLUENCE INTERACTION IN FAMILY RELATIONSHIPS?

Although Bowlby (1969; 1973) suggested that attachment bonds are relevant across the life span, initial research on attachment focused primarily on infant-parent relationships. This emphasis shifted, however, with Hazan and Shaver's (1987) seminal work proposing that romantic relationships serve as attachment bonds in adulthood. Adult attachment research follows two lines of thinking. The first, a developmental perspective, uses the Adult Attachment Interview to elicit narrative accounts of relationships with parents in childhood. Based upon the coherence of their narratives, adults are classified as secure, insecure-dismissing, or insecure-preoccupied. Researchers then investigate the relationship between these representations of childhood attachment experiences and orientations toward adult personal relationships (i.e., Cohn, Silver, Cowan, Cowan, & Pearson, 1992). The second, a social psychological perspective, focuses on individuals' current attachment orientations in adult attachment relationships, most frequently focusing on romantic relationships (i.e., Hazan & Shaver, 1987).

According to Hazan and Shaver (1987), comfort with closeness and interdependence and anxiety concerning abandonment are key components of adult romantic relationship attachment orientations. Specifically, they proposed that *secure* individuals are comfortable with intimacy, willing to depend on others and be depended upon, and have relatively few fears of rejection or abandonment. *Avoidant* individuals maintain emotional distance and are uncomfortable with intimacy, and *anxious-ambivalent* individuals desire closeness, yet fear not being loved enough and worry about abandonment. Bartholomew and Horowitz (1991) further divided avoidance into two categories: *fearful avoidants* fear rejection but desire intimacy, and *dismissive avoidants* deny their need for intimacy and emphasize independence. Consistent with Hazan and Shaver's (1987) expectations, a number of studies have demonstrated a relationship between attachment security and relational quality in dating and marital relationships (see Feeney, 1999; Mikulincer, Florian, Cowan, & Cowan, 2002 for reviews).

Developed from past attachment experiences, internal working models contain beliefs and expectations that influence cognition, emotion, and communication in adult attachment relationships. Given the basic assumptions of attachment theory, three key communication functions have received particularly close attention in attachment research: approach/avoidance behaviors, support-seeking and provision, and conflict resolution and problem solving.

Both cognitions and behaviors related to relational closeness play a central role in attachment theory across the life span. Bowlby (1969, 1973) focused on children's proximity-seeking behavior as a key attachment behavior. Hazan and Shaver (1987) argued that attachment security, in part, reflected individuals' comfort with intimacy, and Mikulincer et al. (2002) proposed a theoretical model in which interaction goals related to intimacy and closeness moderate the relationship between attachment security and relationship satisfaction. Approach behaviors such as self-disclosure, emotional expression, and nonverbal involvement may contribute to the development of intimacy or closeness in the relationship, whereas avoidance behaviors serve a distancing function. Different expectations for, and comfort with, intimacy in attachment orientations, then, should influence self-disclosure and nonverbal involvement behaviors.

At the individual level, secure and avoidant individuals exhibit the clearest patterns of difference in self-disclosure and nonverbal involvement. Compared with avoidant individuals, secure partners engage in more open communication, both in terms of amount and content of disclosure as well as comfort with and flexibility in disclosure (e.g., Bradford, Feeney, & Campbell, 2002; Le Poire, Haynes, Driscoll, Driver, Wheelis, Hyde, Prochaska, & Ramos, 1997; Mikulincer & Nachshon, 1991). In addition, secure individuals report greater reciprocity of high disclosure by partners (Mikulincer & Nachshon, 1991) and more confidence in their ability to elicit disclosure from others (Bradford et al., 2002). Avoidants tend to have a more negative response to others' disclosures (Mikulincer & Nachson, 1991). Secure individuals are more nonverbally expressive than avoidant individuals in conversations with romantic partners (Guerrero, 1996). These patterns fit with the assumption that avoidant individuals desire distance and detachment in personal relationships. Findings regarding anxious-ambivalent relational partners are more mixed for both disclosure (Le Poire et al., 1997; Mikulincer & Nachshon, 1991) and nonverbal cues (Guerrero, 1996), with similarities to secure individuals in amount of and comfort with disclosure and similarities to avoidants in flexibility, topical reciprocity, and honesty of disclosure.

In addition to closeness and intimacy more generally, attachment theory focuses specifically on behaviors activated by distress, directing attention toward supportive communication. According to Ainsworth et al.'s (1987) classification system, for example, secure infants use their caregivers as a source of comfort and support when distressed. Avoidant infants, on the other hand, make no effort to actively seek support from caregivers—they cope internally, and anxious-ambivalent infants make inconsistent attempts to gain support. In adulthood, support-seeking behaviors take different forms given developmental differences. Also, given the mutual nature of adult attachment relationships, support provision becomes an added dimension of attachment behavior.

Generally, secure partners are more likely to provide and seek support than avoidants, whereas highly ambivalent individuals may have more negative perceptions of their partners' support provision (Crowell, Treboux, Gao, Fyffe, Pan, & Waters, 2002; Rholes, Simpson, Campbell, & Grich, 2001). For couples experiencing the transition to parenthood, highly ambivalent women who felt they received minimal support from their husbands prior to the birth reported greater declines in spousal support and sought less support than women in other categories (Rholes et al., 2001). Men married to these women reported providing less support. Avoidant women, on the other hand, sought less support both before and after the birth, perhaps reflecting a greater desire for independence.

Attachment orientation also predicts support behavior in sibling relationships. Secure older siblings were more likely than insecure older siblings to respond to infants' distress with comfort attempts (Teti & Ablard, 1989).

In addition to intimacy and support functions, individuals' attachment patterns also impact their responses to, and regulation of, negative emotion in close personal relationships (Kobak & Hazan, 1991). Because conflict in attachment relationships may elicit distressing emotions that must be managed and raise questions about partners' availability, attachment researchers have also investigated the links between attachment style and conflict management.

Patterns in research indicate that secure attachment relates to more harmonious and constructive conflict strategies in marital and parent-child relationships. In marital relationships, secure individuals reported fewer arguments with partners, and less verbal aggression and defensiveness and more validation and negotiation during conflict (Crowell, Treboux, & Waters, 2002; Kobak & Hazan, 1991; Wampler, Shi, Nelson, & Kimball, 2003). These studies found that insecurely attached spouses, however, displayed more rejection behaviors, ambivalents reported greater anxiety and displayed more hostility and anger, and avoidant men expressed less warmth and supportiveness. In mother-teen disagreements, Kobak, Cole, Ferenz-Gillies, Fleming, and Gamble (1993) found that secure teens and their mothers displayed less avoidance and less dysfunctional anger.

Although individual attachment orientations clearly impact family communication, scholars also have identified partner and couple effects on interaction. *Partner effects* refer to the relationship of individuals' behaviors to their partners' attachment orientation. For example, individuals tended to disclose less relationship information overall to avoidant spouses, and disclosures were less intimate and more negative in emotional tone with anxious partners (Bradford et al., 2002). Husbands of securely attached women listened more as the wife confided about a distressing event, whereas wives of insecurely attached husbands were more rejecting in problem-solving conversations (Kobak & Hazan, 1991). Feeney (2003) found that wives were more likely to avoid conflict when married to men with high relationship anxiety.

In contrast with partner effects, *couple effects* direct attention to ways in which the pair's particular combination of attachment styles influences communication. For example, insecure women married to secure men engaged in less conflict and more positive interaction than insecure women married to insecure men (Cohn et al., 1992), and coercive conflict behaviors, such as threats and verbal or physical aggression, were more likely in couples in which wives had high anxiety and husbands had low anxiety (Feeney, 2003). In relationships in which both husbands and wives are securely attached, couples reported greater intimacy in marriage and less-frequent verbal aggression and withdrawal in conflict than did couples in relationships with mixed attachment types (Senchak & Leonard, 1992). Both partner and couple effects suggest that interaction patterns reflect responsiveness to partners' attachment styles and the relational context, as well as individual differences.

Individuals bring different attachment orientations to a relationship, but the interaction between partners, as well as the interaction of partner attachment orientations, influences the individual and relational impact of that orientation (i.e., Le Poire et al., 1997). Although partner and couple effects have been identified in research, the processes of mutual influence in relational partners' negotiation of the attachment relationship are less clear. Also, as with understanding attachment in childhood, a systemic approach to adult attachment would provide a more coherent understanding of the relationship between working models and communication behaviors within particular contexts (Feeney, 2003; Mikulincer et al., 2002).

HOW MIGHT FAMILY INTERACTION CONTRIBUTE TO CHANGES IN ATTACHMENT SECURITY?

Researchers of attachment patterns in adulthood traditionally treat internal working models as if they are stable personality traits. Although he suggested that working models are open to modification based on relationship experiences, Bowlby (1988) conceptualized attachment patterns as relatively stable. More recently, however, both research investigating patterns of attachment in adulthood over a relatively short period of time (i.e., Ross & Spinner, 2001) and longitudinal research comparing attachment patterns in infancy to patterns in adolescence or young adulthood (i.e., Waters, Merrick, Treboux, Crowell, & Albersheim, 2000) suggested that attachment security can change over time as internal working models undergo revision. Although some evidence exists that stability may be typical (i.e., Waters et al., 2000), working models are not set in stone, particularly when individuals experience emotionally positive or negative life events (i.e., Davila, Karney, & Bradbury, 1999; Weinfeld, Sroufe, & Egeland, 2000).

The stability of children's attachment security depends upon ongoing parenting behaviors (Crowell et al., 2002). As Crowell et al. point out, after infancy caregivers "continue to play an important role in organizing and helping to consolidate secure base behavior, and they co-construct representations of attachment-related experiences throughout childhood and adolescence" (p. 467). Changes in parental sensitivity at least partially explain shifts in children's attachment security (Teti et al., 1996). Given the potential for change, attachment processes might better be understood with research considering the relevance of parental sensitivity beyond infancy (i.e., Belsky & Pasco Fearon, 2002; Trees, 2000). Interactional sensitivity may change over time, given life events in the family (Teti et al., 1996). The sensitivity of parental behaviors after attachment patterns develop interacts with attachment security to impact children's psychological development (Belsky & Pasco Fearon, 2002). To complicate matters, what counts as sensitive interaction may be different at different stages of development (Clausen & Crittenden, 2000).

In adulthood as well, communication likely contributes to the revision of working models. Attentive and responsive interactions in a close personal relationship, for example, may make the secure schema accessible, even if an individual generally has an avoidant or anxious attachment (Baldwin, Keelan, Fehr, Enns, & Koh-Rangajaroo, 1996). The presence of partner and couple effects in adult attachment research also supports the idea that working models may change, depending upon the relational context. Additionally, Le Poire et al. (1997) found that partners' attachment styles predicted the final form of individuals' attachments in romantic relationships. Specifically, the combination of individuals' own secure attachment to parents and their partners' secure attachment styles predicted their secure attachment in that specific romantic relationship. The relationship between attachment security and communication patterns is probably a reciprocal one in which security affects interaction patterns, but communication experiences influence security, although more research needs to be done to understand how this process works.

DIRECTIONS FOR FUTURE RESEARCH

Attachment theory predicts connections between early childhood experiences in the family and interpersonal experiences across the life span. Along with cognitive and affective components, communication plays a central role in attachment theory and its application to family relationships. Future family communication research can both contribute to knowledge about how attachment processes work and use attachment theory to illuminate our understanding of family communication processes.

Investigating processes of mutual influence in parent-child and marital interaction could help to explain the development of relationship-specific attachment patterns, partner and couple effects in attachment research, and changes in attachment patterns over time. For example, how do patterns of interactional sensitivity influence attachment styles in marriage? Do matching or differing patterns of intimacy behaviors help explain the development or erosion of security in family attachment relationships? Related to this, research needs to investigate the intersection of different attachment relationships and their consequences for family communication. For example, how does an individual's spousal attachment pattern in combination with parental attachment patterns impact parenting behaviors?

Additionally, attachment theory provides a theoretical frame for investigating important family communication processes, particularly for families experiencing life transitions or stressful events when attachment systems are likely to be activated. Stepfamily formation illustrates one potential application of attachment theory. Stepfamilies bring together individuals with different past relational experiences during a time of relational transition when role negotiation and development, managing relational ambiguity and feelings of being caught, and regulating boundaries become important communicative activities (Golish, 2003). Attachment models likely shape and are shaped by interaction processes during stepfamily formation and also impact relational and individual outcomes. For example, how do attachment orientations influence stepparents' warmth and control behaviors and the negotiation of the stepparent role? How do attachment processes explain responses to feeling caught between relationships?

As research in this area expands, more complex understandings of psychological, sociological, and interactional influences on attachment security and of the influence of attachment security on individual and relational functioning have begun to emerge. As researchers continue to investigate attachment processes, they should keep in mind cultural differences and social changes in family forms and experiences that may influence communication and attachment. These include considering attachment processes in different family forms, attending to various types of child care options available to families, and considering cross-generational influences in attachment processes.

REFERENCES

Ainsworth, M. D. S., Blehar, M. C., Waters, E., & Wall, S. (1978). *Patterns of attachment: A psychological study of the strange situation.* Hillsdale, NJ: Erlbaum.

Baldwin, M. W., Keelan, J. P. R., Fehr, B., Enns, V., & Koh-Rangarajoo, E. (1996). Social-cognitive conceptualization of attachment working models: Availability and accessibility effects. *Journal of Personality and Social Psychology, 71,* 94–109.

Bartholomew, K., & Horowitz, L. M. (1991). Attachment styles among young adults: A test of a four-category model. *Journal of Personality and Social Psychology, 61,* 226–244.

Belsky, J. (1999a). Infant-parent attachment. In L. Balter & C. S. Jamis-LeMonda (Eds.), *Child psychology: A handbook of contemporary issues* (pp. 45–63). Philadelphia: Psychology Press.

Belsky, J. (1999b). Interactional and contextual determinants of attachment security. In J. Cassidy & P. R. Shaver (Eds.), *Handbook of attachment: Theory, research, and clinical applications* (pp. 259–264). New York: Guilford Press.

Belsky, J., & Pasco Fearon, R. M. (2002). Early attachment security, subsequent maternal sensitivity, and later child development: Does continuity in development depend upon continuity of caregiving? *Attachment and Human Development, 4,* 361–387.

Bowlby, J. (1969). *Attachment and loss: Vol. 1 Attachment.* New York: Basic Books.

Bowlby, J. (1973). *Attachment and loss: Vol. 2 Separation: Anxiety and anger.* New York: Basic Books.

Bowlby, J. (1988). *A secure base: Parent-child attachment and healthy human development.* New York: Basic Books.

Bradford, S. A., Feeney, J. A., & Campbell, L. (2002). Links between attachment orientations and dispositional and diary-based measures of disclosure in dating couples: A study of actor and partner effects. *Personal Relationships, 9,* 491–506.

Bretherton, I. (1985). Attachment theory: Retrospect and prospect. *Monographs of the Society for Research in Child Development, 50,* 3–35.

Clausen, A. H., & Crittenden, P. M. (2000). Maternal sensitivity. In P. M. Crittenden and A. H. Clausen (Eds.), *The organization of attachment relationships: Maturation, culture, and context* (pp. 115–122). Cambridge, UK: Cambridge University Press.

Cohn, D. A., Silver, D. H., Cowan, C. P., Cowan, P. A., & Pearson, J. (1992). Working models of childhood attachment and couple relationships. *Journal of Family Issues, 13,* 432–449.

Crowell, J. A., Treboux, D., Gao, Y., Fyffe, C., Pan, H., & Waters, E. (2002). Assessing secure base behavior in adulthood: Development of a measure, links to adult attachment representations, and relations to couples' communication and reports of relationships. *Developmental Psychology, 38,* 579–693.

Crowell, J. A., Treboux, D., & Waters, E. (2002). Stability of attachment representations: The transition to marriage. *Developmental Psychology, 38,* 467–479.

Cummings, E. M., & Cummings, J. S. (2002). Parenting and attachment. In M. H. Bornstein (Ed.), *Handbook of parenting: Vol 5: Practical issues in parenting* (pp. 35–58). Mahwah, NJ: Lawrence Erlbaum.

Davila, J., Karney, B. R., & Bradbury, T. N. (1999). Attachment change processes in the early years of marriage. *Journal of Personality and Social Psychology, 76,* 783–802.

DeWolff, M. S., & van IJzendoorn, M. H. (1997). Sensitivity and attachment: A meta-analysis on parental antecedents of infant-attachment. *Child Development, 68,* 571–591.

Feeney, J. A. (1999). Adult romantic attachment and couple relationships. In J. Cassidy & P. R. Shaver (Eds.), *Handbook of attachment: Theory, research, and applications* (pp. 355–377). New York: Guilford Press.

Feeney, J. A. (2003). The systemic nature of couple relationships: An attachment perspective. In P. Erdman & T. Caffery (Eds.), *Attachment and family systems: Conceptual, empirical, and therapeutic relatedness* (pp. 139–163). New York: Brunner-Routledge.

Golish, T. D. (2003). Stepfamily communication strengths: Understanding the ties that bind. *Human Communication Research, 29,* 41–80.

Guerrero, L. K. (1996). Attachment-style differences in intimacy and involvement: A test of the four-category model. *Communication Monographs, 63,* 269–292.

Hays, S. (1998). The fallacious assumptions and unrealistic prescriptions of attachment theory: A comment on "parents' socioemotional investment in children." *Journal of Marriage and the Family, 60,* 782–790.

Hazan, C., & Shaver, P. (1987). Romantic love conceptualized as an attachment process. *Journal of Personality and Social Psychology, 52,* 511–524.

Howes, C. (1999). Attachment relationships in the context of multiple caregivers. In J. Cassidy & P. R. Shaver (Eds.), *Handbook of attachment: Theory, research, and applications* (pp. 671–687). New York: Guilford Press.

Isabella, R. A. (1993). Origins of attachment: Maternal interactive behavior across the first year. *Child Development, 64,* 605–621.

Kobak, R. R., Cole, H. E., Ferenz-Gillies, R., Fleming, W. S., & Gamble, W. (1993). Attachment and emotion regulation during mother-teen problem solving: A control theory analysis. *Child Development, 64,* 231–245.

Kobak, R. R., & Hazan, C. (1991). Attachment in marriage: Effects of security and accuracy of working models. *Journal of Personality and Social Psychology, 60,* 861–869.

Le Poire, B. A., Haynes, J., Driscoll, J., Driver, B. N., Wheelis, T. F., Hyde, M., Prochaska, M., & Ramos, L. (1997). Attachment as a function of parental and partner approach-avoidance tendencies. *Human Communication Research, 23,* 413–441.

Lundy, B. L. (2002). Paternal socio-psychological factors and infant attachment: The mediating role of synchrony in father-infant relationships. *Infant Behavior and Development, 25,* 221–236.

Main, M., & Solomon, J. (1990). Procedures for identifying infants as disorganized/disoriented during the Ainsworth Strange Situation. In M. T. Greenberg, D. Cicchetti, & E. M. Cummings (Eds.), *Attachment in the preschool years: Theory, research, and intervention* (pp. 161–182). Chicago: University of Chicago Press.

Mikulincer, M., Florian, V., Cowan, P. A., and Cowan, C. P. (2002). Attachment security in couple relationships: A systemic model and its implications for family dynamics. *Family Process, 41,* 405–434.

Mikulincer, M., & Nachshon, O. (1991). Attachment styles and patterns of self-disclosure. *Journal of Personality and Social Psychology, 61,* 321–331.

Raval, V., Goldberg, S., Atkinson, L., Benoit, D., Myhal, N., Poulton, L., & Zwiers, M. (2001). Maternal attachment, maternal responsiveness, and infant attachment. *Infant Behavior and Development, 24,* 281–304.

Rholes, W. S., Simpson, J. A., Campbell, L., & Grich, J. (2001). Adult attachment and the transition to parenthood. *Journal of Personality and Social Psychology, 81,* 421–435.

Ross, L. R., & Spinner, B. (2001). General and specific attachment representations in adulthood. *Journal of Social and Personal Relationships, 18,* 747–766.

Schuengel, C., Bakermans-Kranenburg, M. J., & van IJzendoorn, M. H. (1999). Frightening maternal behavior linking unresolved loss and disorganized infant attachment. *Journal of Consulting and Clinical Psychology, 67,* 54–63.

Senchak, M., & Leonard, K. E. (1992). Attachment styles and marital adjustment among newlywed couples. *Journal of Social and Personal Relationships, 9,* 51–64.

Smith, P. B., & Pederson, D. R. (1988). Maternal sensitivity and patterns of infant-mother attachment. *Child Development, 59,* 1097–1101.

Teti, D. M., & Ablard, K. E. (1989). Security of attachment and infant-sibling relationships: A laboratory study. *Child Development, 60,* 1519–1528.

Teti, D. M., Sakin, J., Kucera, E., Corns, K. M., & Das Eisen, R. (1996). And baby makes four: Predictors of attachment security among preschool-aged first-borns during the transition to siblinghood. *Child Development, 67,* 579–596.

Trees, A. R., (2000). Nonverbal communication and the support process: Interactional sensitivity in interactions between mothers and young adult children. *Communication Monographs, 67,* 239–261.

van IJzendoorn, M. H. (1995). Adult attachment representations, parental responsiveness, and infant attachment: A meta-analysis on the predictive validity of the Adult Attachment Interview. *Psychological Bulletin, 117,* 387–403.

van IJzendoorn, M. H., & De Wolff, M. S. (1997). In search of the absent father–meta-analyses of infant-father attachment: A rejoinder to our discussants. *Child Development, 68,* 604–609.

van IJzendoorn, M. H., Moran, G., Belsky, J., Pederson, D., Bakermans-Kranenburg, M. J., & Kneppers, K. (2000). The similarity of siblings' attachments to their mother. *Child Development, 71,* 1086–1098.

Wampler, K. S., Shi, L., Nelson, B. S., & Kimball, T. G. (2003). The adult attachment interview and observed couple interaction: Implications for an intergenerational perspective on couple therapy. *Family Processes, 42,* 497–515.

Waters, E., Merrick, S., Treboux, D., Crowell, J., & Albersheim, L. (2000). Attachment security in infancy and early adulthood: A twenty-year longitudinal study. *Child Development, 71,* 684–689.

Weinfeld, N. S., Sroufe, L. A., & Egeland, B. (2000). Attachment from infancy to early adulthood in a high-risk sample: Continuity, discontinuity, and their correlates. *Child Development, 71,* 695–702.

12

Attribution Theories: Assessing Causal and Responsibility Judgments In Families

Valerie L. Manusov

Editors' Note: As Manusov notes, this chapter summarizes several theories that are closely related in their common focus on attributions, all with origins in the field of psychology. Although attribution theories emphasize how people interpret their own and others' everyday actions, they are logical-empirical rather than interpretive in nature because of their commitment to explanation, prediction, and generalizability.

A t their most general, attributions involve the processes and products of interpreting or explaining our own and others' actions. When we see someone act in a certain way, we often act as "naïve scientists" (Heider, 1958) and discern various options to determine why a person behaved in a certain way. For example, if a parent is late to pick up a child, that child is likely to make a guess as to the causes of the parent's tardiness. If a husband brings home a surprise gift for his wife, she may think about why her husband brought the gift. The combined body of scholarship exploring these kinds of sense-making functions is known as *Attribution Theory*.

The term "Attribution Theory" is, however, somewhat misleading. The body of scholarship on attributions is perhaps more accurately termed *a set of theories or principles* that help us understand and predict the processes involved when people explain their social worlds to themselves or to others (for a recent critique of Attribution Theory as a theory, see Spitzberg, 2001). To help ground the range of work that makes up attribution theories, this chapter first covers some of the primary bodies of scholarship that attribution researchers have developed. It then turns toward sets of communication studies that focus on attributions generally and reviews some lines of application to family communication and functioning more specifically. As such, this overview is necessarily partial, given the vast amount of attention paid to attributions in a range of academic disciplines.

ATTRIBUTION THEORIES

The earliest writing on attribution processes came from Heider's (1958) argument that people attempt to make sense of one another's actions (i.e., create attributions) as part of a general need to control and predict the world around us. When a person acts in a certain way, we cannot know the cause of the action directly. Instead, according to Heider, we work to assess the likely reason behind it by weighing the probability of various potential causes to determine the most probable cause for an action. Heider argued that evidence for this "natural" form of sense-making can be seen in the everyday ways we talk about others and their actions (e.g., "We have problems in our relationship because my spouse had a difficult upbringing"; "The reason my Mother is strict is that she cares about me").

In what can be described as a *normative* view of attributional processing, Heider and other social psychologists (e.g., Jones & Davis, 1965; Kelley, 1971) accepted certain beliefs about people and how they select and organize information coming from the social world around them. The most important of these are (1) that people are active interpreters of the events occurring in their lives, and (2) that people use consistent and logical (i.e., normative) means to make their interpretations. For Heider (1958), these means or choices are based primarily on what he termed an action's *causal locus:* the judgment of a behavior's cause as internal (i.e., a disposition) or external (i.e., an environmental factor) to a person.

Jones and his colleagues (Jones & Davis, 1965; Jones & Harris, 1967) discussed the idea of causal locus more fully in their theory of correspondent inferences. Jones's concern was primarily with how people came to believe that an internal locus or disposition (rather than some external explanation) was the most likely cause of someone's action. For Jones, inferences to a person's intention are the most informative as they are best for predicting that person's future behavior. He argued that people can and will look at all available evidence to make their inference or attribution. Most notably, Jones contended that people will assess the degree to which a person appeared responsible for an action and had the ability to bring about the consequences of the action, and the relative contribution of luck or chance to bringing that action about. Once these pieces of information are determined, people can make the most accurate inference about the cause of another's behavior.

At about the same time, Kelley (1967) also proposed a normative model of attribution-making that came to be known as the ANOVA cube. Similar to Jones's work, Kelley argued that people make certain assessments about a cause's locus based on rational decision making, given what information is available. In his model, named after the statistical process of analyzing variance in quantitative data, Kelley asserted that people weigh the different sources of variability in people's actions. Most notably, a behavior can be judged on its *consistency* (has the person acted like this before in this situation?), its *consensus* (have others experienced the person acting this way?), and its *distinctiveness* (does this happen only with this person or also with other people?). If an attributor judges that the behavior was high in consistency, consensus, and distinctiveness, the attributor should/will attribute the cause to something about the person (i.e., an internal or "entity" attribution). Other judgments on consistency, consensus, and distinctiveness will rationally lead to other causal attributions.

CRITIQUES OF NORMATIVE MODELS

As with most established models of social behavior, both Jones's and Kelley's theories have been critiqued extensively. In particular, researchers have challenged the degree to which people act with as much rationality as the models predict that they will, leading many to call these first entries into attribution theory building "overly rational" (e.g., Crittenden & Wiley, 1985). Indeed, a large body of evidence supports the idea that attribution-making is "biased" in that it often veers from the normative models proposed. Ross (1977), for example, noted that people tend to make internal attributions far more often than they make external attributions—and much more often than the "available information" demands. He called this tendency to over-attribute internal causes as the "fundamental attribution error" (but see Fiske & Taylor, 1984, for an interesting argument about why it may be an error to call this process an error). Another noteworthy deviation from normative models deals with the tendency for people to make attributions for others' behaviors in a different way than they make attributions for their own behaviors. This is known generally as the "actor/observer effect" (Fiske & Taylor, 1984; Jones & Nisbett, 1972). Although consensus does not exist regarding the degree to which people act in a more normative or "biased" way in their attribution-making, enough evidence has accumulated to suggest that people often (although not always) ignore information vital to making logical causal links (Abelson, Leddo, & Gross, 1987), and many researchers now assert that attribution-making is better seen as part of a larger set of social cognitive processes and subject to the same shortcuts and preconceptions that influence all social judgment (Fiske & Taylor, 1984).

In addition to the work proposing deviations from (or differences in) normative patterns of attribution-making, attribution researchers have made two other important moves that stem from critiques of the original theorizing and both temper and extend the original views. The first critique deals with the actual occurrence of attributional processes, and the second extends the types of attributions people provide. As noted, Heider (1958) contended that causal inference is a typical response to observations of the social world. Some researchers (e.g., Langer, 1978) argue against this belief and say instead that spontaneous attributions (i.e., those not provoked by a researcher but instead occuring spontaneously in "real life") are not cognitively efficient (i.e., they take too much thinking) and so occur rarely in our everyday thoughts. That is, if we made careful attributions for all our actions and those of others around us, we would be unable to handle the large mental load such processing would require. A more tempered argument is that people *do* make attributions as part of our general sense-making, but extensive attribution-making is done only (or at least primarily) at certain times (Berger & Roloff, 1982; Pszyszynski & Greenberg, 1981; Wong & Weiner, 1981; for a more recent application, see Floyd & Voloudakis, 1999).

When these attributions occur, however, they are even more complex than early theories suggested. Weiner (1986) noted that people's attributions for actions do more than assess causal locus and the responsibility for an action's consequences. They also reflect beliefs about the valence, stability, and controllability of a cause as well as how intentional or global the cause is seen to be. So, in addition to assessing whether another person (or some outside influence) was the cause of a behavior, attributions also differ on the basis of how positive or negative and how constant the cause is, how much influence the person had over that cause, how deliberate it was perceived to be, and whether the cause applies only to this specific circumstance or can be seen as a more broad condition. For communication scholars interested in how attributions affect the perceived meanings of message behaviors, the variation allowed within Weiner's model is particularly important (see Manusov, 1990, 2002, for more discussion of this issue; see Fiske & Taylor, 1984, however, for a critique of Weiner's work).

APPLICATIONS OF ATTRIBUTION THEORIES TO COMMUNICATION

Given their concern with how people perceive and think about social actions, it makes sense that attributions have largely been the purview of social psychologists, and most of the theoretical development just discussed is derived from their work. Communication researchers, particularly those interested in how cognitive processes influence interpretations of messages as well as those concerned with the communicative outcomes of attributional processes, have also embraced many of the principles of attribution theory. Although most of the theory-building comes from social psychology, particularly important applications of attribution principles derive from communication studies.

Two noteworthy chapters appeared in the 1980s and provided some of the paths connecting attributions and communication. In 1982, Sillars asked the question, "Are people 'naïve scientists' or just naïve?" (p. 73). He answered that we are a bit of both: "People are both reflective and spontaneous, rational and rationalizing, logical and illogical"

(p. 96). He also contended that attributions are at work when people attempt to reduce their uncertainty with others (see Berger & Roloff, 1982), during metacommunication, and when punctuating or "chunking" communication sequences. For Sillars (1982), attributions also are an integral part of conflict processes and are influenced by relational familiarity. Seibold and Spitzberg (1982) likewise detailed an argument for why communication scholars get value from taking an attributional perspective. Most notably, the authors argued that attribution theories provide a conceptual framework for understanding the interpretation of identities, situations, and relationships we encounter in our everyday lives. They also noted a range of possible applications that communication researchers could make by applying principles from attribution theories to communication action and explanation.

In some of my own work (e.g., Manusov, 1990, 2001), I have continued these authors' previous assertions and specified three of the ways in which attribution processes work as part of communication. First, attributions can be seen *as the explanations*—the socially created, verbal reasons—given for social actions, including communication behaviors (e.g., "She said that to hurt me"); in this way, they are similar to the more general category of "accounts" that people provide in conversation for their own and others' actions. Second, attributions can also be viewed as ways to categorize explanations as more internal or external, more positive or negative, and so on; the dimensions help to show the range of meanings that can be given to communication behavior. Third, we can think of attributions as the actual meaning given to a behavior or the statements we form in our heads or in our speech that reflect an overall meaning we have attached to a behavior (e.g., "It hurt."). All these variations show how attributions become important as or surrounding communicative acts.

APPLICATIONS OF ATTRIBUTION THEORY TO THE FAMILY

Married Couples

Given its concern with explanations, it is not surprising that attribution principles have been studied in the family, a site in which much of our sense-making occurs (Koenig Kellas & Trees, 2005). The majority of empirical work using attribution theory in family relationships focuses on the processes and effects of attributions in married couples.

Only some of this work centers on *communication* processes, but all of it is relevant to understanding the role of attributions in families. Fincham and Bradbury summarized much of this work in their 1992 paper, noting the following:

> [D]istressed spouses . . . make attributions for negative events that accentuate their impact (e.g., they locate the cause in their partner, see it as stable or unchanging, and see it as global or influencing many of the areas of their relationship), whereas nondistressed spouses . . . make attributions that minimize the impact of negative events (e.g., they do not locate the cause in the partner and see it as unstable and specific). (p. 457)

The tendency for nondistressed or satisfied couples to make low-impact attributions for negative behaviors (and, conversely, to allow positive events more influence) has been termed "relationship-enhancing" attributions; the type of attributions more common for distressed or dissatisfied couples is called "distress-maintaining" (Holtzworth-Munroe & Jacobson, 1988). Karney, Bradbury, Fincham, and Sullivan (1994) used the term "maladaptive attributions" to describe the same tendency for distressed couples to make attributions that were harmful for their relationships. Recent scholarship has also been concerned with the causal order of satisfaction and attribution type, with evidence that certain attributions over time will influence satisfaction levels, and that satisfaction levels also have an impact on the types of attributions that spouses make (see Johnson, Karney, Rogge, & Bradbury, 2001).

The occurrence and impact of "distress-maintaining" attributions appear augmented when couples are categorized as "aggressive." In a recent report, Sillars, Leonard, Roberts, and Dun (2002) concluded that "aggressive couples have an acutely negative style of communication, which becomes more negative when husbands drink alcohol" (p. 97). Individuals in what are deemed aggressive relationships tend to hold particular divergent attributions for why they acted as they did and why their partner behaved as the partner did. Thus, one partner may claim he engaged in certain conflict behavior because "I'm trying to get her to talk about it" but might claim his spouse performed the same action for a very different reason: "She's always got to have her way" (see Sillars et al., 2002, p. 97). Most notably, Sillars et al. found that aggressive spouses tended to attribute less-constructive engagement and more avoidance to their partner than they attributed to themselves. Given the tendency for husbands in aggressive relationships to pay heightened attention to communication, and the likelihood that their attributions for their wives' communication will be negative, the link between attributions and communication "presents a combustible situation" (Sillars et al., 2002, p. 101).

Sillars has been one of the primary communication researchers to assess attributions in relationships. Likewise, I have conducted several investigations into couples' attributions from a communication perspective (e.g., Manusov, 1990, 2002; Manusov, Floyd, & Kerssen-Griep, 1997; Manusov & Koenig, 2001). Most of this work centers around attributions for nonverbal behaviors, following the assumption that the ambiguity of many nonverbal cues (e.g., facial expressions, posture, vocal tones) encourages the need for sense-making. Like those working on other behaviors occurring in marriage, I have found a tendency for couples to make "biased" attributions depending on their satisfaction level, consistent with the nature of distress-maintaining and relationship-enhancing attributions (Manusov, 1990, 1995) and consistent with the fundamental attribution error and the actor-observer bias (Manusov et al., 1997; as a caveat, however, Manusov and Koenig [2001] noted that although there is a tendency toward making relationship-enhancing or distress-maintaining attributions depending on satisfaction level, the content of many of these explanations includes elements of both attribution types).

As can be seen, much of the work just discussed, centering on attributions in marriage (and other intimate relationships), focuses on the link that attributions have with overall relational satisfaction. Some, however, expand the connection to other important variables. For instance, Rempel, Ross, and Holmes (2001) looked at the ways in which couples that had different levels of *trust* made attributions for conflict. Specifically, the authors investigated the couples' talk for instances of causal attributions. Interestingly, those at the medium-trust level focused most on negative attributions. Couples with the lowest trust for one another used less-negative attributions that worked to diminish the likelihood that the conflict would escalate, and those with the highest trust levels provided positive attributions. Rempel et al. contended that the results could not be accounted for by the couples' degree of relational satisfaction; thus trust acts somewhat separately from satisfaction to influence attribution-making for couples (see Flora & Segrin, 2001, for an additional application tying couples' attributions to their overall relational and personal well-being).

Although investigated less than would be expected, some research also focuses on the relationship between attributions and couples' *behaviors*. In one study (Manusov, 2002), for instance, I reported evidence that attributions made by one spouse for another's nonverbal cues may also influence the behaviors that the attributor engages in with the other (e.g., when a spouse thought that the partner could or had control over his or her facial expressions , the attributor was more likely to be facially pleasant, gaze more, and use a more upright posture when talking to his or her spouse). Other researchers have found links between the ways in which people assign responsibility and their own anger displays (Fincham & Bradbury, 1992), their overall use of negative behaviors in reaction to an attribution (Bradbury & Fincham, 1992), and their reciprocity of partners' negative behavior (Bradbury & Fincham, 1992). The links between attributions and other affective and behavioral outcomes show the extent to which attribution-making may permeate intimate relationships.

Other Family Relationships

Families are, of course, often made up of more (or other) than a couple, and researchers have sought to look at other ways that attributions occur in families. For example, some scholars have extended the above work by looking at possible ways in which parents' attributions are transmitted to their children. Benson, Arditti, Reguero de Atiles, and Smith (1992) asked young adults about their own intimate relationships as well as about their relationship with their parents. The authors concluded that positive attributions in their mother-child relationships and negative attributions in father-child relationships were both associated with the attributions the children made in their own intimate relationships. The authors suggest that one of the important outcomes of parental attribution-making is its continuance in children's personal relationships. Fincham, Beach, Arias, and Brody (1998) also found a link between children's attributions for their parents' behavior and the positive evaluation of the parent/child relationship.

A particularly salient context of study for attributions in the family revolves around the relationship between abuse and attributions. Bugental and her associates (e.g., Bugental, Shennum, Frank, & Ekman, 2001), for example, argue that children from homes in which they are physically and/or psychologically abused often have "unreliable life experiences" (Bugental et al., 2001, p. 250) that may influence the type of attributions they make. Some of these children respond to their environments by acting "with an exaggerated effort to maintain control" (Bugental et al., 2001, p. 251); others tend toward the perception that they have very little power. Although the context affects the outcomes to some degree, Bugental et al. argue that those abused children who respond by believing they have little power also make the most inaccurate attributions; these attribution errors may be due in part to the parents' own use of inconsistent and disingenuous behaviors.

Wilson and Whipple (2001) likewise found interesting, if troubling, associations between abuse and attributions. In their work, however, the authors were most concerned with the way in which parents who abuse their children provide attributions for their children's "misbehavior" (i.e., the actions the parents deem need changing and that may escalate into abusive encounters; also see Katsurada & Sugawara, 2000, for a study on the relationship between mothers' attributions for a child's aggressiveness and the mothers' own negative behavior). Using a social information-processing model of child physical abuse, Wilson and Whipple argued that physically abusive parents tend toward making attributions for their child's misbehavior (e.g., temper tantrums) that are more internal and general and that assign blame and age-related knowledge to the child for his or her actions (i.e., "She should have known better"). The explanation for the type of attributions made by abusive parents may be due in part to dysfunctional beliefs about child-rearing, noting the important ways in which cognitions may influence one another. (For an investigation of abuse and poor attribution-making in couples, see Schweinle & Ickes, 2002; for an investigation on the relationship between attributions and anger/empathy, see Betancourt & Blair, 1992).

Wilson and Whipple (2001) also learned that dysfunctional attributions in families may be linked in many cases to parents' depression. This tie between certain types of attribution-making and depression has been explored in other studies, some of which center around the family. In particular, "depressed [people may] view themselves as the cause of negative relationship events" (Fincham & Bradbury, 1993); this seems to be particularly likely for women/girls (Gotlib & McCabe, 1990), adolescents (Feiring, Taska, & Lewis, 1999), and abuse victims (Cerezo & Frias, 1994). Ties between cognitions and depression also have been found when viewing couples' interaction (e.g., Kowalik & Gotlib, 1987), and just as in other family relationships, if one couple member is depressed, both that person and his or her partner tend to attribute marital problems to the depressed individual (for a review, see Baucom & Adams, 1987).

The focus on some of the more dysfunctional or problematic occurrences of attribution-making (which also includes incest [McKenzie & Calder, 1993; Monahan, 1997; Staley & Blumberg Lapidus, 1997] and mental illness [Robinson, 1996]) has led a group of researchers to look for ways to use this knowledge to change families' attribution patterns to increase their overall relational quality. Given the particular focus on *couples'* dysfunctional attributions in much of the attribution literature, it makes sense that one of the first, most developed, and most critiqued therapies (Jacobson's [1984] behavioral marital therapy [BMT]) concerns attributions made by and for married partners. BMT is designed to help the quality of relationships by working with spouses to change their patterns of thinking. Part of this change may include decreasing the "hypersensitivity" that distressed spouses may have toward one another's behaviors (i.e., distressed spouses often notice and think more about one another's behaviors—particularly negative ones—than do nondistressed couples) and the degree to which couples react and reciprocate one another's negative behaviors. But positive behaviors may also be an issue. According to Jacobson (1984), "marital therapy will be successful only when spouses perceive each other as responding positively in the absence of any obvious or immediate return" (p. 389).

Other work has focused on the larger family and found that different families in which abuse occurred were more or less likely to be helped by therapy. Specifically, Silvester, Bentovim, Stratton, and Hanks (1995) looked at attributions spoken by family members (i.e., the statements in families' talk that could be categorized as causal or responsibility statements). They found three categories of families based on their likelihood of rehabilitation: good, uncertain, and poor. "In families rated Good, parents were more likely to attribute more control to self than child for negative outcomes. They were also more likely to nominate themselves as causing negative events" (p. 1221).

CONCLUSION

This chapter shows the foundations of attribution theories, their application to communication, and some primary areas of attribution scholarship focusing on families. Overall, attributions can be seen as a common form of causal and responsibility sense-making that is part of people's attempts at understanding the social world around them. When that social world involves their family, the ways in which people make their attributions for behavior is linked to such things as relational quality, trust, and (notably) abuse. The links between attribution-making and other important psychological and communicative factors makes the work in this area particularly important to those who wish to understand family dynamics.

If a reader wishes to take away some primary observations from this body of work, the following may be particularly memorable. As noted, a great deal of consensus exists surrounding the issue of the multidimensionality of attribution-making. That is, to really capture the variety of attributions that can be made, it is best to do so through a range of dimensions or attributes. This chapter mentioned several in its discussion of Weiner's (1986) work. Those that seem most central to intimate relationships, however, appear to be the causal dimensions of stability and of globality as well as a general responsibility index made up of attributions for blameworthiness, intentionality, and un/selfish motivation (Bradbury & Fincham, 1990). Although one family may make most of its attribution for the neglect of a household, and another may try to make sense primarily of why they get along so well, the underlying bases that describe their attributions are likely to be on the preceding dimensions.

Attributions in families also appear to be most likely under certain circumstances. One of these is the unexpectedness of a behavior (Baucom, 1987; Floyd & Voloudakis, 1999). They also tend to be made more often with behaviors thought to be negative rather than positive (Manusov et al., 1997; Wong & Weiner, 1981) and those seen as particularly salient or important (Baucom, 1987). Although it is possible that our sense-making for our own and others' actions can occur for most anything, situations that are unexpected, negative, and/or salient are most likely to take our cognitive time and energy. To change unwanted thoughts and actions in a family, people may do well to focus first on these common attributional tendencies.

Finally, as people who are interested in communication processes primarily, it is useful to look at attributions as involved in communication in at least three ways: (1) attribution-making can be seen as the *process of providing explanations to others*; (2) attributions can be viewed as a series of dimensions that differentiate one way of making sense or "giving meaning to" communication behavior from another; and (3) attributions can be seen as the "stuff of" meanings, as the actual content or meaning provided for our own or someone else's communication behavior. In all of these ways, the intersection between attributions and attribution-making with communication behavior provides fertile ground for understanding our interactions with others.

REFERENCES

Abelson, R. P., Leddo, J., & Gross, P. (1987). The strength of conjunctive explanations. *Personality and Social Psychology Bulletin, 13,* 141–155.

Baucom, D. H. (1987). Attributions in distressed relations: How can we explain them? In S. Duck & D. Perlman (Eds.), *Intimate relationships: Development, dynamics, and deterioration* (pp. 177–206). Newbury Park, CA: Sage.

Baucom, D. H., & Adams, A. N. (1987). Assessing communication in marital interaction. In K. D. O'Leary (Ed.), *Assessment of marital discord* (pp. 139–181). Hillsdale, NJ: Lawrence Erlbaum.

Benson, M. J., Arditti, J., Reguero de Atiles, J. T., & Smith, S. (1992). Intergenerational transmission: Attributions in relationships with parents and intimate others. *Journal of Family Issues, 13,* 450–465.

Berger, C. R., & Roloff, M. E. (1982). Thinking about friends and lovers: Social cognition and relational trajectories. In M. E. Roloff & C. R. Berger (Eds.), *Social cognition and communication* (pp. 151–192). Beverly Hills, CA: Sage.

Betancourt, H., & Blair, I. (1992). A cognition (attribution)-emotional model of violence in conflict situations. *Personality and Social Psychology Bulletin, 18,* 343–351.

Bradbury, T. N., & Fincham, F. D. (1990). Attributions in marriage: Review and critique. *Psychological Bulletin, 107,* 3–33.

Bradbury, T. N., & Fincham, F. D. (1992). Attributions and behavior in marital interaction. *Journal of Personality and Social Psychology, 63,* 613–628.

Bugental, D. B., Shennum, W., Frank, M., & Ekman, P. (2001). "True lies": Children's abuse history and power attributions as influences on deception detection. In V. Manusov & J. H. Harvey (Eds.), *Attribution, communication behavior, and close relationships* (pp. 248–265). Cambridge, UK: Cambridge University Press.

Cerezo, M. A., & Frias, D. (1994). Emotional and cognitive adjustment in abused children. *Child Abuse and Neglect, 18,* 923–933.

Crittenden, K. S., & Wiley, M. G. (1985). When egotism is normative: Self-presentational norms guiding attributions. *Social Psychology Quarterly, 48,* 360–365.

Feiring, C., Taska, L., & Lewis, M. (1999). Age and gender differences in children's and adolescents' adaptation to sexual abuse. *Child Abuse and Neglect, 23,* 115–116.

Fincham, F. D., Beach, R. H., Arias, I., & Brody, G. H. (1998). Children's attributions in the family: The children's relationship attribution measure. *Journal of Family Psychology, 12,* 481–482.

Fincham, F. D., & Bradbury, T. N. (1992). Assessing attributions in marriage: The relationship attribution measure. *Journal of Personality and Social Psychology, 62,* 457–468.

Fincham, F. D., & Bradbury, T. N. (1993). Marital satisfaction, depression, and attributions: A longitudinal analysis. *Journal of Personality and Social Psychology, 64,* 442–452.

Fiske, S. T., & Taylor, S. E. (1984). *Social cognition.* New York: Random House.

Flora, J., & Segrin, C. (2001). The association between accounts of relationship development events and relational and personal well-being. In V. Manusov & J. H. Harvey (Eds.), *Attribution, communication behavior, and close relationships* (pp. 59–78). Cambridge, UK: Cambridge University Press.

Floyd, K., & Voloudakis, M. (1999). Attributions for expectancy violating changes in affectionate behavior in platonic friendships. *The Journal of Psychology, 133,* 32–33.

Gotlib, I. H., & McCabe, S. B. (1990). Marriage and psychopathology. In F. D. Fincham & T. N. Bradbury (Eds.), *The psychology of marriage* (pp. 226–257). New York: Guilford.

Heider, F. (1958). *The psychology of interpersonal relations.* New York: Wiley.

Holtzworth-Munroe, A., & Jacobson, N. S. (1988). Toward a methodology for coding spontaneous causal attributions: Preliminary results with married couples. *Journal of Social and Clinical Psychology, 7,* 101–112.

Jacobson, N. S. (1984). The modification of cognitive processes in behavioral marital therapy: Integrating cognitive and behavioral intervention strategies. In K. Hahlweg & N. S. Jacobson (Eds.), *Marital interaction: Analysis and modification* (pp. 285–308). New York: Guilford.

Johnson, M. D., Karney, B. R., Rogge, R., & Bradbury, T. N. (2001). The role of marital behavior in the longitudinal association between attribution and marital quality. In V. Manusov & J. H. Harvey (Eds.), *Attribution, communication behavior, and close relationships* (pp. 193–210). Cambridge, UK: Cambridge University Press.

Jones, E. E., & Davis, K. E. (1965). From acts to dispositions: The attribution process in person perception. In L. Berkowitz (Ed.), *Advances in experimental social psychology* (Vol. 2, pp. 219–266). New York: Academic Press.

Jones, E. E., & Harris, V. A. (1967). The attribution of attitudes. *Journal of Experimental Social Psychology, 3,* 1–24.

Jones, E. E., & Nisbett, R. E. (1972). The actor and the observer: Divergent perceptions of the causes of behavior. In E. E. Jones, D. E. Kanouse, H. H. Kelley, R. E. Nisbet, S. Valins, & B. Weiner (Eds.), *Attributions: Perceiving the causes of behavior* (pp. 79–94). Morristown, NJ: General Learning Press.

Karney, B. R., Bradbury, T. N., Fincham, F. D., & Sullivan, K. T. (1994). The role of negative affectivity in the association between attributions and marital satisfaction. *Journal of Personality and Social Psychology, 66,* 413–425.

Katsurada, E., & Sugawara, A. I. (2000). Moderating effects of mothers' attribution on the relationship between their affect and parenting behaviors and children's aggressive behaviors. *Journal of Child and Family Studies, 9,* 39–51.

Kelley H. H. (1967). Attribution theory in social psychology. *Nebraska Symposium on Motivation, 14,* 192–241.

Kelley, H. H. (1971). *Attribution in social interaction.* Morristown, NJ: General Learning Press.

Koenig Kellas, J., & Trees, A. R. (2005). Rating interactional sense-making in the process of joint storytelling. In V. Manusov (Ed.), *Sourcebook of nonverbal measures: Going beyond words* (pp. 281–294). Mahwah, NJ: Lawrence Erlbaum.

Kowalik, D. L., & Gotlib, I. H. (1987). Depression and marital interaction: Concordance between intent and perception of communication. *Journal of Abnormal Psychology, 96,* 127–134.

Langer, E. J. (1978). Rethinking the role of thought in social interaction. In J. H. Harvey, W. J. Ickes, & R.F. Kidd (Eds.), *New directions in attribution research* (Vol. 2, pp. 35–58). Hillsdale, NJ: Lawrence Erlbaum.

Manusov, V. (1990). An application of attribution principles to nonverbal messages in romantic dyads. *Communication Monographs, 57,* 104–118.

Manusov, V. (1995). Intentionality attributions for naturally-occurring nonverbal behaviors in intimate relationships. In J. E. Aitken & L. J. Shedletsky (Eds.), *Intrapersonal communication processes* (pp. 343–353). Plymouth, MI: Midnight Oil Multimedia.

Manusov, V. (2001). Preface. In V. Manusov & J. H. Harvey (Eds.), *Attribution, communication behavior, and close relationships* (pp. xvii-xxi). Cambridge, UK: Cambridge University Press

Manusov, V. (2002). Thought and action: Connecting attributions to behaviors in married couples' interactions. In P. Noller & J. A. Feeney (Eds.), *Understanding marriage: Developments in the study of couple interaction* (pp. 14–31). Cambridge, UK: Cambridge University Press.

Manusov, V., Floyd, K., & Kerssen-Griep, J. (1997). Yours, mine, and ours: Mutual attributions for nonverbal behaviors in couples' interactions. *Communication Research, 24,* 234–260.

Manusov, V., & Koenig, J. (2001). The content of attributions in couples' communication. In V. Manusov & J. H. Harvey (Eds.), *Attribution, communication behavior, and close relationships* (pp. 134–152). Cambridge, UK: Cambridge University Press.

McKenzie, B. J., & Calder, P. (1993). Factors related to attributions of blame in father-daughter incest. *Psychological Reports, 73,* 1111–1122.

Monahan, K. (1997). Crocodile talk: Attributions of incestuously abused and nonabused sisters. *Child Abuse and Neglect, 21,* 19–35.

Pszyszynski, T. A., & Greenberg, J. (1981). Role of disconfirmed expectancies in the instigation of attributional processing. *Journal of Personality and Social Psychology, 40,* 31–38.

Rempel, J. K., Ross, M., & Holmes, J. G. (2001). Trust and communicated attributions in close relationships. *Journal of Personality and Social Psychology, 81,* 57–64.

Robinson, E. A. R. (1996). Causal attributions about mental illness: Relationship to family functioning. *American Journal of Orthopsychiatry, 66,* 282–296.

Ross, L. (1977). The intuitive psychologist and his shortcomings: Distortions in the attribution process. In L. Berkowitz (Ed.), *Advances in experimental social psychology* (Vol. 10, pp. 174–177). New York: Academic Press.

Schweinle, W. E., & Ickes, W. (2002). On empathic accuracy and husbands' abusiveness. In P. Noller & J. A. Feeney (Eds.), *Understanding marriage: Developments in the study of couple interaction* (pp. 228–250). Cambridge, UK: Cambridge University Press.

Seibold, D. R., & Spitzberg, B. H. (1982). Attribution theory and research: Review and implications for communication. In B. Dervin and M. J. Voight (Eds.), *Progress in communication sciences* (pp. 85–125). Norwood, NJ: Ablex.

Sillars, A. L. (1982). Attribution and communication: Are people "naïve scientists" or just naïve? In M. E. Roloff & C. R. Berger (Eds.), *Social cognition and communication* (pp. 73–106). Beverly Hills, CA: Sage.

Sillars, A. L., Leonard, K. E., Roberts, L. J., & Dun, T. (2002). Cognition and communication during marital conflict: How alcohol affects subjective coding of interaction in aggressive and nonaggressive couples. In P. Noller & J. A. Feeney (Eds.), *Understanding marriage: Developments in the study of couple interaction* (pp. 85–112). Cambridge, UK: Cambridge University Press.

Silvester, J., Bentovim, A., Stratton, P., & Hanks, H. G. I. (1995). Using spoken attributions to classify abusive families. *Child Abuse and Neglect, 19,* 1221–1233.

Spitzberg, B. (2001). The status of attribution theory *qua* theory in personal relationships. In V. Manusov & J. H. Harvey (Eds.), *Attribution, communication behavior, and close relationships* (pp. 353–371). Cambridge, UK: Cambridge University Press.

Staley, J. M., & Blumberg Lapidus, L. (1997). Attributions of responsibility in father-daughter incest in relation to gender, socio-economic status, ethnicity, and experiential differences in participants. *Journal of Clinical Psychology, 53,* 331–348.

Weiner, B. (1986). *An attributional theory of motivation and emotion.* New York: Springer-Verlag.

Wilson, S. R., & Whipple, E. E. (2001). Attributions and regulative communication by parents participating in a community-based child physical abuse prevention program. In V. Manusov & J. H. Harvey (Eds.), *Attribution, communication behavior, and close relationships* (pp. 227–247). Cambridge, UK: Cambridge University Press.

Wong, P. T. P., & Weiner, B. (1981). When people ask "why" questions, and the heuristics of attributional search. *Journal of Personality and Social Psychology, 40,* 650–663.

13

Critical Feminist Theories:
A Provocative Perspective
on Families

Julia T. Wood

Editors' Note: This chapter brings together several critical feminist theories that share a theoretical commitment to question and reform patriarchal ideologies that give rise to oppressions of a variety of kinds. Critical feminist theories have diverse fields of origin, including sociology, philosophy, linguistics, and cultural studies. The chapter provides a clear exemplar of theorizing within critical meta-theoretical discourse.

> *In their mid-twenties, Pat, Chris, and Lee decide to share their lives. They buy a home and share responsibilities for mortgage payments, mainte-nance, and housekeeping. They also provide each other with emotional support, care during sickness, and financial assistance. After 10 years pass, Pat's unmarried sibling dies, leaving an 8-year-old child, Jamie, who moves in with Pat, Chris, and Lee. Although they never officially adopt Jamie, the three adults share the emotional and financial responsibilities of raising Jamie and the logistical responsibilities for transportation and attending PTA meetings, games, and school concerts. Later, all three accompany Jamie to visit college campuses and as a foursome they decide which college Jamie will attend. Are Pat, Chris, Lee, and Jamie a family?*

A ny theory of the "family" must presuppose a meaning of family. Yet what counts as a family is neither transparent nor universal. Is family defined only by biological and adoptive connections and heterosexual marriage? Or is family defined by the norms of particular societies, in which case polygamy, polyandry, and same-sex unions are families in some societies and interracial or intertribal unions are not families in other societies? Is family an alliance to preserve estates as during the Enlightenment? Is family a matter of legal ownership such as men's ownership of wives, children, and slaves during the early centuries of America's life? Or is family defined by interpersonal processes such as affection and interdependence? If so, some marriages do not qualify as families whereas some extended networks do.

"What is a family?" is not an innocent question. The answer—or answers—depends on the particularities of specific cultures that exist in specific historical moments. For this reason, "family" is ideologically charged. That is, cultural ideas, values, beliefs, structures, and practices shape our understandings of what family is and is not, and how families function. The often unrecognized and unchallenged ideology that informs understandings of family in Western culture marks the starting point of *critical feminist theories* of family, which interrogate values inherent in and reproduced by conventional views of family and explore how alternative perspectives and the ideologies that inform them might reframe understandings of family and aspects of family life that are deemed significant.

This chapter examines critical feminist theories to see what they might teach us about families—as a conceptual category and as lived experience. The first section of the chapter defines critical feminist theories. The second section of the chapter identifies key issues and questions about families that grow out of critical feminist theories. Finally, I assess critical feminist theories.

CRITICAL FEMINIST THEORIES

Critical feminist theories arise from two distinct, yet often overlapping intellectual traditions. First, they belong to a category known as critical theories. Second, because they grow out of feminist theory, they focus on disadvantage based on sex, gender, and other factors, which are not foci of all critical theories. Thus, to understand critical feminist theories we must have working knowledge of both critical and feminist frameworks.

Critical Theories

Critical theories aim to identify prevailing structures and practices that create or uphold disadvantage, inequity, or oppression and to point the way toward alternatives that promote more egalitarian possibilities for individuals, relationships, groups, and societies. Unlike postpositivist theories, critical theories do not embrace explanation and control as primary goals. Instead, critical theories are centrally concerned with social change—with making a difference in how cultures operate and how those operations affect people in material and nonmaterial ways.

Critical theories investigate interactive influence between cultural practices and structures; and the political, material, social, personal, professional, and economic lives of members of a culture, especially those who do not occupy dominant status and the privileges it confers. In other words, critical theories ask how cultural structures and practices shape the lives of members of a culture and conversely, how members' lives and activities shape cultural structures and practices. Critical theorists are particularly interested in identifying how dominant groups manage to privilege their interests and perspectives and impose them on less-powerful groups. At the same time, critical theorists want to understand how oppressed groups become empowered and, in some cases, change dominant patterns and perhaps the ideologies that underlie them.

Critical theorists are intensely interested in struggles between competing ideologies, or sets of ideas that organize groups' understandings of reality (Hall, 1986, 1989). For example, they ask how ideology defines the parameters and sites of struggle between dominant and nondominant races, middle-class and working-class citizens, heterosexuals and nonheterosexuals, and men and women. In each case, there is a dominant group and a less-powerful group or groups, and they participate in what Stuart Hall (1989) called the theatre of struggle, which is an ongoing battle over whose voices, whose perspectives, whose values gain a hearing and cultural legitimacy.

In focusing on ideological control, critical theorists trace how power is deployed and resisted. In doing so, many critical theorists pay attention to both formal kinds of power (e.g., laws that define who can marry) and informal kinds of power (e.g., everyday practices that communicate normative understandings of who is and is not a family). This allows critical theorists to critique not only official forms of power such as laws, but also "tiny, everyday" practices (Foucault, 1984, p. 211) that reproduce and sustain particular ideologies and their attendant inequities. By studying how dominant and marginal groups enact and resist power, critical theorists aim to identify how cultures work and to challenge, disrupt, and remake cultural life so that it better reflects and represents the interests and perspectives of all who comprise it.

Feminist Theories

Influenced by media (mis)representations of feminism and feminists, some people think feminism means hatred of men, burning bras, and so forth. People who have studied feminist history and philosophy, however, are more likely to define *feminism* as the belief that men and women are equal and should have equal respect and opportunities in all spheres of life: personal, social, work, and public. Extending this definition, feminists aim to identify, critique, and change inequities and discrimination, particularly those that are based on sex and gender (Wood, 1995). This broad goal of feminist theorists is a launching pad for diverse intellectual projects.

Central to feminist theories are two widely misunderstood concepts. First, there is confusion between the distinct, yet often conflated concepts: *gender* and *sex*. Sex is a biological category—male or female—that is determined genetically. Gender is social definitions of masculinity and femininity at specific historical moments and in specific cultural contexts. Put another way, gender is the social meanings attached to sex by others and ourselves as well as our ways of embodying—or refusing to embody—those social meanings. Gender influences expectations and perceptions of women and men, as well as the roles, opportunities, and material circumstances of women's and men's lives.

Judith Butler (1990, 1993) argued that there is nothing "normal" or "natural" about gender. She rejected the idea that gender exists prior to particular actions. Instead, claimed Butler, gender comes into being as we perform it in everyday life. We simultaneously enact and produce gender through a variety of mundane, performative practices such as dress, gestures, and verbal acts that embody—and, thus, confer an illusory realness on—normative codes of masculinity and femininity. According to Butler, gender exists if and only if people act in ways that compel belief in the reality of masculinity and femininity. Butler's theory of gender as a learned, performed identity has obvious implications for heterosexuals and their family lives. Perhaps less obviously, Butler's argument that gender is not objective or natural implies that any gendered identity is as real (and as illusory) as any other. Thus, transvestites, gays, transsexuals, lesbians, bisexuals, and interesexed and transgendered people have ontological status equivalent to that of heterosexuals. Their identities are as real—or illusory—as those of heterosexuals.

The second central concept for feminist theories is *patriarchy*, which is a system that reflects primarily the interests, perspectives, and experiences of men as a group. Feminist theorists note that many cultures, including those in the West, were organized predominantly by white, professedly heterosexual men who relied on their experiences, needs, values, preferences, interests, and perspectives to order society. As a result, our social world is set up in ways that do not fully reflect women's or minorities' experiences, needs, values, perspectives, interests, and perspectives. Feminist theorists do not assume that men necessarily organized society in a deliberate effort to oppress women and minorities. The point is that when Western cultures were established, men held positions of public leadership, and women did not. Men's standpoint did not include many experiences typical for women, such as being on call for children 24 hours a day, promoting harmony and cooperation between members of families, engaging in the thankless, repetitive drudgery of keeping a home clean and inviting, and doing all the work to plan, prepare, serve, and clean up after meals. More prominent in a male standpoint would be activities that men routinely enact—working outside of the home, engaging in competitive activities from football to war, and seeing the home as a haven graced by mannerly children, clean clothes, and well-prepared meals.

Patriarchy does not refer to individual men or individual men's oppression of women. Allan Johnson (1997) explained that "'patriarchy' doesn't refer to me or any man or collection of men, but to a kind of society in which men *and* women participate" (pp. 4–5). Agreeing, Dorothy Smith (1987) noted that patriarchy "is not a conspiracy among men that they impose on women. It is a complementary social process between men and women" (p. 34). Because patriarchy was set up a long time ago, it is a system that predates you, me, and others living today. It might be that if today we could organize society from scratch, we would choose a different model. But the patriarchal model is the one that we have inherited—modified in some ways (women are no longer men's property) but still patriarchal.

Critical Feminist Theories

Critical feminist theories identify, question, and seek to reform patriarchal ideologies that give rise to oppression, as well as the asymmetrical rights, opportunities, roles, and so forth. Note that the critique mounted by critical feminists theorists is not confined to matters of sex or gender inequality. Also under critique are efforts to devalue and oppress any groups that do not reflect the standpoint and interests of those who hold dominant positions in cultural life. The dominant masculinist and heteronormative ideology of Western culture produces a decidedly limited understanding of families. We are relatively uninformed about nonheterosexual and nonpatriarchal family forms, processes, and functions. Likewise, we have meager understanding of women's and children's perspectives on family life. Attending to these neglected facets of and perspectives on families is a priority for critical feminist theory and research.

Within the broad category of critical feminist theories there are many specific schools of thought, such as Foucauldian, socialist and Marxist, performative, postcolonial, and psychoanalytic—not all of which are mutually exclusive theoretical camps. In this short chapter, we cannot examine the entire range of critical feminist theories. Instead, we will discuss five broad lines of inquiry that typify—but certainly do not exhaust—the interests of critical feminist theories.

RESEARCH FOCI ENCOURAGED BY CRITICAL FEMINIST THEORIES OF FAMILY

Because critical feminist theories question dominant ideologies, they raise distinctive questions about how conventional Western structures and practices of families tend to create advantage for some people and disadvantage for others. Five questions illustrate critical feminist theories' approach to families.

Who Should Be Included in Families?

Some critical feminist theorists reject the very idea of binary genders, sexes, and sexual orientations. They claim that it is arbitrary to divide humans into two and only two "opposite" sexes and genders, and that sexual orientation is not necessarily fixed. This leads some critical feminist theorists to question why marriage is restricted to heterosexuals (at least if the recent ruling in Massachusetts is vacated). Whose interests are (and are not) served by this limitation? Clearly, the restriction reflects and reinforces heteronormativity as a dominant value in Western culture. Simultaneously, it defines all outside of that realm as other, less legitimate, and less entitled to a substantial set of rights and entitlements. Writing in 2002, Michael Warner asserted that "marriage sanctifies some couples at the expense of others. It is selective legitimacy" (p. 260). This provokes a related question: "How" asked Wendy Brown and Janet Halley (2002), "did we become a people for whom domestic, economically interdependent, long-term, coupled and monogamous intimacy is *the* paradigm of adult intimacy itself" (p. 27)? Why should the state have the right to assume such a central role in defining and regulating intimate human relations?

It is important to distinguish between desiring to marry and desiring to have the right to marry. Not all gays, lesbians, and other people who are denied marriage wish to marry. Some nonheterosexuals do not want to marry; do not want to participate in the institution of marriage as it has been defined. For them, marrying would entail the risk of yielding to the values of normative (hetero)sexuality, which are arguably incompatible with queer politics (Butler, 2002). Speaking to this point, Butler (2002) argued that "a more radical social transformation is precisely at stake when we refuse, for instance, to allow kinship to be reducible to 'family,' or when we refuse to allow the field of sexuality to become gauged against the marriage norm" (p. 255). Concurring, Warner (2002) resisted "the notion that the state should be allowed to accord legitimacy to some kinds of consensual sex but not others, or to confer respectability on some people's sexuality but not others'" (p. 264). And a member of the New York Redstockings pointedly noted that it may be unwise "to fight for the rights of the coupled rather than the rights of *everyone* to have decent health insurance, visit friends in the hospital" (Jay, 2003, p. 213). In other words, there are reasons to be skeptical of policies or laws that would give nonheterosexuals the right to be legally united if doing so gives the state authority to regulate their sexual lives and politics.

Should Marriage Function as a System for Distributing Rights?

Social and legal legitimacy are not all that is at stake in deciding what counts as marriage or family. Warner critiqued "the menu of privileges and prohibitions, incentives and disincentives directly tied to marriage by the state" (p. 274). Why is it, for instance, that a person's ability to pass an estate without taxes to a loved one is tied to the state's sanctioning the legitimacy of the relationship? Why is one's ability to cover a loved one on an insurance plan similarly governed by the state? These are the questions that led Jack Baker, who was in a gay relationship, to apply for a marriage license in Minnesota. In his arguments to the court, Baker claimed that that marriage is "a distribution mechanism for many rights and privileges" (Baker quoted in Warner, 2002, p. 263; see also Warner's discussion of this case including Teal, 1971). Baker argued that denying these rights to gays was discriminatory and that it violated the constitutional guarantee of equal rights. Baker lost.

From a critical feminist perspective, a better solution than allowing anyone to marry would be to uncouple the range of financial, legal, and medical rights and entitlements from marriage. Columnist Michael Kinsley (2003) proposed—half in jest?—that marriage be privatized, which would disjoin consensual unions between adults from government sanction. Religious organizations could still provide union ceremonies to couples; lending institutions could still provide joint tenancy and tenancy in the entirety mortgages to any couples or groups they chose; insurance companies could still provide coverage to dependents, although they might be defined by individual companies. As Kinsley pointed out, this would truly "get the government out of our bedrooms."

As radical as this proposal may seem, it is not entirely fictional. France has instituted pacts of civil solidarity (PACS), which decouple rights from marriage. PACs are an option to marriage for any two people—gay, straight, lesbian, intersexed, transsexed, or transgendered—who are unrelated by blood. (Germany passed similar legislation but it designates the unions as restricted to gays.) PACs give legal recognition on the basis of living arrangements and do not attempt to define or regulate sexual activity. They allow any two people who live together to hold property jointly, inherit, provide health care, gain child custody, and so forth.

How Do Centralized and Decentralized Forms of Power Regulate Families?

Families are regulated by laws and also by normative processes and practices that are entrenched in social life. Assuming a rough equivalence between freedom and individual rights, Western liberal traditions place priority on individuals' equality before the law, or state. Without doubt, laws are important. As Catharine Mackinnon (2003) noted: "while a legal change may not always make a social change, sometimes it helps, and law *un*changed can make social change impossible"

(p. 447). Laws establish rights and responsibilities, financial and otherwise, of parents, spouses/partners, employers, and so forth.

But laws are not the only ways that families are regulated. Many aspects of family life that are not subject to laws or not regulated exclusively by laws are sites of continuing inequality between women and men. Some critical theorists argue that formal and centralized juridical powers such as the law are not the only—and perhaps not the primary—basis by which families are regulated and by which they are granted or not granted legitimacy (Brown & Halley, 2002). While recognizing the importance of juridical power, critical feminist theorists also attend to social-normative forces that define and regulate families. In making this move, critical feminist theorists often draw on the work of French philosopher Michel Foucault (1980, 1983, 1984, 1994), who asserted that the juridical, or sovereign, model of power errs in characterizing power as exclusively centralized, uniform, and repressive. This conception of power, Foucault claimed, neglects dispersed, omnipresent, variable, and often invisible practices that operate locally both to discipline individuals and groups and to resist sovereign power. He reasoned that "the general juridical form that guaranteed a system of rights that were egalitarian in principle was supported by these tiny, everyday, physical mechanisms, by all those systems of micropower that are essentially nonegalitarian and asymmetrical" (1984, p. 211).

According to Foucault (1980), "nothing in society will be changed if the mechanisms of power that function outside, below and alongside the State apparatuses, on a much more minute and everyday level, are not also changed" (p. 60). To pursue analysis of disciplinary power, Foucault declared, "we need to cut off the King's head" (p. 121); that is, we need to develop a political theory that does not center law and sovereign power. In other words, Foucault argued that power is as likely to flow bottom up as to flow top down. To identify, analyze, and negotiate bottom-up power, we need to focus on localized sites of power such as mundane interactions and everyday practices. In analyzing how power is wielded and resisted, Foucault (1980) advised "beginning from the lowest level, [to understand] how mechanisms of power have been able to function . . . at the effective level of the family, of the immediate environment, of the cells and most basic units of society" (p. 100).

Building on Foucault's work, Biddie Martin (1988, 1997) argued that struggles to change existing power relations do not necessarily take the form of a "frontal attack on the state led by the One revolutionary subject, [but consist of] local struggles that undermine institutional power where it reveals itself . . . as it operates in homes, schools, prisons, therapists' offices, and factories, wherever the work of normalization is carried on" (pp. 10–11). Informed by Foucault, many critical theorists assume that individuals are regulated, or disciplined, by a range of social powers such as masculine and heterosexual norms that circulate in everyday life. Within this view of power, equality before the law is insufficient to ensure genuine equality for individuals and groups. Full equality *does* require equality before the law; that is a necessary but not a sufficient criterion for full equality. In addition, genuine equality requires radical changes in normative behaviors and attitudes that shape everyday experiences. Without abandoning insistence that laws and other structures recognize the equality of all people, a critical feminist perspective also notices and critiques the multitude of everyday practices that enforce boundaries on marriage and family.

How Should Responsibility for Family be Structured and Practiced?

Critical feminist theories also raise questions about the responsibilities for caregiving in families. A first question is this: Why are women expected to provide most of the care for the home, as well as children, parents, parents-in-law, and other relatives? Study after study documented the persistence of gendered patterns in caregiving, whereby women do the vast majority, regardless of whether they also work outside of the home (Maushart, 2001; Oakley, 2002; Steil, 1997). This pattern perhaps was functional and even equitable in an earlier era, at least for the minority of heterosexual families that were white and middle- or upper-class, in which the man worked outside of the home and the woman inside of it, and in which the marriage remained intact. This pattern is no longer functional or fair.

A gendered division of labor for home and children is blatantly dysfunctional and unfair today because the vast majority of heterosexual families in the United States today have two wage earners; and in 30.7 percent of married, two-worker households the woman earns more than the man (Tyre & McGinn, 2003). Despite the growing symmetry between women's and men's work in the paid labor force, housework and care of children, parents, and other relatives continues to be done primarily by women (Jena, 1999; Maushart, 2001; Oakley, 2002; Risman & Godwin, 2001). On average, women do 70 percent more housework than men (Johnson, 2002). Dubbing this the "second shift," sociologist Arlie Hochschild (Hochschild with Machung, 2003) reported that the majority of wives employed outside of their homes complete their shifts in the paid labor force only to come home to a second shift of work.

Not only do women work more than men at home, but the work they do is generally more taxing and less gratifying. For instance, whereas many of the contributions men typically make are sporadic, variable, and flexible in timing (for example, mowing the lawn), the tasks women typically do are repetitive, routine, and constrained by deadlines. Women are also more likely to do multiple tasks simultaneously—for example, helping a child with homework while preparing dinner. Whereas mothers tend to be constantly on duty, fathers more typically volunteer for irregular and fun child care activities such as a trip to the zoo.

Another way in which women's contributions to home life are greater is in terms of *psychological responsibility*, which is the responsibility to remember, plan, and make sure that family responsibilities are met (Hochschild with Machung, 2003). For instance, partners may agree to share responsibility for taking children to doctors and dentists, but it is typically the woman who is expected to remember when checkups and inoculations are due, schedule appointments, notice when a child needs attention, and keep track of whose turn it is to take the child. Similarly, partners may share responsibility for preparing meals, but women usually take on the associated responsibilities of planning menus, keeping an inventory of food and cooking supplies, figuring out how to adapt to various family members' shifting dietary preferences and needs, making shopping lists, and doing the shopping. All the planning and organization is a psychological responsibility that is often not counted in couples' agreements for sharing the work of a family.

Illuminating the link between inequity in domestic life and patriarchal and capitalist ideologies, critical feminist theorists point out that Western culture gives lip service to the importance of caring, but it does not reward it with status or income. People who care for others in the home are "just homemakers." Those who take caregiving jobs in the labor force are paid poorly. In the United States, for instance, many child care workers are paid less than people who park cars or clean offices (Folbre, 2001). And in families in the West, as well as elsewhere, the responsibility for providing the care that society does not value tends to fall predominantly on women (Maushart, 2001; Oakley, 2002; Wood, 1994).

But critical feminist critiques of responsibilities for caring are not confined to how individual families operate. Instead, they interrogate the prevailing conception of families as self-contained, self-sufficient entities that can, do, or should take care of themselves (Drusine, 2003; Harrington, 1999; Levine, 2003). Emphasizing that this is neither necessary nor universal, critical feminist scholars note that in other societies— Sweden, France, and Norway, for example—the state assumes substantial responsibility for providing conditions that foster the well-being of families, which are not necessarily defined exclusively by blood or heterosexual union. Social responsibility for caring for families is woven into cultural structures in a variety of ways: making paid parental leaves mandatory for all workers, requiring workplaces to reduce the hours for "full-time" employment for new parents, and providing government-sponsored day care and medical care for all children.

Which Aspects of Family Life Should Be Foci of Research?

In her classic book, *Everyday Life as Problematic,* Dorothy Smith (1987) observed that patriarchal perspectives that are inscribed in social sciences have led researchers to define and study social life from the perspective of men. Relevant to families, one result is a tendency to emphasize what is observable and deemed important from a masculine perspective and, simultaneously, to veil from view a host of activities that are generally performed by women. Activities such as shopping, cleaning, cooking, supervising home maintenance, and caring for children and relatives make it possible for men and women to engage in activities outside of the home. Yet these essential activities have not been a major focus of research on families. They, along with women, have been relegated to the periphery of family research.

Critical feminist theorists ask a question that rattles conventional perspectives on families: What would theories of family look like if researchers focused on aspects of family life that are not accented (and sometimes not evident) from a patriarchal perspective? Put another way, what if research began not with men and men's experiences, but with women and women's experiences in and understandings of families (Harding, 1989, 1991)? If families were not viewed from a patriarchal perspective, we might ask questions such as the following:

- Why are there numerous articles and books about the challenge of reconciling motherhood and a career in the paid labor force, but few on the challenge of reconciling fatherhood and an income-producing career?

- Why do we use language to recognize it when men "help out" with home chores and parenting, whereas women who do the same (or more) are called simply women, wives, or mothers?
- Upon marrying, why does men's participation in housework decline while women's increases (Maushart, 2001)?
- Why do some researchers label child care as "shared" if a father spends time with children without the mother present at least once a week (McMahon, 1999)?
- Why is homemaking typically measured by concrete outcomes (cooking dinner) instead of more holistic processes (talking with family members to learn food preferences, making shopping lists, doing shopping, unpacking and storing purchases, and so forth)?
- Why do married men feel more entitled than married women to leisure time in the home (Coulter & Helms-Erikson, 1997; Greer, 1999)?
- Why is sex discrimination in job assignments illegal in the paid labor force but routine in the family (Maushart, 2001)?
- Why are men at least twice as likely as women to inflict intimate partner violence (Archer, 2000a, 2000b; Department of Justice, 2000; Holtzworth-Munroe, Bates, Smutzler, & Sandin, 1997)?
- How do patriarchal structures limit women's options for leaving violent relationships (Yllo & Straus, 1990; Wood, in press)?

Assessment of Critical, Feminist Theories of Family

By most of the criteria routinely used to assess theories, critical feminist theories of family fare well. They meet the criterion of scope by offering broad frameworks for studying and thinking about family in particular cultural and temporal contexts. They meet the criterion of utility, or pragmatism, by providing practical understandings of how family is currently constructed and by critiquing problems in current family formations and functioning. In limiting themselves to relatively few concepts (gender, power, dominance, and so forth), they meet the criterion of parsimony. How well critical feminist theories meet the criterion of testability is a matter of controversy. Some would say that the evidence of male dominance and privilege is both pervasive and indisputable. Others would say that concepts such as dominance and privilege are so vague that they are not amenable to rigorous testing. What you consider an adequate test and convincing proof will shape your evaluation of the testability of these theories.

Perhaps the criterion on which critical feminist theories most clearly excel is heurism—they spark new thoughts, original questions, and out-of-the-box thinking about what families are and might be. Even if we are uncomfortable with some of the issues and options highlighted by critical feminist theories, they clearly challenge conventional ways of thinking and offer us new insights and choices as we go about the business of organizing our intimate relationships, thinking about how others organize theirs, and reflecting on the ways in which cultural structures and practices impinge on families.

CONCLUSION

So what is family from a critical feminist perspective? From this theoretical viewpoint, which aspects of family merit study? Which aspects of family should be challenged and changed? There are no neat answers to these questions. What is clear, however, is that critical feminist theories do not assume the rightness of dominant definitions of the family, prevailing views of which aspects of family life matter, or domestic conventions with which many people have become comfortable (or resigned). Instead, critical feminist theories question not only established views per se, but also the interests they do and do not serve. In addition, critical feminist theories contest heteronormativity and patriarchy, which underlie conventional Western views of family and, by extension, customary assignments of women's and men's roles in family life. Finally, critical feminist theories ask how alternatives to prevailing views of family might alter both understandings of family life and concrete experiences in the families to which people belong.

REFERENCES

Archer, J. (2000a). Sex differences in aggression between heterosexual partners: A meta-analytic review. *Psychological Bulletin, 126,* 651–680.

Archer, J. (2000b). Sex differences in physical aggression to partners: A reply to Frieze (2000), O'Leary (2000), and White, Smith, Koss, and Figueredo (2000). *Psychological Bulletin, 126,* 697–702.

Brown, W., & Halley, J. (Eds.). (2002). *Left legalism, left critique.* Durham, NC: Duke University Press.

Butler, J. (1990). Performative acts and gender constitution: An essay in phenomenology and feminist theory. In S. Case (Ed.), *Performing feminisms: Feminist critical theory and theatre* (pp. 270–282). Baltimore: Johns Hopkins University Press.

Butler, J. (1993). *Bodies that matter: On the discursive limits of "sex."* New York: Routledge.

Butler, J. (2002). Is kinship always already heterosexual? In W. Brown & J. Halley (Eds.), *Left legalism, left critique* (pp. 229–258). Durham, NC: Duke University Press.

Coulter, A., & Helms-Erikson, H. (1997). Work and family from a dyadic perspective: Variations in inequality. In S. W. Duck (Ed.), *Handbook of personal relationships* (2nd ed., pp. 487–503). West Sussex, UK: Wiley.

Department of Justice. (2000). Washington, DC: Justice Department's Bureau of Justice Statistics. Publication # NCJ 167237.

Drusine, H. (2003). "Just a housewife!" In R. Morgan (Ed.), *Sisterhood is forever* (pp. 342–348). New York: Washington Square Press.

Folbre, N. (2001). *The invisible heart: Economics and family values.* New York: New Press.

Foucault, M. (1980). *Power/knowledge: Selected interviews and other writings: 1972–1977.* C. Gordon (Ed.). Brighton, UK: Harvester.

Foucault, M. (1983). The subject and power. In H. Drefus & P. Rabinow (Eds.), *Michel Foucault: Beyond structuralism and hermeneutics.* Chicago: University of Chicago Press.

Foucault, M. (1984). *The Foucault reader.* P. Rabinow (Ed.). New York: Pantheon Books.

Foucault, M. (1994). (Writing as Florence, M.). Foucault, Michel, 1926. In G. Gutting (Ed.), *The Cambridge Companion to Foucault* (pp. 314–319). New York: Cambridge University Press.

Greer, G. (1999). *The whole woman.* London: Transworld.

Hall, S. (1986). The problem of ideology—Marxism without guarantees. *Journal of Communication Inquiry, 10,* 28–44.

Hall, S. (1989). Ideology. In E. Barnouw et al. (Eds.), *International encyclopedia of communication* (Vol. 2, pp. 307–311). New York: Oxford University Press.

Harding, S. (1989). Is there a feminist method? In N. Tuana (Ed.), *Feminism and science* (pp. 17–32). Bloomington, IN: Indiana University Press.

Harding, S. (1991). *Whose science? Whose knowledge?: Thinking from women's lives.* Ithaca: Cornell University Press.

Harrington, M. (1999). *Care and equality: Inventing a new family politics.* New York: Knopf.

Hochschild, A., with Machung, A. (2003). *The second shift: Working parents and the revolution at home* (Rev. ed.). New York: Viking/Penguin.

Holtzworth-Munroe, A., Bates, L., Smutzler, N., & Sandin, E. (1997). A brief review of the research on husband violence. I: Maritally violent versus nonviolent men. *Aggression and Violent Behavior, 2,* 65–99.

Jay, K. (2003). Confessions of a worrywart: Ruminations on a lesbian feminist overview. In R. Morgan (Ed.), *Sisterhood is forever* (pp. 212–221). New York: Washington Square Press.

Jena, S. (1999). Job, life satisfaction and occupational stress of women. *Social Science International, 15,* 75–80.

Johnson, A. (1997). *The gender knot: Unraveling our patriarchal legacy.* Philadelphia: Temple University Press.

Johnson, D. (2002, March 25). Until dust do us part. *Newsweek,* p. 41.

Kinsley, M. (2003, July 10). My proposal: Privatize marriage. *Raleigh News and Observer,* p. 13A.

Levine, S. (2003). Parenting: A new social contract. In R. Morgan (Ed.), *Sisterhood is forever* (pp. 85–93). New York: Washington Square Press.

Mackinnon, C. (2003). Women and the law: The power to change. In R. Morgan (Ed.), *Sisterhood is forever* (pp. 447–455). New York: Washington Square Press.

Martin, B. (1988). Feminism, criticism, and Foucault. In I. Diamond & L. Quinby (Eds.), *Feminism and Foucault: Reflections on resistance* (pp. 3–20). Boston: Northeastern University Press.

Martin, B. (1997). Foucault and the subject of feminism. *Social Theory and Practice, 23,* 102–128.

Maushart, S. (2001). *Wifework: What marriage really means for women.* New York: Bloomsbury.

McMahon, A. (1999). *Taking care of men.* Cambridge, UK: Cambridge University Press.

Oakley, A. (2002). *Gender on planet earth.* New York: The New Press.

Risman, B., & Godwin, S. (2001). Twentieth-century changes in economic work and family. In D. Vannoy (Ed.), *Gender mosaics* (pp. 134–144). Los Angeles: Roxbury.

Smith, D. (1987). *The everyday world as problematic: A feminist sociology.* Boston: Northeastern University Press.

Steil, J. (1997). *Marital equality.* Thousand Oaks, CA: Sage.

Teal, D. (1971). *The gay militants.* New York: Stein and Day.

Tyre, P. & McGinn, D. (2003, May 12). She works, he doesn't. *Newsweek,* 44–54.

Warner, M. (2002). Beyond gay marriage. In W. Brown & J. Halley (Eds.), *Left legalism, left critique* (pp. 259–289). Durham, NC: Duke University Press.

Wood, J. T. (1994). *Who cares?: Women, care and culture.* Carbondale, IL: Southern Illinois University Press.

Wood, J. T. (1995). Feminist scholarship and the study of personal and social relationships. *Journal of Social and Personal Relationships, 12,* 103–120.

Wood, J. T. (in press). Gendered power, aggression and violence in heterosexual relationships. In D. Canary & K. Dindia (Eds.), *Sex differences and similarities in communication* (2nd ed.). Mahwah, NJ: Lawrence Erlbaum.

Yllo, K., & Straus, M. (1990). Patriarchy and violence against wives: The impact of structural and normative factors. In M. Straus & R. Gelles (Eds.), *Physical violence in American families: Risk factors and adaptations to violence in 8,145 families* (pp. 383–399). New Brunswick, NJ: Transaction Press.

could advance knowledge about family communication and discuss strengths and limitations of the theory.

COMPONENTS AND EMPIRICAL
FINDINGS OF EMOTION REGULATION THEORY

The cornerstone of emotion regulation theory is the concept of *meta-emotion*, that is, one's emotions about emotions. Gottman et al. (1997) proposed that parents' meta-emotion structure exerts a potent influence on their children's developmental outcomes. Meta-emotion structure refers broadly to the executive functions that govern one's experience and expression of emotions. This entails parents' philosophy about emotions, metaphors for characterizing emotions, and thoughts and feelings regarding certain emotions. In their research, Gottman et al. operationalize meta-emotion structure as parents' awareness of specific emotions in themselves and their children, and parents' coaching of emotions in their children.

Gottman et al. (1997) conducted in-depth interviews with parents regarding their meta-emotions for anger and sadness. Their analysis revealed two fundamental and contrasting parental styles. *Emotion-coaching* (EC) parents exhibit five key features. First, the parent is aware of the child's emotions, including lower-intensity emotions. EC parents "connect with their children when their children are being emotional before the negative emotion escalates to a high intensity" (Gottman et al., 1997, p. 85). Second, the EC parent views the child's negative affect as an opportunity for intimacy or teaching. The child's experience of negative emotions is seen as healthy and a vehicle for growth. Third, the EC parent assists the child in translating feelings into words, facilitating the child's labeling of feelings. Fourth, the EC parent empathizes with the child's emotion by communicating an understanding and acceptance of the emotion in the situation in which the child experiences it. Fifth, EC parents help their children in problem-solving. They set limits on behavior, describe consequences for inappropriate behavior, assist the child in setting goals in the emotion-inducing situation, and help the child explore strategies to accomplish those goals. These characteristics of EC parents stand in contrast to the profile of *emotion-dismissing* (ED) parents. ED parents do not possess a detailed language for describing emotions, fail to discern lower-intensity emotions in themselves and their children, and perceive negative emotions as deleterious and aversive. They teach their children that they "should minimize, endure, and get over the negative affective state quickly" (Gottman et al., 1997, p. 85).

Gottman and colleagues (1997) recognized that "meta-emotion variables do not stand alone but are contextualized in a web of variables that describe parenting" (p. 9). Thus, meta-emotions are associated with other aspects of parenting behavior. For example, when engaged in an instructional task with their child, ED parents show frustration; take over for the child as soon as the child has trouble with the task; wait for the child to make a mistake and criticize the child's performance; and escalate the criticism to derisive humor, mockery, and belittling. Gottman et al. (1997) referred to this type of parenting as *Derogatory*. EC parents avoid Derogatory parenting. Instead, they engage in a positive form of parenting labeled *Scaffolding/Praising*, which provides a structured, responsive, engaged, and affectionate frame for conducting the task at hand. Parents high on the Scaffolding/Praising dimension calmly provide the child with just enough information to begin the task, they are uninvolved in the child's mistakes, and they praise the child's performance when the child does something correctly.

Gottman's program of research indicated that EC is associated with a number of desirable developmental outcomes for children (Gottman et al., 1997). Children with EC parents at age 5 demonstrated the following outcomes at age 8: (a) better social relations with their peers, (b) higher scores in math and reading (controlling for IQ), (c) better ability to focus attention, and (d) fewer infectious illnesses. Interestingly, these effects cannot be explained by a simple social learning or modeling of skills exhibited by EC parents. What accounts for the positive developmental outcomes of EC, since it is not modeling of EC skills? The answer, according to Gottman et al. (1997), is that EC cultivates emotional intelligence in children (e.g., Goleman, 1995; Salovey & Mayer, 1990). Their emotional self-awareness allows them to develop the ability to regulate emotions and to self-soothe and focus attention when emotionally stressed. It is this emotional self-awareness that enables children to fare well in middle childhood, when social competence and peer acceptance require kids to act cool and calm and to avoid drawing undue attention to themselves and their emotions (Gottman, 2001). As Gottman et al. (1997) elaborated:

> In middle school these abilities are manifest by inhibiting displays of distress and inhibiting aggression when teased and instead acting emotionally unflappable, and in being able to enter an ongoing

peer group with ease and awareness instead of with the lumbering bravado of the socially rejected child. (p. 102)

This skill at regulating emotions is indexed in two ways: (a) the child's regulatory physiology, and (b) the child's ability to inhibit negative affect.

Gottman et al. (1997) proposed that the influence of parental meta-emotion structures on the developmental outcomes of offspring is mediated by the child's regulatory physiology. Previous research demonstrated that children with higher basal vagal tone (i.e., physiological reactivity mediated by the tenth cranial nerve) are better able to focus attention and regulate emotions (e.g., Fox, 1989; Porges, 1973, 1984; for review see Porges, 1991). Consistent with this line of research, Gottman et al. (1997) discovered that children of EC parents exhibit higher baseline vagal tone, which evidences heightened reactivity to stimuli. At the same time, children of EC parents are better able to *suppress* vagal tone, which means that they can calm themselves more quickly and return to a regulated state. Gottman and Katz (2002) found that children with higher basal vagal tone have both a larger heart rate increase and a faster recovery during stressful interactions with a parent, compared with children with lower vagal tone.

Children of EC parents also show the ability to inhibit negative affect as assessed by the amount of effort parents exert in down-regulating their child's negative affect. The ability to suppress vagal tone apparently facilitates children's emotional regulation. Gottman et al. (1997) found that "the greater the child's ability to suppress vagal tone at age 5, the less the parents had to down-regulate the child's negative affects, inappropriate behavior, and overexcitement at age 8" (p. 171). Similarly, Gottman and Katz (2002) reported that children's basal vagal tone and suppression of vagal tone at age 4–5 predicted mothers' ratings of their children's ability to regulate emotions at age 8. Gottman et al. (1997) provided convincing evidence that most of the connections between EC and children's developmental outcomes are mediated by the children's regulatory physiology (i.e., vagal tone and vagal tone suppression) and ability to regulate emotions (as perceived by their parents).

EC also provides a buffer for children whose parents' marriage is marked by hostile conflict. Gottman et al. (1997) found that although such children still experience daily stress and sadness due to the declining marriage, the negative effects on academic achievement, peer relations, behavioral problems, and infectious illness are mitigated when at least one parent exhibits an EC meta-emotion structure.

The positive effects of parental EC extend beyond the children. There is evidence that the EC dynamics carry over into the marriage. Gottman et al. (1997) demonstrated that EC parents exhibit higher marital satisfaction, fewer serious considerations of separation and divorce, less likelihood of divorce, and better physical health. Moreover, "couples who have an emotion coaching meta-emotion structure are also more validating and affectionate during marital conflict, they are less disgusted, belligerent, and contemptuous during marital conflict, and the husbands are less likely to stonewall" (p. 210). Although causal direction is not determined yet, the authors speculate that meta-emotion precedes marital quality. Interestingly, *discrepancy* between husbands and wives in their emotion coaching tendencies was highly predictive of marital instability.

EMOTION REGULATION THEORY
AND FAMILY COMMUNICATION

If one considers emotion regulation theory to be a framework regarding meta-emotion applied to the family context, then it could be considered a "theory in family communication." However, we feel a strong case can be made that emotion regulation theory qualifies as a "theory *of* family communication." Although the theory has not been employed much by family communication scholars, family communication represents its essential focus. Indeed, the subtitle of the book (Gottman et al., 1997) that synthesizes the theory is *How Families Communicate Emotionally.* The empirical findings we have reviewed demonstrate the theory's fundamental concern with family communication.

Based on our review, emotion regulation theory illuminates our understanding of family communication in the following ways: (a) The theory identifies parental patterns of communication (i.e., EC) that foster in children the ability to regulate emotions, which in turn leads to positive developmental outcomes. (b) Among the developmental outcomes fostered by EC are better child-peer relations, which obviously entail interpersonal communication competencies derived from family interactions. (c) Parental EC buffers children against the otherwise deleterious effects of negative communication patterns between parents in a declining marriage. (d) Positive parent-child communication (i.e., EC) is associated with positive communication patterns between spouses (i.e., constructive conflict management). In the sections that follow, we build upon these findings to suggest some additional ways that emotion regulation theory could advance knowledge about family communication. Although we believe the theory could be applied in numerous additional ways, we focus specifically on the phenomena of conflict and violence in families.

EXTENSIONS OF EMOTION REGULATION THEORY: FAMILY CONFLICT AND VIOLENCE

Emotions play an integral role in the management of conflict and the enactment of violence. Consequently, emotion regulation and meta-emotion structures seem logical constructs for illuminating these forms of interaction among family members. We speculate that parental meta-emotion structures influence conflict patterns and tendencies toward violence in parent-child interactions and in sibling relationships. We also suggest the parental meta-emotion structures that affect children continue to exert influence in their adult relationships.

Meta-emotion Structure and Parent-Child Relationships

We believe that parental meta-emotion structures influence the ways in which children manage conflict with their parents. Recall that couples who embrace an EC parenting philosophy are better able to *regulate* marital conflict. They do not necessarily have less conflict; instead, conflict interactions are less corrosive to marriage. Anger can be expressed, but it is not coupled with expressions of contempt or defensiveness. EC parents are more validating and affectionate during marital conflicts; they articulate a marriage philosophy that emphasizes we-ness and companionship, and they express fondness and admiration for one another (Katz et al., 1999). Thus, children of EC parents have a better model of conflict management to emulate, and this should be reflected in EC children's more constructive conflict interactions with their parents, compared with ED children.

At the heart of parents' constructive conflict management is their ability to regulate their emotionality. Over a period of 25–30 years, Gottman and colleagues have identified significant and specific links between marital affect, conflict, and marriages (for reviews, see Gottman, 1994; Gottman, Murray, Swanson, Tyson, & Swanson, 2002). They have found that the strongest predictor of divorce is the presence of more negativity than positivity in marital interactions. Unhappily married couples engage in long chains of reciprocated negative affect. Negative affective interaction becomes a compelling and "absorbing state" for couples who are dissatisfied. In contrast, happily married couples avoid excessive expressions of criticism, contempt, defensiveness, and stonewalling. They experience positive sentiment override, which fosters shared symbolic meaning. This process, according to Gottman et al. (2002), helps a couple avoid marital gridlock and heightened negativity, thus preventing relationship dissolution.

Children who receive EC are also better able to regulate their own emotions (like their parents), compared with children who do not receive EC. Indeed, this ability to regulate emotions accounts for EC children having smoother relations with their peers and being able to recover from arousal more quickly during stressful interactions with parents. The abilities to self-soothe and focus attention on solving problems that EC promotes should be evidenced in children's conflict behavior with parents. EC children do not necessarily have less conflict with parents than ED children. Rather, they should exhibit more constructive communication during conflict and less protracted expressions of negativity due to their heightened ability to regulate emotions. Empirical support for these predictions would bolster generality of the claim that emotion regulation is key to constructive conflict management.

As Gottman et al. (1997) noted, research on emotion regulation theory has relied exclusively on "normal" families, and it would be useful to expand the range of families studied. In particular, we surmise that parental meta-emotion structures may contribute to an understanding of families whose members enact violence. By violence, we mean the following:

> The ability to impose one's will (i.e., wants, needs, or desires) on another person through the use of verbal or nonverbal acts, or both, done in a way that violates socially acceptable standards and carried out with the intention or perceived intention of inflicting physical or psychological pain, injury, or suffering, or both. (Cahn, 1996, p. 6)

We speculate that EC may reduce the chances of violence occurring in families. EC parents are better able to regulate their own emotions and should therefore be less likely to escalate aggressive conflict episodes into violence. Moreover, unlike EC parents, ED parents tend to equate emotional expression with selfishness, loss of control, passivity, cowardice, or failure (Gottman, 2001). This ED philosophy resembles some of the documented risk factors for committing physical child abuse, such as low frustration tolerance, rigidity, physiological reactivity, anger control problems, deficits in parenting skills, and negative bias/perceptions regarding the child (for review, see Barnett, Miller-Perrin, & Perrin, 1997).

EC parents are also better able to control their negative attacks toward their children than ED parents. ED parents are more likely to exhibit the Derogation parenting style (Katz et al., 1999). When criticizing a child, they display verbal aggression by mocking, belittling, and humiliating. Verbal aggression can be a catalyst for (although not a sufficient cause of) physical violence (deTurck, 1987; Infante, Chandler, & Rudd, 1989; Infante, Sabourin, Rudd, & Shannon, 1990; Sabourin, 1995). Thus, it seems reasonable to suggest that the derogating and disapproving approach to emotions manifested in ED parenting could be a precursor to the display of physical violence by parents against their children. Empirical evidence is needed to discern whether ED parents are at greater risk for committing child abuse, and the extent to which ED parents also possess known risk factors for committing violence.

It also seems reasonable to predict that children of ED parents may be more likely to possess risk factors for parental abuse. Research has shown that some characteristics of children (i.e., difficult child behaviors and physical or mental disabilities) put these children at greater risk of being beaten (see Barnett, Miller-Perrin, & Perrin, 1997). Applying emotion regulation theory, we suspect that such factors could be the *result* of ED parenting. Ironically, in attempting to control the child's emotions, the ED parent actually contributes to the child's dysregulation of emotion (as well as exacerbating the parent's own aggressive tendencies). For example, Gottman and colleagues (1997) have shown that children with ED parents are less healthy, obtain lower achievement scores in school, and exhibit more behavior problems. These characteristics could frustrate ED parents, leading to abuse, which further exacerbates the negative developmental outcomes. In addition to testing these speculations, we suggest exploring whether EC buffers against parental violence when EC children exhibit risk factors for abuse.

Finally, because children who lack EC parenting have more difficulty controlling their negative emotions (e.g., anger) and their high levels of physiological reactivity, they may be more inclined in stressful conflicts to exhibit violent tendencies. Drawing from Freud's hydraulic model of emotion, Katz and Gottman (1995) assert, "when expressive signs of emotion are inhibited they are discharged through other means, namely experiential or physiological channels" (p. 334). If this is the case, then the inhibition of emotional expressivity would be correlated with an individual's propensity for violence. Such behaviors could be related to acts of child delinquency and untoward behaviors in general. More specifically, a child's lack of EC may partially account for the inability to regulate emotions during adolescence when interacting with parents. Millions of parents report experiencing episodes of abuse from their adolescent children (e.g., Straus, Gelles, & Steinmetz, 1980), yet little is known about the causes of such abuse. We contend that ED parents, ironically, could unwittingly foster their own abuse by contributing to their children's inability to regulate emotions. These assumptions await empirical testing.

Meta-emotion Structure and Sibling Relationships

A second familial relationship relevant to a discussion of emotion regulation, conflict, and violence is the one between siblings. We know that there are positive correlations among EC parenting, healthy marital conflict management, and positive child outcomes. We suspect that the relationship between the parents' meta-emotion structure and child outcomes is due in part to the family culture that is communicatively created. In other words, in an EC household, messages (both tacit and overt) convey that emotionality is regarded as healthy, and conflict is something to be regulated constructively. This communication environment influences how all the family members interact. Thus, we believe that not only is the parent-child dyad affected by the family's emotional landscape but so is the sibling relationship. Accordingly, we hypothesize that the behaviors and communication styles of sibling pairings will resemble those of the EC and ED parent-child dyads. Parental meta-emotion structure is expected to influence how children relate to one another and manage their conflicts with each other. Sibling pairs in EC homes should show a propensity to handle their interpersonal conflicts more constructively than siblings in ED households.

When siblings engage in conflict, it often is dismissed as "sibling rivalry"—a normalized, common, and insignificant form of expression in U.S. culture. Yet, according to Straus et al. (1980), the most common form of violence may occur between siblings. In fact, in their first national Family Violence Survey, Straus and colleagues found that 82%

of American children with siblings between 3 and 7 years of age engaged in at least one violent act toward that sibling in the prior year. Although much aggression that occurs between siblings may not qualify as abusive, the prevalence of violence in sibling relationships is nevertheless considerable.

Emotion regulation theory could help explain and predict sibling aggression. For example, the empirical data on emotion regulation show that marital discord interrupts children's ability to regulate their own emotions and interactions with peers, particularly when the parents exhibit an ED style (Katz & Gottman, 1991, 1995; Katz et al., 1999). ED parents experiencing marital distress will use a style of parenting that drives their children's autonomic nervous system to a high state of physiological arousal (Katz & Gottman, 1991). Once in this state of arousal, the children of these parents then show low levels of peer play and high negative affect with peers, including more aggressive and hostile behavior. Although the focus of the empirical analyses thus far has been on friendship groups, we opine that these same negative behaviors may also characterize sibling interactions. It is certainly conceivable that the children within an ED home could be enacting the familial meta-emotion philosophy within the confines of the peer group in their homes; however, whether these patterns exist and become more dispositional ways of managing conflict in their sibling relationships is unclear. Systematic research is needed to examine these links more specifically.

Meta-emotion Structure and Adult Relationships

An important issue yet to be addressed by emotion regulation theory is whether parents' meta-emotion structures influence the way in which their children engage in conflict when they become adults— that is, are the patterns learned in childhood later manifested in marriage and romantic relationships? Will EC children have less chance of divorce (like their parents) when they grow up? Will ED children be less able to regulate conflict and therefore be more likely to divorce? Will ED children have more aggressive relations as adults because they had more aggressive peer relationships during adolescence? Will EC children be less likely to be abusive to their partners when they become adults? These questions boil down to the issue of whether meta-emotion structures learned as a child carry over into adulthood—a challenging but extremely important question that begs for empirical investigation. We will return to this issue of the intergenerational transmission of meta-emotion structures shortly.

On the assumption that one's childhood meta-emotional structure could carry over into adulthood, some testable predictions become obvious. Children who received EC should be more likely to grow up to have stable marriages and more constructive conflict regulation patterns because these outcomes accrue to EC parents. Furthermore, following the logic presented earlier, children whose EC philosophy continues into adulthood should be less likely to exhibit violence in their adult dating and marital relationships. However, it remains unclear how adult partners with discrepant meta-emotion structures will relate to each other as romantic or marital partners. Preliminary research suggests that spouses with different meta-emotion structures have more unstable marriages (Katz et al., 1999). There exists no evidence, however, regarding the stability of meta-emotion structures, how they might be reshaped based upon new relational interactions, and how partners communicatively influence each other's emotion philosophy. Given that parents can be trained to adopt an EC philosophy (Gottman et al., 1997), it seems plausible that significant non-family-of-origin members could influence adult meta-emotion structures over time. This presumably subtle communicative process presents an intriguing possibility for future exploration.

Regardless of the sources that shape an adult's meta-emotion structure, it is clear that emotion regulation processes play a central role in adult relationships. In addition to the evidence provided by Gottman et al. (1997) regarding the positive effects of EC parenting on marital satisfaction and stability, Gottman and associates (1995) illustrated important connections among heart rate activity, emotionally aggressive behavior, and general violence in batterers. They found that these variables combined in unique ways, serving to distinguish between two types of batterers. Type 1 batterers' physiological arousal lowered during the conflict, whereas Type 2 men's heart rates increased. Type 1 men, as compared with Type 2 men, were more generally violent, with aggression extending beyond the marriage; they were more likely to have witnessed aggression as a child; and they were more likely to be classified as anti-social, drug-dependent, and aggressive-sadistic. In a subsequent phase of data collection, Type 1 men's marriages had a separation-divorce rate of zero, compared with 27% of Type 2 men's marriages. Jacobson and Gottman (1998) later referred to Type 1 batterers as *cobras*—they slowly and methodically entrap their victims. Once they have a hold, they never let go. Conversely, Type 2 men were labeled *pitbulls* because, as reflected in their increased physiological arousal during conflicts, they strike fast and hard. This research suggests that aside from influencing abuse propensity, meta-emotion structures, which determine ability to regulate arousal, may discriminate between different types of batterers. Still, we cannot help but wonder whether the seeds of adult emotion regulation and dysregulation are sown in childhood—which returns us to the issue of intergenerational transmission of emotion structures.

Meta-emotion Structure and Intergenerational Transmission

Are parental meta-emotion structures transmitted across generations? Social learning theory (Jasinski, 2001; see also Chapter 17 in this volume) and its correlate, the intergenerational transmission of violence hypothesis, would appear to suggest that there should be a positive correlation between patterns learned in the family-of-origin and those enacted in adult romantic relationships. For example, some researchers assert that violence witnessed or experienced in childhood increases the likelihood of being violent with an intimate partner (O'Leary, 1988). This association is stronger when both the parent and the child are male, when the child identifies with the aggressive parent, and when the frequency and severity of the abuse are greater (MacEwan, 1994). However, although these observations make sense theoretically and intuitively, little substantive empirical evidence supports the claim that such a transmission occurs (Gelles, 1990). Reviewing the literature, Johnson and Ferraro (2000) found that the intergenerational transmission effect was quite small because the correlation between exposure to parental violence and enactment of intimate violence was approximately .10. Based upon these data, the authors assert that the metaphor of transmission is a "gross distortion of the reality of family-of-origin effects of the adult lives of children" (p. 958). Indeed, emotion regulation theory suggests that modeling cannot adequately account for intergenerational transmission effects because effective regulation of emotions entails the developed abilities to self-soothe and focus attention when emotionally distressed. Given the fuzzy association between children's experiences with aggression and their own adult behavior, the connection between the meta-emotional structures learned in childhood and those manifested in adulthood begs for empirical evidence. In addition, we should pursue questions such as the following: How does communication facilitate or hinder transmission processes? Do certain communication behaviors and interpersonal relationships act as buffers, protecting individuals from repeating the patterns learned in childhood? If so, what are they? How and why do they appear to help some and not others?

If it can be demonstrated that meta-emotion structures tend to be transmitted across generations, then how is this process related to the transmission of violence? To what degree would the hostile peer inter-action and other anti-social behaviors learned from the ED family phi-losophy affect one's likelihood to aggress toward an intimate partner? If ED parents are more likely to be abusive (as speculated earlier), is this tendency to abuse transmitted across generations? Is the "cycle of abuse" perpetuated by the inability to regulate emotions, which is grounded in a cycle of dysfunctional meta-emotion structure? Definitive answers to these issues will require longitudinal data. These are all important questions to ask as we continue to explore family con-flict, violence, and emotionality across the life span.

EVALUATION OF EMOTION REGULATION THEORY

Emotion regulation theory merits high marks for its contributions to understanding family communication. The concept of meta-emotion structure offers a powerful mechanism for explaining the quality of marital, parent-child, and sibling interactions. Moreover, the abilities to regulate emotion that are cultivated within the family system have important consequences for interactions outside of the family. In fact, Gottman et al. (1997, p. 39) consider a child's "ability to interact suc-cessfully with peers and to form lasting peer relationships" as the most important empirical outcomes in their program of research. Thus, emo-tion regulation theory reveals the importance of family communication in both family processes (i.e., parenting, managing marital conflict, enacting sibling rivalry) and relational functioning outside the family. One can easily imagine the concepts of emotion regulation being extended to account for communicative competence in friendships, work relationships, and so forth. The extensive, ongoing program of research by Gottman and his team, and the copious and intriguing findings it has yielded, evidence the heuristic value of the theory. As we hope to have illustrated in this chapter, there are numerous addi-tional ways to apply the theory in an effort to advance knowledge about family communication. Space limitations forced us to limit our application of the theory to family conflict and violence. It seems obvious, however, that meta-emotion structure could very well account for other forms and functions of family communication such as seeking and providing social support, managing privacy and intimacy, and coping with loss.

Perhaps the biggest limitation of emotion regulation theory is that its empirical support has been derived from traditional middle-class families. It is important to test the theory with other types of families, including single-parent, blended, and gay and lesbian families, as well as those representing different socioeconomic, racial, and cultural groups. Aside from assessing the generality of the theory, this could reveal that (co-)cultural differences in family communication are attributable to cultural differences in meta-emotion structures.

Finally, the evidence thus far supporting emotion regulation theory rests on data about meta-emotions for anger and sadness only. Gottman (2001) indicates that his team is now studying fear, pride, love, guilt, and embarrassment. To these we would recommend adding hate, shame, and jealousy. Pursuit of these lines of research will dramatically advance our understanding of how parental coaching of emotions influences a host family members' personal and relational outcomes.

REFERENCES

Barnett, O. W., Miller-Perrin, C. L., & Perrin, R. D. (1997). *Family violence across the lifespan.* Thousand Oaks, CA: Sage.

Cahn, D. D. (1996). Family violence from a communication perspective. In D. D. Cahn & S. A. Lloyd (Eds.), *Family violence from a communication perspective* (pp. 1–19). Thousand Oaks, CA: Sage.

deTurck, M. A. (1987). When communication fails: Physical aggression as a compliance gaining strategy. *Communication Monographs, 51,* 106–112.

Fox, N. A. (1989). The psychophysiological correlates of emotional reactivity during the first year of life. *Developmental Psychology, 25,* 364–372.

Gelles, R. J. (1990). Methodological issues in the study of family violence. In G. R. Patterson (Ed.), *Depression and aggression in family interaction* (pp. 49–74). Hillsdale, NJ: Lawrence Erlbaum.

Goleman, D. (1995). *Emotional intelligence.* New York: Bantam Books.

Gottman, J. M. (1994). *What predicts divorce? The relationship between marital processes and marital outcomes.* Hillsdale, NJ: Lawrence Erlbaum.

Gottman, J. M. (2001). Meta-emotion, children's emotional intelligence, and buffering children from marital conflict. In C. D. Ryff & B. H. Singer (Eds.),

Emotion, social relationships, and health (pp. 23–40). New York: Oxford University Press.

Gottman, J. M., Jacobson, N. S., Rushe, R. H., Shortt, J. W., Babcock, J., La Taillade, J. J., & Waltz, J. (1995). The relationship between heart rate reactivity, emotionally aggressive behavior, and general violence in batterers. *Journal of Family Psychology, 9,* 227–248.

Gottman, J. M., & Katz, L. F. (2002). Children's emotional reactions to stressful parent-child interactions: The link between emotion regulation and vagal tone. *Marriage & Family Review, 34,* 265–283.

Gottman, J. M., Katz, L. F., & Hooven, C. (1997). *Meta-emotion: How families communicate emotionally.* Mahwah, NJ: Lawrence Erlbaum.

Gottman, J. M., Murray, J. D., Swanson, C. C., Tyson, R., & Swanson, K. R. (2002). *The mathematics of marriage: Dynamic nonlinear models.* Cambridge, MA: MIT Press.

Infante, D. A. Chandler, T. A., & Rudd, J. E. (1989). Test of an argumentative skill deficiency model of interspousal violence. *Communication Monographs, 56,* 163–177.

Infante, D. A., Sabourin, T. C., Rudd, J. E., & Shannon, E. A. (1990). Verbal aggression in violent and nonviolent marital disputes. *Communication Quarterly, 38,* 361–371.

Jacobson, N. S., & Gottman, J. M. (1998). *Why men batter women: New insights into ending abusive relationships.* New York: Simon & Schuster.

Jasinski, J. L. (2001). Theoretical explanations for violence against women. In C. M. Renzetti, J. L. Edleson, & R. K. Bergan (Eds.), *Sourcebook on violence against women* (pp. 5–21). Thousand Oaks, CA: Sage.

Johnson, M. P., & Ferraro, K. J. (2000). Research on domestic violence in the 1990s: Making distinctions. *Journal of Marriage and the Family, 62,* 948–963.

Katz, L. F., & Gottman, J. M. (1991). Marital discord and child outcomes: A social psychophysiological approach. In J. Garber & K. A. Dodge (Eds.), *The development of emotion regulation and dysregulation* (pp. 129–158). Cambridge, MA: Cambridge University Press.

Katz, L. F., & Gottman, J. M. (1995). Marital interaction and child outcomes: A longitudinal study of mediating and moderating processes. In D. Cicchetti & S. L. Toth (Eds.), *Emotion, cognition, and representation* (pp. 301–342). Rochester, NY: University of Rochester Press.

Katz, L. F., Wilson, B., & Gottman, J. M. (1999). Meta-emotion philosophy and family adjustment: Making an emotional connection. In M. J. Cox & J. Brooks-Gunn (Eds.), *Conflict and cohesion in families: Causes and consequences* (pp. 131–166). Mahwah, NJ: Lawrence Erlbaum.

MacEwan, K. E. (1994). Redefining the intergenerational transmission hypothesis. *Journal of Interpersonal Violence, 9,* 350–365.

O'Leary, K. D. (1988). Physical aggression between spouses: A social learning theory perspective. In V. B. Van Hasselt, R. L. Morrison, A. S. Bellack, & M. Hersen (Eds.), *Handbook of family violence* (pp. 31–55). New York: Plenum Press.

Porges, S. W. (1973). Heart rate variability: An autonomic correlate of reaction time performance. *Bulletin of the Psychonomic Society, 1,* 270–272.

Porges, S. W. (1984). Heart rate oscillation: An index of neural mediation. In M. G. H. Coles, J. R. Jennings, & J. A. Stern (Eds.), *Psychophysiological perspectives: Festschrift for Beatrice and John Lacey* (pp. 229–241). New York: Von Nostrand Reinhold.

Porges, S. W. (1991). Vagal tone: An autonomic mediator of affect. In J. Garber & K. A. Dodge (Eds.), *The development of emotion regulation and dysregulation* (pp. 111–128). Cambridge, MA: Cambridge University Press.

Sabourin, T. C. (1995). The role of negative reciprocity in spouse abuse: A relational control analysis. *Journal of Applied Communication Research, 23,* 271–283.

Salovey, P., & Mayer, J. D. (1990). Emotional intelligence. *Imagination, Cognition, and Personality, 9,* 185–211.

Straus, M. A., Gelles, R. J., & Steinmetz, S. K. (1980). *Behind closed doors: Violence in the American family.* New York: Doubleday/Anchor.

15

Social Theories: Social Constructionism and Symbolic Interactionism

Wendy Leeds-Hurwitz

Editors' Note: This chapter addresses two closely related interpretive theories: social constructionism and symbolic interactionism. Both theories focus on how people create meaning through language in use, but in slightly different ways. Further, although both have origins in sociology, they have developed different intellectual histories.

This chapter discusses the theories of social constructionism and symbolic interactionism, the methodological implications of choosing one of these theories, and how either or both of these theories has been used in the past and may prove useful to future research in family communication. Briefly, because a family is a social construct, these theories are particularly appropriate to choose for studying family communication. Both take as their goal the understanding of how people create meaning for themselves and others, although they have different intellectual histories and different emphases in practice. The fact that these theories have not often been applied to family communication should be understood as evidence of the theoretical orientation of those in communication who have studied families rather than as a measure of their potential value to the topic.

Social constructionism had its start as a theory with Berger and Luckmann's publication in 1967 of their book, *The Social Construction of Reality*. Reflecting the background of the authors, this theory combined the assumptions of sociology and philosophy, but it has since been taken up by other disciplines as well, including communication (Burr, 1995). Berger and Luckmann's primary intent was to understand how knowledge is constructed, not how communication is constructed, so many of their points are actually irrelevant to what is studied today under the label "social constructionism." Two elements are most relevant to social constructionism as applied to communication behavior. First is the central assumption that people make sense of experience by constructing a model of the social world and how it works (Schwandt, 2000). Gergen (1985) expanded upon this when he explained that "social constructionist inquiry is principally concerned with explicating the process by which people come to describe, explain, or otherwise account for the world (including themselves) in which they live" (p. 266). In his terms, describing, explaining, and accounting for the world are all parts of constructing it. Second is the emphasis on language as "the most important sign system of human society" (Berger & Luckmann, 1967, p. 36), and the resulting implication that "the most important vehicle of reality-maintenance is conversation" (p. 152; see also Potter & Wetherell, 1987; Shotter, 1993; Shotter & Gergen, 1994). In other words, we use talk to make things happen: by naming things, we give them substance. Berger and Luckmann (1967) discussed the largest social construction (society) and the smallest (the individual), leaving room for others to apply their ideas to the family, a structural unit standing between these two in size and influence.

Central to social constructionism is the implied metaphor of building, of making, of bringing something into being that had no existence before (Hacking, 1998). It implies studying how it is that people make something inchoate (like a family) appear to have substance and definition. But other words and phrases have come to be used as well. Often the social world is said to be "constituted" through interaction, or language specifically (Potter, 1996); also, there are often references to the "discursive practices" (meaning, talk) through which interaction is constructed (Wood, 1994).

One of the implications of a social constructionist approach is the acknowledgment that "the process of making social reality happen requires the interaction of two or more people" (Harris & Sadeghi, 1987, p. 483). So it is *social* construction in the sense of requiring joint, rather than individual, effort. The basic assumption here is that "nothing exists in the social world unless it has been introduced into that world by a human social and constructive act" (Harré, 2002, p. 24). As a result, Jorgenson (1989) suggested, "Family research undertaken from the constructivist perspective ... is directed toward elucidating the shared understandings that form the basis for social interaction in everyday life" (p. 28). That is, the emphasis belongs on how the entire family as a unit jointly constructs meaning, rather than analyzing any one individual, or one person's ideas, at a time.

Social construction incorporates four elements: construction, maintenance, repair, and change (Carey, 1989). First, we develop a concept, and then figure out ways to make it concrete. But if we stop displaying a concept, such as a family's identity, over time, it dissipates, dissolves, ceases to be true. We need to actively maintain it if it is to remain relevant. We also need to periodically repair our social construction, for aspects may be inadvertently forgotten or changed over time. And, finally, there are many times when the construction that worked in one time period needs to be changed in another, and so we also must consider the ways in which social constructions, such as family identities, change over time. Gergen emphasizes the ongoing nature of meaning creation when he argues that "Meanings are subject to continuous reconstitution" (1994, p. 267), and further that social constructionists "think of the objects of the world as social accomplishments" (1985, p. 40). Because people are constantly displaying one or another of these steps, we can easily observe construction, maintenance, repair, and change through the study of actual behavior. However, because people are not generally aware that this is what they are doing, asking them to describe their behavior or intent is not always the best method of research. David Reiss, one of the few authors to have explicitly applied social constructionist theory to studies of family communication, suggested "that the transactions of individuals in a family with the outside world are coordinated by a shared conception–held by all of them–of the fundamental nature or structure of that world" (1981, p. 377).

Symbolic interactionism has an entirely separate intellectual history. Named by Herbert Blumer in 1937, and most explicitly described by him in 1969, it grew out of the Chicago School of Sociology, with strong ties to social psychology by way of George Herbert Mead (Blumer, 1969). Although Mead did not label his work "symbolic interactionism," others frequently cite *Mind, Self and Society* (1934) as the central publication on the topic. Symbolic interactionism emphasizes meanings, the self, and the ways in which the self is constructed through interaction with others. There is a focus on social roles because "actors . . . name one another, in the sense that they recognize each other as occupants of positions, and in naming one another invoke expectations with respect to one another's behavior," and on the self because "actors . . . name themselves as well—it is to these reflexively applied positional designations that the concept of self is typically intended to refer—and in so doing they create their own internalized expectations with respect to their own behavior" (Stryker, 1968, p. 559).

Sandstrom, Martin, and Fine (2001) provide a particularly tidy summary of symbolic interactionist theory, highlighting six assumptions:

- People are unique creatures because of their ability to use symbols.
- People become distinctly human through their interaction.
- People are conscious and self-reflexive beings who actively shape their own behavior.
- People are purposeful creatures who act in and toward situations.
- Human society consists of people engaging in social interaction.
- To understand people's social acts, we need to use methods that enable us to discern the meanings they attribute to these acts (pp. 218–219).

One of the implications of these assumptions is that, like social constructionism, symbolic interactionism implies paying particular attention to the actual use of language in interaction. As Atkinson and Housley (2003) put it, "Language allows for the creation of culture, in that human social actors can exchange experiences, cumulate experiences and share meanings" (p. 6). In both theories, we use language to create the self as well as others and our sense of the social world around us, therefore it behooves researchers to study the words actually used by social actors in interaction.

Unlike social constructionism, symbolic interactionism has a long history of influencing research on families, although mostly within sociology rather than communication (Handel, 1992; Stryker, 1959), and is often named as an appropriate theory to use in studying families (Arliss, 1993; White & Klein, 2002). LaRossa and Reitzes (1993) proposed that "Symbolic interactionism's unique contribution to family studies is, first, the emphasis it gives to the proposition that families are social groups and, second, its assertion that individuals develop both a concept of self and their identities through social interaction, enabling them to independently assess and assign value to their family activities" (p. 135). The early major studies are Bossard and Boll (1950), Hess and Handel (1959), and Kantor and Lehr (1975), all of which used qualitative methods to study the structure of the family, including interviews and observations.

Social constructionism and symbolic interactionism are both interpretive theories. As such, both emphasize the study of meaning construction. Like social constructionism, symbolic interactionism emphasizes the centrality of social interaction, and the joint action necessary to maintain it, as well as stressing the significance of symbols, including most especially language. Because of these overlaps, they have occasionally been treated as two parts of the same theory within communication, and especially within the family communication tradition, although this is not really appropriate. Most briefly, what separates them is that social constructionism is centrally concerned with how people make sense of the world, especially through language, and emphasizes the study of relationships; whereas symbolic interactionism's central concern is making sense of the self and social roles.

The fact that both social constructionism and symbolic interactionism are interpretive links them together with other theories studied within communication, such as ethnomethodology or the coordinated management of meaning. As interpretive approaches, they are centrally concerned with understanding meaning and meaning-making; all of them take as their central question how people construct meaning for themselves and others through their language and their behavior. Thus the emphasis is on how language (or any other form of communication) makes or constructs the social world for its inhabitants. To date, none of these theories has been central to the tradition of family communication research conducted by scholars within communication, but they are potentially useful and ought to be studied at greater length.

As with every theory, choosing either social constructionism or symbolic interactionism has implications for the choice of method to be used in investigating a particular research question. As a result of their focus on language, Berger and Luckmann explicitly emphasized the importance of studying everyday social interaction because "the most important experience of others takes place in the face-to-face situation"

(1967, p. 28; see also Burr, 1995). Likewise, Blumer stated that symbolic interactionism assumes that:

> Its empirical world is the natural world of such group life and con-
> duct. It lodges its problems in this natural world, conducts its
> studies in it, and derives its interpretations from such naturalistic
> studies. If it wishes to study religious cult behavior it will go to
> actual religious cults and observe them carefully as they carry on
> their lives . . . Its methodological stance, accordingly, is that of
> direct examination of the empirical social world. (1969, p. 47)

Others have been even more explicit in outlining the methodological implications of symbolic interactionism. Charon (1989) argued that
"Symbolic interactionists believe that it is important to gather data
through observing people in real situations" (p. 182). Rock (2001) suggested that "Interactionist research hinges on participant observation:
participant because it is only by attempting to enter the symbolic life-
world of others that one can ascertain the subjective logic on which it
is built and feel, hear and see a little of social life as one's subjects
do . . . but *observer* because one's purposes are always ultimately distinct and objectifying" (p. 32).

Social constructionism and symbolic interactionism, then, equally
imply documentation of actual words and behavior in interaction, thus
emphasize methods such as conversation analysis or ethnography
(Atkinson & Housley, 2003). What people say they do and say is not the
same as what they can be observed to do and say; therefore, it is taken
for granted by those assuming a social constructionist or symbolic
interactionist stance that such techniques as interviews, survey ques-
tionnaires, or diaries cannot be relied upon as entirely accurate. In the
study of families, it may appear to be intrusive to use techniques
implying direct observation of behavior, but there are enough
examples of research by now to demonstrate that this is not only possible, but appropriate. The studies of dinner table conversation are but
one strand of research, proving this (e.g., Blum-Kulka, 1997). The fact
that this research has been framed as contributing to understanding
social interaction generally rather than family communication particularly does not mean it is not useful to the latter as well. Those having
concerns about intrusions have, at times, invented unusual methods of
data collection. Edwards and Middleton (1988) provided an especially
creative way to document actual conversations within families: They

asked parents to set a tape recorder next to them when looking at photograph albums with their child/ren, thus combining direct data collection with minimal intrusion.

Past research within family communication has occasionally used the language of either social constructionism or symbolic interactionism, but even the best work has rarely followed up on the implications for methodology as outlined previously. Golden (2002) said that she was "reframing work and family as a matter of development and sustaining shared meanings, including role-identities" (p. 138). In studying social construction within the family, Jorgenson (1994) looked at language, specifically forms of address. She assumed that meaning "is not transparently evident from the words themselves, but emerges in the interplay among their contexts of use" (p. 197) and that "choosing a particular term implies constructing the relationship in a particular way" (p. 203). Weigel (2003) explicitly applied a symbolic interactionist framework, but then adds the vocabulary of social constructionism at the end of the study. He looks at construction of commitment but uses only one interview of a single couple. Applying the criteria given previously about methodological implications, this study (as is the case with many others) only examines reports of language, rather than language in use, which is the more appropriate focus for either of these theories. Similarly, social constructionism shows up often in titles, without being utilized in any real way (Beall & Sternberg, 1995; Kahn & Coyne, 1985).

Whitchurch and Dickson (1999) argue that "The emphasis of the family communication specialty area is on interaction among communicators" (p. 697), but this is not supported by the research published to date, so their comment is more appropriately read as a suggestion for where the research could go in the future than a description of where it has been in the past. Social constructionism and symbolic interactionism are certainly appropriate theories to use if interaction is to become the focus. Specifically, I would argue that family communication scholars need to follow up on the implications of these theories for methodology. Given their complexity, families are difficult to study in significant ways, but it is worth at least seriously attempting to resolve the methodology problem.

There are at least two obvious major directions to pursue in future research. The first would be to make better use of existing scholarship in the area of language and social interaction, such as the studies of dinner conversations mentioned previously, even to the point of collaborating with language and social interaction researchers. The logic of linking to language and social interaction research is that it "gives primary emphasis to the discursive practices themselves through which persons construct or produce the realities of social life" (Sanders, Fitch, & Pomerantz, 2001, p. 386), exactly what both social constructionism and symbolic interactionism privilege. Mandelbaum (2003) provides a good example of what the existing language and social interaction research has to offer the study of family communication—in this case, specifically relationships—for she assumes that "the character of a relationship is built moment by moment, by interactants, in and through interaction" (p. 207). Similarly, Taylor (1995) demonstrates what social constructionist assumptions, combined with conversational analysis, adds to an examination of family communication, although the concern here, as with Mandelbaum (2003), is more with the construction of conversation than families. It will be up to family communication scholars to reverse the emphasis, using conversations as a way to study families.

Second, moving outside the discipline of communication, there is currently much relevant research in sociology, which takes an explicitly social constructionist point of view. In the United States some recent sociological work focuses on the family (Gubrium & Holstein, 1990; Gubrium & Lynott, 1985), specifically on *"accomplishing* family in and through descriptive practice" (Holstein & Gubrium, 1994, p. 246). Even more research is being conducted in England, where there has been a special emphasis on children, not only by sociologists but also geographers, doing a good job of showing how it should be done, through direct observation (usually ethnography). The basic assumption of this strand of research is that childhood is a social construction, and "Children must be seen as actively involved in the construction of their own social lives, the lives of those around them and of the societies in which they live" (James & Prout, 1990, p. 4; see also Christensen & James, 2000; Holloway & Valentine, 2000; James, 1993; James, Jenks & Prout, 1998). These studies emphasize what one author describes as "children's ability to interpret and construct the world which they inhabit" (Cook, 2002, p. 2). Stainton-Rogers and Stainton-Rogers (1992) characterize this set of what are being termed "social studies of childhood" as "explicitly social constructionist" (p. 103), so they could serve as a corrective to the distinct lack of studies emphasizing not only social constructionism as a theory but also children as a topic in family communication (Socha, 2003). Given that the family socializes the child, studies of childhood are particularly important, yet negligible in communication to date. Just as symbolic interactionism was the early theory of choice by those studying families, so social constructionism is the theoretical orientation of those who take the study of children seriously today.

The primary strength of both social constructionism and symbolic interactionism is the potential they offer for future studies of family communication. They are cutting-edge theories for multiple disciplines, not just communication, and so much research currently takes either of them as the basic starting point. Their primary limitation within family communication is that scholars have either not attended to them (especially social constructionism) or have misunderstood the methodological implications. Better grounding in the key scholars (Blumer [1969] for symbolic interactionism, and Berger & Luckmann [1967] for social constructionism) would help considerably, as would wider reading outside of the communication discipline and outside of the United States.

There are many specific topics to which either social constructionism or symbolic interactionism fruitfully can be applied within the study of family communication. Symbolic interactionism would be especially appropriate to a study of the various roles family members take (Golden, 2001). Social constructionism has already been widely applied to the construction of gender, and it is particularly appropriate to examine the socialization to gender that occurs within the family, for, as Allen and Walker argue, "families are the primary arena in which gender is taught, learned, and transformed" (2000, p. 1; see also Aitken 2000; Ervin-Tripp, 2001).

Narratives have already been studied extensively by scholars in many disciplines, using various theoretical approaches and in many contexts, although not primarily through the lens of social constructionism or with a specific focus on family contexts. But they are particularly important as a vehicle for studying social constructionism because "we become who we are through telling stories about our lives and living the stories we tell; our stories are a cornerstone of our identity" (Andrews, 2002, p. 75). A rare exception within family communication research with a focus on narratives is Jorgenson and Bochner (2004), who argue that stories "are resources through which family members create shared realities of family life" (p. 517).

Two especially inviting new directions for research are applying social constructionist assumptions to family interactions surrounding the definition of social age and the social definition of the appropriate use of space. Solberg (1990) argues that "social age" is different from biological because control of space, time, and money all vary by family for the same-age children. The social construction of appropriate space is a complex process (Wood & Beck, 1990). For example, children and parents appear to bring different assumptions to decisions about where children should be allowed to play (e.g., Holloway & Valentine, 2000; Sibley, 1995; Sibley & Lowe, 1992; Valentine, 1997).

Other possible applications of social constructionism include the study of how family members utilize symbols and combine symbols into rituals. Bossard and Boll (1950) began the study of rituals within families, but many others have pursued that direction since. As with stories, "rituals are symbolic links to the past, performed in the present" (Jorgenson & Bochner, 2004, p. 518). There is much work to be done in the examination of material culture symbols, because this is a topic rarely studied within communication to date. But families are known for passing objects down through generations, and there is potential for studies of what is passed to whom and under what conditions, or how dispersal of estates is handled, because these topics primarily occur within the family setting. Other potential topics include nonverbal communication patterns within the family; family rules; religion, especially the socialization to religious beliefs; race and ethnicity, again, especially the socialization to cultural identities; changes in family structure; use of time; analyzing the various metaphors used by family members to describe the social unit; and family discipline practices.

In conclusion, obviously there are numerous topics in family communication that might benefit from examination using social constructionist or symbolic interactionist theoretical assumptions. Both theories make good sense for a study of family communication, but neither has been used as often as might seem obvious. This means that there is much work yet to be done. The strength of both theories is their value in a study of meaning creation; the weakness of both is that they have hardly been explored by scholars of family communication. This chapter has argued that future researchers should give careful consideration to the methodological implications of these theories and should try hard not to inadvertently confuse them. Symbolic interactionism emphasizes making sense of self and social roles, whereas social constructionism focuses more broadly on making sense of the nature and structure of the social world.

REFERENCES

Aitken, S. C. (2000). Play, rights and borders: Gender-bound parents and the social construction of children. In S.L. Holloway & G. Valentine (Eds.), *Children's geographies: Playing, living, learning* (pp. 119–138). London: Routledge.

Allen, K. R., & Walker, A. J. (2000). Constructing gender in families. In R. M. Milardo & S. Duck (Eds.), *Families and relationships* (pp. 1–17). Chichester, UK: John Wiley.

Andrews, M. (2002). Generational consciousness, dialogue, and political engagement. In J. Edmunds & B. S. Turner (Eds.), *Generational consciousness, narrative, and politics* (pp. 75–87). Lanham, MD: Rowman & Littlefield.

Arliss, L. P. (1993). *Contemporary family communication: Messages and meanings.* New York: St. Martin's Press.

Atkinson, P., & Housley, W. (2003). *Interactionism: An essay in sociological amnesia.* Thousand Oaks, CA: Sage.

Beall, A. E., & Sternberg, R. J. (1995). The social construction of love. *Journal of Social and Personal Relationships, 12,* 417–438.

Berger, P. L., & Luckmann, T. (1967). *The social construction of reality: A treatise in the sociology of knowledge.* New York: Doubleday Anchor.

Blumer, H. (1969). *Symbolic interactionism: Perspective and method.* Englewood Cliffs, NJ: Prentice Hall.

Blum-Kulka, S. (1997). *Dinner talk: Cultural patterns of sociability and socialization in family discourse.* Mahwah, NJ: Lawrence Erlbaum.

Bossard, J. H. S., & Boll, E. S. (1950). *Ritual in family living.* Philadelphia: University of Pennsylvania Press.

Burr, V. (1995). *An introduction to social constructionism.* London: Routledge.

Carey, J. W. (1989). A cultural approach to communication. In *Communication as culture: Essays on media and society* (pp. 13–36). New York: Routledge.

Charon, J. M. (1989). *Symbolic interactionism: An introduction, an interpretation, an integration* (3rd ed.). Englewood Cliffs, NJ: Prentice Hall.

Christensen, P., & James, A. (Eds.). (2000). *Research with children: Perspectives and practices.* London: Falmer.

Cook, D. T. (2002). Introduction: Interrogating symbolic childhood. In D. T. Cook (Ed.), *Symbolic childhood* (p. 1–14). New York: Peter Lang.

Edwards, D., & Middleton, D. (1988). Conversational remembering and family relationships: How children learn to remember. *Journal of Social and Personal Relationships, 5,* 3–25.

Ervin-Tripp, S. M. (2001). The place of gender in developmental pragmatics: Cultural factors. *Research on Language in Social Interaction, 34,* 131–147.

Gergen, K. J. (1985). The social constructionist movement in social psychology. *American Psychologist, 40,* 266–275.

Gergen, K. J. (1994). *Realities and relationships: Soundings in social construction.* Cambridge, MA: Harvard University Press.

Golden, A. G. (2001). Modernity and communicative management of multiple roles: The case of the worker-parent. *Journal of Family Communication, 1,* 233–264.

Golden, A. G. (2002). Speaking of work and family: Spousal collaboration on defining role-identities and developing shared meanings. *Southern Communication Journal, 67,* 122–141.

Gubrium, J. F., & Holstein, J. A. (1990). *What is family?* Mountain View, CA: Mayfield.

Gubrium, J. F., & Lynott, R. J. (1985). Family rhetoric as social order. *Journal of Family Issues, 6,* 129–152.

Hacking, I. (1998). On being more literal about construction. In I. Velody & R. Williams (Eds.), *The politics of constructionism* (pp. 49–68). Thousand Oaks, CA: Sage.

Handel, G. (1992). The qualitative tradition in family research. In J. Gilgun, K. Daly, & G. Handel (Eds.), *Qualitative methods in family research* (pp.12–21). Newbury Park: Sage.

Harré, R. (2002). Material objects in social worlds. *Theory, Culture and Society, 19* (5/6), 23–33.

Harris, L. M., & Sadeghi, A. R. (1987). Realizing: How facts are created in human interaction. *Journal of Social and Personal Relationships, 4,* 481–495.

Hess, R., & Handel, G. (1959). *Family worlds.* Chicago: University of Chicago Press.

Holloway, S. L., & Valentine, G. (Eds.). (2000). *Children's geographies: Playing, living, learning.* London: Routledge.

Holstein, J. A., & Gubrium, J. F. (1994). Constructing family: Descriptive practice and domestic order. In T. R. Sarbin & J. I. Kitsuse (Eds.), *Constructing the social* (pp. 232–250). Thousand Oaks, CA: Sage.

James, A. (1993). *Childhood identities: Self and social relationships in the experience of the child.* Edinburgh: Edinburgh University Press.

James, A., Jenks, C., & Prout, A. (1998). *Theorising childhood.* New York: Teachers College Press.

James, A., & Prout, A. (Eds.). (1990). *Constructing and reconstructing childhood: Contemporary issues in the sociological study of childhood.* Basingstoke, UK: Falmer Press.

Jorgenson, J. (1989). Where is the "family" in family communication? Exploring families' self-definitions. *Journal of Applied Communication Research, 17*(1–2), 27–41.

Jorgenson, J. (1994). Situated address and the social construction of "in-law" relationships. *The Southern Communication Journal, 59,* 196–204.

Jorgenson, J., & Bochner, A. P. (2004). Imagining families through stories and rituals. In A. Vangelisti (Ed.), *Handbook of Family Communication* (pp. 513–538). Mahwah, NJ: Lawrence Erlbaum.

Kahn, J., & Coyne, J. C. (1985). Depression and marital disagreement: The social construction of despair. *Journal of Social and Personal Relationships, 2*, 447–461.

Kantor, D., & Lehr, W. (1975). *Inside the family.* San Francisco: Jossey-Bass.

LaRossa, R., & Reitzes, D. C. (1993). Symbolic interactionism and family studies. In P. G. Boss, W. J. Doherty, R. LaRossa, W. R. Schumm, & S. K. Steinmetz (Eds.), *Sourcebook of family theories and methods: A contextual approach* (pp. 135–163). New York: Plenum.

Mandelbaum, J. (2003). Interactive methods for constructing relationships. In P. J. Glenn, C. D. LeBaron, & J. Mandelbaum (Eds.), *Studies in language and social interaction in honor of Robert Hopper* (pp. 91–102). Mahwah, NJ: Lawrence Erlbaum.

Mead, G. H. (1934). *Mind, self and society.* Chicago: University of Chicago Press.

Potter, J. (1996). *Representing reality: Discourse, rhetoric and social construction.* Thousand Oaks, CA: Sage.

Potter, J., & Wetherell, M. (1987). *Discourse and social psychology: Beyond attitudes and behaviour.* Thousand Oaks, CA: Sage.

Reiss, D. (1981). *The family's construction of reality.* Cambridge, MA: Harvard University Press.

Rock, P. (2001). Symbolic interactionism and ethnography. In P. Atkinson, A. Coffey, S. Delamont, J. Lofland, & L. Lofland (Eds.), *Handbook of ethnography* (pp. 26–38). Thousand Oaks, CA: Sage.

Sanders, R., Fitch, K., & Pomerantz, A. (2001). Core research traditions within language and social interaction. *Communication Yearbook, 24,* 385–408.

Sandstrom, K. L., Martin, D. D., & Fine, G. A. (2001). Symbolic interactionism and the end of the century. In G. Ritzer & B. Smart (Eds.), *Handbook of social theory* (pp. 217–231). Thousand Oaks, CA: Sage.

Schwandt, T. A. (2000). Three epistemological stances for qualitative inquiry. In N. K. Denzin, & Y. S. Lincoln (*Eds.*), *Handbook of qualitative research* (2nd ed., pp. 189–213). Thousand Oaks, CA: Sage.

Shotter, J. (1993). *Cultural politics of everyday life.* Buckingham, UK: Open University Press.

Shotter, J., & Gergen, K. J. (1994). Social construction: Knowledge, self, others, and continuing the conversation. *Communication Yearbook, 17,* 3–33.

Sibley, D. (1995). Families and domestic routines: Constructing the boundaries of childhood. In S. Pile & N. Thrift (Eds.), *Mapping the subject: Geographies of cultural transformation* (pp. 123–137). London: Routledge.

Sibley, D., & Lowe, G. (1992). Domestic space, modes of control and problem behaviour. *Geografiska Annaler 74B* (3), 189–197.

Socha, T. J. (2003, November). *It all begins at home: Implications of development in communication.* Paper presented to the National Communication Association meeting, Miami, Florida.

Solberg, A. (1990). Negotiating childhood: Changing constructions of age for Norwegian children. In A. James & A. Prout (Eds.), *Constructing and reconstructing childhood: Contemporary issues in the sociological study of childhood* (pp. 118–137). Basingstoke, UK: Falmer Press.

Stainton-Rogers, R. S., & Stainton-Rogers, W. (1992). *Stories of childhood: Shifting agendas of child concern*. Toronto, Canada: University of Toronto Press.

Stryker, S. (1959). Symbolic interaction as an approach to family research. *Marriage and Family Living, 21,* 111–119.

Stryker, S. (1968). Identity salience and role performance: The relevance of symbolic interaction theory for family research. *Journal of Marriage and the Family, 30,* 558–564.

Taylor, C. E. (1995). "You think it was a *fight?*": Co-constructing (the struggle for) meaning, face, and family in everyday narrative activity. *Research on Language and Social Interaction, 28,* 283–317.

Valentine, G. (1997). "Oh yes I can." "Oh no you can't.": Children and parents' understanding of kids' competence to negotiate public space safely. *Antipode, 29,* 65–89.

Weigel, D. J. (2003). A communication approach to the construction of commitment in the early years of marriage: A qualitative study. *Journal of Family Communication, 3,* 1–19.

Whitchurch, G. G., & Dickson, F. C. (1999). Family communication. In M. Sussman, S. K. Steinmetz, & G. W. Peterson (Eds.), *Handbook of marriage and the family* (2nd ed., pp. 687–704). New York: Plenum Press.

White, J. M., & Klein, D. M. (2002). *Family theories* (2nd ed). Thousand Oaks, CA: Sage.

Wood, D., & Beck, R. (1990). Dos and don'ts: Family rules, rooms and their relationships. *Children's Environments Quarterly, 7,* 2–14.

Wood, J. T. (1994). Saying it makes it so: The discursive construction of sexual harassment. In S. G. Bingham (Ed.), *Conceptualizing sexual harassment as discursive practice* (pp. 17–30). Westport, CT: Praeger.

16

Social Exchange Theories: Interdependence and Equity

Marianne Dainton

Elaine D. Zelley

Editors' Note: The authors note social exchange as a group of theories coming out of sociology, psychology, and cultural anthropology. They are logical-empirical theories focused on how persons communicate and make rational choices with the goal of maximizing rewards and minimizing their costs.

One of the most frequently "borrowed" theories from disciplines outside of communication studies for understanding marital and family communication is social exchange theory. Not an individual theory *per se* but a constellation of theories that share common attributes, social exchange theory emerged from the fields of sociology, psychology, and cultural anthropology in the 1950s and 1960s. Communication scholars quickly adopted exchange principles, particularly in their study of interpersonal relationships. Of the many different social exchange theories, two have emerged as central to the study of family communication: Thibaut and Kelley's (1959; Kelley & Thibaut, 1978) theory of interdependence, and Walster and colleagues' (Walster, Walster, & Berscheid, 1978) equity theory. This chapter presents an overview of these social exchange approaches, particularly as they relate to marital and family communication. We also offer several research exemplars and emerging uses of the theories. Finally, we conclude with strengths and weaknesses of exchange approaches while noting future research directions for the study of family communication.

NATURE AND ASSUMPTIONS OF SOCIAL EXCHANGE APPROACHES

Using an economic metaphor to explain interactional life, social exchange perspectives assert that all human interaction involves the voluntary and reciprocal trade of resources from one person to another (Roloff, 1981). Much like economic market trades, social exchange perspectives posit that people hold a number of *resources*, which are defined as any symbolic or physical commodity that can be exchanged through interpersonal behavior (Foa & Foa, 1976). When talking about "social" exchanges—as opposed to economic exchanges—typical resources include love, attraction, acceptance, social approval, respect, status, information, and compliance/power (Blau, 1964; Foa & Foa, 1976). Importantly, not all resources are created equally; each individual has preferred resources, which are termed *rewards*. Moreover, because exchange processes involve both the giving and receiving of resources, all exchanges also involve costs. *Costs* refer to benefits foregone in the exchange process.

Although the language is that of economic exchanges, the reality is that few, if any, social exchange theories are grounded purely in market economics. Behavioral reinforcement theories and social structural approaches to culture have also played a role in the development of these theories. Specifically, there are two distinct and contradictory intellectual influences on exchange theories: utilitarianism and structuralism (Sabatelli & Shehan, 1993). Utilitarian perspectives assert that humans act rationally to maximize their benefits through exchanges with others (e.g., Homans, 1974; Thibaut & Kelley, 1959). Using the language of social exchange, then, through interaction people will make rational choices to maximize rewards and minimize their costs.

Structural perspectives, however, suggest that exchange patterns that produce payoffs for interactants (i.e., rewards) are preferred, and over time such exchanges lead to enduring patterns of social interaction (Levi-Strauss, 1969; Mauss, 1954). Thus, cultural norms for interaction are created by social exchanges, and these norms later constrain the types of exchanges that are permissible in given networks or cultures. (Structuration processes are discussed in more detail in Chapter 19 of this volume.)

In practice, then, social exchange approaches can provide a means for a microanalysis of the decisions made by individuals in developing and maintaining their relationships, as well as a macroanalysis of how exchanges create social structures that constrain individual choice and reflect power differentials. Within the domain of family communication, most scholars have focused on the former rather than the latter (see Chapter 19 of this volume for emerging uses of structural exchange theories). Discussed in turn, the present chapter focuses on interdependence theory and equity theory, the guiding frameworks that social exchange scholars have most frequently used.

INTERDEPENDENCE THEORY

Interdependence theory predicts relationship satisfaction, dependence, and stability by examining the interplay of three distinct yet overlapping (interdependent) variables (Thibaut & Kelley, 1959). These variables include relational outcomes, comparison levels, and comparison levels of alternatives.

Simply defined, *relational outcomes* are the perceived ratio of rewards to costs within a given relationship (Thibaut & Kelley, 1959). Noted earlier, interdependence theory posits that rewards and costs emerge within any social relationship. Relational rewards include interpersonal resources that an individual perceives as enjoyable or helpful in achieving specific goals; for instance, companionship, social support, and intimacy are all possible rewards. Conversely, relational costs include limitations or drawbacks that an individual perceives as disagreeable or as obstacles that prevent goal achievement. For example, negotiating holiday visits with in-laws or stepfamilies, loss of social independence with the arrival of the firstborn child, or setting aside career aspirations because of family obligations all could be potential costs for members of a family. Although individual preferences for rewards and perceptions of costs will vary, the concept of relational outcomes suggests that individuals have an awareness of these benefits and drawbacks. Relational outcomes are often represented by a simple mathematical equation: Rewards − Costs = Outcome. When perceived rewards overshadow costs, a positive outcome value results; conversely, a negative outcome value occurs when perceived costs outweigh rewards.

Notably, this positive or negative outcome value is not enough to predict relational satisfaction and stability. Instead, the outcome value serves as a benchmark to compare current rewards and costs in relation to one's *comparison level* (CL). CL represents what rewards and costs a person expects from a particular relationship (Thibaut & Kelley, 1959). Individuals typically base these expectations on their own models for relationships (e.g., parents) and on one's own relational experiences; television and other media representations of relationships may also shape a person's expectations. According to interdependence theory, then, individuals compare their relational outcomes with their CL. For instance, if, as a new father, Brett perceives more rewards than costs, and this outcome matches or exceeds his expectations for parenthood, interdependence theory predicts that Brett will be satisfied with his family relationships (Outcome > CL). In contrast, if Brett expects more rewards than he currently perceives, a sense of dissatisfaction is predicted (CL > Outcome). Thus, one's satisfaction with a relationship is based on a positive outcome value that also meets or exceeds one's expectations (CL).

According to interdependence theory, determining a person's relational satisfaction (or lack thereof) is still not enough to predict whether the relationship will continue or terminate. For example, Mona's expectations exceed her perceived relational outcomes, leaving her deeply dissatisfied with her marriage; yet, she remains in the relationship—why? According to Thibaut and Kelley (1959), an individual considers the *comparison level of alternatives* (CL_{alt}), that is, the options to the current relationship. Should she leave her relationship? Is there someone better out there? When individuals perceive that their alternatives are greater than their current outcome or greater than their expectations (CL), interdependence theory predicts that they will seek to end the relationship. Even if satisfied with a current relationship (i.e., Outcome > CL), a person who perceives that the alternatives surpass the current situation may end the relationship (represented mathematically by CL_{alt} > Outcome > CL). Only when considering an individual's perception of *Outcomes : CL : CL_{alt}*, then, can researchers make predictions about the state and status of a relationship.

EQUITY THEORY

A second social exchange approach, equity theory, relies on the principle of distributive justice; that is, whoever contributes the most to the relationship should receive the most benefits from the relationship (Deutsch, 1985). According to equity theory, individuals are aware of their own contributions and benefits, as well as those inputs and outcomes of their partner (Canary & Stafford, 1992). An *equitable relationship* is one in which the ratios of benefits to contributions is the same for both partners. Conversely, when partners' ratios of outcomes to inputs are not the same, an *inequitable relationship* results with two opposing conditions. First, the individual who receives more outcomes in relation to inputs is considered *overbenefited*. That is, this person receives more than is given when compared with the partner. Conversely, the individual who contributes more in relation to benefits received is termed *underbenefited*. In other words, this individual gives more and receives fewer benefits than the partner.

Similar to interdependence theory, equity theory also maintains that people want to maximize outcomes while minimizing inputs. When relationships become inequitable, however, equity theory also suggests that relational partners will typically seek to restore equity rather than exploit the situation (Hatfield, Traupmann, Sprecher, Utne, & Hay, 1985; Roloff, 1981). For example, underbenefited individuals can decrease their inputs (e.g., stop doing laundry), adjust their perceptions of behavior to balance equity ratios (e.g., "I like to do the cooking"), or end the relationship (Sprecher & Schwartz, 1994). Conversely, the overbenefited person can increase the inputs to restore equity.

Theoretically, individuals in equitable relationships are more satisfied than are persons in inequitable relationships (Hatfield et al., 1985). Understandably, underbenefited persons feel dissatisfaction because they put more into the relationship and receive fewer benefits than do their partners. Notably, equity theory also predicts that those who are overbenefited also feel discontent, likely due to feelings of guilt. Despite the finding that both inequitable conditions lead to dissatisfaction, being underbenefited is considered more destructive because it is positively related to anger, depression, and sadness (Sprecher, 1986).

USES OF INTERDEPENDENCE AND EQUITY THEORIES

Scholars have most often used social exchange perspectives to study dyads, particularly marital dyads, rather than the entire family system. This section highlights research that has used social exchange principles within these contexts.

Relational Development and Maintenance

Current understandings of relationship initiation and development have largely been grounded in theories of social exchange. For example, Levinger's (1972, 1974, 1980) incremental exchange theory uses social exchange processes to explain interpersonal attraction. Similarly, Altman and Taylor's social penetration model (1973; Morton, Alexander, & Altman, 1976) uses exchange elements to argue that the process of relational development is a function of increased depth and breadth of disclosure. Likewise, Knapp's (1978) staircase model of relational development and dissolution is also grounded in social exchange principles.

Similarly, both interdependence theory and equity theory have been used to study relational maintenance processes. For example, Ragsdale (1996) used interdependence theory to uncover whether satisfaction (which was assessed via a measure of comparison levels) predicted maintenance use among married couples. He did not find the predicted link between comparison levels and the use of maintenance, however. Dainton (2000) also tested interdependence principles in her study of maintenance within romantic relationships. She found that meeting or exceeding one's expectations for maintenance behaviors predicted satisfaction, but that the sheer use of maintenance strategies was a stronger predictor. Together, these studies cast doubt on the predictive ability of interdependence theory in explaining relational maintenance processes.

Equity theory has been more successful in predicting relational maintenance. In adapting equity theory to the process of relational maintenance, Canary and Stafford (1992, 1993, 2001) proposed that maintenance behaviors are resources in a relationship; one's own maintenance behaviors count as inputs, and the partner's maintenance behaviors count as rewards. Canary and Stafford (1992) predicted that individuals in equitable relationships would be most likely to use maintenance behaviors, as by definition, maintenance behaviors are used to sustain desired relational states (such as equity). They have found partial support for these predictions within married and romantic relationships.

One of the few studies to examine equity within the family context, Vogl-Bauer, Kalbfleisch, and Beatty (1999) extended the understanding of maintenance to include parent-child relationships. Following the methods of Canary and Stafford (1992), they used equity theory in their investigation of the maintenance of relationships between parents and adolescent children. Vogl-Bauer et al. (1999) found that although parents were most satisfied when their relationship with an adolescent child was equitable, the teens reported more satisfaction when they were overbenefited. This finding partially contradicts the theory's prediction that individuals seek to maintain equity. Vogl-Bauer et al. speculated that the discrepancy for adolescents may exist because of teens' egocentric tendencies to view the world as centered on them. In this manner, adolescents may expect to be overbenefited, and an equitable relationship may be perceived as dissatisfying. Due to such developmental reasons, it may be that equity theory is better understood within the context of adult-to-adult relationships.

Relational Conflict and Power

Social exchange theories suggest that the root cause of relational conflict is a violation of expectations, including perceived inequity. Violations might occur because of actual changes in the distribution of rewards or because of changing perceptions of what should be considered fair (Roloff, 1981). Social exchange theories extend several techniques for restoring perceptions of fairness. According to equity theory, for example, individuals can change their own or their partner's behavior by either increasing or decreasing inputs; they can also distort perceptions of behavior to change equity calculations, or they can leave the relationship (Sprecher & Schwartz, 1994). If the partners can resolve the conflict, social exchange theories suggest that the relationship will continue; failure to resolve conflicts can lead to relational termination (Roloff, 1981).

Historically, social exchange approaches have focused on how differential access to resources leads to power differentials in marriage. For instance, Scanzoni (1979) proposed that husbands typically have more power than their wives because of increased financial resources (also see the discussion on feminist approaches to the family in Chapter 13 of this volume). This has not always been supported empirically, however. Sexton and Perlman (1989) used equity theory to study whether gender or career status affected marital power. They found that single-career and dual-career couples did not vary in perceived power. Moreover, gender roles did not explain variations in power. Instead, factors unique to the couple were perceived as important to equity in resource exchange.

One way in which the issue of power manifests itself is with the division of household labor. In their review of research into inequity in this area, Canary and Stafford (2001) concluded that women have historically been underbenefited in the distribution of domestic labor. Moreover, for women, this type of inequity is positively associated with divorce, with little evidence that marital satisfaction mediates the two (Frisco & Williams, 2003).

Most research using interdependence theories to study maintenance has emphasized romantic relationships, marital dyads, and even friendships, but with little investigation of families. One possible reason for this oversight is that family relationships are the most permanent type of interpersonal relationship. Individuals don't often "break up" with siblings or "divorce" their parents. Actively working to maintain relationships that are bound by blood ties seems counterintuitive: Why examine rewards and costs of a relationship that will never end? No matter how good someone else's family looks (CL_{alt}), we can't have it. Likewise, interdependence approaches may not be used widely to study family communication because of the assumed hierarchy and power differences within traditional conceptualizations of family. One probably does not and should not expect equity between a parent and a toddler. As family composition becomes increasingly complex, however, examining issues of family inequity may prove fruitful. For example, maintaining relationships with in-laws, adult siblings caring for elderly parents, and managing shared custody in blended families are all modern family arrangements in which issues of inequity may arise. Such emerging issues are discussed next.

EMERGING USES

New domains of study and uses for social exchange theory continue to emerge in the study of family interaction. This section focuses on recent research using social exchange theories.

Benefits and Costs of Parenthood

Sabatelli's (1984) Marital Comparison Level Index has served as one of the first measures of satisfaction that incorporates Thibaut and Kelley's (1959) notion of comparison level. More recently, Waldron-Hennessey and Sabatelli (1997) created the Parental Comparison Level Index to assess the experience of parenthood relative to expectations. As Waldron-Hennessey and Sabatelli (1997) argued, understanding contemporary families requires understanding the experience of parenthood. Their measure allows for examinations of parental perceptions over the lifespan of the family. As such, it might allow for counselors and scholars to better understand the transition to parenthood, the impacts of family stressors on the parent-child dynamic, and the extent to which expectations might be negotiated within the parental and parent-child systems.

Changing Family Dynamics

In recent years, researchers have used a social exchange approach to explain nontraditional family dynamics. In a study comparing international and domestic adoption, for example, Hollingsworth and Mae Ruffin (2002) identified the benefits and cost associated with adoption. They argued that a social exchange approach explains these families' decisions.

In their examination of second marriages, Buunk and Mutsaers (1999) compared participants' perceptions of equity in former and current marriages. Not surprisingly, these researchers found that those who had remarried reported much more inequity in the former marriage as compared to the current marriage. Of particular interest, remarried women reported more satisfaction when they experienced equity in their second marriage, whereas remarried men were more satisfied when they were overbenefited in the second marriage.

Caregiver burden is another pertinent issue in family communication. Increasingly, adult children are taking responsibility for care of their elderly parents; yet the burden for this care is not always equally distributed among siblings. Ingersoll-Dayton, Neal, Ha, and Hammer (2003) found support for inequity as an explanatory mechanism in efforts to rectify imbalances among siblings in caring for older parents. This inequity can be personally detrimental; for example, unequal exchanges lead to caregiver burden (Call, Finch, Huck, & Kane, 1999).

The "Dark Side" of Families

Certainly, caregiver burden straddles the dark side of family relationships. Other dark side issues can be explained by social exchange as well. In focusing on the marital dyad, Prins, Buunk, and VanYperen (1993) found that inequity was associated with women's desire for and involvement in an extramarital affair. In fact, inequity was independent of other reasons for having an affair, including relational or sexual dissatisfaction, or normative disapproval.

Another dark side issue is alcoholism. Ruben (1998) applied blended systems principles and social exchange approaches to explain how family alcoholism exacerbates perceptions of inequity and lack of reciprocity in the exchange of positive resources such as love, affection, and nurturing. He provided methods for clinical assessment in alcoholic families.

Finally, social exchange processes may explain sibling rivalry. McHale, Updegraff, Jackson-Newsom, Tucker, and Crouter (2000) studied parents' differential treatment and perceptions of fairness in middle childhood and adolescence. They found that perceived fairness was a stronger predictor of children's self-esteem and sibling positivity than was perceived differential treatment alone, supporting a social exchange approach to this phenomenon.

STRENGTHS AND LIMITATIONS

Because the exact nature of social exchange theories vary, it is difficult to present a critique that holds true across all theories. In his definitive book on the use of social exchange theories in interpersonal communication, Roloff (1981) identified five social exchange approaches and subsequently argued that each social exchange theory should stand separately rather than be grouped together, arguing that

> I fear that some may be tempted to treat the five approaches as food on a smorgasbord tray, choosing a little of each and disregarding the rest. I think the theories should be treated as separate entities rather than patched together like the Frankenstein monster. (p. 135)

Nevertheless, because the present chapter focuses on the class of theories associated with social exchange rather than one specific theory, we will present the most common strengths and weaknesses associated with exchange approaches.

The first major criticism identified with social exchange theory is the problem of measuring rewards and costs (Hinde, 1981; Roloff, 1981). Because of the subjective nature of what is considered rewarding and what is considered costly, rewards and costs can be determined only after they are administered. Thus, the process of assessing rewards and costs has been condemned as tautological; something is considered a reward if the individual finds it rewarding (Bochner, 1985; Roloff, 1981).

A second major criticism of social exchange principles is the problem of what is considered "fair" (Roloff, 1981). Some scholars use the principle of equality to assess fairness, which implies that fairness is achieved if outcomes are equal among relational partners, regardless of investments (Cate, Lloyd, Henton, & Larson, 1982). Equity theorists, however, propose that fairness is achieved when partners perceive that the proportion of outcomes to investments is equal between the partners (Walster, Walster, & Berscheid, 1978). Importantly, however, when considering family relationships, fairness is very complicated and difficult to judge, especially within particularly complex systems such as stepfamilies, blended families, foster families, and intergenerational families. Third, some scholars criticize that social exchange processes are overly rational. For example, Duck (1988) argued that researchers "assume too easily that information processing is rational and intelligent in relationships when much of the time our subjects and our own personal lives reveal that it is not so" (p. 146). Regarding social exchange processes specifically, Duck (1986) asserted that "we do not go through a ritual each breakfast time where we treat each other like strangers and run through a whole range of rewarding techniques to re-establish the relationship" (p. 90). In other words, Duck believes that relational maintenance is less strategic and more mundane, occurring through the use of routine, everyday behaviors and not through continuous, formal reassessments of rewards and costs.

Defenders of social exchange address all three of these criticisms while identifying a number of strengths. First, social exchange principles tend to be highly formalized and present clear directions for research (Roloff, 1981). That is, the specific theories under the social exchange rubric have testable hypotheses and a clear logical structure. Second, social exchange approaches are useful for the study of a number of different relationship contexts (Roloff, 1981). Described earlier, these theories have most often been used to study romantic relationships and marriage in particular, but exchange processes can also be applied to larger family networks. Third, social exchange theories bridge the gap between practitioners and theorists (Roloff, 1981). That is, these theories can be used in pursuit of academic understanding, but they also can be used in therapeutic contexts (e.g., Nelson & Nelson, 1982; Winstead, Derlega, Lewis, & Margulis, 1988). Finally, and perhaps most importantly, social exchange processes strike many people as an accurate way to understand their real, everyday relationships (Roloff, 1981).

FUTURE DIRECTIONS

Despite the well-established and emerging areas of research described earlier, there are several sources of untapped opportunities that might benefit from more careful observation. First, we described structural approaches to social exchange at the beginning of this chapter, (and Chapter 19 of this volume focuses on the use of structuration theory specifically). However, a gap in the research exists that could be bridged by more careful attention to the macro processes that influence the micro exchange principles described by interdependence and equity theories. For example, a true systems approach to family communication (see Chapter 20 of this volume for a review of systems approaches) would call attention to larger network and cultural influences on what is considered rewarding and what is considered fair. Topics such as cultural expectations for motherhood, normative prescriptions for "healthy family functioning," and formalized family leave practices all constrain the types of exchanges that take place in families. Social exchange approaches have yet to address the role of these larger social structures. Perhaps most problematic is that social exchange approaches largely ignore culture. Research indicates that neither equality nor equity are consistently linked to relational satisfaction or stability in other cultures, suggesting that the social exchange theories described in this chapter might not work cross-culturally (Berman, Murphy-Berman, & Singh, 1985; Lujansky & Mikula, 1983).

On the other hand, Thibaut and Kelley's (1959) concepts of CL and CL_{alt} imply recognition of network effects because an individual's expectations and perceived alternatives are part of one's network. The influence of social networks *can* be examined through existing social exchange theories. Consider again the notion of parental expectations.

Denise expected that parenthood would be extremely difficult and require a great number of sacrifices. She has found parenthood better than expectations and is feeling very connected with her new infant. Six months later, Denise's sister-in-law Carrie finds out that she is pregnant. Carrie formulates her expectations for parenthood based on Denise's experience. However, Carrie's newborn suffers from colic. Her parenthood experience is below expectations, resulting in a lack of connection with her infant and a strain on her marital relationship. In this case, the interdependence of family members is highlighted *because* of the use of social exchange principles.

A second untapped area of opportunity involves a bridge between social exchange approaches and symbolic interaction theory (described in Chapter 15 in this volume). Stephen (1984), for example, proposed and found support for a symbolic exchange framework, which blends symbolic interaction and social exchange. Specifically, he has argued that meaning is the primary resource that individuals exchange within relationships. In support for this assertion, Stephen found that relationship length positively correlated with symbolic interdependence. That is, the longer relational partners were together, the more similar their relational reality—a relational worldview that defines the meanings given to behaviors in interaction. Likewise, Stephen (1984) found that higher levels of symbolic interdependence were associated with greater relational satisfaction and commitment. This more narrow focus on symbolic exchange, rather than on the broader concept of social exchange, seems ideal for the study of marital and family interaction.

Researchers have not yet adopted this view, however, which may be because symbolic interaction theory and social exchange are grounded in distinct metatheoretical assumptions; symbolic interaction theory tends to be an approach embraced by more humanistic scholars, who eschew quantitative research methods. Social exchange tends to be used by social scientists who use quantitative methods. Strong philosophical commitments about the nature of human beings and appropriate ways to study them may prevent scholars from utilizing the blended approach.

Finally, social exchange principles might become even more valuable by incorporating the role of emotion in decision making. For instance, Planalp (2003) has argued that emotion might be the currency of social exchange; likewise, judgments would not be made by computing profits but by assessing how exchanges made people feel. Her ideas present a fresh way of reconsidering social exchange processes.

In sum, social exchange approaches have provided popular and useful theoretical lenses for communication scholars interested in marriage and the family. If these approaches are to explain family communication processes more fully, however, the scope must simultaneously expand to comprise the entire family system, including networks as well as cultural contexts, and constrict to focus more clearly on communicative exchanges.

REFERENCES

Altman, I., & Taylor, D. (1973). *Social penetration: The development of interpersonal relationships.* New York: Holt, Rinehart & Winston.

Berman, J. J., Murphy-Berman, V., & Singh, P. (1985). Cross-cultural similarities and differences in perceptions of fairness. *Journal of Cross-Cultural Psychology, 16,* 55–67.

Blau, P. (1964). *Exchange and power in social life.* New York: Wiley.

Bochner, A. P. (1985). The functions of human communication in interpersonal bonding. In C. Arnold & J. Bowers (Eds.), *Handbook of rhetorical and communication theory* (pp. 544–621). Boston: Allyn & Bacon.

Buunk, B. P., & Mutsaers, W. (1999). Equity perceptions and marital satisfaction in former and current marriage: A study among the remarried. *Journal of Social and Personal Relationships, 16,* 123–132.

Call, K. T., Finch, M. A., Huck, S. M., & Kane, R. A. (1999). Caregiver burden from a social exchange perspective: Caring for older people after hospital discharge. *Journal of Marriage and the Family, 61,* 688–699.

Canary, D. J., & Stafford, L. (1992). Relational maintenance strategies and equity in marriage. *Communication Monographs, 59,* 243–267.

Canary, D. J., & Stafford, L. (1993). Preservation of relational characteristics: Maintenance strategies, equity, and locus of control. In P. J. Kalbfleisch (Ed.), *Interpersonal communication: Evolving interpersonal relationships* (pp. 237–259). Hillsdale, NJ: Lawrence Erlbaum.

Canary, D. J., & Stafford, L. (2001). Equity in the preservation of personal relationships. In J. H. Harvey & A. Wenzel (Eds.), *Close romantic relationships: Maintenance and enhancement* (pp. 133–151). Mahwah, NJ: Lawrence Erlbaum.

Cate, R. M., Lloyd, S. A., Henton, J. M., & Larson, J. H. (1982). Fairness and reward level as predictors of relationship satisfaction. *Social Psychology Quarterly, 45,* 177–181.

Dainton, M. (2000). Maintenance behaviors, expectations, and satisfaction: Linking the comparison level to relational maintenance. *Journal of Social and Personal Relationships, 17,* 827–842.

Deutsch, M. (1985). *Distributive justice: A social-psychological perspective.* New Haven, CT: Yale University Press.

Duck, S. (1986). *Human relationships: An introduction to social psychology*. Beverly Hills, CA: Sage.

Duck, S. (1988). *Relating to others*. Milton Keynes, U.K.: Open University Press.

Foa, E., & Foa, U. (1976). Resource theory of social exchange. In J. Thibaut, J. Spence, & R. Carson (Eds.), *Contemporary topics in psychology* (pp. 99–131). Morristown, NJ: General Learning Press.

Frisco, M. L., & Williams, K. (2003). Perceived housework equity, marital happiness, and divorce in dual-earner households. *Journal of Family Issues, 24*, 51–73.

Hatfield, E., Traupmann, J., Sprecher, S., Utne, M., & Hay, M. (1985). Equity in close relationships. In W. Ickes (Ed.), *Compatible and incompatible relationships* (pp. 91–171). New York: Springer-Verlag.

Hinde, R. A. (1981). The basis of a science of interpersonal relations. In S. Duck (Ed.), *Personal relationships 1: Studying interpersonal relationships*. New York: Academic Press.

Hollingsworth, L., & Mae Ruffin, V. (2002). Why are so many U.S. families adopting internationally? A social exchange perspective. *Journal of Human Behavior in the Social Environment, 6*, 81–97.

Homans, G. C. (1974). *Social behavior: Its elementary forms* (Rev. ed.). New York: Harcourt, Brace, Jovanovich.

Ingersoll-Dayton, B., Neal, M. B., Ha, J. H., & Hammer, L. B. (2003). Redressing inequity in parent care among siblings. *Journal of Marriage and the Family, 65*, 201–212.

Kelley, H. H., & Thibaut, J. W. (1978). *Interpersonal relations: A theory of interdependence*. New York: Wiley.

Knapp, M. (1978). *Nonverbal communication in human interaction*. New York: Holt, Rinehart & Winston.

Levinger, G. (1972). Little sand box and big quarry: Comment on Byrne's paradigmatic spade for research on interpersonal attraction. *Representative Research in Social Psychology, 3*, 3–19.

Levinger, G. (1974). A three-level approach to attraction: Toward our understanding of pair relatedness. In T.L. Huston (Ed.), *Foundations of interpersonal attraction* (pp. 100–120). New York: Academic Press.

Levinger, G. (1980). Towards the analysis of close relationships. *Journal of Experimental Social Psychology, 16*, 510–544.

Levi-Strauss, C. (1969). *The elementary structure of kinship*. Boston: Beacon.

Lujansky, H., & Mikula, G. (1983). Can equity theory explain the quality and stability of romantic relationships? *British Journal of Social Psychology, 22*, 101–112.

Mauss, M. (1954). *The gift*. New York: Free Press.

McHale, S. M., Updegraff, K. A., Jackson-Newsom, J., Tucker, C. J., & Crouter, A. C. (2000). When does parents' differential treatment have negative implications for siblings? *Social Development, 9*, 149–172.

Morton, T., Alexander, J., & Altman, I. (1976). Communication and relationship definition. In G. Miller (Ed.), *Explorations in interpersonal communication* (pp. 105–126). Beverly Hills, CA: Sage.

Nelson, M., & Nelson, G. K. (1982). Problems of equity in the reconstituted family: A social exchange analysis. *Family Relations, 31,* 223–231.

Planalp, S. (2003). The unacknowledged role of emotion in theories of close relationships: How do theories feel? *Communication Theory, 13,* 78–99.

Prins, K. S., Buunk, B. P., & VanYperen, N. W. (1993). Equity, normative disapproval and extramarital relationships. *Journal of Social and Personal Relationships, 10,* 39–53.

Ragsdale, J. D. (1996). Gender, satisfaction level, and the use of relational maintenance strategies in marriage. *Communication Monographs, 63,* 354–369.

Roloff, M. E. (1981). *Interpersonal communication: The social exchange approach.* Beverly Hills, CA: Sage.

Ruben, D. H. (1998). Social exchange theory: Dynamics of a system governing the dysfunctional family and guide to assessment. *Journal of Contemporary Psychotherapy, 28,* 307–325.

Sabatelli, R. M. (1984). The marital comparison level index: A measure for assessing outcomes relative to expectations. *Journal of Marriage and the Family, 46,* 651–662.

Sabatelli, R. M., & Shehan, C. L. (1993). Exchange and resource theories. In P. G. Boss, W. J. Doherty, R. LaRossa, W. R. Schumm, & S. K. Steinmetz (Eds.), *Sourcebook of family theories and methods: A contextual approach* (pp. 385–411). New York: Plenum.

Scanzoni, J. (1979). Social processes and power in families. In W. Burr, R. Hill, F. Nye, & I. Reiss (Eds.), *Contemporary theories about the family: Research based theories vol. 1* (pp 295–316). New York: Macmillan.

Sexton, C. S., & Perlman, D. S. (1989). Couples' career orientation, and perceived equity as determinants of marital power. *Journal of Marriage and the Family, 51,* 933–941.

Sprecher, S. (1986). The relation between equity and emotions in close relationships. *Social Psychology Bulletin, 49,* 309–321.

Sprecher, S., & Schwartz, P. (1994). Equity and balance in the exchange of contributions in close relationships. In M. J. Lerner & G. Mikula (Eds.), *Entitlement and the affectional bond: Justice in close relationships* (pp. 11–41). New York: Plenum Press.

Stephen, T. D. (1984). A symbolic exchange framework for the development of intimate relationships. *Human Relations, 5,* 393–408.

Thibaut, J. W., & Kelley, H. K. (1959). *The social psychology of groups.* New York: Wiley.

Vogl-Bauer, S., Kalbfleisch, P. J., & Beatty, M. J. (1999). Perceived equity, satisfaction, and relational maintenance strategies in parent-adolescent dyads. *Journal of Youth and Adolescence, 28,* 27–49.

Waldron-Hennessey, R., & Sabatelli, R. (1997). The parental Comparison Level Index: A measure for assessing parental rewards and costs relative to expectations. *Journal of Marriage and the Family, 59,* 824–833.

Walster, E., Walster, G., & Berscheid, E. (1978). *Equity: Theory and research.* Boston: Allyn & Bacon.

Winstead, B. A., Derlega, V. J., Lewis, R. J., & Margulis, S. T. (1988). Understanding the therapeutic relationship as a personal relationship. *Journal of Social and Personal Relationships, 5,* 109–125.

17

Social Learning Theory: Modeling and Communication in the Family Context

Adrianne Kunkel

Mary Lee Hummert

Michael Robert Dennis

Editors' Note: Social Learning Theory is firmly rooted in the logical-empirical paradigm, coming out of psychology and behaviorism. The theory focuses on the cognitive processes involved in learning from the environment; thus cause-effect generalizations.

Social Learning Theory (SLT) explains the process by which human beings acquire behaviors through observation of their external environments and provides a useful framework for the study of communication within the family. In this chapter, we present a condensed history of Social Learning Theory, with an emphasis on the major constructs and predictions of its most recent and highly influential articulation: Social Cognitive Theory (Bandura, 1986, 2001). In addition, we acknowledge the contributions of prior social learning research to the understanding of communication behavior in family settings. Finally, we contemplate promising future applications of social learning principles to scholarship that examines acquisition, within the family context, of communication behaviors, skills, and cognitions pertaining to health maintenance, social support, and stereotypes of age and gender.

OVERVIEW OF SOCIAL LEARNING AND SOCIAL COGNITIVE THEORIES

Although Social Learning Theory (SLT) is neither generally attributed to one academic discipline nor to a single theorist, the earliest formulations of SLT within psychology featured predictions drawn from the tradition of behaviorism (e.g., Skinner, 1938). Essentially, behaviorism purports that behavior is "cued by the stimuli that precede it and shaped and controlled by the reinforcing stimuli that follow it" (Bandura, 1986, p. 12). Miller and Dollard (1941) characterized social learning as a form of operant conditioning by emphasizing the roles of reward/ reinforcement and punishment in the production of imitative (i.e., learned) behaviors.

More recent formulations of SLT have moved beyond a strict behaviorist, stimulus-response explanation for how people acquire behaviors and considered how motivational, personality, and cognitive processes are involved in learning from the environment. Critical to those of us involved in the study of communication, these later formulations also recognized the "role of other people as the agents of reinforcement" (Howard & Hollander, 1997, p. 45). Although many scholars have contributed to the development of SLT, we focus here on the contributions of two scholars whose work is particularly relevant to the study of family communication: Julian Rotter (1954, 1966) and Albert Bandura (1977, 1986, 2001).

Julian Rotter and the Importance of Beliefs in the Reproduction of Behaviors

In his 1954 book, Rotter, a clinical psychologist, advanced SLT by showing that an individual's expectancy (or belief) that a behavior will lead to particular reinforcements strongly influences the likelihood of that behavior's occurrence. In subsequent work, Rotter (1966) introduced the notion that individuals have a general tendency to think of outcomes as either under their personal control (internal locus of control) or under the control of outside forces such as other people or luck (external locus of control). These individual differences helped to explain variance in behavioral responses to similar environmental factors.

Albert Bandura and the Evolution of SLT to Social Cognitive Theory

If there is one name most closely associated with Social Learning Theory, it is Bandura's. His emphasis on the role of cognition in the acquisition of observed behaviors led to Bandura's (1986, 2001) reformulating Social Learning Theory as Social Cognitive Theory. Bandura argued that *learning theory* implies a conditioning model associated only with response acquisition, whereas *Social Cognitive Theory* recognizes the individual learner as agentic (i.e., in control) in the "learning" process. His contributions included the stages of social learning and the development of the psychological construct of self-efficacy.

Stages of social learning. Bandura (1977, 1986) noted that social learning occurs in four stages. In the first stage, the individual attends to the behavior of another—either directly via a live model, or indirectly via a mediated source such as television. In the second stage, the individual acquires and retains knowledge of the behavior. The third stage occurs when the individual can reproduce what has been seen or heard. In the final stage, the individual chooses whether to accept the model's behavior as a guide to performance, a decision that is determined largely by the perceived consequences of the behavior for the model.

Bandura and his colleagues tested these stages in the classic "Bobo doll" studies (e.g., Bandura, 1965; Bandura, Ross, & Ross, 1963). In this paradigm, children watched a film of an adult acting aggressively toward a large, inflated clown doll named "Bobo." In the film, the adult was either rewarded, punished, or received no consequences for the aggressive behaviors. The children were subsequently left alone with the Bobo doll and their behaviors monitored. Bandura's results (1965) were illustrative of the paradigm. Consistent with Bandura's description of the fourth stage of social learning, the children who saw the adult being punished engaged in significantly fewer aggressive behaviors toward the doll than did those in the other two groups. However, all children were then offered a reward if they could demonstrate some of the behaviors from the film. This eliminated any differences between the three groups in the production of the behaviors, supporting the conclusion that all children had proceeded through the attention, knowledge, and behavioral acquisition stages hypothesized by Bandura.

Self-efficacy. Bandura (1986) also introduced the notion that one factor influencing whether individuals choose to imitate behaviors of others is their *self-efficacy;* that is, their confidence in their ability to perform those behaviors. Whereas locus of control (Rotter, 1966) refers to the belief that one's own actions *can* (internal locus of control) or *cannot* (external locus of control) determine outcomes, self-efficacy centers on the belief that one *can produce* effectively the behaviors necessary to achieve desired outcomes. Accordingly, Bandura, Barbaranelli, Caprara, and Pastorelli (2001) found that children's perceived self-efficacy in social and academic arenas more strongly predicted the children's career and academic goals than did their actual academic achievement.

Summary of Social Learning Concepts

SLT focuses primarily on the dynamic interplay between observation of action, consequences of the action, and the enactment of imitative modeling. Modern conceptualizations of SLT involve much more than a simple stimulus-response relationship, and instead emphasize the importance of psychological or cognitive factors (e.g., beliefs about personal control, self-efficacy, outcome expectancies, values placed on particular outcomes) in behavioral modeling. These commitments of SLT make it a useful theory for the study of family communication.

CONTRIBUTIONS OF SOCIAL LEARNING TO UNDERSTANDING FAMILY COMMUNICATION

An interest in the family as the social unit in which critical social learning occurs has dominated social learning research. Bandura believed social learning to be the key to understanding the perpetuation of aggressive behavior from one generation to the next (Bandura & Walters, 1959). Likewise, Patterson (1971) saw social learning as the vehicle by which parents become the catalysts for family-based behaviors such as children eating well and going to bed when asked. Moreover, communication is implicitly understood to be part of the social learning process. Indeed, Rosser (1981) observed that the stimuli pertinent to the learning of prosocial behaviors include "sources of verbal information" (p. 69) that may instruct "under what conditions and why the behavior should be performed" (p. 75). Accordingly, a number of social learning studies have examined family communication, as described in the following section.

Social Learning of Family Interaction Patterns

Dixson (1995) noted that "children usually enter the parent-child relationship with no expectations," assume that their relationships are "normal," and use the relationship with parents to model their expectations "of what relationships are supposed to be like" (p. 49). For example, family communication patterns that emphasize either conversation or conformity orientation have dramatic effects on children's communication apprehension (Elwood & Schrader, 1998) and future relationships (see Chapter 4 of this volume). Also, in his exhaustive examination of family research studies published in peer-reviewed journals from 1990 to 2001, Stamp (2004) identified 18 articles that were guided by SLT, and a recurrent theme among them was the reproduction of family violence across generations. Furthermore, Gelles (1994) found that both the abused person and observers of abuse might socially learn to become abusers.

Social Learning and Family Therapy

Social learning has been studied not only as a source of negative communication patterns within the family but also as a potential remedy for those patterns. Chamberlain and Rosicky (1995) stated that Social Learning Family Therapy (SLFT) is "based on the notion that conduct-problem behavior is inadvertently developed and sustained through daily maladaptive parent-child interactions" and "is designed to alter the pattern of dysfunctional techniques and focuses on building parental skills in reinforcement" (p. 443). SLFT involves discipline (e.g., time-out, loss of privileges, extra chores) and reinforcement outcomes (e.g., allowance, point systems), as well as the development of family communication skills. Numerous investigations of the SLFT model indicated successful treatment and maintenance of productive behavior in adolescents, as well as more cohesion and less conflict in targeted families (Chamberlain & Rosicky, 1995). It is especially encouraging that aggression in children has been effectively reduced via SLFT (e.g., Horne & Van Dyke, 1983). Clearly, the prospects for family intervention based on tenets of social learning are bright.

OPPORTUNITIES FOR APPLICATION: SOCIAL LEARNING OF BEHAVIOR AND COGNITION IN THE FAMILY CONTEXT

As the prior research and Bandura's Social Cognitive Theory suggest, the lessons to be learned from the family may include not only communication behaviors, but also (and perhaps more critically) the perceptual sets and cognitions that underlie behavior. The subsequent sections of this chapter show how constructs borne of social learning can be applied to further our understanding of health maintenance behaviors, social support skills, and age and gender stereotypes within the family communication context.

Health-Related Behaviors

Undoubtedly, family members observe each other's health-related practices and messages and, to some extent, shape their relevant beliefs, attitudes, and habits accordingly. It seems reasonable to assume that, just as with prosocial and antisocial behaviors, the cognitions that inform individuals' hygiene, diet, and disease prevention decisions may be learned from those nearest them on an everyday basis. Moreover, the specific constructs that arose from social learning and social cognition theories, locus of control (Rotter, 1954, 1966), and self-efficacy (Bandura, 1986) have made great contributions to our understanding of health-related cognition and to models of health-related decision making.

Results of research linking the internal locus of control and the performance of particular preventive health behaviors have been mixed. Investigations have associated internal "health locus of control" (Wallston, Wallston, & DeVellis, 1978) with the performance of aerobic activity, breast self-examination, and smoking cessation, although these findings are countered by studies that do not uncover such relationships (see review by Norman & Bennett, 1996). In fact, Wallston's (1992) modified SLT of health behavior posits that an individual's internal health locus of control is merely a condition that promotes the relationship between self-efficacy and healthy action.

The "can do cognition" (Schwarzer & Fuchs, 1996, p. 163) of self-efficacy has not only received strong support on its own as a predictor of a variety of health-related behaviors—such as exercise, breast self-examination, dental flossing, and safe sex practices (see review by Schwarzer & Fuchs, 1996)—but has also been featured as the most significant variable in important health cognition models such as Witte's (1992) Extended Parallel Process Model (EPPM). If sufficiently motivated by a fear appeal or other threat to health, EPPM predicts that an individual who believes in his or her ability to adopt recommended preventive behaviors (i.e., danger control) will do so, whereas one who lacks self-efficacy will instead engage in denial, reactance, or defensive avoidance of recommendations (i.e., fear control). EPPM has been validated in studies of threat and efficacy messages, as delivered within health campaigns, relative to tractor safety, skin cancer, dental hygiene, and STDs (see review by Witte, Meyer, & Martell, 2001).

Although Bandura (1977) noted that self-efficacy perceptions may be developed from verbal persuasion, such as that found in mediated campaign messages, he also nominated vicarious experience (such as watching someone else effectively use sunscreen to ward off skin problems) as a viable source of efficacy information. Family settings are likely, then, to be key contexts for the social learning of health-related behaviors and beliefs about the feasibility of enacting them. As parents brush regularly, eat well, avoid smoking, enjoy the subsequent benefits of these behaviors, and provide consistent messages, their children may come to believe they are also capable of achieving healthy outcomes and choose to emulate parents' actions. Conversely, when motivated to do so by mediated campaigns and community or school-based interventions, children can healthfully influence their elders. Moreover, unhealthy behaviors may also be promoted within the family (Jones, Beach, & Jackson, 2004), and future research should identify messages that best counteract the unhealthy habits of relatives.

One representative opportunity for family communication scholars to assist the promotion of health comes with the prevalence of Type II diabetes onset among young people and its origins in lifestyles that lead also to obesity (Knowler, W., Barrett-Conner, E., Fowler, S., Hamman, R., Laching, J., Walker, E., & Nathan, D., 2002). "A Su Salad En Accion" was a San Antonio campaign directed at Latinos with slogans such as "you can easily arm yourself against diabetes" and "you have control over your life," and with suggestions regarding lower-fat diets and healthier food preparation (Ramirez, Villarreal, & Chalela,

1999). The campaign inspired Latina women to make healthier meals but did not attempt to convince their families that they were capable of eating in ways that were contrary to their acquired tastes and culture. The challenge for health and family communication scholars lies in discovering effective ways to model behaviors advocated in such well-meaning campaigns at home and to advance household members' beliefs in their abilities to bring about desired health outcomes.

Social Support

As people experience emotional distress caused by everything from daily hurts and hassles to severe trauma, emotional recovery is essential and emotional support is a fundamental form of communication in relationships (Goldsmith, 1994). Comforting and social support can motivate substantial changes in the emotional states of distressed others and may result in significantly enhanced mental and physical health (Cohen & Wills, 1985; Cutrona, 1996). Burleson (1984) defined comforting (or emotional support) as "the type of communicative behavior having the intended function of alleviating, moderating, or salving the distressed emotional states of others" (p. 64). In general, social support within the family has been studied within three types of relationships: marriage, sibling relationships, and parent-child bonds (Gardner & Cutrona, 2004). We focus here specifically on the parent-child relationship because a great deal of research emphasizes this bond and it seems most pertinent to the notion of social learning.

Traditional social support research tended to focus on situations and coping with particular stressors (Cohen & Wills, 1985; Pierce, Sarason, Sarason, Joseph, & Henderson, 1996), whereas family relationship research focusing on the parent-child bond has gravitated toward a "developmental approach" (Pierce et al., 1996, p. 4) in which social support contributes to personality and social development. For example, although children who receive sensitive and effective support from their parental caregivers are likely to expect the same from others outside the family and thus benefit from the existence of perceived social support such as higher self-esteem (e.g., Franco & Levitt, 1998), children who are neglected regarding support are likely to miss out on such benefits. Likewise, children who use more prosocially oriented behaviors and who provide more sensitive support to others tend to be better-liked and more accepted by others (including peers) than those who fail to provide such support (e.g., Burleson, Delia, & Applegate,

1992). The most compelling issue that intersects family and support scholarship may concern support and comforting skill that is gleaned from interactions with and observations of others, especially family members (e.g., Burleson & Kunkel, 1996, 2002).

Within the parent-child bond, Burleson, Delia, and Applegate (1995) testified to the transmission "from one generation to the next" (p. 69) of the person-centered communication style, one that is widely recognized for its supportive properties. Person-centeredness refers to "message behavior that reflects an awareness of and adaptation to the subjective, affective, and relational aspects of communicative contexts" (Burleson, 1987, p. 305). Consistent with Bandura's (1986) emphasis on cognition, Burleson et al. (1995) suggested that parental performance affects a child's interpersonal cognitive structures and these, in turn, shape his or her acquisition and performance of person-centered communicative behaviors. Thus, a child becomes more supportive with recognition of the importance of face maintenance, identity and relationship management, and consideration of long-term impacts of interactions. Additional research regarding how the "learning" of support varies in different types of family relationships and how to enhance the social support skills of family members is needed.

Stereotypes of Age and Gender

Because the critical elements in social learning may be the acquisition of cognitions and constructs that bear on behavioral decisions (Bandura, 1986), important perceptions of those we interact with may be informed by our representations of them as members of particular demographic groups. These perceptions may also be shaped by our observations of family members' enactment of such beliefs and the consequences of that enactment. For instance, if an individual's brother displays disdain for the residents of a neighboring state and is reinforced for doing so by their father, the individual may be likewise encouraged to possess and recite such sentiments. Two perceptual sets that have been shown by researchers to shape our communication profoundly are those pertaining to age and gender roles.

Age stereotypes and communication. Two models grounded in communication accommodation theory (see Chapter 2 in this volume) have guided research on the role of age stereotypes in interpersonal communication: the Communication Predicament of Aging (CPA) model

(Ryan, Giles, Bartolucci, & Henwood, 1986) and the Age Stereotypes in Interactions (ASI) model (Hummert, 1994, 1999). Both models view age stereotypes as person perception schemas and illustrate how negative age stereotypes can lead to an age-adapted communication style with an older person (e.g., using slower, louder, simpler speech than usual) that can be perceived as patronizing and foster loss of self-esteem and age-related declines in the older individual. In addition, the ASI model specifies characteristics of communicators (e.g., age, contact with older adults) and the context that account for the influence of positive as well as negative age stereotyping in the communication process. Both models are strongly supported by empirical research (see review by Hummert, Garstka, Ryan, & Bonnesen, 2004).

From a social learning perspective, these models are unique in their emphasis on the ways in which the age-adapted communication of younger family members can reinforce age-stereotypical beliefs and behaviors in older family members. For instance, older participants who were addressed in an age-adapted style within the context of a referential communication task gave lower assessments of their own communication abilities than participants addressed in a standard adult style (Kemper, Othick, Warren, Gubarchuk, & Gerhing, 1996). Additional research on the ways in which the communication of younger family members affects the self-efficacy judgments of older family members would provide insights into the complex relational dynamics of intergenerational relationships, as well as into the social learning of age stereotypes and age-appropriate behavior.

Also of relevance to our discussion of social learning in the family context are studies documenting (a) age group differences in stereotypes about older adults, beliefs about communication, and communication behaviors; and (b) self-stereotyping in communication behaviors of older persons. First, the age group differences that have been identified indicate "a developmental increase in the richness and complexity of age stereotype schemas" (Hummert, 1999, p. 190) across the life span. For example, older people not only have more age stereotypes (both negative and positive) for their age group than do younger persons (Hummert, Garstka, Shaner, & Strahm, 1994) but they also are less likely to use an age-adapted communication style with a negatively stereotyped individual than are younger people (Hummert, Shaner, Garstka, & Henry, 1998). These findings suggest a lifelong social learning process that enables people to use their experiences to modify their age stereotype schemas and to reduce their association of negative stereotypes with the need for age-adapted communication behaviors. The family provides the ideal context for study of this process.

Second, Hummert et al. (2004) noted research demonstrating that in choosing some communication behaviors, older adults may be self-stereotyping; that is, categorizing themselves as "old" and reinforcing negative stereotypes of age in listeners as well as in themselves. These behaviors include self-disclosures centering on such topics as illness or loss, age excuses for memory failure, and repetitions in conversation. For example, Ryan, Bieman-Copland, Kwong See, Ellis, and Anas (2002) found that participants evaluated forgetful older people in their 70s who used an age excuse as more likely to forget in the future and as older than those using other excuse types (e.g., lack of ability or effort). Clearly, such communication behaviors of older persons may play a powerful role in the social learning of age stereotypes and age-appropriate communication behaviors by younger family members, and deserve further study. Recent research on the grandparent-grandchild relationship (see Chapter 2 in this volume) supports this view, showing that grandparent communication styles affect not only grandchildren's perceptions of the grandparent, but also their perceptions of older people in general.

Gender stereotypes and communication. Gender stereotypes are "common, culturewide beliefs about how men and women differ in personal qualities and characteristics" (Haslett, Geis, & Carter, 1992, p. 29). A wide variety of studies have indicated that conceptions of men include characteristics such as being objective, competitive, independent, aggressive, and responsible, whereas women possess characteristics such as being emotional, intuitive, dependent, illogical, and nurturing (see review by Kunkel, Dennis, & Waters, 2003). Much research also provides evidence of stereotypes of men as "instrumentally-oriented" communicators and of women as "affectively-oriented" communicators (see review by Cutrona, 1996), although a newer paradigm is also emphasizing similarity between the sexes (e.g., Kunkel & Burleson, 1999; see review by Burleson & Kunkel, in press). These perceptions influence our expectations of others as communicators and of our own constraints as we operate communicatively within our gender-based roles.

The socialization approach to gender roles holds that "children learn to internalize prescriptions and proscriptions (do's and don'ts) for being appropriately masculine and feminine" (Howard & Hollander,

1997, pp. 28–29) from others around them. Howard and Hollander (1997) recognized that through repetition of "only rewarded behaviors, children develop gendered repertoires of behavior" (p. 46).

The origins of the perceptions and stereotypes that influence our intergroup communication might literally reside with us, in our homesteads. Our "models" of social information may be relatives or media representations that we evaluate in discussions with family members. We must examine how stereotypes about age, gender, and other demographic sources of bias (e.g., ethnicity, religion) are introduced, reinforced, and passed among generations of families.

CONCLUSIONS: LIMITATIONS AND PROSPECTS OF SOCIAL LEARNING FOR UNDERSTANDING FAMILY COMMUNICATION

Social Learning Theory (SLT) offers the promise of insight into family communication processes related to health behaviors, social support, and transmission/reduction of stereotypes. Researchers need to remain alert to the danger of adopting only the early behaviorist view of social learning in the family (e.g., Miller & Dollard, 1941), a perspective in which children are passive learners doomed to repeat the actions of their parents. Instead, the cognitive mediators of the social learning process identified in the Social Cognitive Theory of Bandura (1986, 2001) and the work of Rotter (1954, 1966) must be the guiding principles. For maximum effect in understanding family communication processes, what is recognized as SLT must address not only emulated behaviors, but also the acquisition of perceptions and cognitive structures that affect their selection. The existence of bidirectional influence between generations should also be examined because to date, only children modeling the actions of their elders have been studied. For instance, researchers in the future may investigate whether the values of young adults regarding political and social issues, as well as their voting behaviors, are adopted by older relatives.

Family communication scholarship recognizes that families are systems, that family members "simultaneously influence, and are influenced by, each other" (Vangelisti, 2004, p. ix), and that families are constituted through social interaction wherein messages and meanings establish parent and child roles, maintain rules for communication topics, perform functions such as emotional support, and sustain behavioral patterns. Clearly, social learning is, and shall continue to be, integral to family communication.

REFERENCES

Bandura, A. (1965). Influences of models' reinforcement contingencies on the acquisition of imitative responses. *Journal of Personality and Social Psychology, 1,* 589–593.

Bandura, A. (1977). *Social learning theory.* Englewood Cliffs, NJ: Prentice-Hall.

Bandura, A. (1986). *Social foundations of thought and action: A social cognitive theory.* Englewood Cliffs, NJ: Prentice-Hall.

Bandura, A. (2001). Social cognitive theory: An agentic view. *Annual Review of Psychology, 52,* 1–26.

Bandura, A., Barbaranelli, C., Caprara, G. V., & Pastorelli, C. (2001). Self-efficacy beliefs as shapers of children's aspirations and career trajectories. *Child Development, 72,* 187–206.

Bandura, A., Ross, D., & Ross, S. A. (1963). Vicarious reinforcement and imitative learning. *Journal of Abnormal Social Psychology, 67,* 601–607.

Bandura, A., & Walters, R. H. (1959). *Adolescent aggression: A study of the influence of child-training practices and family interrelationships.* New York: The Ronald Press.

Burleson, B. R. (1984). Comforting communication. In H. E. Sypher & J. L. Applegate (Eds.), *Communication by children and adults: Social cognitive and strategic processes* (pp. 63–104). Beverly Hills, CA: Sage.

Burleson, B. R. (1987). Cognitive complexity. In J. C. McCroskey & J. A. Daly (Eds.), *Personality and interpersonal communication* (pp. 305–349). Newbury Park, CA: Sage.

Burleson, B. R., Delia, J. G., & Applegate, J. L. (1992). Effects of maternal communication and children's social-cognitive and communication skills on children's acceptance by the peer group. *Family Relations, 41,* 264–272.

Burleson, B. R., Delia, J. G., & Applegate, J. L. (1995). The socialization of person-centered communication: Parental contributions to the social-cognitive and communication skills of their children. In. M. A. Fitzpatrick & A. L. Vangelisti (Eds.), *Explaining family interactions* (pp. 34–76). Thousand Oaks, CA: Sage.

Burleson, B. R., & Kunkel, A. W. (1996). The socialization of emotional support skills in childhood. In G. R. Pierce, B. S. Sarason, & I. G. Sarason (Eds.), *Handbook of social support and the family* (pp. 105–140). New York: Plenum.

Burleson, B. R., & Kunkel, A. W. (2002). Parental and peer contributions to the emotional support skills of the child: From whom do children learn to express support? *Journal of Family Communication, 2,* 79–97.

Burleson, B. R., & Kunkel, A. W. (in press). Revisiting the different cultures thesis: An assessment of sex differences and similarities in supportive communication. In D. Canary & K. Dindia (Eds.), *Sex, gender, and communication: Similarities and differences* (2nd ed.). Mahwah, NJ: Erlbaum.

Chamberlain, P., & Rosicky, J. G. (1995). The effectiveness of family therapy in the treatment of adolescents with conduct disorders and delinquency. *Journal of Marital and Family Therapy, 21,* 441–459.

Cohen, S., & Wills, T. A. (1985). Stress, social support, and the buffering hypothesis. *Psychological Bulletin, 98,* 310–357.

Cutrona, C. E. (1996). *Social support in couples.* Thousand Oaks, CA: Sage.

Dixson, M. D. (1995). Models and perspectives of parent-child communication. In T. J. Socha & G. H. Stamp (Eds.), *Parents, children, and communication: Frontiers of theory and research* (pp. 43–61). Mahwah, NJ: Erlbaum.

Elwood, T. D., & Schrader, D. C. (1998). Family communication patterns and communication apprehension. *Journal of Social Behavior and Personality, 13,* 493–502.

Franco, N., & Levitt, M. J. (1998). The social ecology of middle childhood: Family support, friendship quality, and self-esteem. *Family Relations, 47,* 315–321.

Gardner, K. A., & Cutrona, C. E. (2004). Social support communication in families. In A. L. Vangelisti (Ed.), *Handbook of family communication* (pp. 495–512). Mahwah, NJ: Erlbaum.

Gelles, R. J. (1994). Family violence, abuse, and neglect. In P. J. McKenry & S. J. Price (Eds.), *Families and change: Coping with stressful events* (pp. 262–280). Thousand Oaks, CA: Sage.

Goldsmith, D. J. (1994). The role of facework in supportive communication. In B. R. Burleson, T. L. Albrecht, & I. G. Sarason (Eds.), *Communication of social support: Messages, interactions, relationships, and community* (pp. 29–49). Thousand Oaks, CA: Sage.

Haslett, B., Geis, F. L., & Carter, M. R. (1992). *The organizational woman: Power and paradox.* Norwood, NJ: Ablex.

Horne, A. M., & Van Dyke, B. (1983). Treatment and maintenance of social learning family therapy. *Behavior Therapy, 14,* 606–613.

Howard, J. A., & Hollander, J. A. (1997). *Gendered situations, gendered selves: A gender lens on social psychology.* Thousand Oaks, CA: Sage.

Hummert, M. L. (1994). Stereotypes of the elderly and patronizing speech style. In M. L. Hummert, J. M. Wiemann, & J. F. Nussbaum (Eds.), *Interpersonal communication in older adulthood: Interdisciplinary theory and research* (pp. 162–185). Newbury Park, CA: Sage.

Hummert, M. L. (1999). A social cognitive perspective on age stereotypes. In T. M. Hess & F. Blanchard-Fields (Eds.), *Social cognition and aging* (pp. 175–195). New York: Academic Press.

Hummert, M. L., Garstka, T. A., Ryan, E. B., & Bonnesen, J. L. (2004). The role of age stereotypes in interpersonal communication. In J. F. Nussbaum and J. Coupland (Eds.), *Handbook of communication and aging research* (2nd ed.) (pp. 91–114). Hillsdale, NJ: Erlbaum.

Hummert, M. L., Garstka, T. A., Shaner, J. L., & Strahm, S. (1994). Stereotypes of the elderly held by young, middle-aged, and elderly adults. *Journal of Gerontology: Psychological Sciences, 49,* 240–249.

Hummert, M. L., Shaner, J. L., Garstka, T. A., & Henry, C. (1998). Communication with older adults: The influence of age stereotypes, context, and communicator age. *Human Communication Research, 25,* 124–151.

Jones, D. J., Beach, S. R. H., & Jackson, H. (2004). Family influences on health: A framework to organize research and guide intervention. In A. Vangelisti (Ed.), *Handbook of family communication* (pp. 647–672). Mahwah, NJ: Erlbaum.

Kemper, S., Othick, M., Warren, J., Gubarchuk, J., & Gerhing, H. (1996). Facilitating older adults' performance on a referential communication task through speech accommodations. *Aging and Cognition, 3,* 37–55.

Knowler, W., Barrett-Conner, E., Fowler, S., Hamman, R., Laching, J., Walker, E., & Nathan, D. (2002). Reduction in the incidence of type 2 diabetes with lifestyle intervention or metformin. *The New England Journal of Medicine, 346,* 393–403.

Kunkel, A. W., & Burleson, B. R. (1999). Assessing explanations for sex differences in emotional support: A test of the different cultures and skill specialization accounts. *Human Communication Research, 25,* 307–340.

Kunkel, A. W., Dennis, M. R., & Waters, E. (2003). Contemporary university students' ratings of the characteristics of men, women, and CEOs. *Psychological Reports, 93,* 1197–1213.

Miller, N., & Dollard, J. (1941). *Social learning and imitation.* New Haven, CT: Yale University Press.

Norman, P., & Bennett, P. (1996). Health locus of control. In M. Conner & P. Norman (Eds.), *Predicting health behaviour* (pp. 62–94). Philadelphia, PA: Open University Press.

Patterson, G. R. (1971). *Families: Applications of social learning to family life.* Champaign, IL: Research Press.

Pierce, G. R., Sarason, B. R., Sarason, I. G., Joseph, H. J., & Henderson, C. A. (1996). Conceptualizing and assessing social support in the context of the family. In G. R. Pierce, B. S. Sarason, & I. G. Sarason (Eds.), *Handbook of social support and the family* (pp. 3–23). New York: Plenum.

Ramirez, A. G., Villarreal, R., & Chalela, P. (1999). Community-level diabetes control in a Texas barrio. In R. M. Huff & M. V. Kline (Eds.), *Promoting health in multicultural populations: A handbook for practitioners* (pp. 169–187). Thousand Oaks, CA: Sage.

Rosser, R. A. (1981). Social learning theory and the development of prosocial behavior: A system for research integration. In R. W. Henderson (Ed.), *Parent-child interaction: Theory, research, and prospects* (pp. 59–81). New York: Academic Press.

Rotter, J. B. (1954). *Social learning and clinical psychology.* New York: Prentice-Hall.

Rotter, J. B. (1966). Generalized expectancies for internal and external control of reinforcement. *Psychological Monographs: General and Applied, 80*, 1–28.

Ryan, E. B., Bieman-Copland, S., Kwong See, S. T, Ellis, C. H. & Anas, A. P. (2002). Age excuses: Conversational management of memory failures in older adults. *Journal of Gerontology: Psychological Sciences and Social Sciences, 57B*, 256–267.

Ryan, E. B., Giles, H., Bartolucci, G., & Henwood, K. (1986). Psycholinguistic and social psychological components of communication by and with the elderly. *Language and Communication, 6*, 1–24.

Schwarzer, R., & Fuchs, R. (1996). Self-efficacy and health behaviours. In M. Conner & P. Norman (Eds.), *Predicting health behaviour* (pp. 163–196). Philadelphia, PA: Open University Press.

Skinner, B. F. (1938). *The behavior of organisms: An experimental analysis.* New York: Appleton-Century-Crofts.

Stamp, G. H. (2004). Theories of family relationships and a family relationships theoretical model. In A. Vangelisti (Ed.), *Handbook of family communication* (pp. 1–30). Mahwah, NJ: Erlbaum.

Vangelisti, A. (2004). Preface. In A. Vangelisti (Ed.), *Handbook of family communication* (pp. ix-xii). Mahwah, NJ: Erlbaum.

Wallston, K. A. (1992). Hocus-pocus, the focus isn't strictly on locus: Rotter's social learning theory modified for health. *Cognitive Therapy and Research, 16*, 183–199.

Wallston, K. A., Wallston, B. S., & DeVellis, R. (1978). Development of multidimensional health locus of control (MHLC) scales. *Health Education Monographs, 6*, 160–170.

Witte, K. (1992). The role of threat and efficacy in AIDS prevention. *International Quarterly of Community Health Education, 12*, 225–249.

Witte, K., Meyer, G., & Martell, D. (2001). *Effective health risk messages: A step-by-step guide.* Thousand Oaks, CA: Sage.

18

Stress and Adaptation Theories: Families Across the Life Span

Tamara D. Afifi

Jon Nussbaum

Editors' Note: This chapter discusses no fewer than seven theoretical perspectives that cohere around the issue of how families cope with predictable and unpredictable stressors. All these theories are interested in identifying generalizable cause-effect relationships to determine how families cope with a variety of stressors, thereby earning them membership in logical-empiricism. For the most part, these theories have origins in psychology or the interdisciplinary field of family studies.

F amilies are often the source of our most profound happiness and comfort, and yet they simultaneously function as catalysts of frustration and stress. Family members are the people with whom we share our most intimate lifelong experiences. Yet, it is often because of these shared, enduring connections that stress manifests itself. The paradoxical nature of families highlights the importance of examining the types of stress that families experience and how they cope with them. Stress also changes across the life span of a family and is dependent upon the context and developmental stage of a family and the relationships within it. This chapter opens with an overview of the stressors that families commonly face across the life span to provide important background for a discussion of the primary theoretical approaches that help explain how families cope communicatively with stress.

FAMILY STRESSORS

Stressors That Families Experience Across the Life Span

Regardless of a particular historical period and the technological and economic advances that encompass it, many of the life stressors that families experience have remained relatively stable across time. For instance, although more young people are choosing not to marry, are marrying later in life, and are having fewer children than in previous decades (Teachman, Tedrow, & Crowder, 2000), the majority of the population in the United States still choose to marry. Along with the joys of a new marriage come a variety of stressors. Research points to the importance of the early years of a marriage as "testing grounds" for a couple's ability to learn and adjust to each other's conflict-management style, spending habits, division of labor, and sexual preferences (e.g., Christopher & Sprecher, 2000; Stanley, Markman, & Whitton, 2002). In fact, the first seven years of a marriage are often the most predictive of its long-term health (Gottman & Notarius, 2002). A couple's relational satisfaction tends to be highest in the first few years of marriage, but tends to decrease as they begin to confront the sources of stress in their marriage, and then is enhanced again later in the marriage (Mares & Fitzpatrick, 1995).

One turning point that is believed to contribute to marital distress is the transition to parenthood. Researchers often assumed that the introduction of children to a marriage began a cycle of erosion of marital well-being that only led to an increase in satisfaction when children left the home (Huston & Vangelisti, 1995). Indeed, children add a new level of stress to a couple's life that challenges their ability to spend time together, balance their work and family life, organize and divide household responsibilities equitably, and negotiate a sense of autonomy (Grote & Clark, 2001; Stamp, 1994). As Huston and Vangelisti (1995) noted, however, relatively recent research on the transition to parenthood has provided a more complex understanding of why having children enhances some marriages and hinders others. For instance, couples who become distressed after they have children may not have had a solid foundation for their marriage before they had children. Other studies have only examined couples with children and have not used control groups of couples who do not have children to compare changes in marital satisfaction (Huston & Vangelisti, 1995). Thus, the introduction of children can be very stressful for couples, and its impact on marital well-being can be discerned only after considering the numerous factors that contribute to it.

The transition to parenthood is a process that takes place over an extended period of years. This process often becomes increasingly salient as children enter adolescence and young adulthood. Adolescents' attempts to distance themselves from their parents and align themselves with their peer groups often create additional strain in families (Gambier & Piko, 2001). Stress can also arise when parents and their young adult children begin to renegotiate their privacy boundaries. As Petronio (1994) noted, when children go away to college and return home, privacy boundaries that were once "co-owned" between parents and children suddenly have to be renegotiated, which can create turbulence within the home until privacy rules can be coordinated successfully.

Although some parents feel somewhat liberated and reconnected with their spouse when their children leave the home, other parents may experience the empty nest syndrome. Parents who were accustomed to communicating with—and engaging in activities with—their children on a regular basis may suddenly feel lonely, depressed, and uncertain about the direction of their own lives (Magai & Halpren, 2001). For many couples this provides an opportunity to reprioritize their marriage (Walsh, 1999). When there are difficulties in the marriage, however, the exiting of children can exacerbate these preexisting problems. Couples who do not have a strong marital foundation may not want to "let go" of their children for fear of having to confront their rather unsatisfactory or less-gratifying relationship with their spouse (Dankowski, 2001).

Parents are also often still responsible for their children's psychological, physical, and financial security well into adulthood, which can be simultaneously fulfilling and stressful. Research has often focused on the emotional and pragmatic assistance that parents provide for their children until the parents reach a relatively old age (Williams & Nussbaum, 2001). Parents continue to provide social and financial support to their children long past the transition to adulthood (White,

1992). Various life-turning points, such as marriage and family formation, divorce, illnesses, and home ownership often re-integrate parents into their offspring's lives in positive and yet potentially stressful ways (Troll & Fingerman, 1996). For instance, although the introduction of grandchildren often fosters greater closeness between parents and their children, it can also be a source of stress if the grandparents assume too much of a parental role.

When adult offspring reach midlife, they often begin to offer social, emotional, and financial support to parents who once assumed this role. Adult children's caregiving responsibilities for their parents later in life are often perceived as compensation for the inequitable flow of resources from their parents (Stein, 1993). As Stein (1993) argued, such obligations are the result of societal expectations for what is deemed to be an appropriate exchange of resources and caregiving behaviors with family members across the life cycle. Expectations for appropriate connection and helping behaviors are often a part of ongoing communicative negotiations within families (Stein, 1993). For instance, some adult children may restrict the number of phone calls and visits they have with their parents as a way to communicate greater distance. The obligations to maintain regular contact with one's parents often shift from obligations to desires as children grow older (Stein, 1993; Troll & Fingerman, 1996).

As adult children themselves grow into old age, they face a different set of stressors. Adults during this phase of life are at risk for loss of mental functioning, such as Alzheimer's disease, depression, and suicide (Walsh, 1999). The relationship between spouses may become strained because of the fear of dependence, diminishing health, the loss of friends due to death, and one's own mortality (Dankowski, 2001). One spouse is often left to take care of the other due to debilitating physical or mental health. Wives often assume this caretaking position for their husbands in older age, largely because women tend to live longer than men (Nussbaum, Pecchioni, Robinson, & Thompson, 2000). This can pose numerous challenges to the relationship and the individuals involved when one spouse is left to watch the other's "true self" slowly deteriorate (Baxter, Braithwaite, Golish, & Olson, 2002).

Changes in Stressors for American Families

Even though many of the sources of family stress have remained relatively consistent across history, changes in societal structures have created unique stressors for today's families. One of the most notable changes in recent history is the number of women who have entered the workplace. Women occupied 30% of the labor force in 1950, but increased their participation to 47% by 2000 (Toosi, 2002). Approximately 78% of couples also have a spouse who works outside the home (Families and Work Institute, 1998). As a result of these shifts at home and in the labor force, researchers have begun to examine the degree to which work stress spills over into family life (Crouter, Bumpus, Head, & McHale, 2001). Job stressors, such as exhaustion, job intensity, and apathy have been found to spill over into family life by affecting family life and marital quality (Mauno & Kinnunen, 1999). Being a dual-career couple can be especially stressful if both people suffer from fatigue, are preoccupied with work, and are unable to "contain" their stress from each other (Leiter & Dunrup, 1996). Although work is often necessary for economic survival and is a source of great satisfaction, dual-career couples often find themselves struggling in their attempts to balance work and family.

Families are also rapidly changing in their composition, creating newfound challenges for families in the 21st century. As Amato (2000) contended, "Of all the changes in family life during the 20th century, perhaps the most dramatic—and the most far-reaching in its implications—was the increase in the rate of divorce" (p. 1269). The divorce rate has slowly but steadily increased since 1940, with approximately half of all first marriages today ending in divorce (Teachman et al., 2000). The divorce rate increased exponentially during the Women's Movement in the 1970s, but has remained relatively stable since the 1980s. Moreover, the majority of people who divorce remarry at some point in their lives and one-half of marriages involve a second (or higher) marriage (U.S. Bureau of the Census, 1998). These changes in family structure have had a profound impact on the types of stressors that families experience.

The stress associated with marital transitions is often most profound for children of divorce, who often have greater difficulty in school, less contact with both of their parents, greater financial strain, and poorer psychological adjustment than children whose parents remained married (Lamb, Sternberg, & Thompson, 1999). Divorce can have long-term effects on children as well. Adults who experienced parental divorce as children tend to score lower on a variety of psychological, behavioral, and socioeconomic factors than adults who grew up with continuously married parents (Lamb et al., 1999). Researchers have demonstrated, however, that many of the consequences of divorce tend to dissipate over time and that most children are quite resilient to divorce if conflict is kept to a minimum (Hetherington, 1999). Children also tend to vary considerably in how they respond to divorce, and numerous factors— such as the amount of interparental conflict, the length of time since the divorce, and the age of the child—must be taken into account when assessing its impact (Amato, 2000; Hetherington, 1999).

Although some of the stressors associated with divorce may dissipate over time, new stressors may emerge when a stepfamily is formed. The challenges associated with stepfamily development often include a redefinition of family boundaries, roles, and rituals (Braithwaite, Baxter, & Harper, 1998); building solidarity as a family unit (Braithwaite, Olson, Golish, Soukup, & Turman, 2001); loyalty conflicts (Coleman, Fine, Ganong, Downs, & Pauk, 2001); uncertainty, role ambiguity, and consistency in parenting (Schwebel, Fine, & Renner, 1991); establishing the credibility of the stepparent (Cissna, Cox, & Bochner, 1990); and coordinating appropriate privacy boundaries (Afifi, 2003). While these challenges are varied and complex, they are also a natural outgrowth of stepfamily development and are often a function of a lack of familiarity and relational history that can and often do work themselves out over time (Afifi & Schrodt, 2003).

Regardless of what stressors have remained consistent and what stressors have changed throughout history, the stressors that families experience fluctuate and develop across the life span of the family. For instance, what is stressful for a newly married couple changes over the life span of a marriage. As children enter the marriage, the stressors that a couple experience change as the children develop and the couple adapts, or fails to adapt, their parenting practices. In addition, just as families vary in their functionality and form, they may take different paths in their development and management of their stress. For instance, as Huston and Vangelisti (1995) contend, there are multiple trajectories that represent the transition to parenthood and how children affect a marriage over time. Therefore, the stressors that families experience change over time and must be understood within the confines of a particular family.

Stressors within families can also become compounded when the source of the stress is directed from multiple phases of the life span. For example, middle-aged adults often find themselves in the difficult circumstance of being "sandwiched" between caring for their elderly parents at the same time as they are parenting their children (Williams & Nussbaum, 2001). Researchers have speculated that the increased longevity of older adults, the demands of dual-career households, and delayed childbirth have placed an incredible amount of pressure on middle-aged adults (Brody, 1981). These multigenerational responsibilities are especially pressing for women, who are often the primary caregivers at home for their children and are the caretakers for their elderly parents (Dankoski, 2001). These roles are stressful and yet appear to be managed quite well at the present time (Williams & Nussbaum, 2001). However, as the nature of our workforce and multifaceted focus of our caregiving increases, the stress that middle-aged parents face may become more salient for families (Williams & Nussbaum, 2001).

PRIMARY THEORIES OF STRESS AND COPING IN FAMILIES ACROSS THE LIFE SPAN

Numerous theoretical frameworks and bodies of literature have been used to explain the stressors that families experience across their life span and the competencies necessary to cope with them. One area that has addressed these issues is the stress and coping literature. Scholars typically emphasize the cognitive capacities of the individual and how these capacities interact with the magnitude of the stressor and the resources available to manage it (Skinner & Edge, 1998). Although much of coping is cognitively based, the way people cope is largely a function of their interaction with others. Many of the stressors that were identified in the previous sections are experienced and managed individually, dyadically within specific relationships in the family, and within the social fabric of the family as a whole.

Most of the research that has examined the role of communication in coping has been grounded in social support theorizing (Lyons, Mickelson, Sullivan, & Coyne, 1998). In general, this research has shown that people's access to social networks often helps to ameliorate stress, and thus enhances well-being (see Albrecht, Burleson, & Goldsmith, 1994). Although the theoretical nature of social support is contested, research suggests that social support can protect individuals against some of the harmful effects of stress. According to the *buffering hypothesis*, social-support networks mitigate much of the negative impact of stressful events on people's mental and physical health (Kaniasty & Norris, 1997). For example, if an individual has an illness, family members may minimize the severity of the stress by providing comfort, reducing uncertainty, and providing assistance with household chores (Heller &

Rook, 1997). Some of the impact of the stress on the person's well-being may be buffered because of such efforts.

Although social support is often beneficial for families, there are also instances when social support does not enhance, or is potentially detrimental, to family members' well-being. As numerous scholars contend, social support is beneficial to the degree that the support is communicated competently (Goldsmith, 1992), is non-face threatening (Caplan & Samter, 1999), and is acknowledged and perceived as effective by the recipient (Jones & Burleson, 1997). Social support may be ineffective to the extent that the number of people in need of resources exceeds the amount of resources available (Heller & Rook, 1997). In this sense, a *support deterioration model* (Barrera, 1989) may be in effect where changes in social support contribute to the deleterious consequences of the stress (Kaniasty & Norris, 1997). Social support can also be harmful if family members continually disclose too much of their stress to one another (Afifi, Hutchinson, & Krouse, 2004). For instance, research suggests that single mothers are sometimes unable to contain their stress from their children because of their dual-role demands at work and at home and the lack of a relational partner to buffer the stress (Larson & Gillman, 1999).

Even though the research on social support has provided essential information about the theoretical structure of the coping process, it does not readily address the proactive, collective coping efforts of groups of people (i.e., families as a whole). Nevertheless, a relatively new area of research that has focused on collective coping efforts is communal coping (e.g., Lyons et al., 1998). Communal coping (e.g., Lyons et al., 1998; Wells, Hobfoll, & Lavin, 1997) involves people actively combining their resources and problem solving together to overcome adversity as a group. Such collective coping efforts have been investigated in families that attempt to cope together with chronic or terminal illnesses (e.g., Lyons & Meade, 1995), wars (e.g., Khalaf, 2002), natural disasters (e.g., Kaniasty & Norris, 1997), pregnancy (e.g., Wells et al., 1997) and divorce (e.g., Afifi et al., 2004). What this research suggests is that collective coping contributes to greater coping efficacy and well-being of social groups (e.g., Brashers, Haas, Neidig, & Rintamaki, 2002). Communal coping may be a particularly effective form of coping for families, especially under times of severe or chronic family-level stressors, because it fosters resiliency and collective resolve.

Even though theories of collective coping are rare, one theory that has been used to address stress and coping in families as a whole is

McCubbin and Patterson's (1982) *Double ABCX family coping theory.* Their theoretical model was adapted from the original version of the ABCX Family Crisis Model (Hill, 1949). This original model argued that how a family copes with a stressor is dependent upon the magnitude of the type of stressor (A) and the resources of the family to cope with it (B). These factors also interact with the family's perception of the stressor (C), which can turn the stressor into a crisis (X). Thus, how a family manages a stressor depends upon the type of stressor, how threatening it is perceived to be, and the general family resources available to manage it.

McCubbin and Patterson's (1982) revised version of the model provides a more detailed examination of the accumulation of the stressors on a family and the types of resources families use to manage them. The Double ABCX Model recognizes that families are often confronted with multiple simultaneous demands and that these demands or stressors can pile up over time. The severity of the pileup is partially determined by the amount of resources available to the family, which include psychological resources of the individual and the social and financial resources within the family and the community. How a family perceives stress depends upon the meaning ascribed to it, the pileup of the stressors, and the resources available to manage it. The meaning-making process results in degrees of adaptation or maladaptation.

Although McCubbin and Patterson's (1982) theoretical model has proven to be an extremely valuable resource for researchers and practitioners, it is not without its limitations. As with much of the research on stress and coping, the model lacks a developmental focus. McCubbin and Patterson's model recognizes that how stress affects a family can and often does change based upon the meaning that family members give to it and the resources available to manage it. However, it does not readily decipher *the process* through which families learn to adapt (or do not adapt) to stress over time and how their coping abilities, in turn, affect the stress within the family.

McCubbin and Patterson's (1982) model also does not assess the interactive and dynamic nature of stress and coping in families. Communication is viewed as a type of resource within and outside the family that can be used to cope with stress. While this may be true, communication is also the means through which family members cope and is the outcome of such coping efforts. The interactive nature of coping is also more complex than one person simply talking to another about his/her stress. There are diverse communicative ways of coping that are captured in the psychological characteristics of the individual and the efforts of families as social units (see Afifi et al., 2004).

Recent theorizing has also relied on a *risk and resiliency theoretical perspective* to understand the theoretical underpinnings of stress and coping. Risk and resiliency theoretical models emphasize the various stressors or "risk factors" that contribute to poor socio-emotional and interpersonal functioning, as well as the factors that promote resilience to the challenges that accompany various life transitions (Deater-Deckard & Dunn, 1999; Hetherington, 1999). Typically these models have been applied to children to explain the psychological, interpersonal, and environmental factors that enhance or hinder their development (e.g., Afifi & Keith, 2004; Hetherington, 1999). For instance, scholars have used risk and resiliency models to explain psychological and interpersonal risk factors that can contribute to children's post-divorce adjustment (see Deater-Deckard & Dunn, 1999). Such models represent a shift away from models that only examine the variables that deter health to the variables that promote varying levels of functionality.

Family strengths theorizing has also helped move researchers away from a "deficit approach" (Visher & Visher, 1979) to the study of family stress and coping. Scholars within (e.g., Golish, 2003; Kelley & Sequeira, 1997) and outside (e.g., Stinnett & DeFrain, 1985) of the field of communication have focused on typologies of family strengths as a way to understand the characteristics that make families function well. For instance, in their research on family functioning, Stinnett and DeFrain (e.g., DeFrain & Stinnett, 1992) and Kelley and Sequeira (1997) discovered that strong families were qualitatively different than other families in their openness, ability to manage conflict effectively, degree of support, religiosity, and overall sense of unity. Golish (2003) also found in her study of communication in stepfamilies that strong families evidenced greater family problem solving, resolve, rituals, openness, affection, and a willingness to directly confront stressors than families having more difficulty. Overall, such perspectives have enabled researchers to decipher the communicative factors that help some families function better than others.

Researchers have also used trajectories and family development models to examine changes in stress and coping over time. For instance, Baxter, Braithwaite, and Nicholson (1999) and Braithwaite et al. (2001) used turning point analysis to assess the major turning points or changes in stepfamilies in their first four years of formation. They discovered that stepfamilies take many different paths in their attempts to "feel like a family" and that these paths involve intricate layers of discourse patterns. Through their examination of the turning points, these researchers not only were able to better understand how family members made sense of their stressors, but what behavioral and perceptual coping mechanisms altered the development of the families' solidarity over time. While turning point analyses do not provide a true longitudinal analysis of stress and coping in families, they do allow for a more comprehensive picture of the changing nature of stress and coping in families.

Numerous life span theories have also addressed the evolving and multifaceted nature of stress and coping in families. For instance, *life span attachment theory* (Bowlby, 1979; Cicirelli, 1983, 1991; see also, Trees, this volume) suggests that the bonds a child develops with his/her primary caregiver (typically mothers) and other family members early in life become the basis for the adult child's sustained relationships, assistance, and commitment with these family members. The strength of these attachments may be why some families are closer than others and why some families are better able to assist other family members in times of crisis. The greater attachments might produce a more significant amount of social resources, which, as the stress buffering hypothesis suggests, may protect family members against some of the negative effects of stress.

The solidarity of a family also has a strong influence on the social demands and norms of assistance in families in times of stress. *Intergenerational solidarity theory* suggests that solidarity is a multifaceted construct that involves not only cohesiveness, affection, contact, and communication, but also familial norms and rules that govern caretaking behaviors and the exchange of resources (Bengston & Harootyan, 1994). Adult children become socialized to provide assistance and to cope in certain ways (Cicirelli, 1995). Normative prescriptions in families often dictate when and how family members should provide help to one another. For instance, family members are often governed by such norms as "family members should be there for one another" and "family members should keep in touch" (Cicirelli, 1995). Norms that encourage family solidarity help families stay together and cope with the stressors they encounter. When families lack these norms or fail to act on them, it may create strain within the family and make coping more difficult for family members who are attempting to cope alone.

Even though the people closest to us are obliged to provide support during stressful times, some family members and friends are not always helpful and are not equally effective in the type of support they provide. As adult children age, they may become more selective in choosing the people with whom they turn to for support. According to *socioemotional selectivity theory* (Carstensen, 1991, 1992), as people age they reduce the overall number of people with whom they interact, but maintain the relationships that are the most fulfilling and affirming. Thus, adults tend to have fewer but closer relationships as they age and devote more of their resources to those relationships (Nussbaum et al., 2000).

As Nussbaum et al. (2000) note, socioemotional selectivity theory is based upon a social exchange approach (see chapter by Dainton and Zelley, this volume). Although establishing relationships is often highly rewarding, it also invokes costs in terms of time, energy, money, and emotions. As people age they slowly select out and remain closely connected to those who enhance the emotional and social gains in their life and minimize the costs (Carstensen, 1992). As individuals age, they probably become more selective in the family members and friends on whom they rely for social support. Family members who continually provide ineffective support or who perpetuate additional stress are not likely to be sought out for assistance in the future.

CONCLUDING REMARKS

As this chapter illustrates, families are simultaneously a source of joy and stress. The various sources of the joy and stress change over the life course of a family and are embedded within larger societal and cultural structures. The longevity of families and their paradoxical nature provide family communication scholars with fertile ground for serious thought and empirical exploration. Our theories must account for the unique paradox of families as entities facing multiple crises due to the constant renegotiation of their relationships while simultaneously remaining stable and serving as the most consistent sources of comfort and support.

Theories of family stress and life span family change should begin to address the pragmatic causes and adaptations that families manage during certain phases of life. Events such as childbirth, adolescence, the empty nest, and ultimately caring for parents do not occur in isolation of other life events and can create a cumulative reservoir of stress. Family communication scholars are well-placed to view the paradox of joy and stress as a function of interaction and a co-constructed reality best understood by focusing on the communication that serves as the foundation of the family.

Family communication scholars have investigated the day-to-day communicative behavior of families attempting to manage their stressful lives. Many of these same researchers have observed patterns of communication, pointing to support and joy in all of the familial relationships. These researchers, however, have yet to tackle how these communicative behaviors change not only across the life span but between differing contexts of stress. Do families who have successfully managed the birth of their children while maintaining relational satisfaction within their marriage generalize their competent communicative strategies to life with adolescents and then to the ultimate empty nest? What characteristics of families predict successful coping with each of the family stressors? To capture these changes, we need to observe families progressing through their communicative strategies of managing stress and giving comfort.

Family communication scholars have long viewed the isolation of family dyads as potentially problematic. It is time to emphasize theories that incorporate entire family groups into our investigations of stress across the life span. Numerous relationships are simultaneously enacted within families. It seems rather obvious, but we are actively negotiating our roles as fathers, mothers, stepfathers, stepmothers, brothers, sisters, grandfathers, and grandmothers at the very same time, often in the same room! Messages are exchanged that have different meanings to different relational partners because these messages are embedded in a different relationship with a unique relational history. The very nature of the relationship may determine if the message helps to reduce stress or to reinforce the stress.

REFERENCES

Afifi, T. D. (2003). "Feeling caught" in stepfamilies: Managing boundary turbulence through appropriate communication privacy rules. *Journal of Social and Personal Relationships, 20,* 729–756.

Afifi, T. D., Hutchinson, S., & Krouse, S. (2004). *Communicative ways of coping: Variations in communal, social, and individual coping and resilience in post-divorce families.* Manuscript submitted for publication.

Afifi, T. D., & Keith, S. (2004). A risk and resiliency model of ambiguous loss in post-divorce stepfamilies. *Journal of Family Communication, 4,* 65–98.

Afifi, T. D., & Schrodt, P. (2003). Uncertainty and the avoidance of the state of one's family/relationships in stepfamilies, post-divorce single parent families, and first marriage families. *Human Communication Research, 29,* 516–533.

Albrecht, T. L., Burleson, B. R., & Goldsmith, D. (1994). Supportive communication. In M. L. Knapp & G. T. Miller (Eds.), *Handbook of interpersonal communication* (2nd ed., pp. 419–449). Thousand Oaks, CA: Sage.

Amato, P. R. (2000). The consequences of divorce for adults and children. *Journal of Marriage and the Family, 62,* 1269–1287.

Barrera, M. (1989). Models for social support and life stress: Beyond the buffering hypothesis. In L. H. Cohen (Ed.), *Life events and psychological functioning: Theoretical and methodological issues* (pp. 211–236). Newbury Park, CA: Sage.

Baxter, L. A., Braithwaite, D. O., Golish, T. D., & Olson, L. N. (2002). Contradictions of interaction for wives of elderly husbands with adult dementia. *Journal of Applied Communication Research, 30,* 1–26.

Baxter, L. A., Braithwaite, D. O., & Nicholson, J. H. (1999). Turning points in the development of blended families. *Journal of Social and Personal Relationships, 16,* 291–313.

Bengston, V. L., & Harootyan, R. A. (1994). *Intergenerational linkages, Hidden connections in American society.* New York: Springer.

Bowlby, J. (1979). *The making and breaking of affectional bonds.* London: Tavistock.

Braithwaite, D. O., Baxter, L. A., & Harper, A. M. (1998). The role of rituals in the management of the dialectical tension of "old" and "new" in blended families. *Communication Studies, 49,* 101–120.

Braithwaite, D. O., Olson, L. N., Golish, T. D., Soukup, C., & Turman, T. (2001). "Becoming a family": Developmental processes represented in blended family discourse. *Journal of Applied Communication Research, 29,* 221–247.

Brashers, D. E., Haas, S. M., Neidig, J. L., & Rintamaki, L. S. (2002). Social activism, self-advocacy, and coping with HIV illness. *Journal of Social and Personal Relationships, 19,* 113–135.

Brody, E. M. (1981). Women in the middle and family help to older people. *The Gerontologist, 21,* 471–491.

Caplan, S. E., & Samter, W. (1999). The role of facework in younger and older adults' evaluations of social support messages. *Communication Quarterly, 47,* 245–264.

Carstensen, L. L. (1991). Socioemotional activity theory: Social activity in life-span context. *Annual Review of Gerontology and Geriatrics, 11,* 195–217.

Carstensen, L. L. (1992). Social and emotional patterns in adulthood: Support for socioemotional selectivity theory. *Psychology and Aging, 7,* 331–338.

Christopher, F. S., & Sprecher, S. (2000). Sexuality in marriage, dating, and other relationships: A decade review. *Journal of Marriage and the Family, 62,* 999–1018.

Cicirelli, V. G. (1983). Adult children's attachment and helping behavior to elderly parents: A path model. *Journal of Marriage and the Family, 45,* 815–822.

Cicirelli, V. G. (1991). Sibling relationships in adulthood. In S. P. Pfeifer & M. B. Sussman (Eds.), *Families: Intergenerational and generational connections* (pp. 291–310). New York: Haworth Press.

Cicirelli, V. G. (1995). *Sibling relationships across the lifespan.* New York: Plenum Press.

Cissna, K. N., Cox, D. E., & Bochner, A. P. (1990). The dialectic of marital and parental relationships within the stepfamily. *Communication Monographs, 37,* 44–61.

Coleman, M., Fine, M. A., Ganong, L. H., Downs, K., & Pauk, N. (2001). When you're not the Brady Bunch: Identifying perceived conflicts and resolution strategies in stepfamilies. *Personal Relationships, 8,* 55–73.

Crouter, A. C., Bumpus, M. F., Head, M. R., & McHale, S. M. (2001). Implications of overwork and overload for the quality of men's family relationships. *Journal of Marriage and the Family, 63,* 404–416.

Dankowski, M. E. (2001). Pulling on the heart strings: An emotionally focused approach to family life cycle transitions. *Journal of Marital and Family Therapy, 27,* 177–188.

Deater-Deckard, K., & Dunn, J. (1999). Multiple risks and adjustment in young children growing up in different family settings: A British community study of stepparent, single mother, and nondivorced families. In E. M. Hetherington (Ed.), *Coping with divorce, single parenting, and remarriage: A risk and resiliency perspective* (pp. 47–65). Mahwah, NJ: Lawrence Erlbaum.

DeFrain, J., & Stinnett, N. (1992). Building on the inherent strengths of families: A positive approach for family psychologists and counselors. *Topics in Family Psychology and Counseling, 1,* 15–26.

Families and Work Institute. (1998). *The 1997 national study of the changing workforce, executive summary.* New York: Families and Work Institute.

Gambier, R., & Piko, B. (2001). Gender differences and similarities in adolescents' ways of coping. *Psychological Record, 51,* 223–235.

Goldsmith, D. J. (1992). Managing conflicting goals in supportive interaction. *Communication Research, 19,* 264–286.

Golish, T. D. (2003). Stepfamily communication strengths: Understanding the ties that bind. *Human Communication Research, 29,* 41–80.

Gottman, J. M., & Notarius, C. (2002). Marital research in the 20th century and research agenda for the 21st century. *Family Process, 41,* 159–198.

Grote, N. K., & Clark, M. S. (2001). Perceiving unfairness in the family: Cause or consequence of marital distress? *Journal of Personality and Social Psychology, 80,* 281–293.

Heller, K., & Rook, K. S. (1997). Distinguishing the theoretical functions of social ties: Implications for support interventions. In S. W. Duck (Ed.), *Handbook of personal relationships* (pp. 551–670). Chichester, UK: Wiley.

Hetherington, E. M. (Ed.). (1999). *Coping with divorce, single parenting, and remarriage: A risk and resiliency perspective.* Mahwah, NJ: Lawrence Erlbaum.

Hill, R. (1949). *Families under stress.* New York: Harper.

Huston, T., & Vangelisti, A. L. (1995). Parent-adolescent relationships. In M. A. Fitzpatrick & A. L. Vangelisti (Eds.), *Explaining family interactions* (pp. 147–177). Thousand Oaks, CA: Sage.

Jones, S. M., & Burleson, B. R. (1997). The impact of situational variables on helpers' perceptions of comforting messages: An attributional analysis. *Communication Research, 24,* 530–555.

Kaniasty, K., & Norris, F. H. (1997). Social support dynamics in adjustment to disasters. In S. W. Duck (Ed.), *Handbook of personal relationships* (pp. 595–619). Chichester, UK: Wiley.

Kelley, D. L., & Sequeira, D. L. (1997). Understanding family functioning in a changing America. *Communication Studies, 48,* 93–107.

Khalaf, S. (2002). *Civil and uncivil violence: A history of the internationalization of communal conflict in Lebanon.* Cambridge, MA: Columbia University Press.

Lamb, M. E., Sternberg, K. J., & Thompson, R. A. (1999). The effects of divorce and custody arrangements on children's behavior, development, and adjustment. In M. E. Lamb (Ed.), *Parenting and child development in "nontraditional" families* (pp. 125–136). Mahwah, NJ: Lawrence Erlbaum.

Larson, R. W., & Gillman, S. (1999). Transmission of emotions in the daily interactions of single-mother families. *Journal of Marriage and the Family, 61,* 21–37.

Leiter, M. P., & Dunrup, M. J. (1996). Work, home, and in-between: A longitudinal study of spillover. *Journal of Applied Behavioral Science, 32,* 29–47.

Lyons, R. F., & Meade, D. (1995). Painting a new face on relationships: Relationship modeling in response to chronic illness. In S. W. Duck & J. T. Wood (Eds.), *Confronting relationship challenges* (pp. 181–210). Thousand Oaks, CA: Sage.

Lyons, R. F., Mickelson, K., Sullivan, M. J. L., & Coyne, J. C. (1998). Coping as a communal process. *Journal of Social and Personal Relationships, 15,* 579–607.

Magai, C., & Halpren, B. (2001). Emotional development during the middle years. In M.E. Lachman (Ed.), *Handbook of midlife development* (pp. 310–344). Wiley: New York.

Mares, M. L., & Fitzpatrick, M.A. (1995). The aging couple. In J.F. Nussbaum & J. Coupland (Eds.), *Handbook of communication and aging research* (pp. 185–205). Mahwah, NJ: Lawrence Erlbaum.

Mauno, S., & Kinnunen, U. (1999). The effects of job stressors on marital satisfaction in Finnish dual-earning couples. *Journal of Organizational Behavior, 20,* 279–295.

McCubbin, H. I., & Patterson, J. M. (1982). Family adaptation to crisis. In H. I. McCubbin, A. E. Cauble, & J. M. Patterson (Eds.), *Family stress, coping, and social support* (pp. 26–47). Springfield, IL: Charles C Thomas.

Nussbaum, J. F., Pecchioni, L. L., Robinson, J. D., & Thompson, T. L. (2000). *Communication and aging* (2nd ed.). Mahwah, NJ: Lawrence Erlbaum.

Petronio, S. (1994). Privacy binds in family interactions: The case of parental privacy invasion. In W. R. Cupach & B. Spitzberg (Eds.), *The dark side of interpersonal communication* (pp. 241–258). Hillsdale, NJ: Lawrence Erlbaum.

Schwebel, A., Fine, M. A., & Renner, M. A. (1991). A study of perceptions of the stepparent role. *Journal of Family Issues, 12,* 43–57.

Skinner, E., & Edge, K. (1998). Reflections on coping and development across the lifespan. *International Journal of Behavioral Development, 22,* 357–366.

Stamp, G. H. (1994). The appropriation of the parental role through communication during the transition to parenthood. *Communication Monographs, 61,* 89–112.

Stanley, S. M., Markman, H. J., & Whitton, S. W. (2002). Communication, conflict, and commitment: Insights on the foundations of relationship success from a national survey. *Family Process, 41,* 659–676.

Stein, C. H. (1993). Felt obligation in adult family relationships. In S. Duck (Ed.), *Social context and relationships* (pp. 78–99). Newbury Park, CA: Sage.

Stinnett, N., & DeFrain, J. (1985). *Secrets of strong families.* Boston: Little, Brown.

Teachman, J. D., Tedrow, L. M., & Crowder, K. D. (2000). The changing demography of America's families. *Journal of Marriage and the Family, 62,* 1234–1246.

Toosi, M. (2002). A century of change: The U.S. labor force, 1950–2050. *Monthly Labor Review, 125,* 15–28.

Troll, L. E., & Fingerman, K. (1996). Connections between parents and their adult children. In C. Magai & S. McFadden (Eds.), *Handbook of emotion, adult development, and aging* (pp. 185–205). New York: Academic Press.

U.S. Bureau of the Census (1998). *Statistical abstract of the United States* (118th ed.). Washington, DC: U.S. Government Printing Office.

Visher, E. B., & Visher, J. S. (1979). *Stepfamilies: A guide to working with stepparents and stepchildren.* New York: Brunner/Mazel.

Walsh, F. (1999). Families in later life: Challenges and opportunities. In B. Carter & M. McGoldrick (Eds.), *The expanded family life cycle: Individual, family and social perspectives* (3rd ed., pp. 307–326). Boston: Allyn & Bacon.

Wells, J. D., Hobfoll, S. E., & Lavin, J. (1997). Resource loss, resource gain, and communal coping during pregnancy among women with multiple roles. *Psychology of Women Quarterly, 21,* 645–662.

White, L. (1992). The effect of parental divorce and remarriage on parental support for adult children. *Journal of Family Issues, 13,* 234–250.

Williams, A., & Nussbaum, J. F. (2001). *Intergenerational communication across the life span.* Mahwah, NJ: Lawrence Erlbaum.

19

Structuration Theory: Promising Directions for Family Communication Research

Kathleen J. Krone

Paul Schrodt

Erika L. Kirby

Editors' Note: Structuration theory originates in sociology. The theory sits at the border of more than one metadiscourse, as will become apparent in reading the chapter; however, if forced to select only one membership category, it would be the metatheoretical discourse of interpretivism.

S tructuration theory is the intellectual creation of Anthony Giddens, one of the most influential social theorists of our time. From a rather humble beginning as a first-generation college student of sociology, Giddens has constructed an academic career that now spans three decades and includes the publication of 34 books, published in more than 30 languages (Giddens & Pierson, 1998). He currently serves as director of the prestigious London School of Economics and Political Science, a position from which he continues to develop and apply innovative social and political theory (see, for example, Giddens, 1998, 2003). Giddens introduced structuration theory in *New Rules for Sociological Method* (1976), further developed its conceptual contours in *Central Problems in Social Theory* (1979), and went on to present its most detailed exposition in *The Constitution of Society* (1984). Structuration theory is a broad perspective emphasizing the importance of recurrent social practices in the study of human action, structure, and institutions (Giddens, 1984, 1989). The theory has inspired insightful and ground-breaking research across the social sciences, but because social interaction is at the very center of structuration processes (Poole, Seibold, & McPhee, 1996), structuration theory has generated considerable interest among communication scholars.

In general, structuration theory stands as one of the earliest and most influential critiques of functionalism (a perspective focused on determining the functions of social structure) and of the traditional split between functionalist and interpretivist approaches to social theorizing. According to Giddens, functionalist research underestimates the human capacity to make choices in social life, whereas interpretive research overemphasizes it, often overlooking the influence of historical forces and institutional constraints on human action. Structuration theory maintains a balance between human agency and structure by stressing the need to understand interrelationships between the two. Giddens does this by reconceptualizing the traditional dualism between human agency and structure as a duality–the duality of structure in which structure is both the medium and the outcome of social action. Human agents should not be theorized as autonomously creating structures (the bias of interpretivism), nor should structures be theorized as totally determining human action (the bias of functionalism). Rather, human action should be understood as it is both enabled and constrained by social structures.

Communication research inspired by structuration theory has led to the development of more complex, finely nuanced understandings of constructs such as organizational climate (Poole & McPhee, 1983), organizational culture (Riley, 1983), and small group decision making (Poole, Seibold, & McPhee, 1985, 1996). The theory also has inspired fresh insights into practical dilemmas related to managerial communication about organizational structure (Poole, 1988), and the production and negotiation of work-life conflicts in organizations (Kirby & Krone,

2002). In this chapter, our intent is to explore how structuration theory might lead to promising developments in family communication research. First, we turn our attention to a more specific discussion of key elements to the theory.

ELEMENTS OF STRUCTURATION THEORY

Structuration theory offers a number of interrelated theoretical concepts and propositions relevant to the study of family communication. The theory begins by focusing our attention on *structuration*, the processes by which social systems are produced and reproduced through members' use of rules and resources (Giddens, 1984). According to Giddens (1984), "analyzing the structuration of social systems means studying the modes in which such systems, grounded in the knowledgeable activities of situated actors who draw upon rules and resources in the diversity of action contexts, are produced and reproduced in interaction" (p. 25). An important distinction within structuration theory is that between *system*, which refers to the observable pattern of relations within a group (such as a family), and *structure*, which refers to the rules and resources members use to create and sustain the system (Poole, 1999). Structures can be thought of as "recipes" for acting within a given social context (Giddens, 1984), and the relations between structure and system are represented in the concept of *structuration* (Poole et al., 1996). Consequently, a structuration approach to family interaction would focus not only on surface-level behaviors or family functions but also on the structures and structuring processes that support them (c.f., Poole, 1999).

At the heart of structuration is the *duality of structure:* structure is both the medium and the outcome of the interactions that produce social systems. Giddens (1984) argued that structures are produced by human agency and simultaneously are the reproduced conditions of human agency. That is, structures are the medium of action because members draw on structures to interact, and yet they are the outcome of action because rules and resources exist only by virtue of being used in interaction. "Whenever the structure is employed, the activity reproduces it by invoking and confirming it as a meaningful basis for action" (Poole, 1999, p. 117). Take, for example, the structure of parental authority in families. Parents employ certain rules and resources as they discipline their children and establish their own parental authority as a meaningful basis for action within the family system. As parents discipline their children, they draw on certain rules and resources (e.g., power), which in turn perpetuate the structure of parental authority as a meaningful basis for disciplinary action. As such, structural properties constituted in both rules and resources express forms of domination and power (Giddens, 1984), and these structural expressions have a virtual existence–they exist only as memory traces in a continuous process of structuration (Poole et al., 1996). It is important to note, however, that Giddens (1984) sees structural expressions of power as dialectical in nature and he offers the *dialectic of control* to help explain the two-way character of power. Often, the less powerful manage resources in such a way as to exert control over the more powerful in established power relationships. Returning to our example, parents often find themselves conceding to their child's every wish, in part because they may desire the approval and affection of their child. Although parents often hold an established position of power within the family, children exert some level of control over their parents' behavior by managing emotional resources such as affection, thereby demonstrating the potential to negotiate parental authority through the dialectic of control in family structuration processes.

As we noted earlier, juxtaposed with structure is *human agency* (Giddens, 1984). Structuration theory assumes that actors (i.e., family members) are skilled and knowledgeable beings capable of monitoring their activities as they engage in social interaction. Giddens (1984) highlights the *reflexive monitoring of action,* or the purposive character of human behavior, as one source of knowledgeability that human actors possess within a given social context. Each act that facilitates the reproduction of a structure is simultaneously an act of production and may initiate social change by altering that structure that is simultaneously being produced (Baber, 1991). Giddens goes on to describe how actors are knowledgeable about their activities on the basis of both *practical consciousness,* which refers to tacit knowledge that cannot be expressed in language, and *discursive consciousness,* which refers to thoughts and knowledge that can be expressed in language. The knowledgeability of human agents, when placed at the discursive level, can facilitate social change; yet it is the practical consciousness of human agents that simultaneously reproduces the deeply embedded social structures that enable and constrain human action.

Through discursive consciousness, human agents attempt to maintain a sense of *ontological security,* or the "confidence and trust that the natural and social worlds are as they appear to be, including the basic existential parameters of self and social identity" (Giddens, 1984, p. 375). This sense of security, in turn, is maintained through *routiniza-tion*, or the habitual, taken-for-granted character of the vast bulk of activities of day-to-day social life. Routine helps establish and maintain a sense of security in everyday life. In fact, one of the ways in which we manage the tensions that threaten our sense of security is to draw upon mutual tact (i.e., a social structure) in our everyday interactions (Craib, 1992). Through socialization, human agents establish routines of daily life such as tactful behavior, which in turn provide a sense of ontologi-cal security and safety in the world. As such, Giddens sees human action not only as transformative but also as having normative and communicative dimensions that are basic to it (Craib, 1992). Thus, social systems such as families "only exist insofar as they are continu-ally created and recreated in every encounter, as the active accom-plishment of human subjects" (Giddens, 1979, p. 118).

Central to structuration theory is the notion that human agency is bounded by factors that enable and constrain action, as well as by the unintended consequences of action. As Poole et al. (1996) suggest, human agency is bound by the temporal order of action, by the context of action (including situational factors and historical precedents), and by the differential distributions of knowledge and resources among members. Take, for example, the modern development of "expert" sys-tems of knowledge on parenting. Access to this system of knowledge and the ability to apply it in day-to-day parenting can shape parent-child interaction and the communicative construction of family over time. At the same time, because social systems such as families are complex, family members cannot always be fully aware of the conse-quences of drawing upon this knowledge base in their day-to-day interactions with family members. That is, the use of this knowledge may or may not improve family relationships and communication, and can therefore influence the construction of family in unpredictable ways. Giddens (1984) addresses the idea that human agency is fraught with the unintended consequences of action, and these unknown out-comes often constrain future action or lead to unintended problems within the social system. As a further example, consider attachment theory (see Trees, this volume) and the notion that the bond between infants and their primary caregivers is crucial for children's social and emotional development. Certain attachment behaviors, such as crying and clinging, help keep the attachment figure (or primary caregiver) close by, creating an early sense of security from which the infant can explore the environment (Feeney, Noller, & Roberts, 2000). To the extent that primary caregivers are consistent or inconsistent in their care, the unintended consequences of their parenting behaviors can have a profound influence on their children's attachment styles in personal relationships later in life. Thus, the notion of unintended consequences in structuration theory may hold important implications for family communication scholars attempting to understand the intergenerational transmission of such phenomena as family violence patterns, parenting styles, conflict styles, and other micro-level structures that enable and constrain human action within family systems.

In addition, structuration theory examines the link between social institutions at the macro-level of analysis (e.g., globalization, capitalism, democracy) and human interaction at the micro-level of analysis (e.g., day-to-day family communication) across space and time. This approach is illustrated in recent explorations of the implications of global capitalism for "mothering" (Hochschild, 2000, 2003; Parrenas, 2001a, 2001b, 2002). In exploring the intersections between global trends and individual lives, Hochschild sketches out the contours of "global care chains" constructed by Third World women coming to First World countries to provide care for the children of wealthy families, leaving their own children behind to be cared for by others. These care chains produce and reproduce both the commodification and displacement of mothering. Mothering is commodified as highly compensated working women, who lack the time to care for their own families, employ immigrant women to provide that care. Mothering is displaced as immigrant women provide care for the children of others while relying on extended family members to provide day-to-day care for their own children, often for extended periods of time (Parrenas, 2001a, 2001b).

Finally, although family members may create certain structures that seem unique to their own family system, more often they are appropriated by the family from preexisting social institutions, such as larger political, economic, religious, or cultural institutions. The term *appropriation* refers to a process whereby family members adopt structural features from a particular institution and develop a situated version of them (Poole et al., 1996). In stepfamilies, for instance, there is evidence to suggest that some stepfamilies are more or less successful in their attempts to appropriate existing structures from the nuclear family model (i.e., traditional roles and norms), thereby producing different developmental pathways in stepfamilies (Baxter, Braithwaite, &

Nicholson, 1999). As Poole et al. (1996) noted, the appropriation of structural features is a skillful accomplishment that results in different versions of institutional features being adapted to specific contexts. Consequently, the ways in which family members employ and draw upon institutional structures is a critical component of structuration. To address this process, Giddens (1984) turned his attention to the *modalities*, or forms of knowledgeability, that connect levels of human interaction with larger social structures and institutions.

First, Giddens (1984) suggested that institutional features may operate as interpretive schemes in communication processes, referred to as structures of *signification*. These structures invoke certain symbolic orders, modes of discourse, and language that ultimately are only understood in connection with the two remaining structures of domination and legitimation. Structures of *domination* refer to institutional features that facilitate power and influence, invoking the resource authorization provided by political institutions and the resource allocation afforded by economic institutions (Giddens, 1984). Finally, institutional features may operate as norms that guide behavior and undergird judgments about others, referred to as structures of *legitimation*. Structures of legitimation invoke the sanctioning of certain behaviors afforded by legal and religious institutions, as well as by ethical standards and societal customs. It is important to note that although Giddens (1984) identified three distinct institutional structures that surface in human interaction, the distinction is largely analytical and the three elements tend to overlap in every action (Poole et al., 1996). For example, Schrodt, Baxter, McBride, Braithwaite, and Fine (2004) used structuration theory to explore the communicative processes underlying co-parenting relationships in stepfamilies. These researchers identified two structures of signification with respect to the divorce decree, one in which the decree was framed as a legal document, dictating the rights and responsibilities of parents, and one in which the decree was viewed as a negotiating guide or backdrop for more informal co-parenting decision-making processes. Schrodt et al. (2004) found that structures of legitimation and domination were interwoven with these two structures of signification, particularly when co-parents in one household used the structure of "decree as legal contract" as a legitimation resource of domination over the other household by controlling access to the children.

In sum, structuration theory places equal emphasis on both action and structure, thereby providing an appealing theoretical perspective for exploring family communication as a complex social system. Although we have briefly discussed its key elements, Giddens consistently noted that structuration theory is not meant to be tested in its entirety, but is meant to be used selectively as a set of sensitizing concepts (1976, 1979, 1984). Giddens did argue, though, that the starting point for research must be "the analysis of recurrent social practices" (Giddens, 1989, p. 252). In that sense, structuration theory offers an alternative understanding of the nature of social life, rather than a series of formal propositions to test (Craib, 1992). Specifically, a structurationist approach entails conceptualizing and exploring families as they are constructed and reconstructed in the flow of member interaction across space and time, rather than conceptualizing them as simply "containing" communication. We believe that the concepts of structuration theory are beginning to support new ways of thinking about and studying family communication and structures. In the next section, we illustrate additional applications of structuration theory to family communication research and suggest promising avenues for future research.

PROMISING RESEARCH DEVELOPMENTS AND DIRECTIONS

In this section, we illustrate additional uses for structuration theory by advancing directions in family communication research that (a) look across levels of analysis, (b) illustrate the production and reproduction of social structures, and (c) allow for exploring dualities between agency and structure. We focus our discussion on examples of alternative family structures, family socialization and change, and "work-family" processes.

Using Structuration to Look Across Levels of Analysis

Structuration theory offers a framework for exploring macrosocietal processes and the micro-level family communication processes that create, re-create, and sustain change in family structures. Studies of the emergence of transnational families in a global economy are but one illustration of how the theory bridges the gap between micro-level family interactions and the macro-level connections among the family and larger political and economic institutions (Parrenas, 2001a). A more extended example comes from research on work-family processes. Although this research ranges on a continuum from micro-level analyses of individual perceptions of "work-family conflict" (Greenhaus & Beutell, 1985) to more macro-level, cross-cultural comparisons of how work and family are treated in different countries (e.g., Haas & Hwang, 1995), the bulk of this research tends to focus only on one level of analysis at a time. Kirby and Krone (2002) illustrated the potential for structuration theory to examine family and work intersections across these multiple levels of analysis through an exemplar of a new father who has taken off six weeks of paternity leave to spend time with family. They asserted that in making this decision, this new father may have (a) added to the workload of others, (b) raised questions as to his level of organizational commitment, and (c) questioned the macrosocietal expectations that men work outside the home as the primary breadwinner while women stay at home as the primary caregiver. These authors illustrate how an unhappy coworker "can use discourse across these levels in complaining about the arrangement (i.e., 'I have to do his work,' 'I can't believe he took that much leave *here;* that's career suicide,' 'Why should he be staying home? That's the mother's job!') (Kirby & Krone, 2002, p. 55). Kirby and Krone go on to illustrate how such discourse from coworkers can then serve as a constraint on interaction through the duality of structure.

We see a similar application of structuration and its interaction with work-family on the "family" side. To this point, the work-family research that has been done with family as a central focus has mainly been at one level of analysis. Yet discourse from multiple levels—including intrapersonal, interpersonal, family, organizational, and macrosocietal—can impact how families "manage" the interrelated realms of working life and family life. Multilevel family communication research might take as a starting point the fact that even in 2005, an (unspoken) macrosocietal expectation still exists that when a parent does stay home, it will be the mother. Imagine that a father decides to stay home full-time with his children instead. What consequences ensue at the level of interpersonal communication inside and outside the family when the macro-level expectation about who works and who nurtures has been challenged? How does it impact patterns of housekeeping and child-care tasks in the family? What impact does it have on how the mother and father raise and communicate with their children? What (if any) unique communication pattern emerge between marital partners? Between partners and their social support networks?

An additional possibility when looking across levels of analysis from a family communication perspective is to consider which actors have agency at different levels. Notably, in most of the work-family research, critical constituents that are missing are the children (Perry-Jenkins, Repetti, & Crouter, 2000). Family communication scholars have a unique niche to fill in bringing these voices to the fore. For example, the intended consequence of parents working more hours to provide a higher standard of living for their families can have unintended consequences in terms of how the children feel about the arrangements. How do children feel and communicate their feelings about having a mother who works? A father who works? What (if any) opportunities do they have for expressing these feelings in the family? These are just some of the numerous areas of fruitful research that emerge when viewing work-family processes through a structurational lens.

Using Structuration to Illustrate the (Re)production of Social Structures

One area of direct application of structuration research is the realm of family socialization and change. In a recent critique of family socialization research, Dietrich and Picou (1998) described a conspicuous lack of researcher concern with the connections between the family and other institutions involved in primary socialization (i.e., socialization that occurs in childhood). This is a critical oversight given that religious, political, educational, and economic institutions instill beliefs and expectations into the family, thereby socializing individuals as to the culture as well as the structure of both professional and family careers (Moen & Orrange, 2002).

One such institutional system is our economic system. Mortimer and Dennehy (1994) examined economic socialization in the American family by exploring the prevalence, distribution, and consequences of allowance arrangements. Although these researchers confirmed an expected association among parental socioeconomic status and provision of allowance, they also discovered that receipt of allowance was associated with weaker intrinsic and extrinsic work values, in part because most children were receiving allowances in exchange for completing household chores. One interesting extension of this research would be to examine the family messages that create and re-create (or structure) the economic socialization of children. Researchers might consider the ways in which parents communicate financial decision-making processes to their children and how such financial structures are created, sustained, and/or changed through communicative agency.

Adopting a structuration perspective would also enable family researchers to consider how these micro-level messages are tied to larger economic institutions and structures.

Another institutional structure that could be examined is the reproduction of the family itself by exploring the ways in which parental socialization (re)produces religious and economic ideologies that structure adolescents' plans for family formation. Starrels and Holm (2000) recently examined the congruence between parents' and adolescents' expectations for family planning. Evidently, daughters were more likely than sons to learn about and be influenced by their mothers' expectations for family formation, though the overall congruence between parents' and adolescents' expectations was greater for marriage than for parenthood. When compared with nonfamilial influences, familial influences on intentions for family formation were stronger and more robust, emphasizing the role that family communication plays in creating and sustaining certain family expectations for future family development. Using structuration theory, communication scholars might extend this research by examining the ways in which the knowledge-ability of adolescents is bounded by parental constraint. In other words, the possibilities that children envision for family formation and for considering alternative family types may be bound, to some extent, by the expectations and standards parents communicate to their children. Researchers might also consider the intergenerational transmission of family communication processes that perpetuate damaging family structures such as patterns of physical abuse and violence. Through these types of investigations, communication scholars may enhance our understanding of the ways in which family socialization is inherently a process of structuration, thereby locating family talk at the center of the socialization process and highlighting the connections among larger social institutions and family interaction.

Thinking about structuration and work-family socialization, the ways that family members talk about "balancing" work and family constructs reality as to the meaning of what it means to live a balanced life to that particular family. In the United States, family events and routines typically schedule around work expectations (Kanter, 1977; Mortimer & London, 1984). Structuration allows for the exploration of family communication that reproduces the privileging of work (i.e., "not now kids, I have to finish this work."). Yet through the duality of structure, it can also be used to question this privilege—what conversations happen in families where the father chooses to stay home with children? Or where individuals leave high-paying jobs to "spend more time with family"? One of us recalls a recent comment from her husband that "your idea of family time is not enough. You had a mom who worked outside the home and so you think it's okay to be gone more"—suggesting the (re)production of that family structure in another time and space.

Using Structuration to Explore
Dualities of Agency and Structure

Structuration theory's mandate to take both human agency and structure seriously can also be useful in examining the challenges to the traditional/nuclear/patriarchal family and the ways in which day-to-day family interaction produces and reproduces alternative family forms. Giddens (1998) argued that current changes in traditional family structures can be viewed as part of a "democratization in personal life," in which good family relationships share similarities with public democratic practices—in other words, families appropriate democratic ideals. That is, men and women treat each other as equals, issues are discussed with an attempt to reach consensus, all family members have legal rights and obligations, and communication is relied upon to influence behavior rather than using coercion or force (Giddens, 1998).

Risman (1998) illustrates how women and men can exercise agency to successfully challenge institutional and gendered interactional structures to form "fair" marriages through her study of 15 egalitarian families. The wives in this study were well-paid professionals and equal to their husbands in social and economic status. These resources were drawn upon in their day-to-day interaction as couples negotiated "peer marriages" with respect to household work and paid labor, authority and control in child care, and the expression and management of emotion. Such research serves as an exemplar of how structuration theory allows for conceptualizing the family, not just as a source of social stability but also as a site for social change. A more explicit application of the theory might examine family communication as it reflects a dynamic interplay between the opposing forces of stability and change in the emergence of alternative family structures.

Another context for family communication in which dualities between agency and structures are highlighted is in the appropriation processes that characterize stepfamily development. In the case of stepfamilies, it appears as though some stepfamilies are more or less successful in their attempts to appropriate existing structures, such as traditional family roles and norms, from the conventional, nuclear family model (Braithwaite, Olson, Golish, Soukup, & Turman, 2001). The appropriation of structural features is a skillful accomplishment that results in different versions of institutional features being adapted to particular contexts (Poole et al., 1996). Given that stepfamilies must socially construct a shared conception of family through communication (Cherlin & Furstenberg, 1994), it is quite reasonable to suspect that family members use agency to employ different rules and resources (i.e., different structures) during the process of "becoming a family" (Braithwaite et al., 2001). Consequently, structuration theory may shed further light on both developmental and life-course changes that families experience as they create, re-create, and perhaps change the very structures that both enable and constrain family communication.

STRENGTHS AND LIMITATIONS

The theory's complexity and degree of abstraction are both strengths and limitations. Indeed, Craib (1992) likens structuration to a "theoretical omelet" in that all sorts of usual, conventional, and unusual ingredients have been added together to form the theory. The resulting complexity of this theory allows for researchers to address a wide variety of phenomena in the family at several levels—from micro-level, situated interactions to more macro-level institutions and expectations. One great attraction of the theory is the potential to overcome the debate between agency and structure, and instead look at both.

Yet, as Clegg (1992) noted, "major problems of both commission and omission have been identified" in structuration (p. 590). One recurring criticism is that constraint gets short shrift in Giddens's work (e.g., Thompson, 1989). In addition, Craib (1992), like other critics, asserted that Giddens's eclectic style of combining aspects of theories makes him difficult to read, and that ultimately, "a range of concepts can be applied in a variety of situations, but it is always difficult to identify when and where application is appropriate or what can be learnt from it" (p. 5). Clegg (1992) agreed with these criticisms but noted that the theory's complexity also can serve as a unifying device for social researchers of all stripes. In that spirit, we invite family communication researchers to join the growing group of communication researchers utilizing structuration theory and to add empirical work to Giddens's largely theoretical stance. Alternative family structures, family socialization and change, and work-family processes are but three illustrations of how elements of structuration theory can be used to inspire new directions in family communication research. We encourage our readers to remain open to additional possibilities.

REFERENCES

Baber, Z. (1991). Beyond the structure/agency dualism: An evaluation of Giddens' theory of structuration. *Sociological Inquiry, 61*, 219–230.

Baxter, L. A., Braithwaite, D. O., & Nicholson, J. H. (1999). Turning points in the development of blended families. *Journal of Social and Personal Relationships, 16*, 291–313.

Braithwaite, D. O., Olson, L., Golish, T. D., Soukup, C., & Turman, P. (2001). "Becoming a family": Developmental processes represented in blended family discourse. *Journal of Applied Communication Research, 29*, 221–247.

Cherlin, A. J., & Furstenberg, F. F. (1994). Stepfamilies in the United States: A reconsideration. *Annual Review of Sociology, 20*, 359–381.

Clegg, S. (1992). Review article: How to become an internationally famous British social theorist. *The Sociological Review, 40*, 576–598.

Craib, I. (1992). *Anthony Giddens.* New York: Routledge.

Dietrich, K. T., & Picou, J. S. (1998). Theory and methodology in family socialization research. *Marriage and Family Review, 27*, 3–18.

Feeney, J. A., Noller, P., & Roberts, N. (2000). Attachment and close relationships. In C. Hendrick & S. S. Hendrick (Eds.), *Close relationships: A sourcebook* (pp. 185–201). Thousand Oaks, CA: Sage.

Giddens, A. (1976). *New rules for sociological method: A positive critique of interpretative sociologies.* New York: Basic Books.

Giddens, A. (1979). *Central problems in social theory: Action, structure, and contradiction in social analysis.* Berkeley, CA: University of California Press.

Giddens, A. (1984). *The constitution of society: Outline of the theory of structuration.* Berkeley, CA: University of California Press.

Giddens, A. (1989). A reply to my critics. In D. Held & J. B. Thompson (Eds.), *Social theory of modern societies: Anthony Giddens and his critics* (pp. 249–301). Cambridge, UK: Cambridge University Press.

Giddens, A. (1998). *The third way: The renewal of social democracy.* Cambridge, UK: Polity Press.

Giddens, A. (2003). *Runaway world: How globalization is reshaping our lives.* New York: Routledge.

Giddens, A., & Pierson, C. (1998). *Conversations with Anthony Giddens: Making sense of modernity.* Stanford, CA: Stanford University Press.

Greenhaus, J. H., & Beutell, N. J. (1985). Sources of conflict between work and family roles. *Academy of Management Review, 10,* 76–88.

Haas, L., & Hwang, P. (1995). Company culture and men's usage of family leave benefits in Sweden. *Family Relations, 44,* 28–36.

Hochschild, A. R. (2000). Global care chains and emotional surplus value. In W. Hutton & A. Giddens (Eds.), *Global capitalism* (pp. 130–146). New York: The New Press.

Hochschild, A. R. (2003). *The commercialization of intimate life.* Berkeley: University of California Press.

Kanter, R. M. (1977). *Work and family in the U. S.: A critical review and agenda for research and policy.* Newbury Park, CA: Sage.

Kirby, E. L., & Krone, K. J. (2002). "The policy exists, but you can't use it": Communication and the structuration of work-family policies. *Journal of Applied Communication Research, 30,* 50–77.

Moen, P., & Orrange, R. M. (2002). Careers and lives: Socialization, structural lag, and gendered ambivalence. *Advances in Life Course Research, 7,* 231–260.

Mortimer, J. T., & Dennehy, K. (1994). Economic socialization in the American family. *Family Relations, 43,* 23–29.

Mortimer, J. T., & London, J. (1984). The varying linkages of work and family. In P. Voydanoff (Ed.), *Work and family: Changing roles of men and women* (pp. 20–35). Palo Alto, CA: Mayfield Publishing.

Parrenas, R. S. (2001a). Mothering from a distance: Emotions, gender, and inter-generational relations in Filipino transnational families. *Feminist Studies, 27,* 361–390.

Parrenas, R. S. (2001b). *Servants of globalization: Women, migration and domestic work.* Palo Alto, CA: Stanford University Press.

Parrenas, R. S. (2002). The care crisis in the Philippines: Children and trans-national families in the new global economy. In B. Ehrenreich & A. R. Hochschild (Eds.), *Global woman: Nannies, maids, and sex workers in the new economy* (pp. 39–54). New York: Henry Holt.

Perry-Jenkins, M., Repetti, R. L., & Crouter, A. C. (2000). Work and family in the 1990s. *Journal of Marriage and the Family, 62,* 981–998.

Poole, M. S. (1988). *Communication and the structuring of organizations.* Unpublished manuscript, Texas A&M University.

Poole, M. S. (1999). Group communication theory. In L. R. Frey, D. S. Gouran, & M. S. Poole (Eds.), *The handbook of group communication theory and research* (pp. 37–70). Thousand Oaks, CA: Sage.

Poole, M. S., & McPhee, R. D. (1983). A structurational theory of organizational climate. In L. Putnam & M. Pacanowsky (Eds.) *Organizational communication: An interpretive approach* (pp. 195–219). Beverly Hills, CA: Sage.

Poole, M. S., Seibold, D. R., & McPhee, R. D. (1985). Group decision-making as a structurational process. *Quarterly Journal of Speech, 71,* 74–102.

Poole, M. S., Seibold, D. R., & McPhee, R. D. (1996). The structuration of group decisions. In M. S. Poole & R. Y. Hirokawa (Eds.), *Communication and group decision making* (2nd edition) (pp. 114–146). Thousand Oaks, CA: Sage.

Riley, P. (1983). A structurationist account of political culture. *Administrative Science Quarterly, 28,* 414–437.

Risman, B. J. (1998). *Gender vertigo: American families in transition.* New Haven: Yale University Press.

Schrodt, P., Baxter, L. A., McBride, M. C., Braithwaite, D. O., & Fine, M. A. (2004). The divorce decree, communication, and the structuration of co-parenting relationships in stepfamilies. Manuscript submitted for publication.

Starrels, M. E., & Holm, K. E. (2000). Adolescents' plans for family formation: Is parental socialization important? *Journal of Marriage and Family, 62,* 416–429.

Thompson, J. B. (1989). The theory of structuration. In D. Held & J. B. Thompson (Eds.), *Social theory of modern societies: Anthony Giddens and his critics* (pp. 56–76). Cambridge, UK: Cambridge University Press.

Family systems theory, often referred to as family process theory, is one offshoot of General Systems Theory (GST).

General Systems Theory (GST) falls under an organicism world-view (Pepper, 1942) that privileges holism, integration, and emergence. Pioneered by Bertalanffy (1934, 1951, 1955, 1968), GST may be viewed as an overarching theory of systems (Whitchurch & Constantine, 1993) rooted in areas involving cybernetic feedback; or self-monitoring processes encompassing various areas of systemic study in fields as disparate as mathematics, biology, and robotics, as well as sociology and family studies. Originally applied to weapons development and information sciences during World War II, the theory's evolution positioned it as a significant contributor to the understanding of human interaction. Throughout the 1960s, GST infiltrated a number of family-related disciplines; early family applications emerged from the work of the eclectic scholars of the Mental Research Institute (MRI), headed by Gregory Bateson, who applied systems concepts to an understanding of schizophrenia as well as to the nascent family therapy movement (Bateson, Jackson, Haley, & Weakland, 1956). In addition, the Palo Alto Group, including renowned family therapist Virginia Satir, linked systems characteristics to ongoing interactional systems, including marital and family relationships (Watzlawick, Beavin, & Jackson, 1967). These pioneers contributed to the emergence of family therapy that, in turn, influenced later interest in well-functioning families and marital and family enrichment.

The backgrounds of many of the early family communication scholars and teachers included group processes, pastoral counseling, family therapy, and marital enrichment (Galvin & Wilkinson, 1980). Interpersonal and group communication scholars adopted systems theory in their efforts to distinguish groups from a "collection of individuals," focusing on the emergent nature of group processes. The outcome of this systems theorizing was the understanding that "group members (or sets of groups) are bound together as a social system through their communication" (Mabry, 1999, p.72).

The role of systems theory in the development of early marital and family communication research was crucial as it centered attention on the holistic nature of interaction patterns as opposed to attending to individual family members. The studies of marital interaction by the MRI and Palo Alto Groups influenced communication scholars such as Rogers-Millar and Millar (1979), and Sieburg (1985). In her explanation of the roots of the study of family interaction by communication scholars, Rogers (2001) asserted that the shift "was closely tied to the system-based conceptual reformulations of the family therapy movement and early clinical research focusing on the family unit or family subsystems" (p. 25). Systems theory's impact on marital and family communication research, although diffused, remains powerful today. As recently as 1999, Whitchurch and Dickson asserted that "Many, if not most, family communication specialists have a systems theory worldview" (p. 691). Essentially "systems theory is not reality but a way of knowing," (White & Klein, 2002, p. 123) a heuristic device for understanding the world. This worldview supports the thinking of many family communication scholars who integrate systems theory in conjunction with other approaches to form frameworks for communication research.

To fully appreciate the groundbreaking nature of systems theory and its role in the past three decades of family-related research, it is important to examine the following issues: (a) the underlying assumptions and concepts of systems theory at the levels of GST and family systems; (b) the applications of family process theory to understanding family communication; (c) the strengths and limitations of systems theory; and (d) future directions. This examination will reveal the intense focus on the emergent nature of relational patterns, as well as the benefits and costs of focusing extensively on the whole rather than on the individuals in relationships.

SYSTEMS THEORY: UNDERLYING ASSUMPTIONS AND CONCEPTS

Although the scope of GST allows it to be applied to both inanimate and animate objects, it provides a framework for understanding the enormous complexities of human organizations (White & Klein, 2002). Its far-reaching application and distinctive ontological view has warranted its reputation as being a "grand theory." This elevated status suggests that the significance of systems theory lies within its powerful assumptions and paradigmatic worldview. Additionally, Polkinghorne (1983) suggested a rethinking of systems theory as an ontological paradigmatic shift, not merely viewing it as a theory that sits within another paradigm. More specifically, it provides a root metaphor for thinking about family interactions as well as concepts and language for talking about ongoing, changing family interaction. Thus, this discussion will discuss family processes within the overarching framework of GST. In basic terms, a system is a set of components that interrelates with one another to form a whole. When individuals come together to form relationships, the result is larger and more complex than the sum of the individuals, or components. What is created is a social system, frequently a family with all its complexities. Four basic assumptions underlie any systems perspective: "(a) systems elements are interconnected; (b) systems can only be understood as wholes; (c) all systems affect themselves through environmental feedback; and (d) systems are not reality" (White & Klein, 2002, p. 124).

As a unique social system, the family may be viewed as "an example of an open, ongoing, goal-seeking, self-regulating, social system" (Broderick, 1993, p. 37) with unique features of gender and generations. Family systems therapist Salvador Minuchin (1984) captured the essence of family systems by asserting that "Decontexted individuals do not exist" (p. 2). Persons are considered not as individuals but as parts of overall patterns; family members serve as a background while their interaction patterns surface in the foreground; patterns take precedence over persons. Communication is central to understanding these family patterns. When two or more persons form a relational system "the most important feature of such a relationship is communication. Relationships are established, maintained, and changed by communicated interaction among members" (Duncan & Rock, 1993, p. 48).

Although various authors emphasize different sets of family systems characteristics (Broderick, 1993; Galvin, Bylund & Brommel, 2004; Littlejohn, 2002; Whitchurch & Constantine, 1993; White & Klein, 2002), seven characteristics are most commonly stressed for a social system such as the family.

Interdependence. Interdependence implies that a change in one part of the system affects the entire system. Changes in any one family member or unit (e.g., marital pair) impacts the family. The idea of interdependence was captured in Burgess's (1926) definition of the family as a "unity of interacting personalities" (p. 5), parts so interrelated as to be dependent upon each other for their functioning. The family operates as a highly interdependent system because of its centrality to, and long lasting effect on, its members.

Wholeness. Just as the cake that emerges from the oven represents a transformation of its original ingredients of sugar, flour, or chocolate, the family that emerges from the interaction of its members has its own unique characteristics. Interaction patterns "emerge from their specific arrangement in a particular system and from the transactions among parts made possible only by that arrangement" (Whitchurch &

Constantine, 1993, p. 329). Entire families may be characterized by emergent properties that differentially represent each individual member. Distinctive communication patterns between and among family members emerge as a result of this wholeness as siblings engage in incessant teasing or parents engage in predictable arguments.

Patterns /Regularities. Each family system develops patterns that make life reasonably predictable and manageable. Communication rules represent a special type of pattern or relationship agreement that prescribe and limit a family member's behavior over time, establishing a sense of regularity and order. Early family theorists viewed the family system as committed to stability, reflecting a mechanistic sense of stability called calibration. Thus, families are "calibrated" through feedback systems to regulate their behavior in accordance with their rules. Today, theorists recognize the ongoing dialectical struggles of human relationships that keep a system in some continuing level of flux, as well as the need for families to cope with developmental changes and unpredictable crises. Current thinkers support an evolutionary model of family change that incorporates the possibility of spontaneous or unpredictable change (Hoffman, 1990; Yerby 1995).

Interactive Complexity. From a systems perspective, interaction patterns trump cause/effect analysis. The ongoing nature of interaction patterns renders meaningless an attempt to identify "what action came first." Accordingly, it is fruitless to assign cause or blame to one member's behavior because each action simultaneously triggers new behavior and responds to a previous behavior. This position, labeled an "illness-free" lens through which to view relationships (Duncan & Rock, 1993), argues that blaming one member for difficulties is senseless because all members play a part in creating the problematic patterns. Even if a singular instigating event could be identified, the issue is now entwined in their ongoing communication patterns. In alcoholic families the key pattern may become symmetrical as the spouses enact continual opposition (Bateson, 1972). A classic pattern is the nag/withdraw cycle ("He withdraws because she nags; she nags because he withdraws"), demonstrating the pointlessness of finding the "first cause." Focusing on current patterns serves to uncover ongoing complex issues.

Openness. Human systems are considered open, in contrast to mechanical systems such as engines, because they permit interchange with the surrounding environments. Thus, information (people, ideas, and experiences) flows back and forth across the boundary that separates the family from the larger environment. Family members maintain constant interchanges, not only within the family boundary but across the family boundary to the larger ecosystem that includes health, educational, legal, political, and economic institutions—as well as friends and extended family. Although boundaries may be strong, flexible, or almost nonexistent, families require some level of interchange with the environment to manage growth and change. The importance of boundaries is central to examining systems.

Complex Relationships. Families are organized into numerous interpersonal subsystems, made up of two or more persons and the relationships between or among them. Imagine a three-person subsystem that has three dyads (mother-son, brother-sister, mother-daughter) and patterns for each dyad, as well as for the triad. Historically, the critical underlying concept of family organization was the generational hierarchy of power, such as the parental subsystem with its secrets and emotional/sexual boundaries. Today, more families are experiencing generational reversals due to immigration and varying levels of technological sophistication between generations. Finally, each family system reflects the psychobiological system of each individual, as well as cultural norms.

Alliances develop when individuals align through mutual efforts to oppose other members. Coalitions, especially triangles of two insiders and an outsider, may form as members align strongly, establishing highly stable interaction patterns. When a two-person relationship is stressful, the members frequently draw in a third person to serve as the focal point of attention, relieving the stress on the original pair.

Equifinality. Family systems are considered goal-oriented entities. Equifinality implies that a particular final state or goal may be accomplished in different ways from different starting points (Littlejohn, 2002). There are many ways to reach the same end; for example, the goal of "raising well-educated children" or "creating a happy family" may be achieved in various ways across diverse families.

APPLICATION OF SYSTEMS THEORY TO FAMILY COMMUNICATION

Viewing the family as a system provides a distinctive lens from which to study interaction; the system's dynamics are explained by the function they play in the whole system; meaning is derived from the role a practice performs to serve the ends of the whole (Polkinghorne, 1983). A systems view of families is comprehensive and extremely broad in scope. The study of marital and family interaction processes developed throughout the last half of the twentieth century relied heavily on Hess and Handel's (1959) work on the psychosocial interior of the family; Rogers's (1972) early development of measures of relational control based in part on a system-theory definition, and her later studies of relational control (Rogers & Farace, 1975; Rogers-Millar & Millar, 1979); Kantor and Lehr's (1976) examination of patterns of distance regulation within open, closed, and random families; and Gottman's (1982) discussion of temporal form in an attempt to find a new language for describing relationships.

The extensive work of David Olson and his colleagues on the development of the circumplex model of family systems has greatly influenced family communication scholars (Olson, 1997, 2000; Olson, Russell, & Sprenkle, 1983a, 1983b; Olson, Sprenkle, & Russell, 1979). Originally developed using core dimensions of cohesion and adaptability, the current model features three dimensions of cohesion, flexibility, and communication. These dimensions emerged from a conceptual clustering of more than fifty concepts, as well as from theorists' conclusions regarding their critical role in understanding and treating marital and family systems (Olson, 2000). Olson and colleagues developed a variety of self-report instruments: the Circumplex Assessment Package (CAP) provides the insider's perspective, whereas the Clinical Rating Scale (CRS) provides the outsider's perspective. When used together, these instruments provide a comprehensive picture of interaction in marital and family systems (Olson, 2000).

In the past decade, scholars from a variety of family-oriented areas have used systems theory in conjunction with other theories and concepts. O'Connor, Hetherington, and Clingempeel (1997) examined combined influences of systems theory and bidirectional influences, the latter described as containing independent, direct, or linear assumptions. They concluded that such a joint framework holds "considerable promise for describing the complex associations between parent-adolescent and family relationships and adolescent development" (p. 500). Three decades of work by Edna Rogers and colleagues continue, as indicated by recent work on patterns of relational control and nonverbal affect (Escudero, Rogers, & Gutierrez, 1997; see Rogers, this volume). Systems theory has also been used to explain interactions in contemporary families in a variety of areas, including children's attitudes toward their single parent's dating behaviors resulting in themes of inclusion/exclusion (Marrow-Ferguson & Dickson, 1995); mistreatment of children as a violation of boundary ethics (O'Neill & Hern, 1991); the association between spouses' self-reports of attachment styles and family dynamics (Mikulincer, Florian, Cowan, & Cowan, 2002); the "cascade" divorce model incorporating chaos theory (Gottman, 1991); and systemic training programs in the resolution of school problems (Walsh & Williams, 1997).

Systems theory plays both an explicit role as a research model in specific studies and serves as an implicit background to other studies. Earlier studies were more likely to elaborate on systems concepts, whereas current studies may rely on the systems assumptions without explicitly noting the connection. For example, Prescott and Le Poire (2002) utilize systems theory and inconsistent nurturing as control theory in their examination of eating disorders and mother-daughter communication because a systems framework "examines the influence of family members on maintaining the eating disorder system" (p. 63). Barbato, Graham, and Perse (2003) relied on systems-related concepts without direct discussion of systems theory to examine family communication climate and interpersonal communication motives. Other studies (e.g., Braithwaite, Olson, Golish, Soukup, & Turman, 2001) utilize systems concepts such as boundaries and boundary management in their development of a process model of blended family development. They reported that blended family members frequently mentioned dealing with family group membership, feelings of closeness, and flexibility to change during their first four years.

Much of the current research that applies a systemic approach to exploring family dynamics is concerned with the mutual influence among family subsystems. When this lens is applied, issues of interdependence become central. For instance, it is common for problems in parent-child relationships to be associated with marital distress. As a result of this focus, the parent-child relationship problems are difficult to resolve until issues in the marital dyad are identified and treated (Cox & Paley, 1997).

Furthermore, research has found that family subsystems behave differently when they are alone as opposed to being together with other subsystems. Belsky and Volling's research (1987) on the impact of children on marriage is a good example of this. Marital partners report significantly lower levels of satisfaction with the interaction with their spouse when the children are present. Deal, Hogan, Bass, Hetherington, and Clingempeel (1999) support this finding by reporting that parents behave differently when the whole family is together than when they are alone. They reported that when the whole family is present, there is less warm communicative activity and less self-disclosure between partners.

Much of the research that applies systems theory to families incorporates a pathological lens on the family. Examples of this kind of research are seen in studies that examine domestic violence, child abuse, boundary violations, mental illness, and parental conflict from a systemic perspective. This research dissects the identified problem on the family level, not the level of the individual. A good example of this type of research examines the effects of witnessing marital discord on children (Marks, Glaser, Glass, & Horne, 2001). This research indicates that children who witnessed severe marital discord had emotional and behavioral difficulties, impaired social competence, and significant school problems. Studies such as these examine how a problem within a family subsystem (e.g. the marital dyad) may significantly impact the children—another family subsystem.

Another exemplar program of research illustrating the connectedness of family subsystems is demonstrated in eating disorders, which tends to focus on the entire family system and its subsystem instead of the individual experiencing the disease. Minuchin (1974) discussed how highly enmeshed patterns of interaction within the family are related to anorexia within the family. In addition, recovery rates among anorexia nervosa victims tends to be higher when the entire family is treated, not just the individual (Minuchin, 1974; Russell, Szmukler, Dare, & Eisler, 1987). Finally, recovery is also higher when control over eating is taken away from the individual and given to the parents (Robin, Bedway, Siegel, & Gilroy, 1996; Robin, Siegel, & Moye, 1995). Such interventions alter the complex relationships involving enmeshment, triangulation, coalitions/alliances, and hierarchy found in the pathological family system.

The aforementioned studies highlight the utility of a systemic approach when examining family interaction. Yerby (1995) provides a concise and insightful summary of its value, suggesting:

> Systems theory has taught us to see our own and other family members' behavior as interrelated, to locate the predictable patterns of interaction that seem to exert more over the family than do any individual family members themselves, to see problems in terms of relationship struggles rather than the "fault" of one person who is "scapegoated" and "blamed" for others' pain, and to explore the intergenerational legacy of family experience. (pp. 339–340)

While this position is valid, scholars need to recognize not only the strengths of this approach, but also its limitations. The following section discusses strengths and weaknesses associated with systems theory that scholars need to consider when applying this approach.

STRENGTHS AND WEAKNESSES
OF A SYSTEMS PERSPECTIVE

Systems theory "ranks as one of the most influential and generative of all the family conceptual frameworks" (Broderick, 1993, p. 5). In the early years of family research, systems theory opened the door to the consideration of marital and family dynamics. No longer was interviewing one partner, usually the female (Blood & Wolfe, 1960), or surveying numerous married individuals, a way to create generalizations about marriages. Transactional, relational patterns gained prominence over individual or intrapsychic issues. While systems theory has vastly influenced the study of family communication, there are a number of limitations that need to be acknowledged when applying this to family dynamics.

Systems theory's limitations have become apparent over the past decades. Many scholars view this theory as too abstract and global to be of use as a single research approach, arguing it is best utilized in combination with other, more narrowly focused theories.

Further, attention is given to repetitive patterns rather than to continual change. Although most scholars have moved far beyond the old "machine metaphor" of a closed system, claiming that goal-oriented homeostatic models are too simplistic to be of value, few really address recursiveness (Breunlin, Schwartz, & Kune-Karrer, 1997) or kaleidoscopic change (Hoffman, 1990). The powerful emphasis on patterns prevents appropriate attention to emerging shifts or variations.

Another critique of systems theory focuses on the assumptions surrounding gender. Systems theory has been criticized for denying gender inequalities between males and females in families. For example, the concept of mutual influence can mask the obvious difference in physical strength between males and females in an abusive relationship. Even in decision making, the marital pair may be viewed as an equal unit whereas greater power may reside with the male. A systemic view of violence does not adequately address the issue of male domination in the family (McConaghy & Cottone, 1998; Yerby, 1995). Systems theory, in its purest form, claims that no part of the system can have unilateral control or power over another part of the system; supporting the notion of circular causality. This view of causality has come under attack by many feminist therapists such as Walters, Carter, Papp, & Silverstein (1988). This issue becomes more salient when therapists and researchers are examining and treating families that experience domestic violence, incest, marital rape, and wife battering. The claim that all of these occurrences are a product of interactional patterns and repetitive sequences of transactional behavior creates serious issues in the treatment and prosecution of the perpetrator. In fact, this perspective can claim that there is not a perpetrator in events of incest, domestic violence, wife raping and battering (McConaghy & Cottone, 1998). One could argue that the systems approach to these kinds of family problems is inappropriate for the victims and may contribute to blaming the victim. When there is a victim involved, there has to be a view of unequal power in the relationship that the systems approach does not acknowledge.

Further criticism revolves around the attention on relationships at the expense of individuals. This critique represents the other side of the coin emphasizing relational patterns. In recent decades, research in behavioral endocrinology, behavioral genetics, evolutionary psychology, and behavioral psychopharmacology has demonstrated the need to maintain an individual focus while acknowledging relational concerns (Booth, Carver, & Granger, 2000). These research areas call for recognition of health or psychological concerns of a member as they impact relational patterns.

Another limitation that surfaces addresses the static and contrived nature in the traditional language used to "describe" families. Systems theory and its characteristics feature a language structure that tends to privilege a patriarchal family structure. The advantage of this is that systems theory validates the appropriateness of the roles in the hierarchy (e.g., "Parents are parents, children are children."). However, in single-parent or military families in which one of the parents may be absent for extended periods of time, it may be necessary and critical to the family's well-being for an older child to assume parental roles. The implication is that systems theory does not necessarily apply to contemporary family experiences with fluid family roles.

Finally, these limitations challenge the progressiveness and timelessness of systems theory's application to contemporary family experiences. The family model changed much more dramatically than was envisioned when Minuchin first applied systems theory to family interaction. Since the inception of family systems theory, the family form or structure has changed so dramatically that the way in which we experience and envision family is entirely different from its existence in the early 1950s and 1960s. The original lens of systems theory, although powerful, was not powerful enough to accommodate the exponential power of family change.

Although many scholars have criticized systems theory, it has also had a significant positive impact on how researchers and therapists view family interaction. For example, systems theory reinforces the notion that families are in a constant state of change. It acknowledges that families are, conceptually, ever-changing with nonstatic energy. When families experience crises due to developmental transitions (Carter & McGoldrick, 1999), a certain level of comfort can be embraced in knowing that circumstances will be altered with the passing of time. As the old adage states, "This too shall pass." For example, parents of adolescents may choose to believe their offspring will outgrow their "developmentally appropriate" disrespect for authority.

Another strength of systems theory is that the components within the theory work together for the family's common goals. One of the foundations of systems is that all the components work together for the common goal of the family. Although some behaviors can be explained away within the framework of a particular component, other behaviors can be rationalized by the interrelated power of the components working together.

Finally, perhaps the most ingenious strength is its parsimonious nature. The characteristics of interdependence, wholeness, patterns/regularities, interactive complexity, openness, complex relationships, and equifinality provide a sense-making map for understanding everyday and erratic family behavior. Its tenets allow scholars of systems theory to exercise both their conventional wisdom and sophisticated explanations of family dynamics.

FUTURE DIRECTIONS

Although systems theory has been advanced in its totality, we suggest that much family understanding can still be garnered by studying systems theory in terms of its individual components and assumptions. Family communication scholars need to examine not just how the components of systems theory work together for the benefit of the whole, but how breakdowns occur within the individual components within the system. Thus, a paradox emerges with the theory as it is dedicated to the notion of the wholeness of the system. The ultimate assumption within systems theory is that the whole is greater than the sum of its parts. This is accepted knowledge; however, the paradox is that the power of systems theory is only as strong as its individual components. Therefore, the application of systems theory to families becomes more useful when we can incorporate both perspectives—the totality of the system and its individual components. For example, to better understand a family's dynamics, it may be advisable to locate predictable as well as unpredictable patterns of interaction. Often, the nuances in the family's behavioral patterns can better explain its challenges and ultimately enhance the family's interactions. Although some patterns of behaviors can be explained within the framework of a particular component such as roles or family boundaries, other patterns of behavior can be better understood through the interrelated power of the components working together. This enhanced orientation of systems theory allows for a greater illumination of contemporary family experiences.

CONCLUSION

The development of systems theory led to numerous breakthroughs in diagnosing, explaining, and understanding and changing family communication for more than half a century. These cumulative research findings confirm system theory's formidable posture and longitudinal power when applied to the family context. Although this theory cannot be considered a perfect framework for understanding family interaction and functionality, its fluid nature and highly adaptive characteristics yield a theoretical framework with considerable staying power and utility.

REFERENCES

Barbato, C. A., Graham, E. E., & Perse, E. M. (2003). Communicating in the family: An examination of the relationships of family communication climate and interpersonal communication motives. *Journal of Family Communication, 3,* 123–148.

Bateson, G. (1972). *Steps to an ecology of mind.* Chicago: University of Chicago Press.

Bateson, G., Jackson, D. D., Haley, J., & Weakland, J. (1956). Toward a theory of schizophrenia. *Behavioral Science, 1,* 251–263.

Belsky, J., & Volling, B. (1987). Mothering, fathering, and marital interaction in the family triad: Exploring family systems processes. In P. Berman &

F. Pederson (Eds.), *Men's transitions to parenthood: Longitudinal studies of early family experience* (pp. 37–63). Hillsdale, N.J.: Lawrence Erlbaum.

Bertalanffy, L. von (1934). *Modern theories of development* (J.H. Woodger, Trans.). Oxford, UK: Oxford University Press.

Bertalanffy, L. von (1951). Problems of general systems theory. *Human Biology, 23,* 302–312.

Bertalanffy, L. von (1955). General systems theory. *Main Currents in Modern Thought, 11,* 75–83.

Bertalanffy, L. von (1968). *General systems theory.* New York: George Braziller.

Blood, R. O., & Wolfe, D. M. (1960). *Husbands and wives.* Glencoe, IL: Free Press.

Booth, A., Carver, K., & Granger, D. (2000). Biosocial perspectives on the family. *Journal of Marriage and the Family, 62,* 1018–1034.

Braithwaite, D. O., Olson, L. N., Golish, T. D., Soukup, C., & Turman, P. (2001). Becoming a family: Developmental processes represented in blended family discourse. *Journal of Applied Communication Research, 29,* 221–247.

Breunlin, D. C., Schwartz R. C., & Kune-Karrer, B. M. (1997). *Metaframeworks: Transcending the models of family therapy.* San Francisco: Jossey-Bass.

Broderick, C. (1993). *Understanding family process: Basic of family systems theory.* Newbury Park, CA: Sage Publications.

Burgess, E. W. (1926). The family as a unity of interacting personalities. *The Family, 7,* 3–9.

Carter, B., & McGoldrick, M. (Eds.). (1999). *The expanded family life cycle: Individual, family and social perspectives* (3rd ed.). Boston: Allyn and Bacon.

Cox, M. J., & Paley, B. (1997). Families as systems. *Annual Review of Psychology, 48,* 243–267.

Deal, J. E., Hogan, M. S., Bass, B., Hetherington, E. M., & Clingempeel, G. (1999). Marital interaction in dyadic and triadic contexts: Continuities and discontinuities. *Family Process, 38,* 105–116.

Duncan, B. L., & Rock, J. W. (1993, January/February). Saving relationships: The power of the unpredictable. *Psychology Today,* 46–51, 86, 95.

Escudero, V., Rogers, L. E., & Gutierrez, E. (1997). Patterns of relational control and nonverbal affect in clinic and nonclinic populations. *Journal of Social and Personal Relationships, 14,* 5–29.

Galvin, K. M., Bylund, C. L., & Brommel, B. J. (2004). *Family communication: Cohesion and change* (6th ed.). Boston: Allyn & Bacon.

Galvin, K. M., & Wilkinson, C. A. (1980). Family communication as an applied area. *Journal of Illinois Speech and Theatre Association, 34,* 1–8.

Gottman, J. M. (1982). Temporal form: Toward a new language for describing relationships. *Journal of Marriage and the Family, 44,* 943–962.

Gottman, J. M. (1991). Chaos and regulated change in families: A metaphor for the study of transitions. In P. A. Cowan & E. M. Hetherington (Eds.), *Family transitions* (pp. 247–272). Hillsdale: N.J.: Lawrence Erlbaum.

Hess, R., & Handel, G. (1959). *Family worlds.* Chicago: University of Chicago Press.

Hoffman, L. (1990). Constructing realities: The art of lenses. *Family Process, 29,* 1–12.

Kantor, D., & Lehr, W. (1976). *Inside the family.* San Francisco: Jossey-Bass.

Littlejohn, S. W. (2002). *Theories of communication* (7th ed.). Belmont CA: Wadsworth/Thomson Learning

Mabry, E. A. (1999). The systems metaphor in group communication. In L. Frey, D. S. Gouran, & M. S. Poole (Eds.), *The handbook of group communication theory and research* (pp. 71–91). Thousand Oaks, CA: Sage.

Marks, C. R, Glaser, B. A., Glass, J. B., & Horne, A. M. (2001). Effects of witnessing severe marital discord on children's social competence and behavioral problems. *The Family Journal: Counseling and Therapy for Couples and Families, 9,* 94–101.

Marrow-Ferguson, S., & Dickson, F. (1995). Children's expectations of their single parents' dating behavior: A preliminary investigation of emergent themes relevant to single parent dating. *Journal of Applied Communication Research, 23,* 1–17.

McConaghy, J., & Cottone, R. R. (1998). The systemic view of violence: An ethical perspective. *Family Process, 37,* 51–64.

Mikulincer, M., Florian, V., Cowan, P. A., & Cowan, C. P. (2002). Attachment security in couple relationships: A systemic model and its implications for family dynamics. *Family Process, 41,* 405–434.

Minuchin, S. (1974). *Families and family therapy.* Cambridge, MA: Harvard University Press.

Minuchin, S. (1984). *Family kaleidoscope.* Cambridge, MA: Harvard University Press.

O'Connor, T. G., Hetherington, E. M., & Clingempeel, W. G. (1997). Systems and bi-directional influences in families. *Journal of Social and Personal Relationships, 14,* 491–504.

Olson, D. H. (1997). Family stress and coping: A multisystem perspective. In S. Dreman (Ed.), *The family on the threshold of the 21st century* (pp. 259–282). Mahwah, NJ: Lawrence Erlbaum.

Olson, D. H. (2000). Circumplex model of marital and family systems. *Journal of Family Therapy, 22,* 144–167.

Olson, D. H., Russell, C. S., & Sprenkle, D. H. (Eds.). (1983a). *Circumplex model: Systematic assessment and treatment of families.* New York: Haworth Press.

Olson, D. H., Russell, C. S., & Sprenkle, D. H. (1983b). Circumplex model of marital and family systems VI: Theoretical update. *Family Process, 22,* 69–83.

Olson, D. H., Sprenkle, D. H., & Russell, C. S. (1979). Circumplex model of marital and family systems: Cohesion and adaptability dimensions, family types, and clinical applications. *Family Process, 18,* 3–28.

O'Neill, P., & Hern, R. (1991). A systems approach to ethical problems. *Ethics and Behavior, 1,* 10–21.

Pepper, S. C. (1942). *World hypotheses.* Berkeley: University of California Press.

Polkinghorne, D. (1983). *Methodology for the human sciences: Systems of inquiry.* Albany, NY: SUNY Press.

Prescott, M. E., & LePoire, B. A. (2002). Eating disorders and mother-daughter communication: A test of inconsistent nurturing as control theory. *Journal of Family Communication, 2,* 59–78.

Robin, A. L., Bedway, M., Siegel, P. T., & Gilroy, M. (1996). Therapy for adolescent anorexia nervosa: Addressing cognitions, feelings, and the family's role. In E. D. Hibbs & P. S. Jensen (Eds.), *Psychosocial treatment for children and adolescent disorders: Empirically based strategies for clinical practice* (pp. 239–259). Washington, DC: American Psychological Association.

Robin, A. L., Siegel, P. T., & Moye, A. (1995). Family versus individual therapy for anorexia: Impact on family conflict. *International Journal of Eating Disorders, 17,* 313–322.

Rogers, L. E. (1972). *Relational communication control coding manual.* Unpublished manuscript, Michigan State University, East Lansing.

Rogers, L. E. (2001). Relational communication in the context of family. *Journal of Family Communication, 1,* 25–35.

Rogers, L. E., & Farace, R. V. (1975). Analysis of relational communication in dyads: New measurement procedures. *Family Process, 1,* 222–239.

Rogers-Millar, L. E., & Millar, F. E. (1979). Domineeringness and dominance: A transactional view. *Human Communication Research, 5,* 238–246.

Russell, G. F. M., Szmukler, G. I., Dare, C., & Eisler, I. (1987). An evaluation of family therapy in anorexia nervosa and bulimia nervosa. *Archives of General Psychiatry, 44,* 1047–1056.

Sieburg, E. (1985). *Family communication: An integrated systems approach.* New York: Gardner Press.

Walsh, W. M., & Williams, R. (1997). *School and family therapy: Using systems theory and family therapy in the resolution of school problems.* Springfield, IL: Charles C Thomas.

Walters, M., Carter, E., Papp, P., & Silverstein, O. (1988). *The invisible web.* New York: Guilford Press.

Watzlawick, P., Beavin, J. H., & Jackson, D. D. (1967). *Pragmatics of human communication.* New York: W. W. Norton.

Whitchurch, G. G., & Constantine, L. L. (1993). Systems theory. In P. G. Boss, W. J. Doherty, R. LaRossa, W. R. Schumm, & S. K. Steinmetz (Eds.), *Sourcebook of family theories and methods* (pp. 325–352). New York: Plenum Press.

Whitchurch, G. G., & Dickson, F. C. (1999). Family communication. In M. B. Sussman, S. K. Steinmetz, & G. W. Peterson (Eds.), *Handbook of marriage and the family* (2nd ed.) (pp. 687–704). New York: Plenum Press.

White, J. M., & Klein, D. M. (2002). *Family theories* (2nd ed.). Thousand Oaks, CA: Sage.

Yerby, J. (1995). Family systems theory reconsidered: Integrating social construction theory and dialectical processes. *Communication Theory, 5,* 339–365.

21

The Theory of Natural Selection: An Evolutionary Approach to Family Communication

Kory Floyd

Mark T. Haynes

Editors' Note: The theory of natural selection (TNS) is a "grand theory" that has spawned a number of more specific theories. The theory originates in biology with the work of Charles Darwin. When applied to humans, its more recent lineage can be traced to the fields of sociobiology and evolutionary psychology. The theory is logical-empirical in nature.

S cholars working to understand the intricacies of family interaction have a number of theoretic paradigms in which to conduct their work, as the present volume attests. One perspective that has not yet been widely used in family communication research is that associated with evolution and natural selection. This is an unfortunate omission because, as we detail in this chapter, the evolutionary perspective is rich in potential for the breadth of family interactions it can explain and the depth and parsimony of its explanation. In this chapter, we will briefly describe the evolutionary perspective and then discuss some of the many ways in which it can be used by communication scholars to predict and explain a variety of family communication processes and outcomes.

Despite references to *The Theory of Evolution*, there actually is no such theory. Instead, a number of theories—which might be described as *theories of evolution*—explicate different aspects of how evolution works (in fact, attachment theory, described elsewhere in this volume, proposes that attachment motivations are adaptive and innate). Chief among these is Darwin's (1859) *theory of evolution by means of natural selection* (TNS). A number of social scientists have used the logic behind TNS to advance more specific theories about how natural selection shapes human psychology and behavior. In the following sections, we describe the major tenets of TNS. We then illustrate some of many ways in which an evolutionary perspective can inform research on family communication processes and outcomes.

MAJOR FEATURES OF EVOLUTIONARY THEORIES

Understanding an evolutionary approach to explaining human behavior first requires a familiarity with the principles of natural selection. Darwin's TNS advanced four primary ideas. First, *in any generation, many more of a given species are born than can survive to reproductive maturity*. This creates what Darwin referred to as a struggle for existence, and inherent in that struggle are two omnipresent motivations: the motivation to survive and the motivation to reproduce. Second, *individual organisms vary, one from another, in myriad physical and mental ways*. For instance, humans vary in their height, weight, eye color, strength, and bone density; as well as in their intellectual capacity, disposition, and personality. Third, *some of this variation is heritable*, meaning that it is passed from parent to offspring genetically. The fourth and most important proposition in TNS was that *heritable characteristics that advantage organisms in terms of survival and/or procreation will gradually appear with greater frequency in populations*. That is, individuals who have characteristics—such as strength, intelligence, or attractiveness—that give them an advantage in survival and/or procreation will produce more offspring, on average, than will those without such characteristics. To the extent that these characteristics are heritable, they will gradually become more common in the population because increasing numbers of children will be born with them. (Remarkably, Darwin was unaware of genetics when he proposed TNS. That is, he offered that certain characteristics are heritable without an understanding of the mechanisms by which heritability operates.)

An appreciation for the evolutionary explanation of communicative behavior requires attention to specific forms of evidence (see Cappella, 1991). For one, its focus on characteristics that are genetically grounded leads researchers using TNS to look for similarities, rather than differences, among cultures and other socially organized groups. To the extent that communicative dispositions are derived from heritable genetic characteristics created by adaptive pressures, they should not be expected to vary appreciably according to culture, class, gender orientation, political affiliation, or other similar social divisions. Ekman's (1972) research on the pancultural similarities in facial emotion display is illustrative. Second, evidence from neonates and infants can illuminate the effects of heritable behavioral dispositions before the influences of socialization and enculturation have had a chance to take hold. Cappella (1991) summarized a large body of research on neonates and infants with respect to patterns of stimulation regulation and emotional expressiveness, noting that the earlier in life such patterns are observed, the more likely they are to reflect innate dispositions. Third, evidence that physiological processes are reliably associated with observed behaviors suggests that the behaviors are part of an adaptive, regulatory process that may have resulted from adaptive pressures. Booth, Carver, and Granger (2000) reviewed several lines of research applying physiological principles to the study of family dynamics.

Although historically fraught with controversy, the principles of natural selection can be applied to the task of understanding humans and human behavior if two fundamental observations are first made. First, *humans are subject to evolutionary pressures just like any other living organism is.* Early controversies surrounding TNS reflected the perspective that humans, because of their superior intellectual abilities, transcend the evolutionary processes that come to bear on all other organisms. Although evolutionary psychologists do not deny the intellectual superiority of humans, they maintain that humans still face the same struggles for survival and procreation that affect every other living organism, and thus are likewise subject to the process of natural selection. Second, *natural selection influences the mind as well as the body.* This observation is somewhat counterintuitive because people tend to conceive of the mind (or psyche) as being separate from their physical bodies. Evolutionary psychologists counter with the observation that the mind is a product of the brain and the brain is a physical entity just like eyes and hands and legs are. As a physical organ, the brain is no less subject to natural selection than is any other part of the body. Evolutionary theories argue that mental or psychological characteristics that advantage a person in terms of survival and/or procreation are therefore equally as likely to be selected for as are advantageous physical characteristics.

These two observations are central tenets in the growing field of evolutionary psychology, which uses the principles of natural selection to understand human personality, cognition, and behavior. Evolutionary psychologists do not deny that human behavior is influenced by social and cultural learning; rather, they simply maintain that it is *also* influenced by the extent to which it advantages individuals in their quests for survival and procreation. When attempting to understand a human behavior from the evolutionary perspective, therefore, the fundamental questions to consider are *To what extent does this behavior confer survival and/or procreation advantages?* and *To what extent is the cause of this behavior heritable?* Researchers have used TNS and related theories of evolution to understand a variety of human behaviors, including those in family communication.

TNS is clearly an example of a theory developed outside the domain of family communication that offers clear and compelling mechanisms for explaining and predicting numerous aspects of how families communicate. As we address in the following discussion, social scientists have applied evolutionary principles to several aspects of family communication, and many other aspects can be equally well explained from this perspective. We opine here, as we have elsewhere (Floyd & Haynes, in press), that evolutionary theories provide an important level of breadth, depth, and explanatory power for understanding family communication.

HOW HAS TNS BEEN USED (AND HOW COULD IT BE USED) TO UNDERSTAND FAMILIES?

TNS has been used rather extensively by psychologists working to understand the intricacies of family interaction. For instance, a large body of empirical work addresses the formation (e.g., Buss, 1989, 1994a, 1994b; Grammer & Thornhill, 1994) and maintenance (e.g., Bellis

& Baker, 1990; Buss, Larsen, Westen, & Semmelroth, 1992; Fisher, 1999; Tooke & Camire, 1991) of romantic pair bonds. A similarly robust literature applies evolutionary principles to parent-child relationships (Clutton-Brock, 1991; Hrdy, 1999), including those in stepfamilies and adoptive families (Daly & Wilson, 1987, 1993). Still other studies have examined communication between siblings (Bevc & Silverman, 2000; Jankowiak & Diderich, 2000) and between grandparents and grandchildren (Euler & Weitzel, 1996) from the perspective of TNS.

Despite the considerable breadth and depth of its explanatory power, however, TNS has not been widely used by family communication researchers. In fact, as we have acknowledged elsewhere (Floyd & Haynes, in press), TNS has been virtually ignored in introductory family communication textbooks, family research sourcebooks (e.g., Vangelisti, 2003), and empirical research published in the *Journal of Family Communication.*

Of the work done in the communication discipline that has applied TNS to family interaction, most has focused either on marriage and mating strategies or on parent-child relationships. For instance, Trost and her colleagues have written extensively on topics such as attraction, mate selection, and reproduction in romantic relationships from the perspective of natural selection (e.g., Kenrick & Trost, 1989, 2000; Trost & Alberts, 1998). Floyd and colleagues have also used evolutionary principles to understand communication in parent-child relationships, including relationships with stepparents and adoptive parents (e.g., Floyd & Morman, 2001). These efforts have truly only scratched the surface.

There are numerous other ways in which TNS and related theories can illuminate family communication processes. For illustrative purposes, we will focus here on understanding various aspects of the parent-child relationship, including the differences between maternal and paternal care, the incidence of parent-child conflict, and the distribution of resources in biological and stepparenting relationships. Readers should note that these are but three examples of the numerous aspects of family relationships that the evolutionary perspective can explain. For more complete treatments of the topic, see Buss (1999), Daly and Wilson (1983), Floyd and Haynes (in press), and Hrdy (1999).

Maternal and Paternal Care

Why is it that mothers tend to invest more energy than fathers in the raising of their children? Feminist scholars have long maintained that this division of parental labor has come about because of the culturally sanctioned subjugation of women (e.g., Chodorow, 1978). However, this is not a uniquely human phenomenon; in fact, maternal care exceeds paternal care in a huge range of species, including many species of reptiles, insects, amphibia, fish, and birds (Clutton-Brock, 1991). It is certainly reasonable to suggest, therefore, that this division of parental labor is not a cultural or political construction, but rather, is reflective of motivations that are generalizeable beyond the human race. Researchers working within the evolutionary paradigm have offered various explanations for why maternal care exceeds paternal care in so many species. The most widely cited explanation concerns *paternity certainty*, or a father's level of certainty that his children are indeed his biological offspring. Few mothers wonder whether their children are actually "theirs"; indeed, the very act of giving birth gives women high certainty that their children are their own biological offspring. Paternity certainty is never as high, however, because sexual infidelity on the part of the mother (whether voluntary or involuntary) makes fertilization by a man other than her mate a possibility. As Daly and Wilson (1987) noted, "maternity is a fact, paternity a conjecture" (p. 109).

Paternity certainty is important because when men invest resources (including their love, attention, and money) in children who are not their biological offspring, these resources do little to further the men's reproductive success. According to the paternity certainty hypothesis, men invest less energy in child care than women do because they have less certainty about whether the children are their biological offspring. Importantly, no evolutionary psychologists argue that men behave this way intentionally or even conscientiously. Rather, evolution has provided the motivation to maximize one's resources by investing them where they will have the largest reproductive payoff; as a result, men's motivation to invest less in children than women do has already been selected for.

Parent-Child Conflict

One aspect of family life that makes it especially relevant from an evolutionary perspective is that family relationships involve genetic links as well as social bonds. Biological family relationships vary in terms of their level of genetic relatedness, defined as the probability of finding in one person a gene that also resides in another (among those genes that vary from human to human). Identical twins share 100% of their genes with each other, and thus are said to have 100% genetic relatedness. We typically have 50% genetic relatedness with biological parents, biological children, and full biological siblings (including fraternal twins). We are related to our half-siblings, grandparents, grandchildren, aunts, and uncles by 25%; and we typically have 0% relatedness to our steprelatives, adoptive relatives, in-laws, and spouses.

According to Hamilton's (1964) *theory of inclusive fitness*, the level of genetic relatedness between family members is important because when we aid our relatives in ways that further their survival or reproductive abilities, we aid ourselves in the process (to a degree equal to our level of relatedness to that person). Thus, we gain more by helping an identical twin than a fraternal twin, and more by helping a father than an uncle. From this perspective, parents and their biological children are invested in each other's welfare because they share 50% of their genes. Importantly, however, this means that they *differ* genetically by the other 50%, suggesting that although parents' and children's priorities overlap, they do not perfectly coincide. Conflict between parents and children is therefore inevitable. Specifically, evolutionary psychologists argue that parents and children have different stakes in the distribution of resources, including money, time, attention, and love. Parents are motivated to invest their resources in their children in ways that maximize their evolutionary returns, but children are driven to acquire as many resources as they can. As an example, suppose that a mother has $1000 to divide between her two biological children. Assuming that both children are healthy and equally able to reproduce, the mother maximizes her investment by giving each child $500. From each child's point of view, however, it is best to try to get more than $500 because each child benefits more by getting the resources than when the sibling does. This explains, from the evolutionary perspective, why parent-child relationships are prone to conflict. It also explains why parent-child relationships can sustain *both* cooperation *and* conflict to the degree that they often can.

Resource Allocation in Biological and Stepfamily Relationships

From an evolutionary perspective, it is easy to see why parents invest so much of their temporal, economic, and emotional resources in their children: Such investments help children to reach reproductive maturity, allowing them to further the parents' own genetic materials. Again, parents need not be conscientious of this motivation, and it is not the only reason why parents invest in their children. The evolutionary perspective suggests that it is *one* reason, however, and that a failure to attend to the needs of one's genetic progeny would eventually be selected against through the normal process of natural selection.

Although parents of multiple children would most likely claim to invest equally in each of their children, research indicates that they rarely do. Several studies have instead shown that parents invest discriminately, giving more resources to children who are the most likely to contribute the parents' genetic materials to succeeding generations and less to those children who are not likely to do so, either because they are unlikely to reproduce (as in the case of homosexual or reproductively infertile children) or because they do not carry the parents' genes to begin with (as in the case of stepchildren). Daly and Wilson's (1987, 1993) *theory of discriminative parental solicitude* explains this pattern as being an adaptation by which parents are motivated to invest their resources in ways that maximize their return in the form of reproductive success.

Several studies have demonstrated this pattern. Anderson, Kaplan, and Lancaster (1997) looked at patterns of parental investment in children's college educations and found that parents were nearly six times as likely to give money for college to biological children as compared with stepchildren; moreover, they gave biological children an average of $15,000 more than they gave stepchildren. In two studies, Floyd and Morman (2001) found that men received less affectionate communication from their stepfathers than from their biological fathers—and importantly, this difference held even when the closeness and satisfaction levels of the relationships, the fathers' involvement in the relationships, and the ages of the fathers and sons were held constant. Other studies have examined the investments made by grandparents in their grandchildren and have reported results consistent with the theory of discriminative parental solicitude (e.g., Euler & Weitzel, 1996).

Parental abuse appears to follow the same pattern. In a study of 841 Canadian households, Daly and Wilson (1985) found that children living with at least one stepparent were *40 times* more likely to be physically abused than were children living with biological parents, and that this difference could not be accounted for by other factors, such as poverty or socioeconomic status. In a separate project, Daly and Wilson (1988) found that children were *40 to 100 times* as likely to be killed by a stepparent than by a biological parent. There is evidence that this finding replicates cross-culturally (Daly & Wilson, 1988).

These are but three illustrative applications of TNS and evolutionary theories to the study of family communication. Although we have provided examples related to parent-child interaction here, researchers can use the evolutionary approach to illuminate the full range of family relationships.

STRENGTHS AND LIMITATIONS OF THE EVOLUTIONARY APPROACH

Like any other approach, the evolutionary approach offers particular strengths and entails particular liabilities. We begin this section by discussing three strengths of the approach—its breadth, depth, and parsimony—all of which are among the most commonly cited criteria for good scientific theories (Reynolds, 1971). We then discuss three limitations—accessibility of the causal mechanism, common misperceptions, and the specificity of derived hypotheses—that researchers must take into account when working within this theoretical perspective.

Breadth

The evolutionary approach to human behavior is exceedingly broad in the range of family relationships and behaviors it can explain. Whereas many family communication theories are specific to particular relationships (such as marital or parental relationships) or to particular behavior patterns (conflict, exchange, attachment), the evolutionary paradigm is neither relationally nor behaviorally bound. Rather, because evolution and natural selection influence so many aspects of physical and psychological life, they likewise influence multiple aspects of relationships (see Kenrick & Trost, 2000). To be certain, TNS is not a "theory of everything"; however, it can be used to explain and predict multiple types of behaviors in a wide range of family relationships, offering greater breadth than some other theories used to study families.

Depth

Importantly, the evolutionary approach does not sacrifice depth for breadth. In addition to its capability to explain a broad range of family relationships and behaviors, the evolutionary perspective provides a depth of explanation that transcends the level of the individual; the interaction; the relationship; and the social, political, religious, or cultural context. Many other theories used to study family communication explain behaviors with reference to theoretically constructed concepts, such as family rules or roles, cultural prescriptions, or relationship "types." Such constructs may be difficult to locate in the natural world and may be highly subject to the operational definitions used to measure them. By contrast, evolutionary theories explain family relationships with reference to the enduring motivations to survive and procreate that affect all humans and all other living organisms. The evolutionary paradigm places human behavior within a deep and broad understanding of the life cycle, illustrating their connection to two goals—survival and procreation—without which more proximal explanations for behavior would be less compelling.

Parsimony

Because its causal mechanism—natural selection—consists of two omnipresent motivations (survival and procreation), explanations for behavior-derived evolutionary theories are relatively parsimonious. As we noted previously, evolutionary analyses require attention to two fundamental questions: How the characteristic to be explained contributes to survival and/or procreation success, and to what extent the characteristic is heritable. Often, engaging in evolutionary logic to explain a relational behavior—conflict, for example—requires assumptions to be made explicit and erroneous preconceptions to be corrected (see the following discussion). However, the deductive process is a parsimonious one, precisely because the motivations to survive and procreate are so enduring and not subject to shifts in the cultural, social, or political context.

Causal Mechanism

One limitation of the evolutionary approach is that the causal mechanism—natural selection—is not easily accessible to researchers wanting to study it because natural selection is, in most instances, an extraordinarily slow process. Physical and psychological adaptations do not typically occur in a matter of generations, or even dozens of generations, but over millennia. One result is that researchers using TNS to predict human behavior do not assess the adaptability of physical or psychological characteristics for modern living; rather, they assess adaptability for what they term the *environment of evolutionary adaptedness* (EEA), or the time period in which the characteristic would have been adaptive (see Tooby & Cosmides, 1992). Humankind has spent more than 99 percent of its history as hunter-gatherers (Morris, 2001). Agriculture was invented only about 10,000 years ago, and civilization (let alone modern civilization) is an even more recent phenomenon. This is an extremely short period of time on an evolutionary time scale. When appealing to natural selection as a causal mechanism, therefore, evolutionists (including evolutionary psychologists) must deduce how a given physical or psychological characteristic would have been adaptive in meeting an evolutionary challenge in the EEA. This typically involves reasoning about how the characteristic would have advantaged the organism in terms of survival, reproductive success, or both—even if the characteristic is maladaptive in the modern environment. Because the EEA is not accessible to modern researchers (except through archeological records and other artifacts), the evolutionary approach has been criticized as being nonfalsifiable. In truth, however, this is misplaced criticism. Even though the causal mechanism is not directly accessible, hypotheses deduced through evolutionary logic (e.g., conflict varies by genetic relatedness; stepchildren receive fewer resources than do biological children) are empirically verifiable and falsifiable.

Common Misperceptions

Although it is not a weakness inherent to the approach, the evolutionary perspective is plagued with misperceptions that, when uncorrected, call its credibility into question. A full discussion of each of these misperceptions is beyond the scope of this chapter (see Buss, 1999). However, we want to draw attention to two commonly raised objections to evolutionary theories that are grounded in misperception. The first is that calling a behavior *adaptive* implies that *genes determine behavior.* For instance, one may respond to Daly and Wilson's claim that parents invest their resources in their children discriminately (to maximize their reproductive success) to mean that stepfamily relationships are doomed to failure because parental resource-sharing behavior is predetermined genetically. This is an example of what evolutionists call the *deterministic fallacy,* and it is an erroneous extrapolation of Daly and Wilson's claim. When evolutionary psychologists argue that adaptations predispose people to behave in certain ways (given certain circumstances), they are rarely implying that those behaviors are predetermined. Instead, they are merely claiming that, in particular circumstances, people will be more likely to behave in one way than in another. The second objection is that calling a behavior *natural* implies that it is *morally right*. For example, when Thornhill and Palmer (2000) argued that rape is an adaptation that maximizes men's reproductive success, many objected to the idea on the grounds that calling rape a natural adaptation was tantamount to endorsing rape and exonerating rapists. This is an illustration of what evolutionists call the *naturalistic fallacy*. It is fallacious because when evolutionists call something a natural adaptation, all they mean is that the characteristic provided an evolutionary advantage in terms of survival or procreation (or both). There is absolutely no moral, social, or political endorsement inherent in such a statement.

Specificity

A third limitation of the evolutionary approach is that the level of abstraction at which it is pitched often makes it more useful for predicting macro-level behavior patterns than for predicting the micro-level behavioral changes that are often of interest to communication scholars. For instance, Trivers' (1972) *parental investment theory* posits that women are more selective than men when choosing a potential mate because women have a greater required investment in potential offspring. Such a theory can be used to deduce broad hypotheses regarding sex differences in mate-seeking behavior (e.g., women are less likely than men to solicit prostitutes or engage in "one-night stands"); however, it would be less useful at predicting minute-to-minute changes in a conversational encounter (such as whether or not an acute increase in immediacy will be reciprocated). This is not to suggest that *no* micro-level behaviors can be explained by evolutionary theories, only that such theories are often more predictive of macro-level behavioral patterns.

Despite these limitations, evolutionary theories have been extremely fruitful tools for understanding the family, and they have the potential to inform family communication research in numerous new ways. To end this chapter, we look ahead briefly to future research and offer ideas on how family scholars might incorporate evolutionary principles in their work.

DIRECTIONS FOR FUTURE RESEARCH

One important application of the evolutionary perspective in future research is in studying the physiology of family communication processes. Investigating communication physiologically helps researchers understand the links between social behavior and how our bodies respond. Why does conflict cause stress, love make us feel good, or transgression make us feel guilty? Physiologists acknowledge that all communicative behaviors, including family interactions, engage the body in physical, as well as mental and emotional, ways; thus, when scholars investigate only the social or cultural influences on such behaviors, they risk missing a large part of the picture that evolutionary theories can help illuminate. Using evolutionary theories leads researchers to focus on (among other things) the ways in which the body functions to reinforce certain behaviors that are advantageous for survival and/or procreation, while mitigating behaviors that are disadvantageous. Consider romantic love as an example. From the perspective of TNS, love serves an enormously important function: It helps to form and maintain pair bonds, which are useful for procreation. Although norms for the expression of love may be largely culturally derived, research suggests a number of ways in which the brain, autonomic nervous system, and endocrine system act to make love a physically rewarding experience. For instance, the secretion of hormones such as vasopressin, oxytocin, serotonin, and dopamine appears to be associated with the experience of romance and sexual attraction (Panksepp, 1998). Because all these hormones impart pleasurable sensations, they may reinforce bonding and attachment processes and help to form and maintain romantic pair bonds that can further reproductive success (for review, see Floyd, in press). Conversely, relational conflict or distress is often associated with heightened nervous system arousal and secretion of the hormone cortisol, which helps the body deal with acute stress but is extremely damaging to the immune system over time (e.g., Miller, Dopp, Myers, Stevens, & Fahey, 1999). Using evolutionary theories as a guide, family communication researchers can investigate these and other links between relational emotions or behaviors and patterns of physiological response.

Although some empirical attention has been paid to the dark side of family communication, TNS and associated theories can add a great deal of understanding to the origins of several family problems and may also suggest effective clinical and therapeutic interventions. Families may face an array of behavioral problems as a result of evolutionary pressures (e.g., sexual coercion, obsessive relational intrusion, infidelity, sexual addiction) that evolutionary theories can illuminate. A third important direction for future research is the further examination of communication in relationships that are outside of the nuclear family. Many in the field of family communication direct their efforts at understanding marriage and parent-child relationships; and for good reason, because these are perhaps the most significant relationships in the life course. However, the family is a rich array of relationships that are much more infrequently the focus of empirical attention, including those with siblings, grandparents, in-laws, steprelatives, adoptive relatives, cousins, aunts and uncles, and godparents. Existing research offers little understanding about what is consistent across all these family relationships; however, they may all contribute in various ways to individual survival and procreation success. Therefore, researchers working with evolutionary theories can offer understanding about these less frequently studied relationships, thereby adding to a more complete comprehension of the family communication experience.

In sum, TNS offers a number of strengths. First, it is broad enough to account for all family relationships; thus, it is not relationally bound. Second, it offers explanation as to *why* particular relational behaviors occur, rather than just a description of those behaviors. Third, and perhaps most important, it links family communication patterns to enduring motivations—survival and procreation—that transcend social, cultural, racial, gender, and class boundaries and illuminate the "bigger picture" into which family communicative behavior belongs.

REFERENCES

Anderson, J. G., Kaplan, H. S., & Lancaster, J. B. (1997, June). *Paying for children's college: The paternal investment strategies of Albuquerque men.* Paper presented to Ninth Annual Conference of the Human Behavior and Evolution Society, Tucson, AZ.

Bellis, M. A., & Baker, R. R. (1990). Do females promote sperm competition? Data for humans. *Animal Behaviour, 40,* 997–999.

Bevc, I., & Silverman, I. (2000). Early separation and sibling incest. A test of the revised westermarck theory. *Evolution and Behavior, 21,* 151–161.

Booth, A., Carver, K., & Granger, D. A. (2000). Biosocial perspectives on the family. *Journal of Marriage and the Family, 62,* 1018–1034.

Buss, D. M. (1989). Sex differences in human mate preferences: Evolutionary hypothesis testing in 37 cultures. *Behavioral and Brain Sciences, 12,* 1–49.

Buss, D. M. (1994a). *The evolution of desire: Strategies of human mating.* New York: Basic Books.

Buss, D. M. (1994b). The strategies of human mating. *American Scientist, 82,* 238–249.

Buss, D. M. (1999). *Evolutionary psychology: The new science of the mind.* Boston: Allyn & Bacon.

Buss, D. M., Larsen, R., Westen, D., & Semmelroth, J. (1992). Sex differences in jealousy: Evolution, physiology, and psychology. *Psychological Science, 3*, 251–255.

Cappella, J. N. (1991). The biological origins of automated patterns of human interaction. *Communication Theory, 1*, 4–35.

Chodorow, N. (1978). *The reproduction of mothering.* Berkeley, CA: University of California Press.

Clutton-Brock, T. H. (1991). *The evolution of parental care.* Princeton, NJ: Princeton University Press.

Daly, M., & Wilson, M. (1983). *Sex evolution and behavior* (2nd ed). Boston: William Grant.

Daly, M., & Wilson, M. (1985) Child abuse and other risks of not living with both parents. *Ethology and Sociobiology, 6*, 197–210.

Daly, M., & Wilson, M. (1987). The Darwinian psychology of discriminative parental solicitude. *Nebraska Symposium on Motivation, 35*, 91–144.

Daly, M., & Wilson, M. (1988). *Homicide.* Hawthorne, NY: Aldine.

Daly, M., & Wilson, M. (1993). Stepparenthood and the evolved psychology of discriminative parental solicitude. In S. Parmigiami & F. vom Saal (Eds.), *Infanticide and parental care* (pp. 121–134). London: Harwood.

Darwin, C. (1859). *On the origin of species.* London: Murray.

Ekman, P. (1972). Universals and cultural differences in facial expressions of emotions. In J. R. Cole (Ed.), *Nebraska Symposium on Motivation 1971* (pp. 207–283). Lincoln, NE: University of Nebraska Press.

Euler, H. A., & Weitzel, B. (1996). Discriminative grandparental solicitude as reproductive strategy. *Human Nature, 7*, 39–59.

Fisher, H. (1999). *The first sex: The natural talents of women and how they are changing the world.* New York: Random House.

Floyd, K. (in press). *Communicating affection: Interpersonal behavior and social context.* Cambridge, UK: Cambridge University Press.

Floyd, K., & Haynes, M. T. (in press). Applications of the theory of natural selection to the study of family communication. *Journal of Family Communication.*

Floyd, K., & Morman, M. T. (2001). Human affection exchange: III. Discriminative parental solicitude in men's affectionate communication with their biological and nonbiological sons. *Communication Quarterly, 49*, 310–327.

Grammer, K., & Thornhill, R. (1994). Human facial attractiveness and sexual selection: The roles of averageness and symmetry. *Journal of Comparative Psychology, 108*, 233–242.

Hamilton, W. D. (1964). The genetical evolution of social behavior. I & II. *Journal of Theoretical Biology, 7*, 1–52.

Hrdy, S. B. (1999). *Mother nature: A history of mothers, infants, and natural selection.* New York: Pantheon.

Jankowiak, W., & Diderich, M. (2000). Sibling solidarity in a polygamous community in the USA: Unpacking inclusive fitness. *Evolution and Human Behavior, 21*, 125–139.

Kenrick, D. T., & Trost, M. R. (1989). A reproductive exchange model of heterosexual relationships: Putting proximate economics in ultimate perspective. In C. Hendrick (Ed.), *Review of personality and social psychology* (Vol. 10, pp. 92–118). Newbury Park, CA: Sage.

Kenrick, D. T., & Trost, M. R. (2000). An evolutionary perspective on human relationships. In W. Ickes & S. Duck (Eds.), *The social psychology of personal relationships* (pp. 9–35). New York: Wiley.

Miller, G. E., Dopp, J. M., Myers, H. F., Stevens, S. Y., & Fahey, J. L. (1999). Psychosocial predictors of natural killer cell mobilization during marital conflict. *Health Psychology, 18,* 262–271.

Morris, R. (2001). *The evolutionists: The struggle for Darwin's soul.* New York: W. H. Freeman.

Panksepp, J. (1998). *Affective neuroscience: The foundations of human and animal emotions.* New York: Oxford University Press.

Reynolds, P. D. (1971). *A primer in theory construction.* Indianapolis: Bobbs-Merrill.

Thornhill, R., & Palmer, C. T. (2000). *A natural history of rape: Biological bases of sexual coercion.* Cambridge, MA: MIT Press.

Tooby, J., & Cosmides, L. (1992). Psychological foundations of culture. In J. Barkow, L. Cosmides, & J. Tooby (Eds.), *The adapted mind* (pp. 19–36). New York: Oxford University Press.

Tooke, W., & Camire, L. (1991). Patterns of deception in intersexual and intrasexual mating strategies. *Ethology and Sociobiology, 12,* 345–364.

Trivers, R. L. (1972). Parental investment and sexual selection. In B. Campbell (Ed.), *Sexual selection and the descent of man 1871–1971* (pp. 136–179). Chicago: Aldine.

Trost, M. R., & Alberts, J. K. (1998). An evolutionary view on understanding sex effects in communicating attraction. In D. J. Canary & K. Dindia (Eds.), *Sex differences and similarities in communication* (pp. 233–255). Mahwah, NJ: Lawrence Erlbaum.

Vangelisti, A. L. (Ed.). (2003). *Handbook of family communication.* Mahwah, NJ: Lawrence Erlbaum.

Index

About the Editors

Leslie A. Baxter (Ph.D., University of Oregon) is F. Wendell Miller Distinguished Professor of Communication Studies at the University of Iowa. She has published four books and close to 100 articles and book chapters on family communication, relational communication, and research methods. Her scholarly awards include the Berscheid-Hatfield Award for Mid-Career Achievement (INPR), the Gerald R. Miller Book Award (NCA), the Franklin H. Knower Article Award (NCA), and the Legacy Theory Award (CSCA).

Dawn O. Braithwaite (Ph.D., University of Minnesota) is professor of communication studies at University of Nebraska–Lincoln. She focuses her scholarship on communication in personal and family relationships, studying relational dialectics, rituals, and social support in the context of stepfamilies, elderly couples, and people with disabilities. She has published three books and 50 articles and chapters in scholarly books. She is a past president of the Western States Communication Association and is the current director of the National Communication Association Research Board.

About the Contributors

Tamara D. Afifi (formerly Golish) (Ph.D., University of Nebraska–Lincoln) is an assistant professor in the Department of Communication Arts and Sciences at the Pennsylvania State University. Her primary research interests include communication processes in postdivorce families, stress, loss, and uncertainty in families undergoing various life transitions, and information regulation (topic avoidance, privacy, disclosure, secrets) in parent-child relationships.

John P. Caughlin (Ph.D, University of Texas at Austin) is an associate professor in speech communication at the University of Illinois at Urbana–Champaign. His research examines communication in families and other close relationships, focusing on the causes and consequences of avoiding communication. He received the Early Career Award from International Association for Relationship Research and chairs the Family Communication Division of the National Communication Association.

William R. Cupach (Ph.D., University of Southern California) is a professor of communication at Illinois State University. His research pertains to problematic interactions in interpersonal relationships, including such contexts as embarrassing predicaments, relational transgressions, interpersonal conflict, and obsessive relational pursuit. He previously served as associate editor for the *Journal of Social and Personal Relationships* and is past president of the International Association for Relationship Research.

René M. Dailey (Ph.D., University of California, Santa Barbara) is an assistant professor of communication studies at the University of Texas at Austin. Her interests include interpersonal and family communication; specifically her interests focus on the impact of family communication climates on children's development. She has authored numerous articles and has recently published in *Communication Monographs*. She is coediting a volume on socially meaningful applied research in interpersonal communication.

Marianne Dainton (Ph.D. Ohio State University) is an associate professor of communication at La Salle University. Her research focuses on relationship maintenance, with particular interest in routine versus strategic maintenance efforts. She has published in *Communication Monographs* and *Journal of Social and Personal Relationships*. She is the coeditor of the book *Maintaining Relationships through Communication* (with Dan Canary), and is coauthor (with Elaine Zelley) of the forthcoming Sage textbook *Applying Communication Theory for Professional Life: A Practical Introduction*.

Michael Robert Dennis (Ph.D., Purdue University) is an assistant professor of communication studies at the University of Kansas. His teaching interests include health communication, new technology, and social science research methods. His research has investigated persuasive evidence types in health-related decision making, health-related compliance seeking by intimate partners, and the linguistic management of grief.

Fran C. Dickson (Ph.D., Bowling Green State University) is an associate professor and chair of the Department of Human Communication Studies at the University of Denver. Her research interests are in family communication and communication and aging, specifically in marriage and remarriage among later-life adults.

Mary Anne Fitzpatrick (Ph.D., Temple University) is a Carolina Educational Foundation Distinguished Professor of Psychology and founding dean of a newly constituted College of Arts and Sciences at the University of South Carolina. Her research and teaching focus on interaction in social and personal relationships with a special emphasis on marital and family relationships. She is a past president of the International Communication Association and recipient of the ICA Career Productivity Award of 2001.

Kory Floyd (Ph.D., University of Arizona) is an associate professor of human communication and director of the Communication Sciences Laboratory at Arizona State University. His research focuses on the communication of affection in families and other personal relationships and on the physiological correlates of relational communication. He has received a number of awards for his research, including the

New Scholar of the Year award from the International Network on Personal Relationships.

Kathleen M. Galvin (Ph.D., Northwestern University) is a professor of communication studies at Northwestern University. She is senior author of *Family Communication: Cohesion and Change* (6th ed.), coeditor of *Making Connections: Readings in Relational Communication* (3rd ed.) and creator of the PBS Family Communication distance-learning program. Her teaching and research interests are in family and relational communication, specifically communicative construction of family identity. She is an associate editor of the *Journal of Family Communication.*

Jake Harwood (Ph.D., University of California, Santa Barbara) is a professor of communication and chair of the gerontology program at the University of Arizona. His research focuses on intergroup communication with a particular focus on age groups and grandparent-grandchild relationships. He has published more than 50 articles in professional journals, with recent articles in *Personality and Social Psychology Bulletin, Journal of Communication, Journal of Applied Communication Research,* and the *Journal of Social and Personal Relationships.*

Mark T. Haynes (M.S., Illinois State University) is a doctoral student in human communication and an associate of the communication sciences laboratory at Arizona State University. His research focuses on the "dark side" of emotion and communication in romantic relationships and on the behavioral, psychological, and physiological correlates of unrequited love.

Mary Lee Hummert (Ph.D., University of Kansas) is a professor of communication studies at the University of Kansas. Her teaching interests include interpersonal communication, communication theory, and research methods. Her research focuses on the social cognitive processes linking age stereotypes and communication, with grant support provided by the National Institute on Aging/National Institutes of Health.

Jody Koenig Kellas (Ph.D., University of Washington) is an assistant professor of communication studies at the University of Nebraska–Lincoln. She specializes in relational communication, family communication, and narratives of personal relationships. Her research has explored postdissolutional communication, facework, attributions in marital relationships, as well as the processes, identity negotiation, and relational qualities associated with individual and collaborative storytelling in families.

Erika L. Kirby (Ph.D., University of Nebraska–Lincoln) is an associate professor of communication studies and director of Women's and Gender Studies at Creighton University. Her teaching and research interests include organizational, applied and work-family/life communication and discourses and their intersections with gender. Her research has appeared in *Journal of Applied Communication Research, Management Communication Quarterly, Communication Yearbook* and *Communication Teacher.* She lives in Omaha, Nebraska, with husband Bob and daughters Meredith and Samantha.

Ascan F. Koerner (Ph.D., University of Wisconsin) is an associate professor of communication studies and affiliate faculty member of the Interpersonal Relationships Research Minor at the University of Minnesota. His research focuses on the cognitive bases of relationships and their influence on interpersonal communication, as well as marital and family communication.

Kathleen J. Krone (Ph.D., University of Texas–Austin) is a professor of communication at the University of Nebraska–Lincoln. Her research and teaching interests are in organizational communication with emphases on workplace emotion, participation, and conflict. Current projects include stakeholder turning points in community consensus-building, and managerial conflict in Sino-American joint ventures. Her research has appeared in *Management Communication Quarterly, Journal of Applied Communication Research, Women's Studies in Communication* and the *Handbook of Interpersonal Communication.*

Adrianne Kunkel (Ph.D., Purdue University) is an associate professor of communication studies at the University of Kansas. Her research and teaching interests include interpersonal communication, emotional support/coping processes in personal relationships and support group settings, romantic relationship (re)definition processes, and sex/gender similarities and differences.

Kristin M. Langellier (Ph.D., Southern Illinois University) is the Mark and Marcia Bailey Professor at the University of Maine, where she teaches communication and women's studies. Her research and teaching interests are in performance studies, personal narrative, family storytelling, and Franco-American cultural identity.

Wendy Leeds-Hurwitz (Ph.D., University of Pennsylvania) is a professor of communication at the University of Wisconsin–Parkside. Her research and teaching interests are in language and social interaction, ethnography of communication, intercultural communication, semiotics, communication theory, childhood socialization, and history of the discipline.

Beth A. Le Poire (Ph.D., University of Arizona) is a professor of communication at University of California, Santa Barbara. Her interests are in family communication and nonverbal communication, and on substance abuse, attachment, and stigma. She has published 45 articles and chapters with recent publications in *Human Communication Research, Communication Monographs,* and *Journal of Applied Communication Research.* She is author of the textbook *Family Communication* (Sage, 2006) and coeditor of a forthcoming volume on socially meaningful applied research in interpersonal communication.

Mei-Chen Lin (Ph.D., University of Kansas) is an assistant professor in the School of Communication Studies at Kent State University. Her research and teaching interests are in aging, group and intercultural communication, specifically communication and aging across cultures, age identity, intergenerational communication and grandparent-grandchild relationship. Her research has appeared in *Communication Monographs, Journal of Communication,* and the *Journal of Social and Personal Relationships,* and *Journal of Cross-Cultural Gerontology.*

Valerie L. Manusov (Ph.D., University of Southern California) is a professor in the Department of Communication at University of Washington. Her work focuses primarily on the interpretation for and patterns of nonverbal communication in social interaction. She has published this work most recently in *Human Communication Research, Communication Monographs, Western Journal of Communication, Journal of Communication,* and *Journal of Social and Personal Relationships.*

Sherilyn R. Marrow (Ph.D., University of Denver) is an associate professor of communication at the University of Northern Colorado. Her research focuses on contemporary family excellence, emotional expressiveness in marriage, and family teamwork. Her research has appeared in the *Journal of Applied Communication* and the *Journal of Family Communication.* She received the "Qwest-Dex Excellence in Education" award and her university's annual recognition as its "Outstanding Woman."

Wendy M. Morgan (M.A., Northwestern University) is a doctoral student in the Department of Communication at Purdue University. Her research focuses on parent-child interaction, and her dissertation proposes a theory of "safe ground" which clarifies parent-child interaction patterns that are fundamental for establishing child self-esteem and behavioral competence. She has coauthored publications in *Communication Monographs*, *Communication Yearbook*, and the *Handbook of Family Communication*.

Jon Nussbaum (Ph.D., Purdue University) is a professor of communication arts & sciences and human development & family studies at Pennsylvania State University. President-elect of International Communication Association, former editor of *Journal of Communication*, a Fulbright Research Fellow in the UK (1991–92) and a Fellow within the Adult Development and Aging Division of APA, he has a well-established publication record (10 books and more than 70 articles and chapters) studying communication behaviors and patterns across the life span.

Loreen N. Olson (Ph.D., University of Nebraska–Lincoln) is an assistant professor of communication at the University of Missouri–Columbia. Her research focuses on many salient social issues facing today's couples and families, including, for example, intimate and family aggression, family secrets, effects of adult dementia on relational functioning, and communication issues in various family forms. She recently was awarded the Steve Duck New Scholar award from the International Association for Relationship Research (formerly INPR).

Eric E. Peterson (Ph.D., Southern Illinois University) is a professor of at the University of Maine, where he teaches communication. His research and teaching interests are in narrative performance, media consumption, nonverbal communication, and communication diversity and identity.

Sandra Petronio (Ph.D., University of Michigan) is a professor in the Department of Communication Studies at Indiana University–Purdue University, Indianapolis; core faculty in the IU Center for Bioethics; and adjunct faculty in the IU School of Nursing and the School of Informatics. She focuses on management of private disclosures. Her book *Boundaries of Privacy* won the International Association for Relationship Research Book Award and NCA Miller Book Award, and she received the 2002 National Communication Association's Brommel Family Communication Award.

L. Edna Rogers (Ph.D., Michigan State University) is a professor of communication at the University of Utah and a past president of the International Communication Association. Her research interests include interpersonal and relational communication with a central focus on the interactional study of marital and family relationships.

Paul Schrodt (Ph.D., University of Nebraska–Lincoln) is an assistant professor of communication studies at the University of Kansas. He specializes in family and relational communication and instructional communication. His research explores communication cognitions and behaviors that facilitate family functioning, specifically examining co-parenting and step-parenting relationships in stepfamilies and the associations among family communication schemata and family functioning. His research has appeared in *Human Communication Research, Communication Monographs,* and *Communication Education.*

Jordan Soliz (Ph.D., University of Kansas) is an assistant professor of communication at the University of Nebraska–Lincoln. His teaching and research interests are in interpersonal and family communication with an emphasis on intergenerational interactions, intergroup/intercultural dynamics within the family, group differences in supportive interactions, and communication and intergroup prejudice. His research has appeared in the *Journal of Applied Communication Research.*

April R. Trees (Ph.D., University of Washington) is an assistant professor of communication at the University of Colorado, Boulder. Her research and teaching interests are relational communication, social support, and nonverbal communication, specifically verbal and nonverbal dimensions of supportive communication and accounting and narrative processes in close personal relationships.

Anita L. Vangelisti (Ph.D., University of Texas at Austin) is a professor of communication studies at the University of Texas at Austin. Her research focuses on the associations between communication and emotion in the context of close personal relationships. She is coeditor of the Cambridge University Press series on Advances in Personal Relationships and has served on the editorial boards of numerous journals. She has published numerous articles and chapters as well as several books.

Steven R. Wilson (Ph.D., Purdue University) is a professor and director of graduate studies in the Department of Communication at Purdue University. His research focuses on interpersonal influence in families, the workplace, and health-care settings. He is the author of *Seeking and Resisting Compliance: Why People Say What They Do When Trying to Influence Others* (Sage, 2002) as well of more than 40 scholarly articles and book chapters.

Julia T. Wood (Ph.D., Pennsylvania State University) is the Lineberger Professor of Humanities and professor of Communication Studies at the University of North Carolina at Chapel Hill. She teaches and conducts research on personal relationships, intimate partner violence, feminist theory, and intersections between gender, communication, and culture. She also consults with attorneys on cases of sex and gender discrimination. During her career, she has received 12 awards for her research and 11 awards for her teaching.

Elaine D. Zelley (Ph.D., Pennsylvania State University) is an assistant professor of communication at La Salle University. Her research explores the relationships between friendship, competition, conflict, social support and the occurrence of eating disorders among women. She has recently published in *Communication Yearbook* and the *International Encyclopedia of Marriage and Family Relationships,* and is the coauthor (with Marianne Dainton) of the forthcoming textbook *Applying Communication Theory for Professional Life: A Practical Introduction.* (Sage, 2006).